Managing Domestic Dissent in First World War Britain

Brock Millman
Royal Military College, Kingston, Ontario

FRANK CASS
LONDON • PORTLAND, OR

First published in 2000 in Great Britain by
FRANK CASS PUBLISHERS
Newbury House, 900 Eastern Avenue
London, IG2 7HH

and in the United States of America by
FRANK CASS PUBLISHERS
c/o ISBS, 5804 N.E. Hassalo Street
Portland, Oregon, 97213-3644

Website: www.frankcass.com

British Library Cataloguing in Publication Data

Millman, Brock
    Managing domestic dissent in First World War Britain.
    – (Cass series. British politics and society)
    1. World War, 1914–1918 – Protest movements – Great Britain
    2. Great Britain – Politics and government – 1910–1936
    I. Title
    940.3'16

ISBN 0-7146-5054-4 (cloth)
ISBN 0-7146-8105-9 (paper)
ISSN 1467-1441

Library of Congress Cataloging-in-Publication Data

Millman, Brock, 1963–
    Managing domestic dissent in First World War Britain / Brock Millman.
        p.   cm. – (Cass series–British politics and society)
    Includes bibliographical references (p.   ) and index.
    ISBN 0-7146-5054-4 (cloth) – 0-7146-8105-9 (paper) (alk. paper)
        1. Great Britain–Politics and government–1910–1936. 2. World War,
    1914–1918–Protest movements–Great Britain. 3. Peace movements–Great
    Britain–History–20th century. 4. Dissenters–Great Britain–History–20th century.
    5. World War, 1914–1918–Great Britain. I. Title. II. Series.

DA577.M55 2000
940.3'41–dc21

00-025434

Typeset by Vitaset, Paddock Wood, Kent
Printed in Great Britain by
Creative Print and Design (Wales), Ebbw Vale

Contents

Figures

Series Editor's Preface

The deluge of the First World War swept away not only millions of lives, but thrones and empires. As the conflict settled into a war of attrition without obvious end, states found themselves forced into an ever-more intense management of both the war and domestic fronts. Societies were tested to destruction by the demands placed by the war upon their economies, manpower reserves and social fabric. By the war's end all the major combatants were experiencing dissent either in the armed forces or domestically, or both.

Brock Millman's excellent and innovative work examines how the state coped with the rising tide of dissent unleashed by the supreme social stresses of the First World War through a meticulous case study of how one major combatant, Britain, dealt with these problems. Placing dissent centre-stage as a problem to be managed in the conduct of war gives a very different perspective from that of traditional military history. Not only that, it also helps to illuminate some aspects of war policy that can otherwise seem obscure, such as the retention of troops in Britain for which Lloyd George was to be censured in the Maurice debate in 1918. The perspective Millman provides makes it clear that there were two wars going on, one in the trenches and one for retention of control at home to ensure that the other could still be supplied. In the process, he skilfully interweaves these two conflicts, making clear the extent to which they impacted upon each other.

This was more than a matter of the passage of the Defence of the Realm Act (DORA) 1914, and its various manifestations. Millman makes it clear that dealing with dissent involved far more than DORA, or the elaboration of the necessary machinery in the Home Office or other departments of state. By clarifying the often informal structures, not dissimilar to the Crown and Anchor Clubs and other such bodies of the Napoleonic era, through which a patriotic alliance was forged, he provides a much more textured account of social conflict and its management during the First World War. At the same time, he illuminates the way in which the war and its consequences gradually provided the occasion for an alignment between mainly middle-class opponents of the conflict and working-class opposition to the degree of coercion it seemed to entail, into a broad-based, cross-class dissenting movement

The significance of this account, accordingly, lies not only in its contribution to military history. Nor is it confined to the light it undoubtedly sheds upon the way in which Whitehall and Westminster sought to manage social conflict during the First World War. In laying bare the changing nature and articulation of this social conflict it also helps to demonstrate that propaganda, whether patriotic or dissenting, is not just a matter of public meetings, films or newspapers addressed at an undifferentiated audience, but something that had to work with and helped to structure patriotic and dissenting alliances. Furthermore, in the process Millman explicates that realignment at the level of low politics wrought by the war, a realignment that was to consign Liberal England to the history books and forge an electoral alliance that was to ensure the Conservative dominance of the inter-war years.

Peter Catterall
Series Editor

Abbreviations

AEU	Amalgamated Engineering Union
AG	Adjutant General
AJAG	Assistant Judge Advocate General
ASE	Amalgamated Society of Engineers
BL	British Library
BLIO	British Library India Office
BLO	Bodleian Library, Oxford
BSP	British Socialist Party
BWNL	British Workers' National League
CCC	Churchill College, Cambridge
CID	Criminal Investigation Department
CIGS	Chief of the Imperial General Staff
CMA	Competent Military Authority
CO	Conscientious Objector
DE	Dalmeny Estate
DMI	Director of Military Intelligence
DORA	Defence of the Realm Act
DPP	Director of Public Prosecutions
DRR	Defence of the Realm Regulations
DWRGWU	Dockers, Wharf, Riverside and General Workers' Union
ELFS	East London Federation of Suffragettes
FO	Foreign Office
FOR	Fellowship of Reconciliation
GFTU	General Federation of Trade Unions
HLRO	House of Lords Records Office
HMG	His Majesty's Government
HO	Home Office
ILIREE	Industrial League for the Improvement of Relations between Employers and Employees
ILP	Independent Labour Party
IWM	Imperial War Museum
IWW	International Workers of the World

JAG	Judge Advocate General
JP	Justice of the Peace
KCL	King's College, London
LBU	London Busworkers' Union
LSE	London School of Economics
MEPO	Metropolitan Police
MFGB	Miners' Federation of Great Britain
MI7	Military Intelligence, Bureau Seven
MIN	Ministry of Information
MP	Member of Parliament
MUH	McMaster University, Hamilton
MUN	Ministry of Munitions
NAC	National Council Against Conscription
NAEE	National Association of Employers and Employees
NAM	National Army Museum
NASFU	National Amalgamated Seamen's and Firemen's Union
NAUL	National Amalgamated Union of Labour
NCCL	National Council for Civil Liberties
NCF	No-Conscription Fellowship
NSL	National Service League
NSP	National Socialist Party
NUDL	National Union of Dock Labourers
NUM	National Union of Miners
NUPPO	National Union of Police and Prison Officers
NUR	Nation Union of Railwaymen
NUWSS	National Union of Women's Suffrage Societies
NWAC	National War Aims Committee
PLP	Parliamentary Labour Party
PRO	Public Record Office
RAF	Royal Air Force
RN	Royal Navy
SDF	Social Democratic Federation
SDP	Social Democratic Party
SNDC	Socialist National Defence Committee
SRO	Scottish Record Office
SWC	The British Stop the War Committee
SWMF	South Wales Miners' Federation
TA	Territorial Army
TF	Territorial Force
TGWU	Transport and General Workers Union
TUC	Trades Union Congress
TUC WEC	Trades Union Congress, War Emergency Committee

UB	University of Birmingham
UDC	Union of Democratic Control
VF	Volunteer Force
WAC	War Aims Committee
WC	War Cabinet
WEC	War Emergency Committee
WIL	Women's International League for Peace and Freedom
WO	War Office
WPC	Women's Peace Crusade
WSF	Women's Suffrage Federation
WSPU	Women's Social and Political Union

Introduction

IT IS a commonplace that modern warfare is not a conflict of armies so much as a contest of societies. Defeat can come as much from the collapse of the home front as from military failure. The maintenance of a nation's will to fight is as important as its physical ability to continue the struggle. Total war, as it emerged during the twentieth century, broadens the scope of the conflict and links aspects of the contest in an organic manner, to the point where weakness anywhere can become weakness everywhere. Lack of military success can easily give rise to dissent on the home front, which, taking the form of industrial unrest, may deprive the army of those things it requires to prevent new and greater defeats. Failure on the home front is therefore as likely to produce total disaster as is defeat at the battle front.

Never was this more the case than during the First World War, when the victorious allies triumphed over Germany largely because the latter's will to carry on the fight had collapsed with its power to do so. The allies did not fight better; with the exception of Russia, they fought longer. Even Russia was never comprehensively defeated in the field, however; it dissolved from within, and this necessarily produced a collapse at the front. By 1917, similarly faced with political and national discontent they did not have the power to contain, Germany's allies were finished. Italy was a noneffective ally by the end of 1917 not simply because of what was happening on the Isonzo, but because of what was transpiring at home. Indeed, defeats at the front derived in part from social–political dislocation. The Italian army was not simply weak in itself, but feeble because Italy was failing. Germany itself might have continued the war through 1919 (as it was expected that it would) except that disappointments at the front combined with war weariness to produce social–political disarray. Dissent was clumsily handled, and national cohesion was lost. In the end, Germany had to end the war or risk comprehensive failure. France and Britain, on the other hand, survived the challenge of total war, if only narrowly, and crossed the finish line first not because they were fastest but in large measure because other competitors had collapsed along the way. Perhaps more appropriately Britain dragged its failing ally, France, across the line on 11 November 1918.

An understanding of the techniques by which each combatant mobilized and sustained civilian effort and morale, therefore, is crucial to accounting for the course and verdict of the war. An understanding of the reasons for Britain's exceptional endurance is especially critical. By the autumn of 1918, of the original combatants Britain alone continued to field an effective force while preserving national cohesion. The Russian, Austro-Hungarian and Ottoman empires were dead. Italy was practically comatose. France was failing. Germany was plainly dying. Britain's fortitude was, at least in part, a function of the fact that Britain of all the combatants was most effective in dealing with dissent on the home front. It follows that to understand why this was so is to take one of several necessary steps toward comprehending why the war ended as it did.

The subject of what follows is the ways in which order was maintained on the British home front (with the exception of Ireland) through to victory in 1918.[1] Important work has been done here on what might be termed the 'positive' means by which civilian morale was sustained and the fruits of civilian endeavour maximized.[2] What remains a blank spot, however, is consideration of the negative efforts by which the government buttressed the home front by limiting, or directing into harmless channels, the expression of dissent. The spotlight has been on the ways in which participation in the war was encouraged and the effectiveness of the national effort maximized, rather than the methods by which opposition was discouraged and the disruption occasioned to the war effort by dissent minimized. It is with this second category that this book is principally concerned.

While specific studies do not exist, some notion of government activity can be glimpsed in works on wartime protest movements of which there are plenty; in a few of the better of these some notion is given of government actions. Here, of course, the government is the enemy, and mention is made of its activities only to provide a background against which the development of dissent can be highlighted. Some, however, are valuable sources. Honourable mention, in this regard, must surely go to Marvin Swartz, who, in *The Union of Democratic Control in British Politics during the First World War*[3] gives what is probably the best existing description of British policy as it developed through the war. This, however, is not his primary focus.

Specific studies which reverse Swartz's priorities are almost totally lacking. About the best that can be found are some monographs dealing with government strike-breaking.[4] These, unfortunately, consider the government's reaction to only one type of dissent. Only one of them devotes any space to the First World War period.[5] Another explicitly indicates that this was a time during which the government was not much worried about industrial action.[6] Another suggests the same.[7] None has used existing wartime material very adventurously. Richard Thurlow's *The Secret State* and Gerard De Groot's *Blighty* are sound, but, once again, their focus is broad and their primary interest elsewhere.[8] Aside from these, a novel, Pat Barker's *The Eye in the Door*, is the best account there is.

This is a major lacuna in the history of the First World War. After all, if a workman can be bought or convinced, he can equally well be confused, intimidated, or deprived of the leadership which alone can make his disaffection in the mass a challenge to the war effort. Ultimately co-operation can be compelled, and it is a mistake to think that no democratic, no *British*, government would consider such a step. The costs of uncontained dissent are simply too high. If dissent reaches major proportions and cannot be silenced then defeat must follow.

Why does this lacuna exist? Perhaps part of the reason that measures to combat dissent have not received much attention is because crucial records have not been available. Consider the British case. Many of the most important files in the most important collections were to be closed for one hundred years. Much of this material has only recently been opened; and even at this late date it is obvious that many files are incomplete. Police correspondence and reports, 'black lists', Criminal Investigation Department (CID) surveillance records and domestic threat assessments may simply have been as embarrassing for the compilers after the war as for those then surveyed, or indeed, for those caught up in waging the war against internal enemies. Documents like these may have been purged; they may simply remain closed. Some important collections appear to have been almost completely sanitized. Correspondence between the Commissioner of the Metropolitan Police (MEPO) and the Home Office (HO), for instance, is almost entirely absent for the war and the immediately postwar period. This correspondence may never have existed. Letters between the Commissioner and the Home Secretary were pasted into exercise books. Between 1914 and 1922, there are almost no letters. Pages were not excised. There were no pages.[9] Along the same lines, we know that Admiralty Intelligence was very active in combating dissent, but such activities have left almost no trace in Admiralty files.

The government, of course, was not the only actor with a selective memory and a bad conscience. Most of those personally engaged on the government side left little record of their activities against dissent.

Assistant Commissioner Basil Thomson, with responsibility for directing the police response to dissent, is a partial exception. Those parts of his memoirs which deal with his activities against dissent, however, are few, obviously sanitized, and included, it seems probable, for curiosity value.[10] Nor do many wartime dissenters have very good postwar memories. This was probably by choice. In his memoirs, Philip Snowden confessed that he had deliberately omitted the long passage he had initially planned concerning the wartime utterances and activities of his opponents. Why? They were too terrible and shaming for those implicated, he thought, to be recalled.[11] Equally shaming may have been remembrance of his own wartime statements (some of which were certainly seditious) once the passions produced by the war had abated and he had taken high office in His Majesty's Government (HMG).[12] It is unlikely that Snowden was the only person who practised this type of self-censorship. About the only memoir writers prepared to tell all were Clydeside Reds – John McGovern and William (Red) Gallacher for instance. Unfortunately, while useful and entertaining, their recollections are of doubtful general utility.[13]

The result? Many questions which cannot be definitively answered and much information lacking detail. Here are a few examples. We can, for instance, establish from the surviving correspondence that there were lists of those to be pre-emptively arrested in certain eventualities without being able to know who was on them because the lists themselves, in all probability, no longer exist. Similarly, we can know that there was infiltration of suspect organizations – trade unions, and suspicious political and peace organizations for instance – without being able to establish the scale or effectiveness of such penetration. We know there were informers. Who they were and how they were recruited and selected remains a mystery. We know that, by 1917, information concerning the activities of dissenting organizations was being passed to civilian organizations for their pre-emption, without being able to establish the scale or global effectiveness of such co-ordination. We know that Lloyd George and other leading members of his administration were associated with the war against dissent, both officially and unofficially, but it is difficult to ascertain how complete was their personal responsibility for much that occurred. We can, finally, sketch out a system of repression functioning effectively by 1917, but it is difficult to know just how much this system was the product of chance or forethought. These are only a few of the more provoking questions. Tentative answers will be suggested for some of them in what follows.

What exists teases and invites speculation without permitting the construction of a comprehensive narrative. Nonetheless, while the complete story cannot be told, enough documentation remains and is now open to give some, provisional, idea of method. What follows is a brief discussion of the highly effective negative methods by which British dissent was marginalized, those persons and organizations which might have mobilized it were rendered impotent, and the type of internal dissension which drove Russia from the war and brought about the collapse of Germany was prevented. It was not that Britain was peculiarly without dissenters, just that the British government dealt with them particularly effectively. Such methods grew from very humble beginnings to the point where, by the end of 1917, a highly effective if not always consistent system of repression had emerged, capable of silencing the dissent which existed, while a more thorough-going structure was already being prepared against the eventuality that dissent might develop in more dangerous directions still. And, while the British government never assembled the formal powers of the autocracies – or even of Clemenceau's administration in Republican France – its policies were, perhaps, more effective for that fact. A covert practice of repression ensured that few ever knew how extensive were the activities inspired, if not always carried out, by the government. Nor were repressive practices ever implemented in such a fashion as was obviously inconsistent with civilian, peacetime practice. Civilian governments, characterized by liberal intentions if not always by liberal practice, remained in control throughout the war. This ensured that all repressive measures were carried through only so far as astute judges of the matter considered that a critical mass of British society was willing to follow, indeed, was disposed to lead. What this meant was that while the government came to operate comprehensively against dissent, repression remained a solution without becoming unnecessarily, disproportionately provocative.

If, therefore, as Ludendorff saw it, the British army might be conceived of as being the instrument of victory, this must be construed not only as an acknowledgement of the fighting prowess of British and dominion troops, but at least in part, as a tribute to the efficiency with which Britain's home front was policed and the private disaffection of many prevented from bringing about national collapse.

NOTES

1. Ireland is excluded not because it is of no interest, but owing to constraints of time and space. Ireland, properly considered, would require a whole volume to itself.
2. For the propaganda war, for instance, see G. Bruntz, *Allied Propaganda and the Collapse of the German Empire in 1918* (Stanford: Stanford University Press, 1972);

P. Buitenhuis, *The Great War of Words* (Vancouver: University of British Columbia Press, 1987); A. Ponsonby, *Falsehood in Wartime: This Containing an Assortment of Lies Circulated Throughout the Nations During the Great War* (New York: E. D. Dutton, 1929); J. Read, *Atrocity Propaganda 1914–1918* (Oxford: Oxford University Press, 1941); N. Reeves, *Official British Film Propaganda During the First World War* (London: Dover, 1986); C. Roetter, *Psychological Warfare* (London: Batsford, 1974); M. Saunders and P. Taylor, *British Propaganda During the First World War* (London: Macmillan, 1982); J. Squires, *British Propaganda at Home and in the United States 1914–1917* (Cambridge, MA: Harvard University Press, 1986).

3. M. Swartz, *The Union of Democratic Control in British Politics During the First World War* (Oxford: Clarendon, 1971).

4. R. Desmarais, 'Lloyd George and the Development of the British Government's Strike Breaking Organization', *International Journal of Social History*, 20 (1975), pp. 1–15; R. Geary, *Policing Industrial Disputes. 1893–1985* (Cambridge: Cambridge University Press, 1985); K. Jeffery, *States of Emergency: British Governments and Strike Breaking since 1919* (London: Routledge & Kegan Paul, 1983); J. Morgan, *Conflict and Order: The Police and Labour Disputes in England and Wales 1900–1939* (Oxford: Clarendon, 1987); S. Peak, *Troops in Strikes: Military Intervention in Industrial Disputes* (London: Cobden Trust, 1984).

5. Morgan, *Conflict and Order*, pp. 65–71.

6. Geary, *Policing Industrial Disputes*, p. 48.

7. Keith Jeffery begins his discussion of the government strikebreaking apparatus by indicating that it was a product of the period immediately following the war, Jeffery, *States of Emergency*, p. 1. In fact, it is more appropriate to see the mechanism surviving into peacetime as the much reduced quantification of wartime practice.

8. R. Thurlow, *The Secret State: British Internal Security in the Twentieth Century* (Oxford: Blackwell, 1994), pp. 47–63, especially pp. 60–3; G. De Groot, *Blighty: British Society in the Era of the Great War* (London: Longman, 1996), pp. 140–60. Thurlow, most importantly, avoids Jeffery's error. For him, the First World War was a seminal period, during which roles were assumed, never to be renounced, and inhibitions lost, never to be regained. De Groot is good, but tends to understate the potential of dissent. For him, the dissenters were 'leaders without followers … fringe ideologues who maintained a lonely and futile opposition to the government' (p. 143). This confuses social–political reality with the effect of government policy.

9. See PRO, MEPO 1/68, and MEPO 1/69. Virtually nothing remains from the period 1914–22 aside from a few letters dealing with spies, and alterations to the police force – the enrolment of special constables, and the retention of retired men, for example.

10. B. Thomson, *The Scene Changes* (London: Doubleday, 1937); idem, *The Story of Scotland Yard* (London: Grayson & Grayson, 1935).

11. Lord Snowden, *Autobiography* (London: Ivor Nicolson & Watson, 1934), p. 416.

12. Snowden was a dynamic platform speaker who, if many of his wartime speeches are taken at face value, was also a revolutionary firebrand and a strong admirer of the Bolsheviks – advocating, through the later war years, that their solution for Russia be applied to Britain. By 1920, his tune had changed considerably (see, for example, in addition to sources indicated below, B. Russell, *The Autobiography of Bertrand Russell* (Toronto: McClelland & Stewart, 1968; London: George Allen & Unwin, 1968), Vol. II, p. 102, etc.). He had become a convinced anti-Bolshevik, and the memory of his wartime utterances must have caused him considerable mortification.

13. W. Gallacher, *Revolt on the Clyde* (London: Lawrence & Wishart, 1949); J. McGovern, *Neither Fear Nor Favour* (London: Bloomfield Press, 1960).

—1—

War and Dissent, 1914–1915

IN AUGUST 1914 Britain declared war on Germany. In Britain, as in all combatant countries, such few voices as were raised in dissent were overwhelmed by a chorus supportive of the decision to resort to arms. It would have been strange had it been otherwise. While its entry to the war had been controversial, attended by the resignation of several members of the Asquith government, Britain entered the war to defend well-defined and long-established interests. It was widely believed that the war would be over quickly and that victory would not require any fundamental change to peacetime ways of doing things.

This is not to say that there were no dissenters. From the beginning, there were prominent men who associated themselves in opposition to the war. During its first year, however, they were without a coherent body of followers, agreed programme, or effective organization. While these things existed in embryo, dissent had not yet developed to the point where it could be a threat to the war effort. Such would remain the case until an increasingly total war, requiring greater levels of sacrifice and necessitating wartime departures such as conscription, began to produce mass disaffection associated, ultimately, with elite dissent. It is, however, important that we understand the basic nature of British anti-war dissent because, while dissent grew in scope and significance, it grew from particularly British roots and its nature did not change. Repression can only be effective if it is constructed to account for the particular characteristics of a given dissent.

Ramsay MacDonald and the faction of the Independent Labour Party (ILP) opposing Britain's entry to the war must surely have pride of place in any discussion of anti-war dissent in Britain. From the time of the first ILP peace meeting in Trafalgar Square, even before the declaration of war, much of the party leadership never looked back.[1] Many of them – Keir Hardie, Ramsay MacDonald and others such as Philip Snowden, Fenner Brockway and Clifford Allen – were either pacifists or convinced, at least, that war between nations did not serve the interests of the working class.

Brockway was a good example of a socialist dissenter and a pacifist. The son of missionary parents, he had graduated from liberalism to advanced socialism by 1907. Throughout he was an uncompromising pacifist. No Marxist, he considered that only pacifism was reconcilable with socialist principles. The only exception he was ever willing to make to this general rule was in the case of colonial peoples struggling for independence. Even this exception was still some decades away in development, and hardly covered Britain's case in 1914.[2] As well, for socialists like Brockway, many of them perhaps less convinced pacifists than he was, the conflict between nations was of less relevance than the struggle for the rights of labour. The secret of the bayonet – need it be said? – was that there was a worker on either end. 'We are told that international Socialism is dead', began the ILP Christmas card for 1914,

> that all our hopes and ideals are wrecked by the fire and pestilence of European war. It is not true. Out of the darkness and depth we hail our working class comrades of every land. Across the roar of guns, we send sympathy and greetings to the German Socialists.
>
> In forcing this appalling crime upon the nations, it is the rulers, the diplomats, the militarists who have sealed their doom. In tears of blood and bitterness, the greater Democracy will be born.
>
> With steadfast faith we greet the future; our cause is holy and imperishable, and the labour of our hands has not been in vain.
>
> Long Live Freedom and Fraternity!
> Long Live International Socialism![3]

While these sentiments were certainly those of a minority, they were, nevertheless deeply held.

For his part, Ramsay MacDonald, in 1914 the leader of the ILP, the umbrella Labour Party and the Parliamentary Labour Party (PLP),[4] represented a greater constituency within British politics: the perplexed – those who combined socialism with religious motives and who, if internationalist by creed, were patriots by instinct. While certainly considered 'pacifists' at the time, adherents of this persuasion would be more correctly labelled today, following Martin Ceadel, 'pacific-ists': anti-war, but not in all cases, convinced that sometimes recourse to war might be a regrettable necessity.[5] This was certainly not a very well defined, nor comfortable position. One of his biographers, Bernard Sacks, is probably most correct in describing MacDonald as a 'practical pacifist'.[6] That is, while not a pure pacifist like Brockway, he was so opposed to war in principle that he could scarcely identify a single case which would justify it. 'I do not think', he wrote to another of the perplexed, in May 1916,

> that [in the event of war] a socialist would be inconsistent if he performed work of national importance such as teaching and farming. I am quite sure that if a Socialist Government were in power conditions might arise when it would have to defend itself, but it would do so on a philosophy of individual conscience and not of State tyranny over the individual. That is where the difference comes in between us and the militarists. … If, in addition to being a Socialist, one is a member of the Society of Friends or a Tolstoyan, then of course, one's Socialist principles must be mixed up with the others, only do not say that the combination of principles which results is pure socialism because it is not.[7]

One, perhaps, could fight if a citizen of a socialist country under attack, if one was a volunteer, and provided that there were no conflicting religious principles. Britain was not a socialist country in 1914. MacDonald was not sure that it had been attacked. With MacDonald there *were* religious scruples. Moreover, like many dissenters MacDonald believed that conscription must inevitably follow from involvement in a European war. Conscription, as Keir Hardie put it, was 'the badge of the slave'.[8] MacDonald, quite plainly, was not likely to provide very effective support for Britain's war effort.

On the other hand, like many of the perplexed, MacDonald was well able to distinguish between combatants. If the war had to be fought, then he certainly hoped that Britain would win it. Britain's participation was a crime; yet a German victory would be a disaster. Overcoming his loathing for the idea of war, in August 1914 MacDonald even offered to work for the national interest provided that his fundamental objections were understood. He was made to understand by Lloyd George, however, that this was simply not good enough.[9] Going further, in October MacDonald took up a challenge to put his principles into practice by volunteering to work for a field ambulance unit. He crossed over into France to see what he could do. He was not at the front for very long, however, before he was arrested by the military authorities and deported back to Britain.[10] He withdrew thereafter into an opposition more extreme than it need have been. Confused MacDonald may have been: he was also already peripheralized and identified as a leader of dissent.

In August 1914 MacDonald withdrew from leadership of the Labour

Party when it became clear that the dissenters would be in the minority. To prevent permanent disunion, Arthur Henderson, his successor, allowed him to remain as treasurer.[11] MacDonald had already found an alternative forum for political activity. With other, like-minded dissenters, he became a prominent, founding member of the Union of Democratic Control (UDC).[12] MacDonald's primary objection, always, was less with the war (which he hated) than with the way in which Britain had entered the war, and the prewar diplomacy which had brought it about (which he absolutely abhorred). The only rational policy, he considered, was to fight until a tolerable peace could be made, and then to work to ensure that there was never a repetition.[13] Moreover, as a socialist, MacDonald was not slow to indict social inequalities as the root of the political evil which had led to the war. If the war had to be fought, he considered, then the rich should be made to finance it out of their own pockets, thus reducing their liking for conflict, avoiding placing a burden on future generations, and accomplishing wealth redistribution.[14] MacDonald, needless to say, very quickly became rather unpopular with very many people.

Both the convinced socialists and the perplexed, combined against the war, were a minority within the Labour Party, labour movement and working class. If all had answered the cry found, for instance, in the ILP Christmas card, dissent might have been vigorous and effective from the beginning of the war. Within Labour ranks, however, a split had already developed in August 1914. When MacDonald proposed that Labour MPs vote against war credits, he had found himself opposed by a solid block of ILP Trades Union Congress (TUC) members led by John Hodge. Patriotism rather than socialist or pacifist principle was the guiding light of this faction. Hodge insisted that the question was an easy one: 'either we are for our country or we are against it'.[15] Even where full-blooded, bellicose patriotism was not in evidence, the majority Labour view was that it would be a political mistake, both strategic and tactical, to compromise the allied war effort. Disagreement within the Labour Party reflected division within the working class. About the only place where Labour unity was preserved through the war was in London. Here, Herbert Morrison – Labour's coming man – managed to preserve a fragile unity by deliberately avoiding the question of the war altogether.[16]

Elsewhere, division was the rule, and the patriots in the ascendance. Throughout the war, the Webbs tell us, five-sixths of the PLP and nine-tenths of the aggregate membership of the Labour Party supported the government's war policy.[17] 'From the beginning of the war to the end', they affirm, the Labour Party, alike in all its corporate acts, and by the individual efforts of its leading members ... stuck at nothing in its determination to help the Government win the war.[18]

The Webbs were certainly over-stating the case, but not much.[19] Even in the ILP – both as a party, and the Labour grouping most accepting of dissent – dissenters were a minority in 1914 and remained so until the Leeds conference of 1917 at least. Marwick provides a useful illustration. In 1918 (with dissent at its high point), in Bradford (a town notorious for its militancy), and in the local ILP (that organization most opposed to the war), absent membership 'was accounted for as follows – 429 in His Majesty's Forces, nineteen in His Majesty's Prisons, with, in addition, twenty-nine conscientious objectors on Alternative Service'.[20] In a place, a time and an organization in which we would expect dissenters to be disproportionately over-represented within a general working-class membership, serving soldiers outnumbered objectors of all types, by 9 to 1, and absolutists by almost 23 to 1.

There were exceptions to the general rule that patriotism overruled dissent in the early years of the war, places where the outbreak of war did not lead to immediate social consolidation. Clydeside was one. The reasons, however, were particular to the region. In Glasgow, for instance, a class divide of the most dangerous kind existed which was not at all lessened by the clumsy policies adopted by the Scottish Office in 1914–15.[21] There was, in addition, a substantial immigrant Irish population in Glasgow, and wherever they were found, the Irish were fodder for dissent during the First World War period.[22] On the Clyde, moreover, the local dissenting leadership almost immediately attempted to turn wartime grievances and fears of approaching conscription to political purposes. Dissent's national leadership did not learn this trick until the later months of 1915. The local Labour leadership tended, finally, to be far more radical than was usual. John MacLean, for instance, the most prominent local Marxist, was not only very popular, but almost unique among British Marxists in being against the war from the beginning. Here only were the most radical voices in British political life against the war; here only did these voices find a ready-made mass audience; here only were the tactics of dissent effective from the start of the war.[23]

The result? In a departure from more permissive policies elsewhere, far left journals were simply suppressed (*Forward* and *Worker* in January 1915) and the most intransigent leaders – John Muir, John MacLean, William Gallacher and Tom Bell – imprisoned. Muir and Bell (the printer) were sentenced for association with *Worker*, which carried an article in January 1915, entitled 'Should Workers Arm?', judged to be blatantly seditious. MacLean got three years, Gallacher six months, and Bell, Muir and Maxton one year each.[24] At the end of the year, Gallacher and Emanuel Shinwell conspired to humiliate Lloyd George during a trip north.[25] First of all, they convinced most prominent Labour leaders to boycott the powerful Minister of Munitions. Ultimately, David Kirkwood was the only local Labour leader prepared to meet him. Later, a packed meeting booed Lloyd George off the stage, and ended by singing the Red Flag. Three days later, nine prominent, radical Labour leaders were arrested and deported.[26] In 1916, Maxton and MacLean were imprisoned, yet again, for speaking against conscription.[27] Thereafter, to a certain extent, Glasgow quietened down under the patient handling of David Kirkwood, who, despite his growing radicalism, was determined to use the war in the interests of the working class. While recalcitrant, and always violent, Glasgow ceased to be so much of an exception.

Somewhere between the Labour dissenters, and the TUC patriots such as Hodge stood Arthur Henderson – the perfect leader for a split party. An officer of the British Section of the Second International, he had assisted Keir Hardie's efforts to stop the war. With Ramsay MacDonald, he had joined the UDC. While he was later to resign from the executive, Henderson never fully repudiated his association with the UDC and returned to it by the end of the war.[28] On the other hand, Henderson did not believe that British diplomacy had been responsible for the war. He believed that Britain's cause was just, and that Germany was evil.[29] He went further and promised to support even conscription and government workplace restructuring if the emergency required it.[30] To do anything else, he considered, would make him a traitor to Britain's soldiers – three of whom were his own sons.[31] Ultimately, Henderson took office in the government: first as PLP whip in the Asquith coalition government, and later as a member of the Lloyd George War Cabinet. He was also an energetic participant in wartime recruiting campaigns.[32] 'If being secretary of the Labour Party', he answered an opponent, 'is in any way to preclude me from doing my duty to my country in this crisis, then I want my hon[ourable] friend and others to know that I chose my country before my party.'[33] When Henderson resigned as leader of the ILP, he was replaced by Fred Jowett, a man of similar convictions – inclined to oppose war, but likewise inclined to support this one. While a dissenter of pacifist tendencies, and pro-UDC, Jowett was also convinced that Britain needed to fight this war to win.[34]

Labour dissenters were by no means alone. Many Liberals hated war, power politics and most of all conscription, so far were these out of keeping with the Gladstonian inheritance. Liberals were, however, like

Labour, divided on the issue of when policies designed to win the war became simply unacceptable. They were, moreover, as vulnerable to patriotic considerations. Nor did the fact that a Liberal government was in power make the situation any easier. A few Liberal-Imperialists of the Rosebery school, such as Winston Churchill, then First Lord of the Admiralty, were exultant and were vigorous supporters of the war effort. A few others – Sir Edward Grey, the Foreign Minister, Haldane, the War Minister and Lloyd George, the Chancellor of the Exchequer – accepted what could not be avoided. Asquith, the Prime Minister, needed to be convinced. In the end, he was brought to throw his weight on the side of his friends, and principal political allies, Grey and Haldane.[35] Most other Liberals were appalled by what had happened. Lord John Morley, Charles Trevelyan and John Burns withdrew from the government at the prospect of war, so much did they disapprove of the 'secret diplomacy' which they believed had brought it about. They could not countenance participation in a war which, they considered, had been caused by unprincipled diplomacy, and was being conducted by immoral means towards ignoble ends. Few, however, moved to overt opposition. That would be, if nothing else, party treason. It would also surrender the party to Grey, Haldane, Lloyd George and Churchill.

Charles Trevelyan, alone among the principal men of the Liberal Party, broke not only with the government but with his party, and became a notable dissenter. It would have been strange had he not. A Gladstonian, he was, in 1904, the founder of the National Peace Council, and a constant critic of the foreign policy of Sir Edward Grey. With war imminent, he became a founder and financial backer of the British Neutrality Committee, and with the declaration of war, a founding father of the UDC.[36] In the early months of the war, he bent his best efforts to the construction of a united anti-war front in Parliament, drawn both from the Liberal and Labour parties.[37] His opinion of the existing Liberal leadership was already highly unfavourable, and steadily declined. As early as 1915 his disapproval was near total. '[W]hen you have reached the depth of dishonesty of Asquith and Grey over the French alliance', he wrote to Sir Arthur Ponsonby in the early months of 1915, 'you are capable of any immorality.'[38] Trevelyan was not only worried about how the war began, but horrified at the crimes which, he was certain, must follow. He believed, for one thing, that the war would certainly be long and hard. It would necessarily involve conscription. But what to do? The best policy, he considered, would be to wait things out, dissociating at least a remnant of the Liberal and Labour parties from the war's conduct, and prepare this rump to organize the inevitable revulsion which would develop.[39]

Certain leading Liberals who remained in the government agreed with much of Trevelyan's assessment. They were not willing, however, to go so far, so openly. It was a sign of the dilemma presented for Liberalism by the war that even leading Liberals and allies of Asquith such as Reginald McKenna, the Home Secretary in 1914, his successor in 1915 (Attorney General in 1914), Sir John Simon and the Chairman of the Board of Trade, Walter Runciman, had their qualms.

Simon was widely expected to leave the government on the outbreak of war, and only stayed after Lloyd George convinced him that the Germans had sought war.[40] Even then, it took a personal appeal from Asquith to ensure Simon's continued loyalty. He would stay, he promised, 'though with a heavy heart'.[41] By 1916, Simon had had enough and, on the issue of conscription, followed those who had left the government at the outset – taking with him 'about three dozen' other Liberal members of the House of Commons 'into opposition to attack the measure'.[42]

McKenna and Runciman disapproved of the way in which Britain had entered the war, and of conscription. However, like many others, they were confused by events for which there was no recent precedent. McKenna, for instance, considered that the army would have to grow if Britain were not to default on its obligations to its allies, but also believed that the growth of the army would imperil Britain's ability to remain in the war by undermining other aspects of national strength.[43] He was, therefore, only too keenly aware of the central dilemma of British domestic war management without having any insight as to how it was to be solved. After the spring of 1915, McKenna and Runciman were only maintained in the government with the most explicit assurances from Asquith that the Unionists,[44] then entering the national government, did so with an open mind on divisive issues such as Ireland, conscription, free trade and taxation.[45] Of course, the Unionists had only accepted Asquith's equivocations (particularly on conscription) because they considered them the best that could be obtained at the moment, and certain to be expanded in the future.[46]

Having made their personal opposition known, most dissenting Liberals remained silent thereafter so as not to harm the party. McKenna, for instance, promised that despite his disagreement with government policy, he would never go into opposition or split the party – even on the issue of conscription.[47] A divided party would fall to the Unionist wolves. Asquith would be isolated within the party and the Liberal 'militarists' would have a clear field.[48] 'What will the country say', Mrs Asquith pleaded at a time when McKenna appears to have been contemplating a real break, 'when it hears that you, Runciman &

Simon – all *real* Liberals – all heart & soul in agreement with Henry have left him?'[49] What the country would say, however, was probably less important for McKenna than what the country would do: turn to Bonar Law or Lloyd George, operating without any effective check.

When Asquith began to renege on his promises, McKenna remained in the government, serving in a succession of posts, increasingly marginalized, unhappy and without influence in the formation of a war policy the defining features of which he could never accept. Runciman resigned.[50] Both remained silent. McKenna was silent, as well, to cries that if Liberalism failed to provide a lead to dissent it would fail, and the Liberal Party would lose leadership of the 'progressive forces' in the nation.[51] In the end, silence seemed like complicity. Apparent acquiescence in a policy dominated by the Unionist agenda was the major reason why dissent, in the end, came to flow through Labour rather than Liberal channels.

Simon was an exception to the rule. Unlike most other Liberal dissenters, he did formalize his break with the party. His dissent, however, remained strictly parliamentary, and therefore, ineffective. Like McKenna and Runciman, he refused to provoke division, however divisive the issue. 'Sir John desires to assure your Majesty', his letter of resignation went,

> that no effort on his part will be wanting to promote a renewal of the national unity which this proposal has jeopardised. He has done, and will do, everything in his power to confine the opposition to this Bill to protests, on grounds of conviction and policy, against its enactment; and has already made it clear, as Mr Balfour admitted in Thursday's debate, that this unhappy difference does not and must not imply any division as to the supreme national purpose for which your Majesty's subjects, one and all, have entered the war.[52]

Having moved into opposition, like McKenna, he refused dissenting appeals to lead the cause against the war,[53] while he himself saw service with the staff of the Royal Flying Corps (RFC) in France.

Another prominent Liberal who, like Trevelyan, not only left the party but moved into overt opposition, was Sir Arthur Ponsonby. While not a party figure of the stature of Trevelyan, Ponsonby was a long-time critic of British foreign policy. As chairman of the Liberal foreign affairs group, he had been a gadfly afflicting whichever government happened to be in power. Even before the war, scenting danger, he had authored a number of books highly critical of what he perceived to be the new, and, as he saw it, unconstitutional way of forming foreign policy.[54]

Like Trevelyan, Ponsonby did not simply oppose the government for the way in which it had entered into the war. He opposed the war itself. Like Trevelyan, he considered the war an unmitigated disaster. 'The matter we are dealing with', he told his Stirling constituents on 25 March 1915,

> is not just a party question, a passing dispute or a matter of small concern which can be left in abeyance. It is a shattering catastrophe the consequences of which will last our life times. The result of which will be felt for generations to come.[55]

And why had this happened? Largely because of the prewar arms race. This was Ponsonby's bugbear, just as conscription was Trevelyan's. Both, of course, were carried over into the UDC critique. 'When nations devote', Ponsonby wrote,

> all their enterprise, their inventive genius, their labour & wealth and the best of their manhood to the manufacture & perfecting of engines of war it is inevitable that an opportunity will sooner or later be made to test their efficiency ... *I feel very strongly about this and think it must be fully dealt with.*[56]

The war could have been avoided. Nothing could possibly be gained sufficient to justify even the effort already made. Who could possibly gain anything from a continuation of the conflict? Only the sinister armament interests. They, Ponsonby charged, had created the environment which had produced the war, and stood ready to rake in the blood money. Ponsonby less broke with the Liberal party than formalized an existing breach when he came together with like-minded men to build the UDC.[57]

Other intellectual Liberals, outside parliament – J. A. Hobson, Norman Angell, Bertrand Russell,[58] Philip Morrell, F. W. Hirst – followed Ponsonby and Trevelyan into active opposition. From the beginning of the war, these men (Angell, Russell and Morrell especially) had been meeting with Liberal and Labour parliamentary dissenters in an attempt to orchestrate a campaign against the war.[59] From this seed grew the UDC. The intellectuals, quite simply, agreed that the war was a crime and a danger on which Britain had embarked due to bumbling, manipulation and its overly enthusiastic participation in a flawed and morally bankrupt international system. They agreed, moreover, that conscription was inevitable and a crime, and that armament interests had both helped cause, and would solely benefit from, a conflict which was otherwise a universal catastrophe. We should not wonder at such concurrence. These men had erected much of the intellectual framework employed by the dissenters. In moving into dissent they were simply associating themselves with the wartime political expression of their own prewar ideas.

A minority faction of the suffragette movement, drawn on by the wider radicalism of which their feminism was a feature, accompanied the socialists and Liberals into dissent. F. W. Pethick Lawrence (later honorary treasurer of the UDC) and Sylvia Pankhurst, leader of the East London Federation of Suffragettes (ELFS), were leaders of this tendency which had begun to split, for tactical reasons, from the mainline Women's Social and Political Union (WSPU) in the months immediately before the war.[60] Kindred movements supported them: the Women's International League for Peace and Freedom (WIL) and Margaret Haley's Women's Peace Crusade (WPC), for instance. The WIL and the WPC were direct responses to the war formed following the suspension of general WSPU activity.[61] Catherine Marshall of the National Union of Women's Suffrage Societies (NUWSS) had also, even before the war, been drawn towards a social, rather than a strictly gender critique of contemporary Britain. Like these others, she quickly became a prominent leader of dissent.[62]

The dissenting suffragettes believed that the struggle of women for political rights was simply part of a greater conflict pitting the disadvantaged against the powers that were. For women, the vote was a beginning. There were other issues of interest to women, they believed, which were more amenable to class or political than gender analysis.[63] Moreover was it not bad tactics to fail to support anti-war dissent? Against the status quo, dissenters of all kinds would have to form a common front or risk being defeated in detail. Support for anti-war dissent, in part, would simply reciprocate backing already received in the struggle for the vote. The ILP had been the only prewar party which had supported, consistently and whole-heartedly, the demand for a female suffrage. Asquith, Grey and the rest (with the exception of Lloyd George and Churchill) were not just Britain's war leadership, but the prewar leaders of the anti-suffrage movement. How would helping to keep them in power further any feminist platform, however modest?

While a suffragette anti-war movement certainly existed from the beginning, for our purposes it does not require separate treatment. From 1914, the dissenting suffragettes were ILP fellow-travellers and, by the end of the war, this faction of the movement had practically disappeared into the Labour Party. The ELFS, for instance, became in March 1916 the Women's Suffrage Federation, devolved into the

Workers' Socialist Federation in 1918 – its male component larger at each stage, its suffragist message more subordinate to socialist content.[64] Despite this fact, however, and even though they were small in numbers, the dissenting suffragettes represented a considerable accretion of strength for dissent. The WIL, in particular, developed a considerable propaganda apparatus. The WPC was remarkably persistent in attempting to arrange anti-war meetings.[65] As male dissenters, by 1916, began to disappear into prisons and guardhouses, very often it was their female collaborators who kept the colours flying.

Such were the major political sources from which anti-war dissent developed. In all of the greater movements from which it derived, dissent remained a minority tendency. Given these disparate origins, it might be considered that dissent would remain an amorphous, divided and impotent force. From the beginning of 1915, however, dissent was beginning to gain coherence, to solidify into an effective force. Why was this?

One factor which certainly contributed enormously to the consolidation of dissent, and which is far too often forgotten in studies of the subject, was the religious provenance of British pacifism. Whatever political form anti-war dissent might take, whether Liberal or Labour (or suffragette for that matter), all were rooted in the traditional abhorrence of large portions of British nonconformity for war of any kind and whatever the cause, and distrust of the state both as foreign policy actor, domestic oppressor and in and for itself.[66] With the exception of the few anti-war British Marxists (John MacLean and Tom Bell for example), doctrinaire non-Christian socialists of other varieties (Clifford Allen and Fenner Brockway for instance), and intellectual humanists (such as Bertrand Russell and Norman Angell), it was a fact that most prominent dissenters were religious. In significant ways, their dissent was as much a product of their religiosity as a response to the circumstances of the day. MacDonald, for instance, was a radical because religious, and became a Christian socialist because a radical. The integrating factor throughout was the nature of his piety.

It is not surprising, of course, that British anti-war dissent should spring from this source. Both the Liberal and Labour parties had begun, in large measure, as conventions of reform-minded nonconformists, albeit of differing social strata, with different sects predominating, and at different times. Emmeline Pankhurst's autobiography is a monument to nonconformist faith become liberal convictions transformed into gender critique when confronted with particular problems. All, in large measure, were simply manifestations of nineteenth-century religious enthusiasm become political radicalism when applied to the resolution of real grievances. In this respect, the dissenting doctrine, rather than simply representing a political challenge, was as well, a religious challenge to the state church represented politically by the Conservative Party – the established church in politics. When Liberalism combined with Labour and the suffragettes in dissent it was as much a fusion of Fox, Wesley and Hannah Moore as it was an association of Mill, Marx and Mary Wollstonecraft.

Among dissenters whose formal religious belief had atrophied, it was generally replaced by a secular humanism which, in most of its particulars, was virtually indistinguishable from the nonconformist Christian social ethic. Consider, for instance, the Allen, Brockway and Russell examples. Allen had studied for a career in the Church before his conversion to socialism. By his later admission, he came to socialism exactly because he considered it to be the only way to carry through the ethical reform of international and political life.[67] The type of reform he had in mind was virtually identical to that envisioned, for instance, by Ramsay MacDonald. What made him different was that his socialism superseded his Christianity rather than proceeded from it – as it did, for instance, with MacDonald, Hardie and Lansbury. Similarly, Brockway's missionary socialism carried much of the same content as the missionary religion he had learned as a child. Likewise, Russell's pacifism is difficult to justify except by reference to principles whose religious origin Russell formally repudiated. Even the Clyde Communists were no different. It was to Catholicism, for instance, that John McGovern and Red Gallacher first looked for an answer. When it proved insufficient to satisfy them, they rejected revealed religion in favour of another faith (Marxism: revealed politics) suggestively like, in many respects, that discarded.

As with the leaders, so with the followers. Christianity, rather than socialism, provided the surest and most reliable link to the working class, itself still in the final throes of nineteenth-century enthusiasm. The best, most popular and most effective propaganda produced by the dissenters was directed primarily, particularly in the early years, at a Christian, nonconforming audience. The religious polarity of dissent did not truly begin to shift until 1917, when the socialist element began to receive equal prominence. A unifying basic belief system, whatever their politics, must certainly be counted as a factor of tremendous importance, linking dissenters of all kinds.

Religion was not the only factor lending coherence to dissent. There was, as well, the fact that both the Labour and Liberal leadership shared an intellectual critique of the prevailing practice of foreign affairs in particular, in which dislike of secret diplomacy, armaments and conscription occupied pride of place. To some extent, concurrence of analysis had been formalized in organization even before the war. The ultimate unifying mechanism, the UDC, was less a striking departure than a natural and inevitable response to the war. Finally, whatever the agenda and membership, it seems to be the case that almost all dissenting organizations, before and during the war, appear to have shared common sources of funding.

Let us consider the extra-political organizations consolidating dissent. Before the war, many who would become dissenters were already associated with various 'Norman Angell' organizations – study groups convened to discuss the ideas of Norman Angell, author of the *Great Illusion*, published in 1910. Ponsonby, E. D. Morel and Ramsay MacDonald had all contributed before the war, for instance, to *War and Peace*, a 'Norman Angell monthly'. Angell himself, of course, was to be a principal founder of the UDC, who, by the summer of 1915, had left off writing general critiques and had begun to pen specific condemnations of Britain's war policy.[68] Similarly, E. D. Morel had been secretary-general of the Congo Reform Association in the years immediately before the war. Among those inclined to dislike British foreign and imperial policy, he was already a notable figure, and the membership of this organization, in large measure, carried over into anti-war dissent.[69]

Another factor which served to consolidate dissent was membership of the UDC, which grew naturally from the foundations established by Angell and Morel. From the beginning, the UDC was envisioned by its political leadership – MacDonald, Ponsonby, Trevelyan – as an organization capable of linking Labour and Liberal opponents of the war. It would become, they hoped, something like a non-partisan, super 'Norman Angell' pressure group, pursuing an agenda already established by the prewar foreign policy critics.[70] E. D. Morel was identified as a probable secretary, also from the beginning. He was a good catch for the UDC. While he agreed with the general purpose of the leaders, Morel had some ideas of his own. He refused to be 'a mere automaton'.[71] In time, he became an almost predominant influence in the formation of UDC policy. While this dominance did not always sit well with other leaders, Morel possessed organizational ability of the first order and ultimately his vision of the UDC prevailed.[72]

In Morel's view, the UDC should never seek to become a simple, monolithic, single cause organization. Rather, it would assume a similar role in dissent to that of the Labour Party on the British left. It would be the general staff of anti-war dissent, organizing the membership of other agencies as its shock troops. Morel, as secretary, would be chief of dissenting general staff. The first step was for the UDC to find friends.

Morel identified labour, pacifist, dissenting religious, suffragette, adult educational, Norman Angell and international affairs organizations as possible tools. He began to work immediately to attach these rather dissimilar organizations to the UDC, and quite plainly hoped to 'direct prewar dissent ... into the channel of the Union's dissent over foreign policy'.[73] From the beginning, members of all of these tendencies were found within UDC ranks. From the outset, the UDC appeal, less revolutionary than radical, was being heard by all elements of this otherwise diverse audience.[74] The second step would be to identify and convince a mass audience. The UDC, Morel hoped, would 'take [Britain] systematically city by city and town by town' through 'existing organizations which [it would] capture for distribution work and for the subsequent organization of public meetings'.[75] Ultimately, through such organizations, Morel hoped to consolidate dissent behind the UDC so that it would be in a position to dominate the peace. From 1915 Morel was attempting to convert ideological affiliation into structural unity; the UDC was, of course, the designated unifier.[76]

In exchange, throughout the war, the UDC acted as a generator of ideas and a propagandist for all types of dissent – most particularly through its publications and the journal it published from 1915, which provided a forum for a variety of dissenting opinions that might otherwise not have found wide circulation.[77] The UDC was able to provide this service because it was never suppressed. The UDC had been formed specifically to defeat *Daily Mail* charges that a secret 'pro-German' committee was forming to disrupt the war effort.[78] Its membership was known. It was organized nationally and operated openly. Its leadership was hardly underground, including even a party leader and member of the future Lloyd George government, Arthur Henderson. However obnoxious most of its leaders became to the authorities for activities outside the union, there never was any official, overt attempt to crush the UDC. Even its propaganda was generally passed through the censor before publication.[79]

The UDC's open activity was possible because, following the Morel line, its principal, public focus was never on stopping the war, but rather on identifying those aspects of foreign policy making which had contributed to the movement to war, while calling for a more sufficient organization of the peace so that there would not be a recurrence. The UDC would aim to:

1. 'secure real parliamentary control over foreign policy, and to prevent it being again shaped in secret and forced upon the country as an accomplished fact';

2. start negotiations on peace, democratic parties and 'influences' corresponding directly to develop 'an international understanding depending on popular parties rather than on governments';
3. conclude a fair, negotiated peace that would not contain the germ of a future war;
4. begin working on a programme of propaganda to make the ideas of the organization known to the general public.[80]

There was nothing very exceptional here, and certainly nothing immediately dangerous. While individual members might have their own agendas and might act through other, more combative organizations, the UDC never became fully engaged in the fight against this war. It was more interested in establishing a position of moral ascendancy for the aftermath of war than in bringing the war to an early end.

If, therefore, the aims of the UDC were exalted, its agenda was certainly limited. How to explain the apparent contradiction? The answer was tactics. Even many inclined to advocate a more immediately confrontational line than Morel agreed with his insistence that the UDC be kept out of the fray. It should be preserved as something apart – as an embryo party in effect – able to take control of the peace. While Ponsonby, for instance, deplored the fact that chairmanship of the UDC tied MacDonald's hands and prevented him from acting more overtly against the war, he also considered that:

> If as *The Times* foreshadows the war is to be a long business we shall want a very strong vigorous and alive body or party to be gradually growing all the while. It will be the only issue and to lay the foundations of a new European system will be the only object worth working for. You are the best man to lead such a party but you ought to be guilt free to do it.[81]

Long-range and short-term agendas, quite simply, required different tactics and therefore different leaderships. Unity of vision, however, remained.

Yet another factor giving coherence to dissent in the early years appears to have been Quaker money. Quakers disliked the war and hated conscription, for obvious reasons. Quaker wartime activities quite naturally followed from prewar political activities. Nearly all of the prewar pacifist movements received Quaker subsidies. Hardly surprisingly, Quakers were prominent members of Norman Angell study groups. Less surprisingly still, with the declaration of war funds from this source began to flow to the UDC and ultimately to the ILP.[82]

Moreover, from 1915, when conscription was first widely mooted as a probable necessity if the British war effort were to be maintained, the Quakers began to move into organized and vocal opposition to British policy in their own right. Indeed, they did more than this; they formalized their own war aims in June 1915 such that they were virtually congruent with those of the UDC.[83] One of their number, Charles Roden Buxton, by September 1915 had ceased to be a simple paymaster and had become a principal dissenter, in October joining the UDC as a member of the executive committee.[84] Another, Arnold Rowntree, was counted from the beginning as a member of the 'controlling ring' of the UDC, although he later left the Union as it moved to indict more forcibly prewar Liberal foreign policy.[85]

Looking ahead, by January 1916 the Society of Friends was virtually at war with the government – the Home Office (HO) receiving in that month an ultimatum which simply confirmed how far things had come since the beginning of the war. 'On behalf of the Committee of the Society of Friends specially appointed to have charge of this matter', it went,

> we write to inform you that if any measure having the above [conscription] for its object should become law, the opposition of our Society to it will in no sense be modified or withdrawn. Such opposition is fundamental and is based upon a conscientious objection to all warfare.
>
> We are further to inform you that if any such measure should become law the support and co-operation of Members of the Society will be available for those outside their own body whose conscientious objection is based upon the same grounds as their own ...[86]

It should be noted, however, that the Quakers were always a voice of compromise on other issues. As an organization, the Society of Friends tended to something like MacDonald's pacific-ism, while as individuals Quakers might, or might not, refuse military or alternative service. Conscription, of course, was abhorrent, but Quakers were not necessarily against force and were often enthusiastic volunteers. Unlike the Anabaptists, moreover, the Quakers did not hate the state. Once their position was established and understood they tended to retreatism rather than rebellion.[87] They could be counted upon, therefore, to reinforce the moderate voices in the UDC. On several occasions in 1914, for instance, Arnold Rowntree – one of the more important, and richer, Quaker leaders – wrote to Morel advocating caution. Britain, he felt, might not be entirely without blame for the war, and it was agreed that conscription was certainly wrong. The military situation, however, remained difficult. The Germans had been wrong in 1914. The invasion of Belgium had been a tremendous wickedness. People were making great sacrifices and might not forgive anybody who jeopardized the war effort. The long-term agenda, therefore, would have to be kept in mind, and dissent kept moderate.[88] If, therefore, the Quakers helped to bring cohesion to the dissenting movement, they also exercised a restraining influence, reinforcing the dominance of the UDC line within dissent in general and of Morel and the moderates inside the UDC.

Let us set out as a series of propositions the principal characteristics of British anti-war dissent. As has been suggested, the basic nature of dissent did not change, and any government response could only be effective if it took account of the characteristics of a particular form of dissent.[89]

1. *British dissent was an elite response.* British anti-war dissent was, particularly in the early years, restricted to those few people whose principles outweighed, or were inextricable from, their patriotism. This meant that:

2. *British dissent was driven by a mobilizational imperative.* If dissent was to be effective it would have to acquire a mass following. Other, more easily explained issues and immediate causes would have to be attached to an intellectual opposition which few shared in full. If this could be done, conscription would be a non-starter, and the war might be stopped.[90]

An attempt to expand the dissenting constituency would be aided by the fact that, while it was an elite response,

3. *British dissent was religious and religious/political in origin* and developed from widespread popular roots. If dissent was essentially elite, then it certainly grew from ideological elements common to much of British society, and dominant in much of the working class. Unlike Lenin, British dissenters did not have to educate anybody. They simply had to speak plainly in a social–political language they shared with many Britons. As well,

4. *Dissent could be expected to grow with the war.* Britain had no experience of total war organization. Even conscription (commonplace on the continent) was a tremendous, and hated, innovation. Therefore, as the government took the steps required if the war were to be won, it would inevitably provide a fillip for dissent.

For its part, dissent would certainly seek to capitalize on whatever residual cleavages in British society were widened as a result of the war, in an attempt to expand its scope. The class and trade union questions, very dangerous and divisive issues in the last years before the war, could be expected to produce exactly the type of breach which the dissenters could be expected to attempt to widen and use. Finally,

5. *Both dissent and the government shared liberally and democratically based inhibitions.* However high they might attempt to turn up the heat, as a group, the dissenters would always pull back from the brink of political disturbance, unless things just got out of hand. They were not revolutionaries.

Similarly, His Majesty's Government, in attempting to manage dissent, would violate as few political taboos as possible. Unless a consensus existed in British society that it was necessary, a truly heavy hand was unlikely. Political assessment of costs and benefits, for both sides, would produce the ultimate criteria for action.

So much for basic dissent. What was the government's initial response?

NOTES

1. Lord Elton, *The Life of James Ramsay MacDonald* (London: Collins, 1939), p. 194.
2. CCC, Fenner Brockway papers. See also F. Brockway, *Thirty Years Inside the Left* (London: George Allen & Unwin, 1947).
3. CCC, Fenner Brockway papers, FEBR 13/2, ILP Christmas Card 1914.
4. In this period the Labour Party was still very much an omnibus organization. Founded to separate representatives of organized labour from the Liberal Party, it was essentially a coalition of distinct political societies moving in the same direction. The most important of these societies were: the ILP (founded to be the political expression of trade unionism); the Social Democratic Federation (SDF: a Marxist grouping); and the Fabian Society (elite British socialists, aiming at achieving democratic socialism by evolutionary rather than revolutionary means). The PLP was composed of the representatives of all Labour tendencies, sitting together in parliament.
5. M. Ceadel, *Thinking about Peace and War* (London: Oxford University Press, 1987), pp. 101–34; idem, *Pacifism in Britain 1914–1945: The Defining of a Faith* (Oxford: Clarendon, 1980), p. 3. In what follows, the convention of the time of lumping pure pacifists and pacific-ists together as 'pacifists' will be followed unless greater accuracy is required. When a more exact definition is unnecessary, 'dissenter' or 'dissenting' will be used in preference, and should be taken to cover all forms of dissent: pacifist, pacific-ist, anti-conscriptionist, socialist, Christian and others. While these generalizations are slightly false, they do reflect government thinking at the time, and it is probable that more clarity is gained than lost by this simplification. To make too much of the distinction between the various positions is to forget the fact that most *were* at least against the First World War, while all tended to co-operate with one another.
6. B. Sacks, *J. Ramsay MacDonald in Thought and Action* (Albuquerque, NM: University of New Mexico, 1952), pp. 470–514.
7. PRO 30/69/1160, MacDonald to A. Lewis, 11 May 1916.

8. N. Young, 'War Resistance and the British Peace Movement Since 1914', in N. Young and R. Taylor (eds), *Campaigns for Peace: British Peace Movements in the Twentieth Century* (Manchester: University of Manchester, 1987), p. 27.
9. C. Wrigley, *Lloyd George and the Challenge of Labour* (New York: St Martin's Press, 1990), p. 9.
10. D. Marquand, *Ramsay MacDonald* (London: Jonathan Cape, 1977), pp. 187–8.
11. T. Lloyd, *Empire to Welfare State* (Oxford: Oxford University Press, 1986), p. 78.
12. Swartz, *Union of Democratic Control*, pp. 20–1.
13. See, for instance, H. Tiltman, *James Ramsay MacDonald* (London: Jarrold, 1929), p. 90.
14. LSE, MacDonald Papers, MacDonald, J8 Vol. VI, 'The Conscription of Wealth', 1915.
15. C. Wrigley, *Arthur Henderson* (Cardiff: GPC Books, 1990), pp. 77–8.
16. B. Donoughue and G. Jones, *Herbert Morrison: Portrait of a Politician* (London: Weidenfeld & Nicolson, 1972), pp. 38–40. Morrison's line was:

    Everyone knows that the Labour movement has been split from top to bottom on the issue of the War. By avoiding the issue at conferences, the London Labour Party has preserved a unity which would have been impossible in other circumstances.

17. S. and B. Webb, *The History of Trade Unionism* (London: Longman, Green, 1920), p. 690.
18. Ibid., p. 693.
19. The Webbs, of course, were Fabians who supported the war both for its immediate objectives and in the hope that it would produce a decisive social–economic realignment.
20. A. Marwick, *The Deluge: British Society and the First World War* (New York: Norton, 1965), p. 211. These orders of magnitude were standard through the war. In the Bradford ILP in February 1916, of 1,473 members, 461 had been fit for service. Of these: 113 were serving; four were dead, nine were wounded and recuperating and three were prisoners of war; 118 were undergoing military training; six were in the Royal Navy; and 207 were attested workers. The total? Rather more than the number of men were serving, or attested and exempted, than should have been the case. Within a year, 351 were with the colours, while only 48 had declared a contentious objection. See K. Laybourne, *Philip Snowden: Biography* (London: Temple Smith, 1988), p. 64.
21. K. Middlemas, *The Clydesiders* (London: Hutchinson, 1965), pp. 51–69.
22. Young, 'War Resistance and the British Peace Movement Since 1914', p. 28.
23. M. Shaw, 'War, Peace and British Marxism, 1895–1945', in Young and Taylor, *Campaigns for Peace*, pp. 158–9. MacLean was almost the only prominent British Marxist of whom Lenin approved.
24. Middlemas, *Clydesiders*, pp. 65–8.
25. D. Mitchell, *Women on the Warpath* (London: Jonathan Cape, 1966), p. 73.
26. P. Slowe, *Manny Shinwell: An Authorized Biography* (London: Pluto, 1993), pp. 55–7; Wrigley, *Arthur Henderson*, pp. 93–4. While Arthur Henderson was later blamed for this, the decision appears to have been made by Lloyd George and Christopher Addison, following a recommendation by Lyndon Maccassey and the Clyde dilution commissioners (whose function was to consider the restructuring of industry to permit limitation of exemptions). Wrigley, *Arthur Henderson*, p. 95.
27. Slowe, *Manny Shinwell*, p. 60.
28. BLO, Ponsonby Papers, 'Report on the Statement Made by Mr E. D. Morel … 22 June 1915'. In leaving the UDC executive, Henderson renewed his 'full sympathy with the four principals of the Union'.
29. Wrigley, *Arthur Henderson*, pp. 77–91; F. Leventhal, *Arthur Henderson* (Manchester: Manchester University Press, 1989), p. 50.

30. Wrigley, *Arthur Henderson*, pp. 82, 91, 94.
31. Leventhal, *Arthur Henderson*, p. 50.
32. Wrigley, *Arthur Henderson*, p. 81.
33. Wrigley, *Arthur Henderson*, p. 96.
34. Laybourne, *Philip Snowden*, p. 64.
35. See R. Jenkins, *Asquith* (London: Collins, 1964).
36. Swartz, *Union of Democratic Control*, pp. 11–12; A. Morris, *C. P. Trevelyan: Portrait of a Radical* (Belfast: Blackstaff, 1977), pp. 120–1.
37. BLO, Ponsonby Papers, Trevelyan to Ponsonby, 25 March 1915.
38. BLO, Ponsonby Papers, Trevelyan to Ponsonby, 27 May 1915.
39. Ibid.
40. T. Wilson (ed.), *The Political Diaries of C. P. Scott* (London: Collins, 1970), diary entry for 4 August 1914, pp. 96–7.
41. BLO, Simon Papers: Simon to Asquith, 2 August 1914 (attempts to resign); Asquith to Simon, 3 August 1914 (induces him to stay); Simon to Asquith, 4 August 1914 (agrees to stay).
42. D. Lloyd George, *War Memoirs of David Lloyd George* (London: Oldhams, 1938), Vol. I, pp. 436–7.
43. CCC, McKenna Papers, MCKN 5/9, Runciman to Asquith, undated 1915.
44. The term 'Unionists' designates the then parliamentary grouping uniting the Conservative Party and the Union (Chamberlainite) Liberals, as such the predecessor of the current Conservative Party.
45. CCC, McKenna Papers, MCKN 5/8, Runciman to McKenna, 29 May 1915.
46. HLRO, Beaverbrook Papers, C 203, Law Speech, 13 April 1916.
47. CCC, McKenna Papers, MCKN 5/9, McKenna to Asquith, undated 1915. Draft resignation over conscription.
48. CCC, McKenna Papers, MCKN 5/9, Hankey to McKenna, 28 December 1915. By the end of 1915, McKenna's relations with Lloyd George were especially poisonous.
49. CCC, McKenna Papers, MCKN 5/9, Mrs Asquith to McKenna, 28 December 1915.
50. CCC, McKenna Papers, MCKN 5/9, Runciman to McKenna, 23 January 1916. The decision to expand the Army to 70 divisions itself, he felt, made compulsion necessary, and what would happen to the promises then? 'I must decline', he concluded the letter announcing his intention to McKenna, 'to be swindled with my eyes open.' See for McKenna at this juncture: R. Adams and P. Poirier, *The Conscription Controversy in Great Britain* (London: Macmillan, 1987), p. 138.
51. CCC, McKenna Papers, MCKN 5/9, Hobhouse to McKenna, 31 December 1915. If both Runciman and McKenna resigned, Hobhouse thought, then there would be 'an alternative government, and a responsible opposition with leaders'. Moreover, he wrote,

> I am sure you will bear in mind the position of your supporters in the House. What will that position be if you remain in the cabinet and assent to conscription? They will be represented as merely the friends of a few slackers. The cause will have been lost, not in fair fight, but by a side attack of insidious character, and the opportunity of rallying all the progressive forces in the country to a sound policy, will have been lost.

52. BLO, Simon Papers, Simon 52, Announcement of Resignation.
53. BLO, Simon Papers, Simon 52, Circular letter to Simon, 11 January 1916, signed by G. Lowes Dickinson, J. A. Hobson, G. Lansbury, F. W. Pethick Lawrence, Sylvia Pankhurst, Bertrand Russell, A. Salter, Robert Smillie, J. Winstone etc.
54. For instance, A. Ponsonby, *Democracy and the Control of Foreign Affairs* (London, 1912); idem, *Social Reform Versus War* (London, 1912).

55. BLO, Ponsonby Papers, Speech to Constituents, 25 March 1915.
56. LSE, Morel Papers, Morel F6/1, Ponsonby to Morel, 30 August 1914.
57. Swartz, *Union of Democratic Control*, p. 17.
58. Russell, of course, was never properly speaking a true-blooded Liberal, and later, never a real socialist. He was, most properly, an individualist and a nonconformist in the fullest sense of the word. See, for instance, Russell, *Autobiography*, Vol. II, p. 38.
59. A. Morris, *C. P. Trevelyan*, p. 121. Many of these were friends and collaborators from before the war. For example, Lady Ottoline Morrell, Philip Morrell's wife, and a prominent dissenter in her own right, was at this time Russell's lover. For text of Russell's first letter protesting against the war, published in the *Nation* see, Russell, *Autobiography*, Vol. II, pp. 42–3. Dr John Clifford, sometimes included with this group and associated with it before the war, was, as we will see, in his public statements an uncompromising patriot.
60. Sylvia Pankhurst, *The Home Front* (London: Cresset, 1987), p. xviii. See also for Sylvia Pankhurst, Mitchell, *Women on the Warpath*, pp. 271–346.
61. A. Wiltsher, *Most Dangerous Women* (London: Pandora, 1985).
62. J. Vellacott, *From Liberal to Labour with Women's Suffrage: The Story of Catherine Marshall* (Montreal: McGill-Queens, 1993), pp. 364–8.
63. See, for instance, S. Pankhurst, *Home Front*.
64. B. Winslow, *Sylvia Pankhurst: Sexual Politics and Political Action* (New York: St Martin's Press, 1996), p. 75.
65. Wiltsher, *Most Dangerous Women*.
66. Young, 'War Resistance', *Campaigns for Peace*; Ceadel, *Pacifism in Britain*.
67. Clifford Allen (1934): social reform was necessary in order to change politics and the nature of international relations. '[I]n no other way can we escape the physical violence and cruelty which will otherwise overwhelm our civilization', C. Allen, *Britain's Political Future* (London: Longman, Green, 1934), p. 2.
68. PRO, HO 139/23/96, File 4, Norman Angell, July 1915, 'Great Britain and the Freedom on the Sea', appended. Angell had attempted to send this through to Holland for publication. Press bureau to Admiralty, 2 July 1915.
69. From the time of the foundation of the Congo Reform Association (1904) Morel was something of a professional dissenter. Swartz, *Union of Democratic Control*, pp. 13–14; C. Cline, *E. D. Morel 1873–1924. The Strategies of Protest* (Belfast: Blackstaff, 1980), p. 98.
70. LSE, Morel Papers, Morel F 6/1, Trevelyan to Morel, 5 August 1914; Morris, *C. P. Trevelyan*, p. 121. For organization circular, see MUH, Russell Papers, Vol. 530, UDC organizational letter, August 1914.
71. LSE, Morel Papers, Morel F 6/1, Morel to Trevelyan, 6 August 1914.
72. For the ego-clash with Angell see Cline, *E. D. Morel*, pp. 100–1, and with MacDonald see pp. 101–2. For Morel's fairly accurate understanding of his own abilities, see MUH, Russell Papers, volume 410, E. D. Morel to Russell, undated 1916.
73. Swartz, *Union of Democratic Control*, p. 57. For Morel's initial contact with the suffragettes see, for instance, LSE, Morel Papers, Morel F6/2, Morel to Maud Royden, 9 September 1914. He was given his head in large measure, because his vision of what the UDC was to become corresponded closely to an agenda common to the political leadership of the organization.
74. Swartz, *Union of Democratic Control*, p. 46.
75. Swartz, *Union of Democratic Control*, p. 46. Also, LSE, Morel Papers, Morel F6/1, 'Plan of Campaign for Distribution of Literature', 22 August 1914.
76. LSE, Morel Papers, Morel 6/4, Morel Circular Letter, November 1915.
77. Swartz, *Union of Democratic Control*, pp. 64–5.

78. Wilson, *Political Diaries of C. P. Scott*, Trevelyan to CPS, 13 September 1914.
79. Swartz, *Union of Democratic Control*, p. 191.
80. LSE, Morel Papers, Morel F6/1, UDC First Circular Letter, August 1914.
81. PRO 30/69/1158, Ponsonby to MacDonald, 17 August 1914. MacDonald certainly benefited from this policy, though he did not always like it. Part of Morel's ascendancy in the UDC derived from the fact that MacDonald, disliking the subordinate role he was compelled to play even as chairman, distanced himself from the organization – thus insulating himself even further from complicity. C. Cline, *E. D. Morel*, pp. 101–2.
82. The Rowntree, Cadbury and Buxton families appear to have been especially free with their cash. See, Swartz, *Union of Democratic Control*. When the police began to examine the books of dissenting organizations in 1917, it became apparent that they were dependent far more on Quaker than on any German money (which could not be traced at all). See, for instance, PRO CAB 24/35, GT 2980, 'Pacifism' [B. Thomson], 13 December 1917.
83. Swartz, *Union of Democratic Control*, p. 94.
84. Ibid., pp. 30, 95.
85. Ibid., p. 31.
86. Signed by Edward Grubb, Joan Mary Fry, Robert O. Mennell. PRO HO 10782/278537, Anti-Conscription 1915–1916, file 46, Society of Friends Central Office to HO, 3 January 1916.
87. Young, 'War Resistance', *Campaigns for Peace*, p. 25; Ceadel, *Pacifism in Britain*, pp. 21–6. According to Ceadel's typology, the Quakers were not pacifists as the term would be applied today, but more appropriately, quasi-pacifists of an esoteric persuasion.
88. LSE, Morel Papers, F6/3, Arnold Rowntree to Morel, 1 and 5 October 1914.
89. Consider, for instance, how different was the British from the German case. The German anti-war movement was based on the Social Democratic Party of Germany (SPD), then a mass, Marxist party, linked to the trade unions, and already the largest political force in Germany. Anti-war dissent, in Germany, was neither elite, nor necessarily mobilizational (the potential mass already existed). It was, on the other hand, always politically motivated and avowedly revolutionary. It was a much different threat, requiring much different handling. A German solution to the British problem – pre-emptive arrest, backed by the militarization of society – would fail miserably. On the other hand, a British solution to the German problem – attempting to convince doctrinaire socialist revolutionaries to support the war effort voluntarily by appealing to national and Christian principles – might not work any better.
90. Young, 'War Resistance', *Campaigns for Peace*, p. 28. If the TUC, the Liberals, Labour, the religious pacifists and the Irish had been united against the war, Young tells us, conscription would never have happened, and the country would have been disastrously divided. He is certainly correct.

2

McKenna at the Home Office, August 1914–May 1915

HOW TO handle the threat to the British war effort represented by dissent? The first thing to keep in mind, of course, was that whichever strategy was adopted, the inhibitions implicit in British political life would have to be remembered. A pre-emptive rounding up of the dissenting leadership, for instance, was simply out of the question. The government response, quite plainly, was going to have to grow in keeping with the threat, with nothing ever done to violate constitutional practice which the majority of the population did not consider justified. Peacetime practice, at least in form, would have to be preserved.

Given this constraint, and it was a powerful one throughout the war, the principal, permanent job for the government was to stop the dissenting leadership from reaching the mass audience which alone could make their criticism effective, while mounting an effective counter-propaganda. It had to be considered, on the other hand, that the use of the state machine to advertise the government's policy would be a tremendous and resented innovation, inconsistent with the existing constitution. Domestic propaganda as understood elsewhere was a tool of near last, rather than of first, resort. Given the enthusiasm with which the war was welcomed in 1914, the government could, at least initially, count on volunteer propagandists to do this work. Most importantly, the dissenters would have to be prevented from linking issues – anti-war dissent, for instance, with existing, war-accentuated class or trade union issues perhaps accentuated by the war – the linkage occurring even by means of the medium of the predominant religious and political modes of discourse. This, of course, was the great threat. One thing to consider, always, was simple palliation: addressing the grievances of the working class, for instance, before they could become operative factors.

Another method was direct action. Censorship could be employed to defeat the mobilizational imperative and to keep the dissenters an isolated elite. Regulations could be imposed to circumscribe dissenting activities. Direct action, moreover, could be directed at the elite itself, and at the organizations which structured it into a political force. Eliminate the elite and the threat would much abate. Grumbling would continue, but without organizers it was unlikely to be structured into active, effective opposition. Destroy its integrating organizations, and dissent's effectiveness would be much reduced. Of course, to attack prominent dissenters in what would be viewed as an improper fashion could only, in liberal, democratic Britain, rebound to the discomfiture of the government. Any direct attacks would necessarily, once again, have to be seen as lawful, and consistent with near-universal political ideals. While not impossible, direct attacks would be difficult, and would have to be carefully modulated.

The ultimate direct action – pre-emption – the militarization of civilian society and pre-emptive arrest of opponents, as occurred in Germany and Russia, could be prepared, but could never be implemented before circumstances sufficiently dire had developed to convince a critical mass in British society that such a departure from the liberal, democratic norm was essential. Indeed, this would be necessary if a political leadership which itself shared the inhibitions of the population were to be brought to countenance simple, and naked, rule by force. Pre-emption would only be possible if rebellion, or something very like it, were considered to be imminent.

Could the government defeat dissent with the tools at its disposal? The answer, certainly, must be yes, because in the end it did. What was required, however, was first and foremost an astute political judgement of just what response would not only be effective, but most tolerable. As the scope and effectiveness of dissent increased, society would be prepared to tolerate more repressive measures. As a general rule, palliation and counter-mobilization were always preferred to direct action. While pre-emption was certainly prepared, it was almost never employed, if sometimes threatened. Government policy? No time without its appropriate policy, and no policy before its time.

In the first year of the war, however, the mood of the country being what it was, the government had to do very little. Extra-governmental agencies were more than willing to produce propaganda sufficiently powerful to counteract the best efforts of a dissent just getting under way. Supporters of the war, moreover, could appeal to the same ideological heritage as the dissenters. To counter Christian pacifist anti-war dissent with a Christian patriotic, pro-war response was a logical development. Similarly, if the dissenters could seek to play on social divisions and labour grievances, then supporters of the war effort could evoke the nation beyond class. Failing complete success, pro-war propaganda might still succeed in driving wedges between sections of those domestic audiences most vulnerable to the dissenting message. The churches, initially, were the most important pro-war propagandists. Given what we have seen of the nature of dissent, pro-war religious propaganda could only be particularly effective.

Almost all British churches and most Christians supported the war effort not only as a national, but as an ethical duty. Had not Germany betrayed Western civilization by its actions? Was it not a power-mad state, the activities of which in Belgium had already indicated that its guiding ideology was no longer Christianity but 'scientific animalism'; the Holy Trinity replaced by an unholy trinity of Bernhardi, Treitschke and Nietzsche; its message not that contained in the New Testament, but 'the gospel of the bully'?[1] For most, it appeared to be so.

For Anglicans – the majority of the English population – the question of the war was phrased rather differently than for religious dissenters.

> Granted, Germany and her Myrmidons represented militarism, a false, anti-Christian philosophy, and a religion barely distinguishable from Devil worship; but from a religious standpoint, could even this justify a Christian in slaying his fellowman?[2]

The Anglican answer was not long in doubt. The answer provided by Bishop Winnington-Ingram, the very popular and patriotic Bishop of London, was more typical than the more tentative answer coming out of Canterbury.[3] 'I think', he said in 1915,

> the Church can best help the nation first of all by making it realize that it is engaged in a Holy War. Christ died on Good Friday for Freedom, Honour and Chivalry, and our boys are dying for the same thing ... MOBILIZE THE NATION FOR HOLY WAR.[4]

England, he thought, was manifestly the Sword of the Lord.[5] The war quite plainly pitted 'the Nailed Hand against the Mailed Fist'.[6] The idea that Britain was engaged in a crusade was not unique to the Bishop of London. It was the predominant Anglican response to the war.[7]

What is truly notable about the Anglican response to the war is how little internal opposition to it there was. Albert Marrion, in his study of the Church at this time, can identify only one Anglican divine anywhere who was a dissenter – Bishop Paul Jones of Utah, forced to resign from his diocese in 1918.[8] Amongst the prominent dissenters, only George Lansbury came from an Anglican background. Ultimately, only 7.5 per cent of all conscientious objectors (COs) would be Anglicans – less than the percentage of confirmed atheists, a tiny minority in the general population.[9] In contrast, by Christmas 1914, 30 per cent of all Anglican ordinands had already enlisted, while the bishops announced that they would not accept any candidate for ordination, after Trinity Sunday 1915, who was fit for service.[10] In the Canadian Expeditionary Force, in the early war years largely composed of British ex-patriots, 70 per cent of soldiers were Church of England by denomination. The pro-war sermons of prominent divines were printed, widely distributed, and cited against dissent and in support of the government.[11] In 1916, going still further, the Anglican diocese of London placed itself at the government's disposal for war loan work, producing and distributing half a million copies of a patriotic message from the bishop.[12]

The ultra-patriotic response of the national church encouraged other denominations and sects to rally to the war effort to avoid seeming insufficiently patriotic. While many nonconforming denominations and sects were pacific-ist, none were willing to renounce recourse to arms in all cases. Some had opposed the Boer War. The First World War, most quickly concluded, was a just war, even a crusade. While looser discipline sometimes meant that individual members of non-conforming denominations felt freer to denounce the war, the churches themselves quickly fell into line. Soon many of them were competing with the Anglican Church in the intensity of their support for the war. Dr John Clifford, for instance, the prominent Baptist divine, was little different from Bishop Winnington-Ingram in his views. 'War is anti-Christian', he admitted, but

> this is a fight between the forces of freedom and those of slavery ... The progress of humanity in my judgement hinges upon this war ... We were forced into it.[13]

'[H]e would rather see', he indicated on another occasion, 'every single living soul blotted off the face of the earth than see the Kaiser supreme everywhere'.[14] In the Welsh mining villages, dissenting clergymen adopted a line of 'praise the Lord and kill the Germans'.[15]

The widespread identification of this war as a crusade was important. Undoubtedly it encouraged many nonconformists to support the war effort.[16] From the beginning, anti-war dissenters were a minority among nonconformists.[17] Of 206,000 men of military age subscribing to primitive Methodism, 150,000, the Methodists were proud to note, saw service during the war. Of these, 15,000 were killed. While the Society of Friends was, as we have seen, associated with dissent as an organization, a third of Quaker men of military age ultimately served.[18] J. A. Pease, a prominent Quaker and the president of the Board of Education in 1914, convinced that the war was a fight between good and evil, went so far as to resign as chairman of the London Peace Society rather than leave the government at this moment of peril.[19] Here looser discipline cut the other way. The churches did not only mobilize the nation behind the government: a principal by-product of their agitation was that religious dissenters could, from the beginning, be safely characterized as militant, stiff-necked and wrong-headed sectarians.

Another type of propaganda, particularly suited to British scruples, was provided by the early war recruiting campaigns. In 1914 Britain had neither conscription nor a standing army sufficiently large to play a useful part on continental battlefields. As during the Boer War, an army had to be recruited. Advertising was urgently required, and energetically undertaken, often on a voluntary basis. The highly patriotic press proprietors especially – Gwynne of the *Morning Post*, Aitken (hereafter referred to as 'Beaverbrook') of the *Daily Express*, and the Northcliffe–Rothermere combine – pumped out freelance propaganda of a high order of virulence. While the population was being sold on enlistment, it was also being sold on the war. Note, once again, that while recruiting efforts were certainly domestic propaganda – it popularized the war; it helped create stereotypes of 'patriots', 'slackers' and foreign enemies which remained powerful for the duration – they were not provocative because they appeared less an innovative attempt to influence British minds, than a necessary recourse to time-honoured methods, much of it not organized by the government at all, and therefore entirely consistent with the Victorian volunteer ethic. Official propaganda or not, the results were the same. For the moment, men flowed into recruiting centres, patriotic and anti-foreign demonstrations became commonplace, and a constituency was created with a personal stake in the war which was to prove, thereafter, almost entirely resistant to the slowly developing dissenting message. In the contest of mobilization for and against the war, the government and its collaborators were first out of the blocks and in some respects gained a lead that they never thereafter relinquished.

If propaganda provided the government with one advantage, the ideological and social–political split among possible opponents provided another. We have already seen something of the different ways in which Christians could interpret the same war. The Labour, working class reaction was equally split and, once again, the majority instinctively supported the war. This fact was particularly important since the working class had shown signs of a developing class-consciousness in the years immediately before the war. If the working class had remained united, and if social and workplace grievances had been linked to dissent, then the war effort would have been truly imperilled. This never happened. What we see, instead, is a splintered working-class reaction, with most supporting, but some opposing the war. The split between Labour leaders, already noted, was in large measure a reflection of this greater working-class dilemma. Which loyalty came first – that to class or that to nation? Were the two even separable? On the other hand, was it possible to protest against some elements of the government's war policy, without ceasing to support the war? These were good questions, and ones which exercised the working class for the duration of the war. No uniform response ever developed. The chasm between the factions so created widened steadily during the war, each growing more radical in the process. This divide, for reasons we shall see, became significant in the war against dissent.

Particularly important was the reaction to the war of organized labour. While the workforce disliked many aspects of early war organization and became increasingly restive as the war proceeded and the screws tightened, it never entirely associated itself with dissent. Even in the most militant workplaces a split reaction to the war was discernible, and opposition to the government's subordinate policies should not be taken to imply concurrence with dissent. The idea, for instance, that the government might assume the power to restructure workplaces was provocative. The notion that conscription might lead to universal manpower controls was, for many, simply abhorrent. When the Munitions of War Act (1915) was passed at a time when conscription was first being mooted, Britain experienced its first significant industrial unrest: 200,000 miners in south Wales struck in defiance of the Act. The miners of south Wales were known for having advanced political ideas, and had been notably restive in the years prior to the war (see Chapter 6). Even a strike so large and dangerous in such a volatile environment, however, did not necessarily signal opposition to the war, though it is sometimes taken to have done so.[20] The miners' grievance was not with the war necessarily. The immediate trigger for the strike was a rejected wage demand.[21] This was most provoking because unprecedented demands were being made of the miners when, as they saw it, the owners were making excessive war profits. Prewar notions of workplace equity were violated.[22] The miners' strike of 1915, in short, was a labour dispute but not necessarily a political statement, though it could not but have political implications. The motivation of the strikers is unclear. Were they against the war and using the particular circumstances of the day as an excuse, or were they for the war and simply determined not to be pushed around? Unclear motivation was the product of an uncertain, splintered social–political response to the war evident from the beginning. We do not have too look far for further signs of divergence and inconsistency among the miners. A few months after the strike was settled, and while the mines remained restive, in the by-election which followed the death of Keir Hardie, the miners of south Wales overwhelmingly elected C. B. Stanton – one of the most violent and uncompromising British patriots – rather than his official ILP, dissenting opponent, James Winstone (see Chapter 6). Meanwhile the miners elected Robert Smillie to represent them nationally on the Miners' Federation of Great Britain (MFGB). Smillie was a convinced dissenter in the ILP and later as president of the TUC War Emergency Committee (WEC).[23] On the other hand, the recently elected leader of the South Wales Miners' Federation (SWMF), William Brace, was a notable patriot who was shortly to enter the government.[24]

What appears to be the case is that while they might strike from time to time, and would often grumble, the majority of the working class and most of the rank and file union membership supported the war effort for the duration. This does not mean that there were no dissenters, nor that the proportion of dissenters to patriots remained constant through the war. It should not be taken to suggest, either, that workplace grievances and anti-war attitudes were not radicalized and did not coalesce in the latter war years. It is simply to say that for most of the working class, in 1918 as in 1914, nation came before class. Indeed, basic working-class patriotism was demonstrated in the most effective way possible. The years 1910–1914 had seen an orgy of labour violence.[25] In the early months of 1914, there were, on average, 150 strikes a month. 'British Trade Unionism', the Webbs tell us, was, 'in the summer of 1914, working itself up for an almost revolutionary outburst of gigantic industrial disputes'.[26] The war changed this. In 1915 there were fewer labour disputes (674) than in any year since 1910. The first few years of the war were 'a time of peace in the labour world such as had never existed before and has not existed since'.[27] It was not until 1916, at the earliest, that a dangerous level of industrial dissent began to emerge. Still, however, labour remained quiet relative to provocation.

Dissent, quite plainly, was more marked in labour leadership than working class constituency. In the leadership, it was more conspicuous among political than TUC notables. The reason should be obvious. Neither trade union leaders nor the general working class had class analysis, Marxist theory, or pacifist principles to set against what were less nationalist beliefs than visceral tribal convictions. Indeed, for many, class and nation shared the same wartime agenda. Had the Germans not started the war? Did a ruthless, militarist clique, headed by an autocrat, not lead them? Would not the victory of Germany, therefore, represent the continental triumph of aristocratic, militaristic principles?

Would not Germany, in the aftermath of such a victory, represent a terrible, permanent threat to the commonality of Britain? Were not the armed services (far from being the tools of an unjust diplomacy, product of a rotten social structure) the shining weapons with which right was defended?[28] Class interest was national interest was victory.[29] In Britain, such perceptions were not heresy. They were common, orthodox, predictable and expected even before the outbreak of war. In 1913, G. D. H. Cole, the Labour theorist, warned that contrary to the orthodoxy of the Second International, nationalism was native, and not imposed upon the working class. 'There is', he wrote,

> a frequent assertion that nationality does not matter: 'the country of the worker is his belly', says one French Syndicalist leader. But however little nationality may matter economically, it still enormously matters morally, socially and politically. The very ease with which the international solidarity of Labour can be swept away by the faintest breath of a war-scare is an illustration of this fact. Nationality can only cease to affect a man sentimentally in the moment when it is not affecting him practically; let his country be threatened, and capitalist exploitation becomes in an instant of secondary importance. Nationality is still the strongest bond which can join men together, and so long as it retains its strength, there will remain a great and fruitful province for the nation state.[30]

Cole was correct, as events were to demonstrate.

Working-class patriotism could erupt, even in the early war years, in a rather brutal form. Men who, in 1915, refused to attest under the Derby scheme were sometimes run in wheelbarrows to the local recruiting office.[31] Quaker meetings were disrupted, and COs and anti-war dissidents were physically assaulted.[32] Germans and other foreigners were the targets of rioting in working class neighbourhoods. Other incidents of patriotic working-class violence we will see in what follows. Even the most prominent dissenting leaders did not always have an easy time of it. Arthur Ponsonby, for instance, faced a constituents' revolt in Stirling in spring 1915; the chairman of his own committee attacking him before a panel of 50 angry men.[33] Charles Trevelyan's experience with his constituency was similar.[34] The violent reaction of a part of the working class to what many viewed not only as national, but class betrayal, quickly became a permanent feature of wartime political life.

In the first year of the war, apart from recruiting, and tolerating freelance propagandists and labour patriots, the government did very little to silence dissent. Whatever dissent was, in 1914–15 political wisdom suggested that the government needed to do very little. For the moment, dissent was marginal and without much popular influence.

Nor, truly, did Britain have in 1914 (outside Ireland) any mechanism by which dissent could have been suppressed. Britain had nothing like a Ministry of the Interior. On the continent, even in peacetime, ministers of the interior possessed broad, ill-defined, coercive powers and exercised general control over all police. As a prewar French Minister of the Interior, Georges Clemenceau had brought in troops and *gendarmes* to suppress strikes when this seemed necessary to maintain public order. He had had deported his own bumptious ex-wife as an illegal alien. On neither occasion did he refer to the Chamber of Deputies. In wartime, when emergency legislation was implemented, and the military assumed much greater authority internally, there was very little a minister of the interior could not do to maintain quiet at home. Permissive, tolerant peacetime practice, it was almost universally assumed, was a luxury a state at war could not afford. In Britain, however, the Home Secretary – the closest analogue to a Minister of the Interior – did not have such powers, in peace or war, either by act or precedent. The Home Secretary in 1914, moreover, was Sir Reginald McKenna, a convinced Liberal as we have seen. If there were to be any repression, McKenna would have had to at least accept, if not orchestrate it. McKenna would have resigned (and was later to resign) if anything other than 'business as usual' had been the policy of the government. Nor would the Prime Minister, H. H. Asquith, have permitted any striking departures from peacetime practice.[35]

Nor was there any truly emergency legislation as understood on the Continent. In continental countries, it was understood, dissent in wartime was too dangerous to be allowed to proceed unhampered. In Germany, for instance, anti-war dissent was dealt with in military courts from the outset. Censorship of unacceptable viewpoints was something for which no explanation was required. In Britain, on the other hand, while the provisions (DRR – Defence of the Realm Regulations) of the 1914 Defence of the Realm Act (DORA) were implemented from the outbreak of war, the only real departures from peacetime practice they produced were designed for spy catching, internal security and home defence, not for the suppression of dissent.[36] Nor would general society have permitted anything more. In 1914 the government was certainly criticized for not doing enough at home, but not for tolerance of dissent. Its activities against enemy agents, it was charged, lacked sufficient vigour. It was a sign of the times, however, that even such criticism was neither very violent, nor long-lived. McKenna simply responded to the most virulent of his critics by thanking the editor of the *Daily Express*, Max Blumenfeld, for his assistance in 'lulling the enemy in our midst into a false sense of security'.[37] There the matter rested: against spies, some activity, against dissenters, none. This was, and was to remain, the McKenna line, and it was to prove sufficient so long as dissent remained weak.

That Britain had, in the beginning, neither proper mechanism nor intention – indeed, need – to limit the expression of anti-war views has not always been realized. John Williams, for instance, writes that with the first passage of DORA 'the traditional freedoms of Britons were signed away at the stroke of a pen'. Civil rights were suspended, Britain placed under martial law, the executive given almost total powers, and the police provided with the authority to act without regard to traditional rights and liberties.[38] Richard Thurlow tells us that DORA was simply 'watered down martial law' which gave 'naval and military authorities virtually unlimited powers'. These 'draconian powers of the state … replaced the workings of the common law'.[39] The truth was far, far more prosaic.

In the war's first years, the application of the various DRRs was muted and had little impact on dissent. A special police 'war duties division' was formed, at the end of July, to co-ordinate police activities during the emergency. For the moment, this meant, in the main, that access to designated vital points was now controlled.[40] In August, soldiers replaced police at military vital positions, where they remained until the end of the war.[41] Meanwhile, important lines of communications came under military control,[42] and certain ports were declared 'defended harbours' and garrisoned.[43] In response to a request from the War Office (WO), persons were prevented from trespassing upon land required for the projected defensive lines around London.[44] Suspected spies were arrested, held under provision of the DRRs,[45] and tried by military courts.[46] It was not difficult to find them. Scotland Yard already possessed a list of all known German spies in Britain.[47] Other suspicious foreigners and enemy aliens were impounded and their property sequestered.[48] In September, 25,000 special constables were enrolled, since so many of the existing police force had been called to the colours.[49] Before 1916, the only office the police established to monitor the home front was staffed by pensioners able to speak foreign languages. The idea of this, once again, was to counter potential espionage.[50] Some of the DRR were later expanded, reinterpreted and redirected against dissent. For the moment, however, that lay in the future. In the early war period, more important for our purposes were the censorship provisions.

From August 1914, under the Postal Act of 1906, the army established a postal censorship bureau under the direction of J. S. Pearson to monitor the correspondence of foreign nationals and suspicious persons. The initial purpose was to prevent leakage of intelligence to the enemy through the mails, as had occurred during previous conflicts.[51] The police, as well, while seeking broader powers of censorship, continued to envision using such powers entirely to combat potential espionage.[52] Of course, as tolerance for dissent began to diminish the equation 'dissenter = pro-German' began to emerge, and the mail of dissenters and dissenting organizations found itself subject to military and police scrutiny. From police files it appears probable that the mail of leading dissenters was being examined on a systematic basis by the end of 1915. While McKenna remained at the HO, however, this was still unacceptable, and until 1916 information gained in this way did not become the grounds for action.

Similarly, very soon after the commencement of hostilities, a press bureau was set up by the army to monitor the nation's press. The press bureau was established under the authority of legislation prepared long before the war (in 1904), continually revised (1908, 1912), and designed for immediate passage upon declaration of war.[53] The general procedure adopted was that an HO and military board would work together, passing off to other agencies – the Admiralty, the Foreign Office (FO), and ultimately the Ministries of Munitions, Shipping and Labour – materials which might interest them. In each office, a censor was always on duty. The general director of the whole was an army officer, General Cockerill.[54] By January 1916, the press bureau had been re-established as bureau MI7a (censorship), responsible to the Director of Military Intelligence (DMI), General Macdonogh. MI7b, meanwhile, was hived off to work with the FO, producing foreign propaganda.[55]

The initial rationale behind the creation of a system of press monitoring and censorship was not to suppress anti-war dissent, but to monitor the press for cryptic communications, and to provide a service to editors capable of advising them that they were about to publish sensitive information, and would, therefore, become vulnerable to prosecution. The system was designed, once again, to combat espionage and to inhibit enemy intelligence gathering. The system was voluntary: there were no penalties for non-compliance. An example of how this system was designed to function came soon after the declaration of war. In September 1914, the *Daily Mail* and *The Times* published troop dispositions for the allied armies, and speculated that a counter-attack was in preparation. Had the Germans been following the British press, they would have had advance warning of the Allied counter-attack on the Marne. The press bureau responded to this leakage by advising that there were to be no maps or speculation for a week, and no accounts of allied troop movements for four days. Editors, realizing how close they had come to compromising operations, and advised that they were now vulnerable to prosecution for betraying military secrets, voluntarily complied.[56]

The question was whether a system designed to ensure military secrecy would prove sufficient to silence dissent, even, in fact, whether there should be any attempt to redeploy press censorship against internal adversaries of the government. There was still no consensus that censoring dissenters was permissible, even if their opinions were likely to be of comfort to the enemy or damaging to the government. How could a democratic system work, after all, without free criticism of government policy? But, on the other hand, how to successfully conduct the war if the solidity of the home front were undermined? This was indeed a rather difficult dilemma. Even if reservations were overcome, and the decision were made to employ press censorship against dissent, then the problem remained that a system which relied for its effectiveness on voluntary compliance would not necessarily work when employed against internal dissent.

If there were inhibitions in the government, there were few in the army. From the beginning, those officers responsible for censorship attempted to silence criticism of British policy. The method was indirect. Warnings that the publication of a specific fact would constitute the passing of sensitive intelligence to the enemy were sometimes accompanied by warnings that certain criticisms of war policy and conduct were taboo. Usually these were heeded. The army was not convinced, however, that its existing powers of caution and admonition would be enough to silence the war's enemies. From August 1915, General Cockerill began to seek coercive powers.[57] In the judgement of Cockerill's political masters, however, a system of compulsory, coercive military censorship was impossible. This sort of censorship, they considered, would certainly have unacceptable political consequences. Society was simply not ready for it. Moreover, real censorship would constitute such a profound alteration of normal practice that it would never be approved by any parliament. Cockerill would have to continue to restrict himself to warnings even when dealing with anti-war dissenters, and when this was not enough, the civilian authorities might choose to act following his suggestion, after another cost/benefit assessment.[58]

While Cockerill might have grumbled, and while he never received the coercive powers he desired, the application of the existing system of press censorship to dissenting opinions was rather effective. Warnings did not have to be explained, and they were generally obeyed.

Most publishers, after all, were not dissenters, and, at least initially, it was they and not the producers of dissenting material who were held accountable for breaches of the DRR. Meanwhile, the impression was preserved (crucial for home and foreign propaganda) that British policy and practice continued to run on traditional, liberal lines. This system never much changed. It was simply reiterated, and applied in a more forceful fashion as the threat grew, and as the tolerance of general society for dissenting opinions diminished.[59]

There was another benefit of a voluntary system. It produced volunteers. Some of these volunteered information. Those patriotic editors, especially, who enjoyed good relations with the censors were eager to bring to the government's attention the manuscripts, ideas and identities of those they considered to be unsound. These, of course, were dissenters, not spies.

Here are some examples. In 1915, an article, 'Why the War Should be Stopped', by a prominent dissenter, C. H. Norman, was brought to the attention of Sir Charles Matthews, the Director of Public Prosecutions (DPP), by Francis Stopford, the editor of *The World*. Norman was, Stopford thought, 'inciting rebellion against the Defence of the Realm Act, and the whole argument is directed towards establishing in the mind of the reader that this war is being waged for the private gratification of a few interested persons'. Surely this was treason? If not, could the man be a lunatic? Was it not the duty of the authorities to restrain him in either case?[60] The press bureau thanked Stopford for his information, and issued a circular leaving publishers in no doubt that it considered Norman a dangerous man.[61] Similarly in 1917, an article by H. W. Nevinson about COs, published in the *Atlantic Monthly*, was brought to the attention of the press bureau not by the FO, but by G. W. Prothero, editor of the *Quarterly Review*.[62] The record for provoking the greatest number of simultaneous denunciations, however, must certainly be held by the radical patriot, Christabel Pankhurst. One of her articles published in the suffragette paper, *Britannia*, concerning the British expedition to Salonika (for the failure of which she blamed Sir Edward Grey), was brought to the attention of the authorities by at least two separate publishers – Gwynne of the *Morning Post* and Phillips of the *Yorkshire Post* – and also Robbins of the Press Association.[63] The article was judged not only contrary to DRR, but libellous. *Britannia* was seized.[64] For some months work on this paper was impossible. Anybody disposed to publish the paper for the WSPU had been given a clear warning. Publication on a small, hand-worked duplicating machine was all that was possible for some time.[65]

Giving information could also become gathering information. In

1915, the Press Association decided on its own not to cover ILP conferences, having perused the motions placed on the agenda paper of the Norwich conference. '[C]onsiderable harm', it concluded, might be done to the national interest 'by the dissemination of such views during the progress of the war'.[66] The Press Association, here, was considerably in advance of government opinion which ultimately advised it to print what it liked.[67] In the end Gwynne's *Morning Post* sent reporters. It did not, however, print their copy but passed it on to the Solicitor General and, for good measure, to Lloyd George.[68] Surely, Gwynne thought, the speeches of C. H. Norman and George Bernard Shaw were actionable?[69] Less convinced than Gwynne, the HO decided that no prosecutions were advisable. A criminal action at this time, it was considered, would give greater attention to the opinions of these men than they might otherwise garner for themselves.[70] A dossier of useful material, however, was collected and stored for future use.

Even a less helpful publisher, unwilling to see profits go up in smoke with condemned material, and therefore resigned to passing material through the censors, could be a useful source of information. In July 1915, for instance, the firm of Ballantyne, Hanson and Company passed to the press bureau a collection of Aleister Crowley's poems which it was considering. Crowley, of course, was a British subject (he was Irish). He was also in the habit of publishing rabidly anti-British articles in pro-German, US Papers (*Fatherland*, for instance). Not only could this book not be published, the press bureau responded, but it would be obliged to receive any information relative to the author's whereabouts. Was Crowley in the UK? When Ballantyne, Hanson and Company refused to provide such information, the press bureau advised that Basil Thomson of the Criminal Investigation Department (CID) was now looking into the case, and would very much like to meet with a representative of the firm. In the end, not only was the book not published, but information on Aleister Crowley gathered. If he had been in the UK, his publisher's compliance with a voluntary system would have resulted in his arrest.[71]

Like publishers, booksellers were often more than willing not only to keep objectionable material off their shelves, but to bring it to the attention of the authorities. In June 1915 H. Musgrave Reade, of the Bible Booklet House, passed to the press bureau a copy of 'Citizens of the World Follow Me' by Yervent H. Iskender, with the brief note that while he 'did not know whether [the press bureau was] informed of this pernicious stuff', he was curious to know whether such material was being passed by the censor. Most of all Reade hoped that the press bureau would be moved to take action.[72]

Even better, in November 1915 Eneas MacKay, one of Ponsonby's constituents, brought to the attention of the censors a copy of *The Crank*, which Ponsonby had co-authored. The UDC had persuaded him to stock it, if it passed censorship. MacKay did not agree with the contents, he informed the press bureau, but he did not consider them to be dangerous since 'we [in Stirling] are pretty unanimous in considering [Ponsonby] a "puir" body with a "bee" in his bonnet'. No approval for publication had been sought, the censor responded. Since the pamphlet might be actionable, and no businessman wishes to court prosecution, *The Crank* was not stocked, therefore, even in Ponsonby's own constituency.[73]

The aggregate result of the redeployment of press censorship against dissent was rather effective. For the duration of 1915 there were only 12 suggested prosecutions brought to the attention of the DPP by the press bureau. Most of these were the product of intelligence willingly passed to the authorities by publishers only too anxious to be helpful. Meanwhile, about three times a week, editors were successfully advised to suppress or alter stories. The most notable nonconformist in the early years was, oddly enough, Lord Northcliffe, who continually bucked the system.[74] He was hardly a dissenter; indeed, Northcliffe opposed censorship because he believed that it hampered his attempts to popularize the war. No news, while perhaps it ensured secrecy, was bad news, in that it depressed morale, sheltered inefficiency and led to rumours.[75] Similarly, Beaverbrook early took to evading censorship in order to organize propaganda better for Canadian consumption.[76] Elsewhere, while application of the system continued to be directed at news of military importance, compliance was nearly universal. The self-congratulation of the official historians of the press bureau was justified. 'It is a curious but indisputable fact', they wrote, 'that the voluntary censorship of this country functioned more efficiently than the compulsory censorship of our Allies.'[77]

While initially created to eliminate passage of information to the external enemy, both postal and press censorship quickly became tools by which dissent was discouraged and intelligence gathered. Since, until 1916, dissent remained an elite tendency, entirely incapable of matching the huge advantage that volunteer propaganda and basic social–political facts had given the government, they were sufficient for the requirement of the moment. They were also tools capable of much greater expansion and wider application as the threat of dissent developed. In 1915, however, nothing like real censorship was necessary. In the first year of the war nothing which the government did to contain dissent was very exceptionable, unreasonable or provocative of much opposition. Real repression simply was not yet necessary.

NOTES

1. A. Hoover, *God, Germany, and Britain in the Great War: A Study in Clerical Nationalism* (New York: Praeger, 1989), pp. 1–37.
2. A. Marrin, *The Last Crusade: The Church of England in the First World War* (Durham, NC: Duke University Press, 1974), p. 125.
3. While Archbishop Davidson deplored the national hatred to which the war gave rise, he considered that 'No household or home will be acting worthily if, in timidity or self love, it keeps back any of those who can loyally bear a man's part in the great enterprise on the part of the land we love' (*Pastoral Letter*, December 1914), A. Wilkinson, *The Church of England and the First World War* (London: SPCK, 1978), p. 47.
4. Marrin, *Last Crusade*, p. 139.
5. Ibid., p. 134.
6. Wilkinson, *Church of England*, p. 47.
7. Marrin, *Last Crusade*, p. 125:

   [W]hat distinguished this phenomenon [i.e. crusading] in the Great War, however, is the degree to which it became part of the imagination of religious people. For a great many Anglicans – we shall never know precisely how many – clergy and laity alike, the conflict that began as a necessary, if somewhat idealized campaign to safeguard national interests and rid the world of a military despotism was transformed under the pressure of events into a holy war, ending as a frenzied crusade against the Devil incarnate.

   See also R. Bainton, *Christian Attitudes Toward War and Peace* (New York: Abingdon Press, 1960), p. 207.
8. Marrin, *Last Crusade*, p. 147.
9. Ibid.; Ceadel, *Pacifism in Britain*.
10. Wilkinson, *Church of England*, p. 37.
11. Marrin, *Last Crusade*, pp. 122–3.
12. Wilkinson, *Church of England*, p. 45.
13. A. Wilkinson, *Dissent or Conform? War, Peace and the English Churches 1900–1945* (London: SCM Press, 1986), p. 23.
14. Wilkinson, *Dissent or Conform?*, p. 24. Clifford went on to contribute with the Bishop of London to a collection of essays entitled *Christ or Kaiser*.
15. K. Morgan, *Rebirth of a Nation: Wales 1880–1980* (Oxford: Clarendon, 1981), p. 162.
16. Ceadel, *Pacifism in Britain*, p. 20.
17. Marrin, *Last Crusade*, p. 147.
18. Wilkinson, *Dissent or Conform?*, pp. 29, 53.
19. Ceadel, *Pacifism in Britain*, p. 32.
20. See, for example, H. Francis and D. Smith, *The Fed: A History of the South Wales Miners in the Twentieth Century* (London: Lawrence & Wishart, 1980), p. 22.
21. H. Pelling, *A History of British Trade Unionism* (London: Macmillan, 1963), p. 153.
22. C. Williams, 'The Hope of the British Proletariate: The South Wales Miners, 1910–1947', in A. Campbell, N. Fishman, and D. Howell (eds), *Miners, Unions and Politics 1910–1947* (Aldershot: Scolar Press, 1996), pp. 126, 140.
23. J. M. Winter, *Socialism and the Challenge of War. Ideas and Politics in Britain* (London: Routledge & Kegan Paul, 1974), p. 208; R. P. Arnot, *The Miners: Years of Struggle* (London: George Allen & Unwin, 1953), p. 158, and for the strike itself, pp. 164–70.
24. Williams, 'The Hope of the British Proletariat', p. 125; H. A. Clegg, *A History of British Trade Unionism Since 1889* (Oxford: Clarendon, 1985), Vol. II, bibliographical appendix.

25. B. Simpson, *Labour: The Unions and the Party* (London: George Allen & Unwin, 1973).
26. Webb, *History of Trade Unionism* (1920), p. 693.
27. J. Williams, *The Home Fronts: Britain, France and Germany* (London: Constable, 1972), p. 52; B. Waites, *A Class Society at War: England 1914–1918* (New York: Berg, 1987), p. 187.
28. In 1914, in a way that is as difficult to imagine today as it would have been in 1800, the armed forces were genuinely popular. See, for example, J. M. Mackenzie, *Popular Imperialism and the Military* (Manchester: Manchester University Press, 1992).
29. B. Waites, *A Class Society at War*, p. 181. See also, P. Ward, *Red Flag and Union Jack: Englishness, Patriotism and the British Left, 1881–1924* (Rochester: Royal Historical Society, 1998).
30. G. D. H. Cole, *The World of Labour* (London: G. Bell, 1913). Somewhat later, George Orwell formulated working class socialism in this fashion:

> The working class Socialist ... is weak on doctrine and can hardly open his mouth without uttering a heresy, but he has the heart of the matter in him. He does grasp the central fact that Socialism means the overthrow of tyranny, and the 'Marseillaise', if it were translated for his benefit, would appeal to him more deeply than any learned treatise on dialectical materialism. (G. Orwell, *The Road to Wigan Pier* (London: Secker & Warburg, 1973 [1937]), p. 220.)

31. Waites, *A Class Society at War*, p. 189.
32. Marwick, *The Deluge*, p. 82.
33. BLO, Ponsonby Papers, Ponsonby to William Robertson, 27 March 1915.
34. Morris, *C. P. Trevelyan*, p. 128. Trevelyan suffered from the problem, moreover, of being repudiated by many members of his family. His father and his brother George hated the position he had taken.
35. See Jenkins, *Asquith*.
36. PRO HO 45 10690/228849, Defence of the Realm Act and Amendments, 1912–1914.
37. HLRO, Blumenfeld Papers, McK 1, McKenna to Blumenfeld, 29 September 1914.
38. Williams, *The Home Fronts*, p. 23.
39. Thurlow, *The Secret State*, p. 48.
40. PRO HO 139 various.
41. PRO MEPO 1/68, Commissioner MEPO to HO, 2 August 1914.
42. PRO HO 45 10600/189180 Sabotage: files 16, 28 January; file 17a, August 1914; file 19, 6 August 1914; file 20, 11 August 1914; file 24, 17 August 1914; file 36, 17 December 1914; file 44, 5 January 1915; file 48, 15 January 1915; file 53, 24 May 1916; file 55, 13 July 1917; file 56, 14 January 1918.
43. PRO HO 45 10690/228849, Defence of the Realm Act and Amendments 1912–1914, file 21, 30 September 1914.
44. PRO HO 45 10690/228849, Defence of the Realm Act and Amendments 1912–1914: file 2, 3 August 1914; file 33, 19 November 1914; file 37, 11 December 1914. The Defensive Line followed a line on the North Downs, from Redhill and then through Godstone and Woldingham, all in Surrey, to Brasted in Kent, and also on the hills above Otford and Wrotham, both in Kent. There were other defences constructed: in Kent, above Lenham; in Norfolk, north and east of Norwich; in Suffolk, along the line Duddenham–Coddenham–Mendlesham; in Essex from Maldon through Great Braxted to Witham and Braintree; and from Fobbing in Essex via Ramsden Heath, Ingatestone, Chipping Ongar, North Weald, Basset, Epping Green and Nazeing, to Hoddesdon in Hertfordshire.
45. PRO HO 45 19765/271164, Courts Martial 1915–1919: file 1, 24 November 1914; file 2, 28 November 1914; file 3, 11 February 1915; file 5, October 1915; files 7, 8 and 9, November 1915; file 11, 16 November 1915; file 12, December 1915; file 13, 7 January

1916; file 15, 7 February 1916; file 17, 21 February 1916. In response to questioning in the House, it emerged that 20 spies had been arrested, and prosecuted under the *Official Secrets Act*. Only one of these was a Briton. While the trials had been closed to the public, McKenna denied that anything had been done contrary to British tradition, and defended the secrecy of the trials as necessary for national security. In the end all death sentences appear to have been commuted.

46. See, for instance, PRO WO 71, files 1236, 1237, 1238 and 1239, which deal with the trial by court martial of four persons, held for suspected espionage: G. Lody (1914), B. Belin (1915), I. Ries (1915), and L. van der Goten (1917).

47. Thomson, *The Scene Changes*, p. 246.

48. PRO MEPO 1/68, various. In 1915, following the spy scare that followed the sinking of the *Lusitania* (June 1915), more foreigners were rounded up and the government received more extensive powers still with DRR 14A which permitted arrest without warrant and detention without charge.

49. PRO MEPO 1/68, Commissioner to HO, 3 September 1914.

50. PRO MEPO 1, MEPO Commissioner to HO, 14 September 1914.

51. PRO INF, 4/1B, 'Military Press Control. A History of the Work of MI7, 1914–1919'.

52. PRO MEPO 1, MEPO Commissioner to HO, 2 October 1914. MEPO were looking for the power (i) temporarily to suspend naturalization; (ii) to restrain British subjects from leaving the country without passports; (iii) to prohibit writing except through the post; and (iv) to control wireless communications. Why? Because it was believed that some naturalized British subjects were communicating with the enemy.

53. PRO INF, 4/1B, 'Military Press Control. A History of the Work of MI7, 1914–1919'.

54. PRO HO 139, various.

55. PRO INF 4/1B, 'Military Press Control. A History of the Work of MI7, 1914–1919'.

56. See Wilson, *Political Diaries of C. P. Scott*, CPS to Hobhouse, 26 September 1914, p. 109.

57. PRO HO 139/25/105, Part 1, File 17, 'Proposed Regulation of D of R Act to Facilitate Prosecution of Press Offenses', August 1915.

58. Ibid.

59. MI7a, for instance, in 1917, was informed that the only way in which prohibitions could be imposed would be for MI to apply for prosecutions to the DPP through the WO. PRO HO 139/25/105, Part 2, File 14, January 1917.

60. PRO HO 139/23/96, Francis Stopford to Sir Charles Matthews, 6 July 1915.

61. PRO HO 139/23/96, Press Bureau Circular, July 1915. 'A perusal of the article in question is enough to convince any patriotic reader that publication of such views in this country could only embarrass the Government, cause anxiety to our Allies, satisfaction to our enemies, and danger to the national cause.'

62. PRO HO 139/21/88, Part 3. Conclusion: nothing could, as yet, be done since the article had probably been hand-carried to the USA. He had not, therefore, violated postal censorship. In 1918, with the expansion of DRRs, Nevinson would have been arrested, as Angell and Morel were, for similar activities.

63. PRO HO 139/23/96, Part 2, File 9, Robbins to Press Bureau, 13 December 1915; Gwynne to Press Bureau, and G. Phillips to Press Bureau, 13 December 1915.

64. PRO HO 139/23/96, Part 2, File 9.

65. Pankhurst, *The Home Front*, p. 270.

66. PRO HO 139/23/96, E. R. Robbins to Sir Stanley Buckmaster (Solicitor General, 1914–15), 30 March 1915.

67. PRO HO 139/23/96, Harris (for McKenna) to Mitchell (Press Bureau), 1 April 1915; Press Bureau to Robbins, 31 March 1915.

68. C. Wrigley, *David Lloyd George and the British Labour Movement in Peace and War* (New

York: Barnes & Noble, 1976), p. 166.

69. PRO HO 139/23/96, H. Gwynne to Buckmaster, 8 April 1915.
70. PRO HO 139/23/96, Buckmaster to McKenna, 8 April 1915; C. Matthews (DPP) to Sir Edward Cook (Press Bureau), 27 April 1915.
71. PRO HO 139/23/96, File 3, Press Bureau to Ballantyne Hanson and Co., 20 and 21 July 1915; Thomson to Cook, 28 July 1915.
72. PRO HO 139/23/96, File 6, H. Musgrave Reade to Press Bureau, 16 June 1915.
73. PRO HO 139/23/96, Part 2, File 8, E. MacKay to UDC, 8 November 1915.
74. T. Clark, *Northcliffe in History* (London: Hutchinson, 1950), pp. 109–10. See also, for example, PRO HO 139/21/84, Part 17.
75. Clark, *Northcliffe in History*, pp. 109–10. See also, PRO INF 1/4B, 'Military Press Control, A History of the Work of MI7, 1914–1919', and 'The Northcliffe Press and Foreign Opinion, 1915'.
76. HLRO, Beaverbrook Papers, C 261 various.
77. PRO INF 4/1B.

3

Simon at the Home Office, May–December 1915

BY THE middle of 1915 the British *Burgenfriede* had begun to break down. Voluntary enlistment was no longer sufficient to maintain the armies. The Western Front had come to reveal more fully its insatiable character. It was obvious that the war would not be quickly won. 'Business as usual', it was apparent, would lead to defeat. A realignment of the home front towards a more ruthless prosecution of the war was required. It also became evident, rather quickly, that all of this was productive of a type of dissent which, if not yet dangerous, was cause for concern. In particular, as HMG during 1915 began to move hesitantly towards manpower compulsion – conscription for both military and industrial service – widespread unrest began to develop. Social and economic tensions, accentuated by wartime realignment, were reawakening. Dissent could now, if it seized the opportunity, begin to organize a mass constituency.

New realities brought a new coalition government, assembled to implement new policies. McKenna, who could not support these policies, left the HO in May 1915 and was replaced by another Liberal, Sir John Simon. As we have seen, however, Simon was hardly an irresponsible chauvinist. While willing to envision them, Simon did not approve of constitutional departures. He could not accept that waging total war and maintaining liberal inhibitions were fundamentally incompatible. Censorship mortified Simon.[1] The press bureau, indeed everything associated with the DRRs he considered a very 'troublesome business'.[2] Of all Asquith's associates, on ideological grounds he was probably the most opposed to compulsion of all kinds.[3] Conscription he would not consider, and he took office only on the understanding that it would not be introduced.[4] He was assured, however, that the National Register Act (July 1915) and the Derby scheme (September 1915 – see page 105) were meant not to precede, but to 'kill compulsion'.[5] These, however, had not been designed to succeed, but to demonstrate to the satisfaction of the majority that there was no alternative to conscription.[6] When the failure of the voluntary system led to the demand for conscription, Simon had to go. He simply could not remain in office when it became apparent that both the war and the threat of dissent had grown to the point where the government was being forced to accept that continuance of the war required acceptance of radically new rules. His period at the HO marked the first, tentative use of the machinery of state to suppress dissent. It was not yet accepted, meanwhile, that an augmentation and systemization of existing machinery was now required.

Let us consider the change to the organization of dissent produced by altered circumstances.

By the time the National Register Act was introduced the UDC had been in existence for some time and was steadily gaining organizational coherence. Three things made it virtually inevitable that at least some of the elements in the UDC would seek to use the organization to attempt to halt the approach of conscription. The first was simple. The battle against conscription would necessarily have to be waged outside Parliament because the leading dissenters were certain that the patriots would sweep the country if opposition gave rise to a general election.[7]

The second was the fact that the leadership of the UDC was almost universally against conscription, and not all were in entire agreement with the Morel line. Ponsonby and Trevelyan, in particular, were becoming increasingly exercised by what they saw as the immoral conduct of the war (particularly conscription); this set them apart from MacDonald and Morel, for instance, who considered it a tactical mistake to shift the focus of UDC activity from war 'origins & the settlement' to more immediate issues.[8] Indeed, when the anti-conscriptionists in the UDC attempted to use the organization to fight this battle, they ended up fighting Morel as well. In June 1915, it was proposed that the UDC use its organization to 'oppose to the utmost any attempt to impose compulsory service either for military or industrial purposes as being unnecessary for the needs of the nation and inadvisable in its best interests'.[9] Morel countered that, in his opinion, this would be 'a tremendously grave step to take', and would be setting the organization up for failure. The government would be certain to fight back. The measure would certainly pass, and the UDC would be forced to adopt a policy of resistance to the law. In the end, to make anti-conscription the centrepiece of UDC opposition would 'bring [it] within measurable distance of prosecution for sedition and rebellion'. Even if the government tolerated a UDC-led anti-conscription campaign, then the UDC would still be committed to what could only become something like a revolutionary course. If the inevitability even of this were accepted and if organized labour did not rally to the UDC, it would face annihilation not only during, but after the war. Finally, if it could be demonstrated that compulsion was necessary to maintain the strength of the army, then the UDC would be driven to declare that it did not care 'whether England is beaten or not'. While, therefore, conscription for anything other than home defence was certainly morally abhorrent, to lead the fight against it would be a tactical error of the first magnitude.[10] For Morel, conscription was certainly important and not an issue to be dropped entirely. It was for its potential usefulness, however, that it was important to him. This issue could not but, if used with circumspection, put impetus and urgency behind the UDC's central question: why was the war being fought at all?[11] It would also, he hoped, give the UDC an entry to a working class audience which it had hitherto lacked. In this last assessment, at least, Morel appears to have been correct. From 1915, we note the gradual association of the UDC and at least a section of the labour movement. In June of that year, seeking to encourage this, the UDC appointed a 'special commissioner' (Egerton Wake, a prewar union organizer) to make contacts with the labour movement.[12] The price of a mass following, however, was probably a much higher level of more directly anti-conscriptionist activity than Morel would have liked.

The opinions of the leadership aside, a third factor pulling the UDC towards more vigorous activity, was the fact that it was, as we have seen, an umbrella organization – incorporating in itself any number of dissenting tendencies or groups, and taking advantage of their local organization and reputation, while providing for them a larger audience than they could have reached by themselves. It depended upon its affiliates to distribute its literature and organize support for its line. The result was that while the UDC used its associates, they were quite capable of using it. This was the trade-off. Many affiliated organizations had a much more immediately pressing agenda than Morel. It was unlikely, for instance, that Christian pacifists, Quakers and socialists threatened with compulsion would be much satisfied with assurances that martyrdom now would pave the way for a more just future. One organization in particular closely associated with the UDC – the No Conscription Fellowship (NCF) – could be counted upon to act with vigour against a measure to which it was entirely opposed.

As anti-conscriptionist feeling began to mount, the UDC began to demonstrate a greater level of public activity than it had done previously, while its agenda, at least for a time, began to slide in an overtly anti-conscriptionist direction. This is the principal fact which made the dissent of the latter half of 1915 more potent than that of 1914. Those opposed to the war as individuals, and in principle, had been given an issue which would attract a mass audience, much more easily understood, and seemingly far more urgent than the rights or wrongs of Britain's prewar diplomacy. The development of the compulsion debate, moreover, came at a time when dissent itself had coalesced to the point where it could, if not contained, begin to grow into a potent political force. Not only had an issue emerged capable of producing mass support, but an organization had emerged coherent enough to lead.

It is hardly surprising that this type of activity seemed dangerous both to the authorities and to much of British society. The government, however, was uncertain how to react. Liberal convictions clashed with immediate requirements. Dissent was becoming effective. A response was required. But could the Asquith government abandon its inhibitions sufficiently to act vigorously, and repressively? Was it even capable of identifying the necessity? A gap, in short, had developed between what seemed to be required, and what had always been permissible.

Into the gap rushed the patriots, a principal mechanism by which dissent was contained until the end of the war. A 'patriot', in First World War British parlance, was someone who was prepared to use force to silence dissenters, with or without official sanction.[13] So predictable was the patriotic response to dissent that some dissenters, remembering the popular mood during the Boer War, had been maintaining a low profile for fear of the inevitable 'jingo mob'.[14] Fear of patriotic violence – even before such violence developed – was a useful method of censorship in itself, due to the self-censorship it produced. It remained so for the duration. Worries that at least part of the British populace would react violently to anti-war dissent were not groundless. As early as October 1914, for instance, MacDonald was informed that a local ILP meeting at Leicester, at which he had been scheduled to speak, had been publicized in the press. Moreover, the local recruiting officer (Captain Pritchard) had warned the local Labour Party organizer (Mr Leeson) that if MacDonald came and spoke as he was wont, a counter-demonstration could be expected and MacDonald would be booed down.[15] In the event, this meeting went off without a hitch. No problems were experienced, and a letter of appreciation was forwarded to the local police for the excellent arrangements they had made to support the meeting.[16]

Half a year later, things had changed markedly on the home front. From spring 1915, the patriotic press – the *Daily Express* especially – was publicizing UDC meetings, exhorting patriots to attend in order to ensure that nothing transpired capable of damaging the war effort. The implication was, of course, that almost anything was permissible to halt the spread of what was now beginning to be characterized as pro-German treachery. By 1915 there were only too many in wartime Britain willing to respond. The police were no longer so co-operative. Booing was the least of the dissenters' worries.

Why was it that the *Daily Express*, which took this role upon itself, was becoming, in short order, an important element in the suppression of dissent? For one thing, the government was hardly ready to do this work for itself. Lord Beaverbrook, moreover, had recently acquired an interest in the *Daily Express*, which he finally purchased in December 1916, exactly as a means of supporting his own political causes. Beaverbrook was a fervent imperialist and patriot who looked to the war to establish the imperial solidarity which remained his lifelong passion. By 1915 he was already the unofficial minister of information for Canada, and would soon be Britain's propaganda chief. From the beginning, Beaverbrook had decided to use the paper to support the war effort. Where the government would not go Beaverbrook was only too ready to lead the patriot rush. There was no opposition from the editorial staff of the *Daily Express*, which welcomed the proprietor's line. The editor-in-chief, Ralph Blumenfeld, had long been rabidly anti-socialist. He had himself founded, in 1908, an Anti-Socialist Union, 'which organized meetings "to counteract the fallacious statements so persistently put about by Socialist writers and speakers, particularly those who speak in parks and open spaces"'.[17] The organization of the patriots by the *Daily Express*, in many ways, was simply a continuation and accentuation of a policy initiated by Blumenfeld years before. Where Beaverbrook scented sedition likely to damage Britain's chances of winning the war, Blumenfeld saw a conspiracy which sought to use the war to further the cause of revolution. Like Beaverbrook, Blumenfeld was a convinced supporter of the imperial programme as it had been defined in the years before the war by Joseph Chamberlain and Alfred Milner.

And, from the beginning, influential members of the government valued Beaverbrook's enthusiastic partisanship, rewarding the *Daily Express* with access to information denied other papers, asking for and returning favours. Beaverbrook's support for conscription was, in particular, partly inspired by his Unionist associates in the government and much appreciated. Sir Henry Chaplin, effectively the leader of the opposition at the time, thanked the *Daily Express*, on 9 July 1915, for its assistance in killing opposition to the National Register Bill then under consideration. 'I am quite sure', he wrote,

> having watched the discussion on the Registration Bill throughout, that what you did so promptly for us at my request in the Daily Express

had undoubtedly a very great effect. The day it appeared there was a very great change in the attitude of our opponents.

Whittaker who led the attack did not show and took no further part in it. The others, though still persistently boring the Committee with useless twaddle, were moderate and even gentle, and though I did not wait for the closing scene when it was practically over, they were evidently trying to re-establish their position.

I owe this for the help which you gave us so promptly and effectively.[18]

Unionist politicians were not the only elements of the British administration with whom the *Daily Express* developed a rather intimate relationship. There is correspondence in the Blumenfeld collection at the House of Lords Record Office (HLRO) which makes it clear that the *Daily Express* was, at various times, acting as unofficial spokesman for the army[19] and the police.[20] It is certain, as well, that Beaverbrook was co-operating with Lloyd George, not simply politically behind the scenes, but editorially, as the Lloyd George coup went forward in December 1916. This was only the beginning. We will return to Beaverbrook in the future. He was a man crucial to the production of the system of suppression, and grew steadily more powerful through the war. Service begot service, and support, information. Control of information is always, as Beaverbrook knew only too well, power.

In fairness to the *Daily Express*, the much more important Northcliffe papers (such as the *Daily Mail* and the *Evening News*) were not much different in their treatment of wartime dissent. During the war, the Beaverbrook–Northcliffe press can be considered to have had a virtually unified editorial line. Beaverbrook himself realized this. 'Really', he wrote to Northcliffe in December 1916,

> my influence is very much the same kind, though on a vastly smaller scale, as yours. I am sure you have [at] the present moment the most tremendous influence for good of any man in this country, and I am convinced that you will use it.[21]

Both were travelling the same road. If Beaverbrook tended to establish the direction, Northcliffe followed close behind, and was perhaps more important, owing to his larger holdings (nearly two-thirds of London dailies, by circulation, were under his control), influence and connections.

The patriotic press campaign, therefore, was much more effective than Blumenfeld's prewar anti-socialist campaign. A much larger proportion of the press was participating. Connections with the authorities had been solidified. Many more Britons were prepared to listen. Violent suppression of dissent followed inevitably and naturally without HMG having to do much of anything more vigorous than avert its eyes and answer a few questions in the House. The patriotic press campaign of 1915 represented an important turning-point in the war on the home front. Trevelyan was later to assert that without the press campaign there would have been no violence, because meetings which were not advertised were never disrupted. For Blumenfeld in particular he developed a poisonous hatred. Nothing, he said, would give him greater pleasure than 'to discharge two barrels into Blumenfeld's backside at thirty yards'.[22] The hatred was natural when we consider that real, physical violence followed from incitement in the press.

Shortly after the *Daily Express* commenced its campaign against dissent, a UDC anti-conscription meeting at Kingston in November 1915 was broken up before a word could be said, and the organizers – Ponsonby for one – physically assaulted.[23] If Trevelyan is to be believed, the patriot ringleader was a notable prewar political thug: 'a man, who has had a hand in the breaking up of Free Trade, Woman Suffrage and Socialist meetings'. Not being content with simply disrupting the meeting, about 30 patriots followed the dissenting leaders to a railway station, 'when, after surrounding and insulting us, they burst into a small waiting room where we ha[d] a free fight, three versus thirty'.[24] Trevelyan was horrified and suggested an approach to the Home Secretary. 'He presumably will have heard something about it', he opined to Ponsonby:

> But he ought to know all the facts, and especially the obvious incite-ment to violence of the *Daily Express*. He ought to take special measures to give us protection if necessary, as he might easily have been on our side of the fence with another ounce weight of moral courage.[25]

The police did nothing. The HO was unsympathetic. It was probably too much to expect that it would either protect the dissenters from what was considered to be the logical consequence of their provocation, or act to prevent any patriot counter-demonstrations which, however widely advertised or violent, were, after all, convened to defend government policy.

A pattern was established. It continued to be followed, with increasing levels of violence, for the duration of the war. The first attack was quickly followed by a second. At Leicester, the following day, another Trevelyan meeting was broken up by soldiers emerging from a public house, one of whom climbed up on the platform and attempted to punch Trevelyan. Fortunately for Trevelyan, his attacker was 'far too gone to be effective'.[26]

Another meeting, the first UDC 'peace' meeting in November 1915, likewise pre-publicized by the *Daily Express*, was broken up by counter-demonstrators led by Cecil Chesterton, son of the author G. K. Chesterton, a perfervid nationalist, notable anti-Semite and editor of the *New Witness*.[27] Chesterton's patriots (mainly soldiers) packed the hall before the meeting commenced, stormed the platform before anybody had a chance to speak, forced the organizers to flee, and used the opportunity to pass a resolution that '[p]eace shall not be made until Prussia is utterly and completely crushed'. The police, while present, offered no resistance.[28] It was a sign of things to come that both Cecil Chesterton and his brother Gilbert – who replaced him as editor of the *New Witness* when he was called up in October 1916 – were already employed by the government writing anti-German propaganda for foreign consumption.[29]

In December a UDC meeting in Ilford was broken up, following the same pattern. At 6.30 p.m., the local organizer of the meeting (Mr H. Purkis) arrived at the hall in which the meeting was to take place to find a great mob of men in khaki attempting to storm the door, while stewards and police attempted to restrain them. When the doors were opened, a crowd of patriots forced their way into the hall. When the speakers appeared (MacDonald and Ponsonby), the patriots stormed the platform from all sides. Ponsonby and MacDonald were expelled from the hall. Purkis himself was badly beaten, 'there being no respect for age & grey hair', he complained to MacDonald. Patriot orators took the stage and what followed, Purkis complained, was 'the grossest misrepresentation of facts I have ever known'. The result? Apparently HO charges that the UDC had done something to provoke the attack.[30] The mainstream press, meanwhile, debated the wisdom of prohibiting 'anti-patriotic meetings' in the interests of public order. The UDC, determined to preserve itself as an organization, retreated to Morel's position that anti-conscription was poor tactics, while working to defeat the charge that it was 'pro-German'.[31]

Glasgow was about the only place in the UK in which this type of violence was not becoming endemic by 1915. Only here and in a few other industrial areas did the UDC conduct openly anti-conscriptionist activities, following a decision to do so only where a sympathetic audience could be assured.[32] As we have seen, however, Glasgow was exceptional. Here the dissenters could always be assured of an audience large enough, convinced enough, and violent enough to protect them. At one meeting, in the summer of 1915, for instance, at which Ramsay

MacDonald was scheduled to speak, an attempt by the Scottish Patriotic League to disrupt the meeting was countered by Emanuel Shinwell and John McGovern, who met the patriots at the door lead pipes in hand.[33] 'Who's this?' a worried MacDonald asked when the big McGovern leapt up beside him. '[Y]ou've no need to worry about him,' Shinwell answered: 'It's only McGovern. He's a pacifist.' 'He's the sort of pacifist I much prefer on my side', the relieved MacDonald answered.[34] Dissent in Glasgow could sometimes even take the offensive. We have already seen how the Glasgow militants were prepared to treat Lloyd George. Later in the war, John McGovern would lead the dissenters in a counter-offensive, on one occasion even disrupting a meeting of 4,500 militant seamen chaired by their union organizer, the redoubtable, vehement and violent patriot, J. Havelock Wilson.[35] Already, by summer 1915, patriot violence had driven dissent in Glasgow entirely into the hands of the militant left as the only force convinced enough and violent enough to provide protection. Glasgow, in this, was in the lead. The rest of the country would follow by the end of the war.

Elsewhere in 1915 the situation was very different, and patriot violence quickly became, in fact and prospect, a rather effective form of censorship useful in stopping dissenters from spreading their message by the spoken word, at least openly and to large audiences. Private communication to small numbers of the convinced was hardly likely to assist the dissenters much in shifting the pro-war consensus. In London, for instance – 'the worst of jingo places' – open meetings had become impossible by summer 1915.[36] Elsewhere, a type of automatic, but unofficial censorship began to operate as larger venues were denied to the UDC and the ILP for fear of the certain, and certainly violent, opposition which would develop. A UDC meeting in December 1915 before a trade union audience was on the point of cancellation before police protection was obtained.[37] In the same month, an ILP meeting was cancelled, for fear of certain violence. Another UDC meeting, scheduled in Shipley, was stopped when the press reported patriot violence in Halifax the night before this meeting was supposed to take place, and the deacons of the chapel in which the meeting was to occur withdrew their permission. A sign of the times: they had been advised by the local police authorities – perhaps seeking to capitalize upon this process to discourage what could not yet be prohibited – that they would be held liable in the event that there was a disturbance of the peace.[38] Some towns, anticipating the patriot reaction, prohibited UDC meetings altogether in the interests of maintaining the peace, as ultimately did Cambridge University.[39]

The UDC, plainly, was not the organization to carry the fight against conscription. Its open nature made it particularly vulnerable to patriotic counter-action, but it could hardly mobilize mass support if it were forced underground. Moreover, as Morel had foreseen, following the passage of the National Register Act, dissenters had to be careful what they said or wrote about conscription if they were not to find themselves accused of sedition, as defined by DRRs. Continued, overt opposition could constitute resistance to the law. Prosecution in the courts would be inevitable. The UDC would have broken the rules of the game, and would not only expose itself to serious legal reprisal but would alienate the mass audience it was seeking to attract. By avoiding this issue the UDC was able to remain openly in operation for the duration of the war. Morel's policy served to maintain the integrity of the UDC for the day when popular sentiment began to turn against the war.

What the UDC could do, however, was continue its support for other, more radical groups.[40] As the UDC returned to the Morel line other organizations – the No-Conscription Fellowship (NCF),[41] the British Stop the War Committee (SWC),[42] the Fellowship of Reconciliation (FOR),[43] the National Council Against Conscription (NAC), the Peace Negotiations Committee (PNC) – began to appear to fight conscription and the war, often with considerable overlap of membership with the UDC. In was no coincidence that it was in the latter months of 1915 that the police began to notice (or at least report on) the activities of what were still rather amorphous collections of activists attacking conscription and the government which was poised to bring it in. Such organizations, eventually operating secretly and contrary to wartime regulations, were composed in large measure of elements already active in dissent. They found in these new campaigning organizations the tool sufficient for the job, while maintaining their association with other dissenting groups, principally the UDC and the ILP. If the UDC remained the message and the ILP represented the hope, these new organizations were the medium through which both were propagated by this point in the war.

The rationale behind such organizations was not to avoid, but rather to invite, suppression, carrying the battle into the courts, thus politicizing and publicizing dissent. At least initially, they, like the UDC, made no attempt to preserve secrecy. The most important, the NCF, was particularly open about its aims. Its meetings were public, its membership enthusiastic and missionary. Copies of its manifestos were sent directly to the Home Secretary, Simon (Home Secretary since May 1915). The Fellowship even offered to send a delegation to the HO to explain its programme.[44] Bertrand Russell, an NCF member, went so far as to write a leaflet contrary to the DRRs and then follow this with a letter to *The Times* claiming authorship. Inevitably, he was arrested and appeared in court. He was fined, but refused to pay. His goods at Cambridge were seized to settle the fine. Russell, it is clear, was actually looking for a prison sentence. This was denied him, but he had still tested the law and gained access to an official platform.[45] Many were sceptical that these tactics would achieve very much. The authorities were simply too clever. Their methods of suppression, it was considered, would certainly develop sufficiently to contain this new threat. '[M]y experience', George Bernard Shaw wrote to Fenner Brockway, in January 1916,

> is that of all useless ways of wasting money the most useless is trying to fight the Government on its own ground in the law courts. Under the Defence of the Realm Act, the Government can do what it likes.[46]

Norman Angell had succeeded in getting the decision that trials of persons arrested for breaches of DRRs could not be held in secret. The result? A further decision that secret proceedings, therefore, were not trials. '[A]t the present pass', Shaw continued, even

> the publication of the facts can do no good. The British Empire has just been handsomely beaten and driven into the sea by the Ottoman Empire [at Gallipoli]; and at such moments jobbery scandals are not opportune: it is more important to get plenty of munitions than to bother about the shareholders who are making the money out of them. The day of reckoning for the jobbery will come when the fighting is over, and the bills come in. If I were you I should wait until then.[47]

Russell, Brockway, Angell and many others were not inclined to wait with Shaw, MacDonald and Morel.

The dissenting, fighting organizations were never able to mobilize the degree of open support that the UDC and ILP did. With their far more immediate goals and outspoken, combative style, however, they were probably the only purely dissenting organizations capable of seriously damaging the war effort. Rather quickly, as might be imagined, such organizations came to the attention of the police and enjoyed, until they were effectively destroyed by 1917, an entirely disproportionate level of police attention. Their membership, police observers reported, was composed of all 'the extremists and cranks of the various political and religious bodies throughout the country'.[48] Nor were the police much fooled by what was essentially a tactical shift by a dissent which remained, by and large, united. The new organizations were, the police considered, only fronts for the UDC – then busy distributing Ramsay MacDonald's pamphlet 'Why we are at War'; it was operating, however, once again within the bounds of the law, and therefore untouchable. If the police were generalizing, they did not do so to the point where significant misapprehension developed. The UDC's purpose according to the Morel doctrine was to consolidate precisely such organizations into an effective whole. The leadership of all of these organizations, moreover, was interlinked, both among themselves, and with the ILP and UDC. Some of them (the NAC[49] and the NCF[50] in particular) still are almost impossible to dissociate from the UDC and the ILP, as so many of the most prominent dissenters were linked to both, and given that co-ordination between them went so far. Moreover, many of the more prominent leaders of the UDC were plainly using it as a propaganda vehicle while organizing direct action through others. The fighting organizations, therefore, *were*, by and large, tactical groups operating within a broader dissenting movement with long-range, strategic goals. Consider, for example, the case of the NCF. Founded in autumn 1914 following the publication of an open letter by Fenner Brockway in the *Labour Leader*, and nationally organized in spring 1915, the NCF was the most active and socialist of the anti-conscription organizations. Clifford Allen, its first chairman, was former manager of the *Daily Citizen*. Fenner Brockway, its first honorary secretary, was editor of the *Labour Leader*, and controlled the National Labour Press which he used to print NCF literature. Both were members of the ILP and the UDC. Until July 1915, when he began to run into trouble with the authorities, the secretary of the NCF was C. H. Norman. He was also a member of the ILP and the UDC, and the treasurer of the SWC. Norman was, moreover, already well known to the police as a syndicalist and supporter of the International Workers of the World (IWW). The police hated him, and considered him to be 'entirely unscrupulous and willing to do anything in order to gain cheap notoriety'.[51] Another leader of the NCF was John Scott Duckers, like the others a member of the ILP and the UDC, and concurrently the president of the SWC. Duckers was another police favourite. The Reverend Layton Richards, a leading member of the first NCF national committee was also, meanwhile, the general secretary of the FOR.[52] Following the eventual arrest of virtually all the original leadership of the NCF (1916–17), Bertrand Russell took over as chairman, by this time having rejoined both the ILP and the UDC. The NCF contained as ordinary members Snowden, Macdonald, Morel and Trevelyan.[53] Throughout, the NCF seems to have been funded largely by the Rowntree family – wealthy Quakers. The purpose of the organization, if a later circular originating from Clifford Allen and Fenner Brockway is anything to go on, was precisely to act as a ginger group within greater affiliated organizations. Members were advised to court prosecution. This would be a valuable 'testimony to the world'. They should act with affiliated organizations – the ILP, BSP, UDC, WIL, FOR, Women's Co-operative Guild, the Society of Friends, the Pope's League for Peace and other bodies; join the PNC, and if there was not a local branch, form one; canvas for signatures for the peace memorial; join the ILP, and work for the peace faction by undertaking propaganda work; boost circulation of the *Labour Leader* (Brockway was editor!).[54] This was not precisely the programme of a distinct, single-issue pressure group. It is truly difficult to blame the police, therefore, for suspecting that the NCF was little more than a ILP/UDC cat's-paw, with a Labour agenda and floated by Quaker money.

The police, however, did not stop at postulating the existence of an essential unity of dissent. The CID was convinced that there was 'little doubt' that the campaigning organizations were inspired and financed by Germany.[55] They were not simply anti-war, but anti-British, even actively pro-German. This, of course, was quite wrong and the product of growing wartime hysteria. The suspicion, however, speaks of the degree to which political perceptions had already become starkly polarized, the extent to which opposition to the war was already being cast as treachery. This perception, that 'dissent equals treason', is highly significant. Ultimately it was to provide the rationale which would allow mechanisms created to combat espionage to be turned against the dissenters. For the moment, however, the campaigning organizations were simply too ineffective to attract much malicious attention. Simon, of course, was already familiar with their activities. Informed by police sources that a new 'Anti-Conscription League' (the NCF) was recruiting members in various British cities, he judged it 'a small & uninfluential body & ... not considered of sufficient importance for action to be taken at present with any useful result', however annoying it might be.[56] In 1915, Simon's thinking was by and large the consensus of the authorities. The new organizations, while reprehensible, were also ineffective. Tolerance was still possible. Before there would be any considerable departure from peacetime practice at home, dissent would have to become more effective, the home front more divided, and the government less inhibited.

This is not to say that there was no action. The, as always, very helpful business community continually urged that something be done. Once again press censorship was employed, at first voluntarily by the publishing community rather than officially by the government. In the case of the new organizations, this was the first stumbling block placed in their path. While never an impassable obstacle, it remained a powerful inhibitor.

'One of our members has received the enclosed advertisement, which of course he has refused to insert', begins a letter by the secretary of the Federation of Northern Newspaper Owners to the press bureau.

> Can nothing be done with the originators of these pernicious advertisements? It might pass into a paper without cognisance of the Proprietors, and lead them to being called to account. I think the right thing to do is to strike at the fountainhead.[57]

Should he print NCF material, a jobbing printer wanted to know. Would he get in trouble by doing so? He was not 'prepared to proceed with the order if there is any feeling against doing so by the Authorities'.[58] Should he post NCF bills, a Stratford businessman enquired. He would not do so if he was simply setting himself up for prosecution.[59] The answer to all of these? No action yet was envisioned. What the NCF was doing was not *yet* against the law, but probably would soon be and in that case, the co-operation of any private business with the NCF would take place at 'personal risk [to the proprietor] and at the risk of his company'.[60] As always, the press bureau absolutely refused to say exactly 'to what point it is safe to go'. Rather, it restricted itself to suggesting when businessmen were moving into waters they were likely to find rising over their head.[61] Official notification that they should use their own judgement in doing work for dissenters, cognisant of possible legal liability, left the NCF with precious few collaborators in its works of dissent.

Despite the reluctance of the business community to assist, there was always the National Labour Press to publish and willing – often suffragette – hands to distribute. Both leaflets and pamphlets, however, were very expensive methods which brought a small return. Moreover, while the dissenters quite plainly hoped to get in touch with the working class, and while Morel agitated for a more aggressive, propagandistic tone, most of the early publications tended to be written by, and directed at, the intellectual elite. A short pamphlet written by Bertrand Russell and distributed by hand was unlikely to have much impact in docklands Liverpool. Public meetings held at Cambridge (prior to their prohibition), where both the UDC and the NCF were active, were hardly likely to produce the mass audience which would be required if the war were to be stopped. Nor was Fenner Brockway speaking on the subject of Foreign Office reform at the University of Manchester likely to have much of an immediate, mass impact.[62] Only access to a much larger audience with more powerful and popular media, conveying a message comprehensible to the people, could produce a mass dissent. By the end of 1915, public venues, except in Glasgow, were no longer available except to the brave or reckless. Sympathetic newspapers were few. The radio and television were non-existent. Film was virtually a government monopoly. While it had an issue, and a potential audience, even the activities of the campaigning organizations did not make dissent effective in 1915. Individual grumbling is not effective opposition. Suitable methods of mobilization were not available, or had not been identified. What was needed, if dissent were to succeed, was more of Glasgow and less of Cambridge. It was not until 1916, even 1917, that the dissenters began to adjust to this reality.

In 1915, official action was restricted to surveillance. The authorities were careful to keep an eye on the new organizations, even if they were not yet ready for action. It was at this juncture that postal censors began opening the mail of dissenters. The intelligence section of the press bureau monitored the dissenting press, without taking action. Police infiltration commenced. From Manchester, for instance, came the report of a certain Detective Inspector A. A. Lewis, who, in the company of a Constable C. H. Haughton, attempted to infiltrate a meeting of the NCF at Milton Hall, Deansgate, Manchester. A socialist delegate, F. V. Jenkins, explained the policy of the Fellowship to the two policemen who were stopped from entering because they had no membership cards.[63] A report from South Shields, much less alarming, included a copy of the NCF membership application, which bound members to refuse to bear arms or to undertake work requiring the swearing of a military oath. The workmen to whom it had been distributed, the report continued, viewed the NCF with suspicion, and believed it to be little better than a flimflam calculated to make money from them.[64] This description of the initial working-class response to the NCF was not entirely untrue. In a survey in June 1916 of its Manchester membership, the NCF was shocked to discover that of 127 members only one was an actual labourer. In its first year, the NCF was essentially a middle-class, non-conformist-socialist association.[65] Not until a year later, in autumn 1916, with conscription a fact and industrial compulsion on the horizon, did the NCF begin to find a wider working-class audience.[66] Even then, Herbert Morrison was by no means alone in viewing the NCF as a middle-class phenomenon, out of touch with working-class issues and apt by its activities to harm labour unity.[67]

The fact that dissent was as yet ineffective and the Home Secretary inclined to be tolerant did not mean, however, that all of the authorities were resigned to sitting on their hands. If the dissenting message was ineffectively broadcast, that did not make it less provoking. And, while the patriots policed the meeting halls and public places of the nation, they were unable similarly to guard against dissemination of the dissenting message through the post and press. If the pamphlet and leaflet campaigns were to be stopped, government initiative would be required. The only answer, of course, was official censorship of some kind. If the HO would not act, indeed, had yet to perceive a real danger, the Attorney General in Asquith's first coalition government, the militant Unionist Sir Edward Carson, was all too willing to supply the wanting impetus. It is from Carson that the first attempts to institute real censorship came.

Horrified by the propaganda being put out by the new organizations, in summer 1915 Carson directed raids against the National Labour Press (responsible for printing most of the offending literature), the head office of the ILP, and the editorial office of George Lansbury's *Daily Herald*, responsible for publicizing the anti-war *Herald* meetings. At the same time, the Glaswegian paper *Forward* was ordered to be seized.[68] Simon, of course, could not be expected to approve. At least for the moment, that was not very important. Carson was seeking to take advantage of the fact that the HO controlled only the MEPO directly. The HO was responsible for police inspection, and co-operation with local police authorities had increased during the war, but each chief constable remained without any constitutional superior.[69] The National Labour Press was in Manchester. While the HO could attempt to restrain and influence local police activities, and while the legal judgement of the Home Secretary would ultimately prevail, Simon could not control the Manchester police. Until the government clarified its policy, an order from the Attorney General was an order from the Attorney General. Carson, in short, was attempting to present Simon and the government with a *fait accompli* while providing an example for more vigorous, direct action against dissent.

When the police went in, four dissenting leaflets were then being printed at the press, along with an edition of the *Labour Leader*. The police seized one copy of everything (including a copy of a pamphlet written by Snowden in 1909 in support of the 'People's Budget'), and told Fenner Brockway that no material, and particularly no UDC material, was to be moved until the judgement of the examining magistrates had been delivered.[70] While the police complied with Carson's direction, these raids were carried through without much enthusiasm, however, in the certain knowledge that the HO was not yet ready to support such activities. If Carson could order raids, and if

Simon could not stop these from taking place, he certainly retained the power to make them pointless by inhibiting legal action.[71] It was unlikely, the Manchester police considered, that Simon would follow where Carson was attempting to go.

The police were correct. The HO refused to back up the Attorney General. When Morel complained to Simon that UDC literature had been seized without an injunction having been issued, and that under existing DRRs responsibility for literature found actionable lay with distributors rather than with producers,[72] Simon could do little but announce his own confusion, and promise to look into the matter.[73] Impounded literature was quickly returned.[74] An embarrassed Simon was forced to offer something like an apology,[75] which became more abject when repeated unofficially by his friend Runciman.[76] So premature had Carson's raid been that, rather than producing effective censorship, it resulted, instead, in open attacks on the government, followed by promises that there would not be a repetition.[77] The only positive development, from a government perspective, was that Morel, having become correctly convinced that the UDC 'had powerful and vindictive enemies in high places', resolved to 'exercise all due vigilance to prevent them from having a handle against us'.[78] A circumspect UDC line became more circumspect still.

The end result? As 1915 gave way to 1916, the groundwork had rather tentatively been laid both for an effective dissent and for its suppression. As yet, however, dissent had not yet found its audience (though it was beginning to perceive it) or identified suitable methods for the expression of its views in a way calculated to appeal to this constituency. The authorities, meanwhile, were largely by chance discovering methods by which dissent could be rendered ineffective, while, for the moment, refusing to accept that these methods should be generally employed, developed and systematized. Dissent would have to become much more effective before any striking policy departures would be considered.

NOTES

1. BLO, Simon Papers, Simon 2, Diary entry 26 October 1915.
2. Lord Simon, *Retrospect* (London: Hutchinson, 1952), p. 103.
3. Adams and Poirier, *The Conscription Controversy*, p. 83.
4. BLO, Simon Papers, Simon 52, Simon to Asquith, 27 December 1915:

   You are aware of my opposition to compulsion & I am not unwilling to worry you with a letter about it. But the situation which now threatens to arise makes it incumbent on me to say this: my firm conviction is that whatever additional numbers may be got by it, compulsion would produce disunion, and would so make the country weaker rather than stronger; consequently, I could not in any circumstances support it.

Hitherto I have assumed that continuance in the Cabinet did not involve assent to the policy of contingent compulsion; and my great desire, alike on public and private grounds, has been to avoid acting in a way which might embarrass you in relation to your 'pledge'. But I should greatly reproach myself if my silence misled you …

5. CCC, McKenna Papers, MCKN 5/9, Mrs Asquith to McKenna, 28 December 1915.
6. Young, 'War Resistance and the British Peace Movement Since 1914', p. 25; Ceadel, *Pacifism in Britain*, pp. 21–6.
7. See for Simon in the last phase, for instance, Wilson, *The Political Diaries of C. P. Scott*, John Dillon to CPS, p. 168. See also for threat of a general election, C. Petrie, *The Life and Letters of the Right Honourable Sir Austen Chamberlain* (London: Cassell, 1940), p. 48.
8. For example, Ponsonby to Trevelyan (May 1915):

   At first I was inclined to think that so far as you, MacDonald & I were concerned there was no real change as it was not the *conduct* of the war but the *origins* & the settlement about which we would want to express ourselves. But I am not quite sure this is the case because we have new elements to deal with.
   (1) The imminence of Conscription …

   Quoted in Swartz, *Union of Democratic Control*, p. 67.
9. LSE, Morel Papers, F6/4, Proposed Resolution, June 1915.
10. LSE, Morel Papers, F6/4, Proposed Resolution, June 1915, Morel objection appended.
11. Swartz, *Union of Democratic Control*, pp. 68–9.
12. Morel, June 1915: 'Our object … has been to gain a solid footing for the Union among the Trade Unions. It is only the first step in a policy which, I hope, will eventuate in thoroughly infusing the Labour World with the Union's creed.' Swartz, *Union of Democratic Control*, p. 60. See also BLO, Ponsonby Papers, 'Report on the Statement Made by Mr E. D. Morel … 22 June 1915'.
13. In what follows, the word 'patriot' will be used in this fashion.
14. BLO, Ponsonby Papers, Gilbert Murray to Ponsonby, 6 January 1915. Murray was not a dissenter in the First World War, though he had been a pro-Boer; indeed, he seems to have gone out of his way during the First World War to avoid the charge of dissent, much to the disgust of those who looked to him to lead dissent this time too. See, for example, Russell, *Autobiography*, Vol. II, p. 17, also pp. 49, 81–2.
15. PRO 30/69/1158, Walter W. Borret to MacDonald, 14 October 1914.
16. PRO 30/69/1158, Walter W. Borret to MacDonald, 27 October 1914.
17. A. Chisholm and M. Davie, *Beaverbrook: A Life* (London: Hutchinson, 1992), p. 208.
18. HLRO, Blumenfeld Papers, Ch. 11, Henry Chaplin to Blumenfeld, 9 July 1915.
19. For instance, HLRO, Blumenfeld Papers, Char 2/1, Charteris to Blumenfeld, 30 December 1917.
20. For instance, HLRO, Blumenfeld Papers, MACR 1, Macready to Blumenfeld, 15 September 1919; MACR 2, Macready to Blumenfeld, 4 October 1920.
21. HLRO, Beaverbrook Papers, BBK C/261, Beaverbrook to Northcliffe, 13 December 1916.
22. Morris, *C. P. Trevelyan*, p. 131.
23. Swartz, *Union of Democratic Control*, pp. 108–9.
24. BLO, Ponsonby Papers, Trevelyan to Robertson, 26 July 1915.
25. BLO, Ponsonby Papers, Trevelyan to Ponsonby, 25 July 1915.

26. BLO, Ponsonby Papers, Trevelyan to Robertson, 26 July 1915.
27. Chesterton had earlier come to national attention during his trial for libelling Rufus Isaacs during the prewar Marconi scandal. He was a power, particularly in the slums of east London where he had worked before the war. See B. Sewell, *Cecil Chesterton* (Faversham: St Albert's Press, 1975), pp. 69, 84, 105.
28. Williams, *Home Fronts*, p. 71; Swartz, *Union of Democratic Control*, pp. 110–11; Wiltsher, *Most Dangerous Women*, pp. 136–7.
29. Sewell, *Cecil Chesterton*, p. 84.
30. PRO 30/69/1159, Purkis to MacDonald, 7 December 1915.
31. Swartz, *Union of Democratic Control*, pp. 111–12.
32. Ibid., pp. 108–9. See also Russell, *Autobiography*, Vol. II, p. 25.
33. Middlemas, *Clydesiders*, p. 72.
34. Slowe, *Manny Shinwell*, pp. 66–7. Slowe has the incident occurring in 1916.
35. McGovern, *Neither Fear Nor Favour*, pp. 46–50.
36. BLO, Ponsonby Papers, Trevelyan to Ponsonby, 25 July 1915. See also Russell, *Autobiography*, Vol. II, p. 25.
37. PRO HO 45/10742/263275/118, Clifford to HO, 2 December 1915. See also for this dynamic Wiltsher, *Most Dangerous Women*, pp. 136–7.
38. PRO 30/69/1159, J. Senior to MacDonald, undated.
39. Swartz, *Union of Democratic Control*, pp. 112–13.
40. Ibid., p. 149.
41. See F. Brockway, *Thirty Years Inside the Left*; Russell, *Autobiography*; and for NCF organization circular, PRO 30/69/1159, No Conscription Fellowship Circular, 25 September 1916.
42. A small, pacifist body, of indeterminate persuasion, and with membership partially interlocking with that of the NCF. S. Duckers was the chairman, C. H. Norman the treasurer. The stated objective of the SWC was to 'demand that Britain's part in the war shall be brought to an immediate, honourable and righteous end'.
43. This was a non-denominational Christian group; its chairman was Dr H. T. Hodgkin, general secretary the Rev. Layton Richards, secretary, Lucy Gardner, and treasurer, J. F. Braithwaite. It was founded by Richard Roberts, a Presbyterian minister, and Henry Hodgkins, a Quaker, in December 1914. Throughout the war, the FOR was predominantly non-conformist and Quaker. See Bainton, *Christian Attitudes*, pp. 207–8; Ceadel, *Pacifism in Britain*, p. 36.
44. PRO HO 45/10782/278537 files 20 and 30, Anti-Conscription 1915–1916, No Conscription Fellowship, 27 October and 9 November 1915.
45. Russell, *Autobiography*, Vol. II, p. 33. Text of offending article, p. 63.
46. CCC, Fenner Brockway papers, FEBR 13/1/16, Shaw to Brockway, 13 January 1916.
47. CCC, Fenner Brockway papers, FEBR 13/1/16, Shaw to Brockway, 13 January 1916. Shaw, while of course a fellow-traveller, was not quite so convinced a dissenter as many of his comrades. This may, in part, account for his differing tactics. Conscription was simply not his issue. Writing to Russell regarding a particular objector, Shaw advised:

> He seems to be, like many literary people, helpless in practical affairs and the army is in some ways the very place for him; for he will be trained to face the inevitable, and yet have no responsibilities. He will be fed and clothed and exercised and told what to do; and he will have unlimited opportunities for thinking about other things. He will not be asked to kill anybody for a year to come; and if he finds his conscience insuperably averse, he can throw down his arms and take his two years hard labour then if he must, and be in much better condition for it. But by that time he will either have been discharged as unfit for service or else have realized

that a man living in society must act according to the collective conscience under whatever protest his individual conscience may impel him to make. I think that is what we are bound to tell all the pacific young men who apply to us. (Russell, *Autobiography*, Vol. II, pp. 64–5.)

48. PRO HO 45 10782/278537 file 18c, Anti-Conscription 1915–1916, CID Report on Anti-War Propaganda, 20 July 1915 (enclosed).

49. PRO 30/69/1159, Johnson to MacDonald, 16 May 1916.

50. Middlemas, *Clydesiders*, p. 69.

51. PRO HO 45 10782/278537 file 18c, Anti-Conscription 1915–1916, CID Report on Anti-War Propaganda, 20 July 1915 (enclosed). We have already seen Norman attempting to publish his pamphlet 'Stop the War', for which he was gagged and ultimately arrested.

52. Ceadel, *Pacifism in Britain*, p. 35.

53. See especially Brockway, *Thirty Years Inside the Left*; Russell, *Autobiography*. For organization circular, see: PRO 30/69/1159, No Conscription Fellowship Circular, 25 September 1916.

54. MUH, Russell Papers, volume 535, 'Circular Letter on Peace Propaganda', undated 1916.

55. PRO HO 45 10782/278537 file 18c, Anti-Conscription 1915–1916, CID Report on Anti-War Propaganda, 20 July 1915 (enclosed).

56. PRO HO 45 10782/278537 file 18a, Cornwall Deputy Chief Constable to HO, 7 August 1915; file 18b, Manchester Chief Constable to HO, 19 August 1915; 18c, South Shields Chief Constable, 22 August 1915.

57. PRO HO 139/23/96, Part 2, File 10, Frank Bird to Press Bureau, 3 January 1916.

58. PRO HO 139/23/96, Part 2, File 10, William Pile Ltd to Press Bureau, 22 January 1916.

59. PRO HO 139/23/96, Part 2, File 10, Borough T Posting Co, Stratford, to Press Bureau, 28 August 1916. This particular query did result in a prosecution. In trying individual members of the NCF at the Mansion House, Judge Bodkin had delivered himself of the opinion that 'war would be impossible if the view that war is wrong, and that it is wrong to support the carrying on of war, were generally held'. Edward Fuller, a journalist member of the NCF, attempted to use this bit of comedy as the basis for an anti-war poster. HMG was not amused. Ultimately Fuller was fined £100, with £25 costs, or 91 days' imprisonment under DORA for committing 'an act preparatory to the commission of an act'. Pankhurst, *The Home Front*, p. 329.

60. PRO HO 139/23/96, Part 2, File 10, Press Bureau to William Pile, 24 January 1916; Matthews (DPP) to Press Bureau, 30 August 1916.

61. PRO HO 139/23/96, Part 2, File 23, Samuel to Troup, 30 October 1916.

62. CCC, Fenner Brockway papers, FEBR 13/9, Notes for a Speech at Manchester University, 1915.

63. The war must be ended, he told them. England had declared war on Germany, not the other way around. The people were happy in Alsace-Lorraine, as were men working for the Germans in Ghent and Brussels. Conscription was an evil which, in the interest of the workers, had to be stopped. 'We owe no allegiance to the King. It's him that is on our backs', Jenkins went on. Messrs Cadbury, Rowntree and Outhwaite were members, he claimed, along with 17,000 others – of whom 7,000 were miners. The only literature the policemen were able to obtain were requests for membership. 'We don't do propaganda', Jenkins explained, 'as the authorities would be upon us.' Having ascertained that there were a total of 28 men, and five women at the meeting, and having obtained Jenkins's address for correspondence (!) the detectives departed. PRO HO 45 10782/278537 file 18b, Manchester Chief Constable to HO, 19 August 1915.

64. PRO HO 45 10782/278537 file 18a, Cornwall Deputy Chief Constable to HO, 7 August

1915; file 18b, Manchester Chief Constable to HO, 19 August 1915; 18c, South Shields Chief Constable, 22 August 1915.

65. MUH, Russell papers, volume 535, 'Conscience and Character', 21 June 1916. Of 126 surveys returned: 94 Manchester NCF members were single; by occupation, 16 were professionals (six teachers), 29 artisans, 29 clerks, 48 white collar workers, four civil servants and one was a labourer; by religion, only six were Church of England, though most were believers; by conviction, 106 had been prewar pacifists; 37 were ILP, and 13 were BSP. 'Nearly all had been Norman Angell Leaguers, Young Liberals, or Single Taxers.' Nineteen had been temperance activists. Most were multiple joiners: the champion was a 23-year-old Quaker who was a member of 12 different political organizations.

66. C. Wrigley, *David Lloyd George and the British Labour Movement in Peace and War* (New York: Barnes & Noble, 1976), p. 182.

67. While Morrison certainly disapproved of the war, and was later to accept alternative service as a CO, he never joined the NCF for the reasons indicated. See Donoughue and Jones, *Herbert Morrison*, pp. 27, 40.

68. Lord Snowden, *Autobiography*, p. 422.

69. Morgan, *Conflict and Order*, p. 65. During the war, the informal influence of the HO over local authorities increased enormously, as did the degree of contact. Already, in 1914, constant liaison between local authorities and the new War Duties Division of MEPO commenced in order to keep the HO war book up to date. Inspection of constabulary continued. Finally, district and central conferences, bringing local chief constables together with MEPO and HO officials were commonplace by 1918. None of this, however, implied any new subordination of local officials to central authority.

70. LSE, Morel Papers, Morel 6/8, Brockway to Morel, 18 August 1915.

71. Swartz, *Union of Democratic Control*, pp. 118–19.

72. LSE, Morel Papers, Morel F6/8, Morel to Simon 19 August, and 25 August 1915.

73. LSE, Morel Papers, Morel F6/8, Simon to Morel, 24 August 1914.

74. LSE, Morel Papers, Morel F6/8, Simon to Ponsonby, 10 September 1915.

75. LSE, Morel Papers, Morel F6/8, HO to Morel, 25 August 1915.

76. LSE, Morel Papers, Morel F6/8, Runciman to Trevelyan, undated 1915.

77. PRO 30/62/1162, Trevelyan to MacDonald, 3 September 1915.

78. LSE, Morel Papers, Morel F6/8, Morel to J. W. Graham, 25 August 1915.

—4—

Samuel at the Home Office, 1916

A S VOLUNTARY enlistment failed to produce the goods, Asquith was forced to honour his promise to move to conscription. A new coalition government with still greater Unionist representation was necessary to implement it. Simon could no longer remain at the HO. His replacement was Sir Herbert Samuel. During the first half of the year, as conscription was implemented first for single men (January) and then for married men (March), dissenting organizations began to demonstrate a new level of activity. They began to find a popular voice, and to identify methods and media with which to amplify it. Almost immediately a harsher attitude to dissent was evident. This was not only due to the change in government, but also to the fact that dissent was becoming more effective.

One thing particularly notable, and frightening for the authorities, was the tone of the material being put out – vigorous, populist, combative. Dissent was obviously learning from its failures. Especially significant in this regard was the pre-emptive, anti-conscription bill-board and leaflet campaign undertaken by the fighting organizations. Their intention was to blanket the country from end to end, reaching the widest possible audience with a message that sold, utilizing media that were still unaffected by censorship. This time there was no laughing in Whitehall.

Taken aback, chief constables across the country forwarded to London copies of dissenting literature with requests for instructions. From South Shields came copies of the leaflets 'Shall Britons be conscripts?', 'What the Compulsion Bill Really Means' and 'Why They Want Conscription',[1] from Surrey, the posters 'Conscription', 'Wealth Before Lives' and 'What Labour Says'.[2] From Nottingham, Liverpool and Cardiff came copies of 'Shall Britons Be Conscripts?';[3] and from Southend on Sea, 'Down With Conscription'.[4] Two examples will serve to illustrate the temper of this first leaflet campaign. One of the more widely distributed leaflets demanded, 'Shall Britons be Conscripts?'. It answered:

The time has come to appeal to those who value our traditional freedom.

A determined resistance must be made to the sinister endeavour to impose upon the people under some such formula as 'compulsory attestation for single men', the evils inherent in Conscription.

National service must not be degraded to national slavery. Freedom of conscience must not be sacrificed to military necessity, nor British liberty to political expediency. Men's deepest religious and moral convictions must not be swept aside.

WE ARE CONFIDENT THIS DANGER CAN YET BE AVERTED.

We appeal to the servants of Christ and to lovers of religious freedom. Is religious persecution once again to stain the life of our country?

We appeal to our fellow-workers in factory, workshop and mine to maintain the right of every man to decide for himself the issue of life and death.

We appeal to those who rejoice in that liberty of conscience, that tolerance of thought and action, which make them honour the name of their country.

THE RESPONSIBILITY IS YOURS TO MAINTAIN INTACT THE LIBERTIES OF THE BRITISH PEOPLE.

If you fail to do this, we – men of military age – must and will resist alone, whatever the consequences.

We believe in human brotherhood, in the sanctity of human life and personality. We will not kill. We will accept no military duties. While the soul of Britain lives our witness cannot be in vain.[5]

'CONSCRIPTION', another leaflet, was headed: 'WHY THEY WANT IT AND WHY THEY SAY THEY WANT IT'. It continued:

They say they want it to punish the slackers.
They want it to punish the strikers.
They say they want it to crush Germany.
They want it to crush labour.
They say they want it to free Europe.
They Want it to enslave England.
Don't let them get what they want because they keep saying
they want something different.
The Cat kept saying to the Mouse that she was a high-minded person,
and if the Mouse would only come a little nearer they could both get
the cheese.
The Mouse said: 'Thank you, Pussy; it's not the cheese you want: it's
my skin'.[6]

This was plainly Glasgow speaking rather than Cambridge, expressing the sentiments of 1910 rather than 1914.

One new, less successful, forum chosen by the pacifists to express their disagreement with government policy was private mailing through the post. Rather quickly this came to the attention of the police. A form letter mailed to a Mr R. Miller, in Birmingham, arrived postage due. Since he refused to receive it, the Post Office opened it to find a return address. When it was discovered that the enclosed material advocated a general strike to end conscription, the letter was passed to the Birmingham police and, from there, to the HO. The letter called the Compulsory Service Bill the 'Thin edge of the wedge (Conscription) Bill', and foresaw its use to suppress all Labour and Socialist papers and organizations. Strikes would be forbidden and questions in Parliament suppressed. To speak against the bill, the letter claimed, would be illegal. 'No conscientious objector', it continued,

> will be allowed unless he has money and influence. All strikes will be a criminal offence. A single man dare not leave his job for any reason or he will be conscripted. His employer can do what he likes with him. The employers and the Government have got you down.
> *Unless*
> You act at once. Arrangements are in hand for a general Strike. Directly the Bill becomes law DOWN TOOLS – forget to get up – There are many ways to stop a Factory or Pit working. If you are all united and firm the Government will give way in a week. If you don't you will have a lifetime of Suffering and the curse of your children. This is a gigantic plot to break Trade Unionism and enslave you. South Wales and the Clyde will not suffer this Slavery though Henderson and Coy. are traitors and paid tools of the Capitalists. Strike *now* or you are Slaves for life.[7]

Startling as this leaflet might have been, and dangerous as its message was, this method of attempting to reach the public met with little success. By its nature, communication through the post could only reach a limited audience and was very apt to come to the attention of the authorities. It could, that is, reinforce an existing belief, but was hardly a tool with which to shift a consensus, while being subject to easy interdiction and possible prosecution. The clumsy attempt, for example, to convert the families of men killed in action by this method was an utter failure, and seems to have hardened them in their determination to see the war through to a victorious finish rather than to move them towards a more pacific viewpoint. Another failure was the

PNC's circulation of a petition demanding that the government start peace negotiations. A total of 200,000 signatures was unlikely to have much of an effect on government policy. The government ignored it, as its predecessor had the Chartists.[8]

Failures aside, dissent was now worrisome. In part this was because, as war weariness developed, and as they found themselves more popular, dissenters began to raise their sights higher than simply stopping conscription, while, once again, attempts were renewed to find a public forum. In spring 1916, for instance, one of the new organizations – the NAC – announced its intention of hosting a series of huge ILP gatherings, outside industrial centres during the summer. Sympathizers would be brought in from outside to hear noted ILP speakers on the subject of 'the necessity for renewed energy in raising the consistent demand for a termination of the War at the earliest possible moment'. Such meetings would begin with picnics and would progress by means of general meetings, when the pitch to stop conscription, by stopping the war, would be made.[9] During 1916, moreover, the NCF made massive efforts to improve contact with disgruntled working men frightened by conscription and the compulsion it seemed to augur. A government increasingly less inclined to tolerate dissent was even less likely to be restrained in dealing with this sort of campaign, which sought to realize its agenda by linking wartime with prewar grievances, programme with class politics.

But what to do? The HO was pushed and pulled in many directions as reaction to the activities of the dissenters began to develop, and was uncertain how to deal with dissent which, while becoming dangerous, was certainly legal. Conscription had only just been introduced, without serious debate in the House. Broader manpower controls were projected. Both were still, therefore, active political issues. From one extreme, police and local authorities consistently advocated the ruthless prosecution of persons responsible for the production and distribution of anti-conscription propaganda. To their voices were added those of certain MPs for whom the dissemination of such ideas in a Britain at war looked very much like treason.[10]

Nevertheless, throughout the Samuel period the HO approach to the question of dissent continued to be inhibited. Samuel was little more likely than McKenna or Simon to permit any great, substantive departure from normal, peacetime practice. He had no ambition to become a minister of the interior. He was backed, moreover, by a prime minister whose liberal inclinations, while tattered, endured. But, while Samuel certainly shared many of the inhibitions of McKenna and Simon, he was without their conviction, clarity or certainty. While, for instance, he believed that conscription was probably necessary however much he hated it, he did not believe that full manpower compulsion would be required.[11] He also believed that absolute certainty that compulsion would not eventually be required alone could give sufficient grounds for leaving the government. He was himself not certain.[12] Samuel was willing to envision the use of methods he hated in order to impose a policy he disliked, hoping that he was helping to make unnecessary a policy he deplored. If Samuel was disoriented, he was also not a very dynamic Home Secretary. He believed that 'in time of war the ideal for the Home Office is to be neither seen nor heard'.[13] An organization invisible by virtue of not doing anything, fixedly determined not to make waves, was not very likely to constitute much of a check on dissent. Even daylight savings time, for instance, struck Samuel as a tremendous innovation which he implemented belatedly 'with some trepidation'.[14] To make matters worse, Samuel was constantly distracted from affairs on the home front by Ireland, then in the throes of rebellion.[15] Samuel, like Simon and McKenna, was a Gladstonian knocked off balance by the collapse of virtually everything in which he had believed. The first of Britain's wartime home secretaries who needed to draw a line against dissent, Samuel was also the last whose distaste for the task often outweighed his sense of its urgency.

Nevertheless, an effective government strategy against dissent began to develop during the Samuel period. Whatever the constitution might have suggested as appropriate, Samuel did not lead this movement. Repressive practices in Britain derived in large measure from the fact that if Samuel was every bit as confused as Simon and McKenna, he was also less masterful and far more distracted. There were others in the government much more inclined than Samuel to take a harsh line towards dissent. He was more a brake on a state system which was increasingly disposed to act decisively than himself being responsible for the greater level of government activity. Albeit he was not a very effective brake. Lloyd George's judgement of Samuel was cruel but probably fair:

> He was a competent and industrious administrator, and I was persuaded that he could preside with neat efficiency over one of the Offices which owing to the War did not demand exceptional gifts of an original kind. Before the War he had won the reputation of being capable and useful in every official sphere he had occupied. During the War he had done nothing in particular, but he had done it very well. … He gradually sank out of sight altogether as a man who attended to odd jobs of a minor but serviceable character.[16]

So why did Samuel become Home Secretary at this juncture? Certainly the reason was largely party political. With every reincarnation of the Asquith coalition, Unionist presence became stronger, Lloyd George more independent, and dependable Liberals close to the top fewer in number. If hardly dynamic, Samuel was certainly dependable. Moreover, Carson's activities in 1915 indicated that a safely Liberal hand would be required on the HO tiller if the Prime Minister were not to lose control of home policy altogether. And, if hardly a ball of fire, Samuel was, at least, liked by his colleagues. Indeed, much of Samuel's utility in the government appears to have been his ability to ginger other Liberals into supporting policies with which they, like Samuel, disagreed at heart.[17] He was a politically useful, but hardly energetic figure, unlikely to lead very decisively in any direction. By October 1916 his days were obviously numbered, as were those of the Asquith government. Like McKenna and Simon, Samuel did not last long.

Like Carson before them, the law officers in the new Asquith government, F. E. Smith (Attorney General November 1915–December 1918) and Sir George Cave (Solicitor General November 1915–December 1916; Home Secretary December 1916–December 1918), were much less inclined to tolerate dissent than certain of their predecessors had been – indeed, than Samuel himself was. They were, as well, Unionists rather than Liberals, and did not, therefore, feel much loyalty to Asquith's policies, or much sympathy for his equivocations. While both Cave and Smith communicated with Samuel, co-operation was never comfortable, and they were increasingly reluctant to wait for a lead which was not apt to come. Having read Morel's pamphlet 'Truth and the War', for instance, both Smith and Cave were strongly of the opinion that it should be suppressed. Samuel, however, refused to act.[18] Failing to find acceptable leadership from the Home Secretary, Cave and Smith began to act both on their own and in co-operation with other government agencies looking for a more vigorous policy against dissent. The armed services were increasingly disposed to act. Lloyd George and the new Ministry of Munitions were very aware of growing unrest at home. The police were growing restive. An unsteady hand now operated the HO brake. The result was, very largely, a coalescence of force disposed to act against dissent, whatever the Home Secretary might prefer.

The first element in the new dispensation was increased censorship. Machinery constructed to deal with espionage, and which had been used to monitor dissent while hampering the dissenters' efforts at propaganda, was ever more directly employed to produce real censorship. As always, however, there was some attempt to mix repression with political sagacity – not to go so far that the act of censorship itself proved more incendiary than the opinion expressed was likely to be.

One way in which stricter censorship could be imposed was simply to employ existing mechanisms to monitor the overseas communications of dissenters. This could be justified on the grounds that if dissenters were not technically German agents, they were certainly apt to pass on to foreign contacts information dangerous to the war effort, while lending comfort to the enemy. No new powers were necessary here. The existing machinery for press, postal and telegraph censorship was tailor-made for this purpose. Not only could the existing system ensure that news and opinions of which the government disapproved neither left nor entered the country, but the dissenters, particularly if they attempted to evade the system, would quickly find themselves moving into a position in which their actions were easily demonstrable as being in contravention of DORA. Moreover, since censorship was an army prerogative, the HO would not need to be consulted. And, since communication with foreigners for purposes of publication except through authorized channels was itself an offence, the censors would never have to justify themselves in court. The offence tried would not be the communication of one or another opinion, but the fact of illegal communication in itself. This was not censorship, so the censors could claim, but simply an issue of law and order. It was important that it was the evasion of the system rather than the substance of the criticism which permitted a response, and that it was the army that directed it, because the Asquith government itself was still not sold on the idea of formal censorship of ideas.[19]

For example, an article which Camille David attempted to send through the mail to the Norwegian Socialist paper, *SocialDemokraten*, was first stopped by the postal censors, and then censored by the press bureau. It was stopped as an

> [u]ndesirable article intended for publication in a neutral country's Socialist Newspaper. The facts stated on the Compulsory Service Act are written in such a way as to give a bad impression if allowed to be published abroad. Writer gives the opinion of several ILP members. Mr Philip Snowden's especially being undesirable.[20]

The article was stopped, in short, because it presented the views of British dissenters to a foreign audience. The stoppage need only be justified by reference to the chosen method of transmission. What had been gained by the opening of David's mail, however, was not simply the interception of an obnoxious article. It was ascertained at the same time that David was writing such material and attempting to send it overseas. This in itself could have led to his prosecution. Even when that was not felt to be justified, by 1916 the discovery that somebody was attempting to send dissenting material overseas invariably resulted in a file being opened on them by the police, while the post and press bureaus began to examine their work and correspondence minutely. In the end, such special treatment often led to arrest for breach of DRRs, generally as the frustrated author did something or another foolish attempting, from sheer vexation, to break through ever more constricting censorship. Meanwhile, in the case we are considering, postal censorship of David meant that the dissemination of the ideas of another dissenter, Snowden, was restricted. Postal censorship of David implied press censorship of both David and Snowden. Rather a good day's work – accomplished, of course, without the Home Secretary having to be consulted at all.

If postal censorship could account for attempts to reach a foreign audience, press censorship could, at least in part, control the attempt to disseminate dissenting ideas via the domestic print media. And, if the press bureau remained without coercive powers, everyone was subject to DRRs which were steadily being reinterpreted in a more restrictive fashion. Even in a system of censorship which, in theory, functioned by compliance rather than compulsion, failure to comply with an always-growing number of 'suggestions' resulted in an ever-greater likelihood of prosecution. And even where prosecution seemed unwise, withholding official sanction could inhibit publication of things that were merely obnoxious. Businessmen would be kept guessing. A printer apt to face prosecution, even to lose his press, is unlikely to be an enthusiastic collaborator.[21] Both mechanisms, while subtle, certainly limited the types of opinion which could be expressed while restricting markedly the audience which any dissenter could reach with the written word. Once again, the Home Secretary did not even have to be consulted.

Even now, no irretrievable step was taken without a political cost-benefit assessment. In general, it was the international stature of a dissenter which determined the nature of the government's response. While, for example, George Bernard Shaw was certainly annoying, he was also famous. An anti-war article penned by Shaw in spring 1916, and filed by the press bureau under the rubric 'self-satisfied article by G. B. Shaw for publication in the USA', was allowed to pass, as was Bertrand Russell's pamphlet 'Political Ideals'. On the other hand, 'Bertrand Russell and the War Office'[22] and 'Why Not Peace Negotiations?' were retained, and censored absolutely, as were Morel's 'Whither is the Nation Being Led?' and Buxton's 'Peace This Winter'. Harassing the prospective publishers hampered other attempts at publication by Morel and Buxton.[23] When, a little later, Troup (press bureau) and Cecil (FO) were inclined to think that Shaw had gone too far and should be prosecuted for his 'Possible Peace Terms: The Republicans' Point of View', despatched to a US publisher, Masterman (HO) and Samuel were convinced that this would be a bad idea because of who he was. 'I am inclined to that opinion also', Samuel wrote, indicating his agreement with Masterman.

> If it is stopped, Shaw will make the most of the stoppage both here and in America, and people there will be convinced that we do not dare to allow our own literary men to express their views freely to the American public. On the other hand, the worst passages will be invaluable material for German propaganda, both in Germany and in all neutral countries. But the very fact that we allow such matter to emanate from England would be a proof of the lightness of our censorship and an indication of the strength of our opinion.[24]

Asquith agreed with Samuel; censorship and prosecution did not follow for Shaw. Note that the level of tolerance shown by the authorities was in direct relation to the popularity of the dissenter in question overseas. The result? Just enough material leaked out, by authors sufficiently well known, to establish the fact that in the UK tolerance for dissenting opinion remained, liberty was preserved and censorship was light. This was a rather clever policy indeed.

The truth was becoming increasingly different from the rather cosy picture created by tolerance of famous people writing for overseas audiences. Closer scrutiny of the dissenting post and press was paving the way for a more thorough-going policing of the home front, as simple prohibition by suggestion began to become prohibition absolute backed by police action. More vigorous methods were available by late spring 1916 with the passage of the Military Service (No. 2) Act. Anti-conscriptionist activity was now often defiance of the law. The dissenters attempted to adapt to changed circumstances by resorting to anonymous publications, and tried to protect their publishers by attributing production of their literature to bogus publishing houses. The government responded with new DRRs which made it an offence to publish anything without indicating both the author and publisher – those persons, that is, who might be held personally liable if the article in question was judged actionable. In addition, police authorities responded to the new secrecy with a series of pre-emptive raids carried out under warrants issued by military authorities under the DRRs.

How was it that the police were operating under military warrant? In 1915–16 the DRRs had been steadily broadened and reinterpreted, so that it was becoming possible to identify opposition to the war, or indeed to an aspect of war management, as sedition or even treason – an equation the police had already made. Need it even be added that, as opposition to conscription developed, the army came to interpret almost any sign of dissent as an attack on its own interests, and therefore as seditious. It was already well established in military minds, for instance, that to oppose conscription in principle was to oppose it in fact, and therefore to interfere with recruiting – an offence. It was equally well established, from a naval perspective, that to advocate any change in terms of work would inevitably have an impact upon its position as a substantial employer of skilled labour exempt from interference by other government agencies, and was, therefore, to employ an argument contrary to the nation's interests in war – perhaps not always an offence, but certainly always a provocation. The Ministry of Munitions, meanwhile, never doubted that to advocate industrial action in a controlled establishment was interference with armament production – possibly an offence both under the Munitions of War Act 1915 and DORA.

The press bureau, meanwhile, was brought directly under military control. In 1916 it was reorganized as MI7a (General Cockerill), responsible directly to the DMI (General Macdonogh). In a further articulation of DRRs, the press and postal censorship bureaux received permission to communicate directly with the legal authorities when a perceived breach of the DRRs had occurred.[25] This established a direct link between the censors and the DPP. The army, virtually without reference to the HO, could now obtain a warrant whenever it felt that a dissenter had gone too far either in publicizing his ideas at home or abroad, or when private correspondence indicated that censorship restrictions, or other DRRs, were being evaded or breached.

Moreover, as concerns about the state of the home front developed throughout 1916, communication between military, police, legal and other government agencies began to become routine. Such co-ordination became normative, very probably, because the HO – which should have co-ordinated restrictive activities at home – was not yet ready to lead in the direction desired. Into this gap, armed with new authority, the services began to advance following a trail already blazed by the legal authorities, only too ready to co-operate.[26] Failing an HO lead, under Unionist control even the FO was active in the suppression of dissent. Lord Robert Cecil (Under-Secretary and Minister of Blockade) and Maurice de Bunsen (Assistant Under-Secretary) were energetic proponents of effective censorship and, like Carson, worked to impose this themselves when the HO proved reluctant. It was, for instance, the FO which pushed the HO to cancel E. D. Morel's permission to export UDC literature to neutral states. When Samuel jibbed, it was the FO (Cecil), once again, which worked through the more accommodating WO to implement this prohibition.[27]

On 5 June 1916 the offices of the NCF were raided by warrant issued under the authority of Lieutenant-Colonel the Honourable Alich Russell (Bertrand's first cousin), Competent Military Authority (CMA) at the Adjutant-General (AG)'s office at the WO. The police involved in the raid were directed to seize anything they considered prejudicial to public safety. They therefore impounded all copies of two circular letters signed by Allen and Brockway. Confiscated as well were all copies of the Fellowship newspaper, *The Tribunal*, all organizational documents and all the Fellowship's business correspondence.[28] This made, no surprise, further actions against the NCF leadership and membership all the easier. In November 1916, similarly, in a rather more embarrassing repetition of the Carson–Simon censorship misunderstanding, Samuel's own police, operating under military warrants, raided UDC organizers and offices, despite the fact that Samuel himself was not consulted.[29] This time, however, there was no apology, or restoration of seized material.

The role of the HO in all of this? Samuel was, as yet, unwilling to act himself to assist in the censorship of ideas. The expression of some ideas, on the other hand, he was willing to help curb. The HO had now developed a policy to deal with those types of propaganda which had been employed in the spring campaign and which were, by the summer, contrary to DRRs. Instructions were despatched to local police authorities to guide their actions. Anti-conscription posters, the Guildford chief constable was advised, were to be torn down or defaced. Those posting them, his South Shields counterpart was instructed, should be advised that their actions would appear to contravene DRR 27, a catch-all regulation dealing with the expression of views prejudicial to the conduct of the war, and should be stopped. If necessary, legal proceedings were to be taken against such persons.[30] While it was recognized that such literature contravened DRRs by repudiating the 'obligations that citizenship entails' and were thus '*pro tanto* prejudicial to recruiting', no legal action was to be taken, as yet, against the authors[31] – and this despite the fact that more vigorous action 'would probably', the HO thought, 'be welcomed by the great majority of people'.[32] Thus the HO position for the moment was that, while the authors of such literature remained within their rights in writing such material – and were therefore not in contravention of the law, those who published, distributed or posted anti-conscription material acted in contravention of the DRRs. In short, to hold an opinion was not illegal, but to express it in such a manner as to make an anti-war critique effective might be so construed.

In accordance with this policy legal proceedings were instituted against several individuals for distributing material, the authors of which remained, for the moment, within the law. An Oxford under-graduate, Alan Kaye, was sentenced to two months' imprisonment in 1916 for distributing 'Shall Britons be Conscripts?'.[33] Clara Cole and Rosa Hobhouse embarked on a peace pilgrimage during which they hoped to distribute anti-war literature, including the Pope's appeal for peace. Five days later, they were arrested and sentenced to five months' imprisonment.[34] R. V. Cox, another NCF member, was tried for circu-lating the current issue of *The Tribunal*. Upon hearing evidence from the Provost Marshal that *The Tribunal* was subversive of military discipline, Cox was fined £100 with costs. The presiding judge, in his summing-up, noted his regret that proceedings, to date, had not been taken against the publishers of such material.[35] He was not long disappointed. Publishers had been so ruthlessly harried by the end of the year that the NCF could no longer find anybody willing to do its work. Posters were impossible. Small runs of *The Tribunal* were still produced on a small hand press, constantly disassembled and carried about the country to avoid detection.[36] Meanwhile, the organization came under intense pressure from the patriots. During its second convention, a hostile mob of patriots surrounded Devonshire House (the Quaker national headquarters), where the meeting was being held, and, while it was not dispersed, those attending were reduced to waving handkerchiefs rather than cheering so as not to incite actual violence.[37]

By the summer, the dissenters were ready for jail. Their literature destroyed, their premises raided, even Ramsay MacDonald was brought to admit that the only satisfaction to be obtained would come when the government was forced actually to imprison people.[38] Shortly after the NCF raid, in June 1916, Bertrand Russell – the author of the offending article in *The Tribunal* – was fined for breaches of DORA. Russell refused to pay, courting prison. Instead, his goods at Cambridge were seques-tered and the fine was ultimately paid by his friends. His crime? He had written a pamphlet which told the story of another pacifist, Ernest F. Everett, conscripted and sentenced to two years' hard labour for failure to report for duty.[39] Russell was not the only one prosecuted for this breach of censorship: in total, 18 individuals were tried for distributing the leaflet. The typical sentence was a fine and short prison sentence.[40]

While Russell himself was not yet in jail, this did not mean that his persecution was over. Another way in which the army could, by fiat, deny the dissenters a platform was to simply declare that, as suspicious persons, they were not allowed to visit prohibited areas – those areas in which special military regimes had been established to guard against espionage – under the Alien Restriction Act 1914. Since Britain is an island, and since most of its great cities are ports or lie near the sea (and were therefore prohibited areas), to deny a dissenter access to such areas was to prohibit communication absolutely with the dissenters' target audience. While this could never be a tool of general utility, it was used against Russell in August 1916 to considerable effect.[41] After 1916, there are few records of Russell meetings being broken up – but then again there are few records of effective Russell meetings.[42] There were ways in which this method implied censorship other than simply by restricting access to public platforms. Russell, for instance, was repeatedly assured that when he stopped doing propaganda work the prohibition would be withdrawn.[43] Failing such a promise, visits would be considered by a CMA on a case-by-case basis, which involved his submission to the press bureau for clearance of all speeches he planned to make in prohibited areas.[44] As always, the censors would not oblige by stating beforehand what was unacceptable.[45] They did not hesitate, however, to draw Russell's attention to topics best avoided – if, that is, he were to be allowed to travel.[46] When Russell would not undertake to comply, permission was refused.[47] The censors went still further. Russell was not permitted even to publicize the fact that if he refrained from propaganda he would be allowed to travel. He was left worrying, therefore, that the natural coloration which would be placed on events would be that he was, in fact, a dangerous, suspicious person.[48] This particular repressive tool, therefore, could never become the source of propaganda against the government (Russell badly wanted and never got a formal, publishable definition of 'propaganda' from the press bureau)[49] and helped to solidify perceptions important to the patriot reaction. When Russell sought to evade censorship by seeking a pass-port to the United States, he was denied – the reach of his message, therefore, was restricted to only those pamphlets the censors were willing to pass.[50] As always in the Samuel period, these were not new tools of repression, but rather the redirection of a mechanism con-structed with foreign espionage in mind. The army could do this, once again, without reference to an HO which was still not ready to authorize such truly restrictive practice.

Much of this still lay in the future. In 1916, following Russell's first arrest, both the NCF and its publishing house came under closer police surveillance. Most of the leadership, at least, was soon on its way behind bars. Brockway, even less lucky than Russell, was arrested four times between 1916 and the end of the war and spent most of the latter war years in Walton prison. His most famous trial came in June 1917 after he was arrested for his pamphlet 'Repeal the Act'. Lord Derby and Brigadier-General Child giving as their opinion that the pamphlet was harmful, the presiding magistrates judged that it was so, and sentenced Brockway to imprisonment.[51] Despite the fact that he attempted to keep abreast of events, and to contribute to the cause by publishing a prison paper, the *Walton Leader*, his days of effective anti-war leadership were over.[52] Allen was ultimately arrested three times, emerged from his imprisonment a wreck, and collapsed physically in December 1917. During 1918 he was unable to work. In this case, even a short dose of prison appears to have taken from the dissenters one who had been, until this time, one of their more prominent, convinced and dynamic leaders.[53] Brockway and Allen joined C. H. Norman, of course, who was already in jail. Ultimately, effective leadership of the NCF seems to have devolved to female volunteers continuing to put out and distribute *The Tribunal*.[54] By the end of 1916, the fighting organizations – the NCF in particular – were already besieged remnants, unable to play any truly effective part in opposition.

For new organizations – those just in the process of formation – there was even less tolerance. One of these which we have already seen, the NAC, forcibly came to the notice of police authorities in spring 1916 when it announced its intention to hold a series of monster, dissenting meetings aimed at the working class. Naval intelligence advised the government, quite simply, that it would be best to strangle this new group in its infancy 'and put an end at once to the movement before it gains many adherents and becomes dangerous'.[55] So much for tolerance of dissident opinions. On 23 June 1916, as part of the same campaign which had snapped up Russell, the offices of this fledgling organization were raided, apparently nationwide – as always, in 1916, under military warrant. All the literature seized in this raid was retained or destroyed with the exception of one pamphlet judged innocuous.[56] The presiding judge, who like most was strongly partisan, merely asserted, prior to ordering the destruction of NAC literature, 'I have considered these pamphlets and in my opinion they should be destroyed'.[57] Snowden applied to Samuel for a reason, but received no response. As Samuel had played no part in this campaign, it is likely that he had nothing to say. The central headquarters of the NAC, Snowden was informed, should have ensured that local branches did not do things which were apt to invite response. The NAC was essentially stillborn and its plan for a great series of meetings through the summer appears to have miscarried entirely. Shortly thereafter, a proposed meeting of the Peace

Negotiations Committee – another of the new organizations, and not in itself illegal, since there was nothing in DRRs which prohibited advocacy of peace negotiations – was prohibited outright when police and military authorities came to the conclusion that its activities were likely to lead to civil strife. Compare this with the lackadaisical first response to the NCF a year previously.[58]

As part of their fight against conscription, the dissenters sought a public platform. Public speaking, during 1916, became ever more important as alternative methods of communication were steadily restricted. Meetings, however dangerous, could perhaps take the place of a failing press. A growing constituency interested in the dissenting message would surely provide protection. From the beginning, government policy left the dissenters in little doubt that they would have a battle on their hands if they sought a public platform once again. In response to a question from Charles Trevelyan in the House as to whether the government was prepared to tolerate public agitation against conscription, Samuel answered that

> Meetings which are limited to opposition to the passage of the Military Service (No. 2) Bill, or to advocating its repeal if passed into an Act, or to opposition to any extension of compulsory service, would not be liable to suppression; but if there were violence, or incitement to violence or to illegal action, or if the law were transgressed in any other way, the object for which the meetings were held or the writings published would not, of course, entitle them to any exceptional treatment.[59]

In other words, there would be no suppression of dissent unless it looked like becoming effective – and this regulated by the fact that to refuse to serve or to advocate refusal for others was an offence under the DRRs. The dissenters could say whatever they wanted always provided that they did not say what they really meant – particularly if there were signs that anybody was paying attention. And, if trouble were anticipated, then it might be averted by removing the provocation, which, of course, meant prohibiting dissenting meetings. As in 1915, however, government action against dissenting speakers was not necessary. The patriots remained equal to the challenge.

On 23 January 1916, an anti-conscription rally was held in Finsbury Park under the aegis of the ILP and the BSP, with well-known dissenters such as Sylvia Pankhurst scheduled to speak from the *Herald* platform. *Herald* meetings, in the past, when concerned with other subjects, had always been popular with the British working class, 'who', the police judged, 'are always ready to listen to attacks on existing governments or wealthy members of the community'.[60] This meeting, however, was not a success. Advertisements for the meeting led to 'prominence' being 'given in the national press' (in the *Daily Express* most particularly) to the suggested meetings of 'Peace Cranks' in Finsbury Park. In the resulting disturbances, 'the Herald platform was overturned and smashed and supporters of the League hounded out of the Park by a large crowd of "patriots"'. 'This may mean', Acting Superintendent of Police, Sergeant William Lange, thought, 'the discontinuance of such meetings there.'[61] The HO noted Lange's conclusion with something like relief and approval.

In April 1916 there was an attempt to mobilize a monster demonstration in Trafalgar Square on Easter Sunday, to oppose conscription. The NCF, the ILP, the BSP, the Herald League, the SWC, the Women's International League and the Workers' Suffrage League would come together with representatives from the UDC, the NAC and the FOR. This was the short list. The meeting was obviously designed by its organizers to give the dissenters a renewed foothold in the city of London.[62] It would be massive and, it was hoped, this alone might provide security. As was usual, by this time, the usual warnings, and provocations appeared in the press. 'Sir', one letter published in the *Morning Post* (like the *Daily Express* a notoriously patriotic newspaper) began,

> the 'Stop the War Committee' and other societies announce a peace meeting in Trafalgar Square next Sunday. After the scenes that occurred a week ago ... the authorities will surely not permit this advertised meeting to be held ... At present the ILP, the UDC and the rest of them are holding peace meetings all over the country, and are circulating leaflets, demanding an immediate peace. Every effort is being made by these friends of Germany to prevent the defeat of Germany. These meetings do little harm here, but they certainly do harm to the Allies in neutral countries, and among people who do not understand how insignificant these people really are.[63]

'Among their objectives', another letter began,

> the last and most important was ... 'To aim to secure such terms that this war will not, through humiliation of the defeated nation or an artificial rearrangement of frontiers, merely be the starting point for new national antagonisms and future wars'. In other words, the object was to secure Germany from the consequences of defeat ...[64]

As was also usual, by this point in the war, an anti-war meeting compromised by preliminary and adverse publicity stood no chance of actually taking place. The Easter meeting never got off the ground. It was broken up by patriot violence – crowds of uniformed, often dominion, soldiers playing a significant role here as elsewhere – before it ever took place.[65]

Sometimes in apprehension of violence police authorities would attempt to inhibit dissenting activities. An NCF meeting at Grimsby, for instance, at which prominent religious and socialist figures were to speak against conscription, scheduled for May 1916, was prohibited by the local chief constable under DRR 27. Apprised of this, the HO informed him that he had no powers under Regulation 27 to prohibit a meeting. An HO official suggested, as an alternative, that DRR 9A be employed, on the grounds that 'it is probable that grave disorder will ensue'. Another concurred, since

> such a meeting is likely to arouse the most intense resentment among people at Grimsby. There is a very rough population at Grimsby: the Ch. Constable says nothing about apprehended violence but this may safely be assumed to be probable. In view of the many calls on the police it does not seem to be desirable that they should be employed on protecting the speakers from the natural consequences of their acts. The meeting is held for the purpose of expressing views wh. are detestable to the great majority of people & probably will be found to involve breaches of the laws but it would be unwise to leave those responsible for it to 'popular justice'.[66]

Thus, he advised, a new gloss was to be placed upon the Samuel dictum that there was to be no restriction of free speech unless it led to disorder. The disorder, in this case, was not to be that advocated by the speaker, but that generated by the opponents of the speaker's point of view.

Samuel himself was not yet ready to countenance this level of cynicism. He ordered on 19 May that the meeting should be permitted to proceed, with the proviso that a police reporter should be present, and speakers warned that anything said contravening DRR 27 would be taken down and used as evidence in potential proceedings against them.[67] The meeting was, as a result, a rather tame affair. At the HO correspondence relative to this incident was filed under the rubric 'miscellaneous crime'.

In the Samuel period, elements of tolerance still remained. A request, for example, from the Horsham District Council that a meeting scheduled for 9 June, at which Sylvia Pankhurst was to speak, be prohibited, was denied. To forbid the meeting, the HO reasoned, would require police or military action, and since both the police and the army were gravely stretched, prohibition was impolitic as well as impossible.[68]

Similarly, a request from Barrow-in-Furness that an open air socialist meeting be suppressed on the grounds that atheism would be preached, was likewise denied.[69] Government forbearance was natural. In respect to public meetings, Britain's informal censorship continued to operate, and nothing more formal needed to be done. As in 1915, it was not so much what the HO *did* to suppress dissent, but what it did *not do* to protect it. As much as it struck at dissenters directly, it simply refused to protect them from public attack. Dissenters would advertise meetings. The press would publicize the meetings. Patriots would counter-demonstrate against the 'peace cranks' and 'pro-Germans'. Violence would erupt. The patriots, being more numerous and violent, would prevail. The authorities, meanwhile, would watch. By the 1916, the mechanism by which British public opinion became essentially self-policing was well established, and served to a large extent to silence the dissenters.

This was a mechanism tailor-made for British scruples, and one, moreover, of which even Samuel was willing to make use to silence dissent which was otherwise well within the law. It was particularly useful when employed against those dissenting leaders difficult to touch due to their parliamentary immunity, and more difficult still to silence because to strike at one would seem to suggest that all had to be suppressed, along with Morel, the ILP, Labour papers and so on: a course of action which might be expected to produce rather drastic political fall-out.[70] Far better to allow these leaders to be intimidated into silence or deprived of a platform than to resort to direct governmental prohibition, censorship or prosecution. In May 1916, for example, Snowden was advised by Samuel that recent disturbances at meetings had made it impossible for the police to guarantee the safety of either Snowden himself or his wife, if they persisted in speaking from dissenting platforms. Snowden could do nothing but warn Samuel that if anything were to happen to his wife he would hold him personally responsible.[71] Samuel responded by opening a file on Snowden at the HO. Meanwhile, the meeting to which Snowden was to have spoken, and which had produced Samuel's warning – the centenary celebration of the London Peace Society – was cancelled because the authorities responsible for the hall at which it was to have taken place refused to risk having their hall broken up by bands of patriots. There was little the secretary of the Peace Society could do but complain in the *Daily Express* of 19 May that the pacifist movement 'was no new agitation ... grown out of the war'; that members of his Society, had 'always been interested in peace'.[72] It is doubtful that the *Daily Express* readership appreciated the distinction any more than would have its proprietor or editor.

It was not until the end of June that Snowden found an alternative platform from which to express his views, only to have this engagement cancelled as well. He had intended to address a meeting at Abertillery, in Wales. The manager of the theatre at which the meeting was to be held was advised, however, by the local police commissioner, Inspector Lewis, that the owner would hold the meeting entirely at his own risk, would be personally liable for all damages, and would be an accessory, aiding and abetting Snowden in the contravention of DORA if Snowden spoke as he was wont to speak.[73] On 25 June, Snowden was finally able to make an anti-conscription speech at Merthyr Tydfil.[74] He did so despite the fact that the UDC had earlier refused to supply a speaker for this meeting, on the grounds that this was an 'unconditional "stop the war" campaign', and therefore contrary to the predominant Morel line.[75] A transcript of this speech was handed to the police by the editor of the *Western Mail*, the latter having judged it actionable under DRR 27. The pattern of widespread popular-self-policing and active co-operation with the mainstream press continued.[76]

While Snowden's speech may indeed have been in contravention of DRRs, there was no arrest or trial of Snowden, in accordance with the HO's tacit policy of not making martyrs. That MPs should receive special consideration was only natural, since the tradition of parliamentary immunity was widely established, and direct action against an MP could not but have been widely noted, and much resented. A few months later, Snowden dared the government to prosecute him.[77] The government did not take up the challenge, considering that, while a successful prosecution might be possible, it would not be worth the 'time & money'.[78] The HO simply permitted Snowden to be deprived of access to larger venues. While, therefore, Snowden later wondered that only four of his meetings had actually been broken up by patriots and considered this a sign of government forbearance,[79] he was perhaps forgetting that many of the larger meetings at which he was to have spoken had been cancelled in apprehension of violence, while the government gathered kudos for its tolerance.

The police likewise handled Charles Trevelyan with kid gloves. A June 1916 pamphlet of Trevelyan's, suspected by the HO of constituting subversion, was laid by but did not become the grounds for prosecution.[80] Similarly, an article published by Trevelyan in the *New York World* in December 1916, carried by hand to New York so as to avoid the censors – this action in itself in contravention of DORA – also passed without legal action.[81]

There was not much need for anybody to deal with Ramsay MacDonald. So obvious a lightning rod had he become that it was virtually impossible for him to find anywhere to speak. In November 1916, for instance, he had been scheduled to speak at the Howard Hall in Letchworth. So far so good. When the news that MacDonald was coming leaked out, however, the town polled itself and a large majority determined to 'refuse to let the Hall to speakers who, while this country is at war, shall endeavour to embarrass the Government by creating internal disunion'. Old Ebenezer Howard, for whom the hall had been named, was disgusted, removed his wife's portrait from the hall, and told the society to change its name. Needless to say, the engagement was cancelled.[82] This was a type of censorship, though once again, the government was not doing anything formally and officially.

For neither Snowden nor Trevelyan nor MacDonald was there ever arrest. There was, however, continuous surveillance. From December 1916, at least, Trevelyan and Snowden, and Bertrand Russell as well, were being closely monitored by the police for suspected violations of DRR 24, which dealt with breaches of censorship.[83] Surveillance of Snowden, in particular, was nothing new; the police had been watching him for some years in connection with his suffragist activities. There might have been other types of harassment as well. Ramsay MacDonald, for instance, was in almost constant correspondence with the tax collectors for not declaring money earned as a journalist and from interest from co-operative societies of which he was a member. It would be interesting to discover if the inland revenue was getting its information from government seizure of UDC materials, or from the censorship of MacDonald's mail.[84]

During the Samuel period, the government began to move into uncoordinated action – of a kind – against the dissenters while, almost accidentally, adopting a much more sophisticated response than was the rule on the Continent. Throughout 1916 the government appeared to have dissent well in hand. Unfortunately, by this time, dissent from conscience was far from being the only worry. In spring 1916, to the battle against pacifist and anti-conscriptionist sentiment was added the first glimmering of the fight against labour unrest. It was at this juncture that Britain experienced its first significant labour difficulties which, if not sufficiently controlled, might have affected significantly its performance in war.

In February 1915 there had been a worrying strike on the Clyde – 8–10,000 strikers walked out, led by their shop stewards – and another, as we have seen, in south Wales.[85] In 1916 there were further outbreaks in the north country, the Midlands and Clydeside. Most disturbingly, perhaps, there was a wage dispute with munitions workers in plants at Abbey Wood and Woolwich in London. The problem was that both of these plants – controlled establishments under the Munitions of War Act – had laid on night shifts, and those workers involved wanted time-and-a-half for working on this shift. The possibility of a strike was being mooted. The disgruntled workers, however, had not applied for arbitration as they were required to under the Act.[86] When police began proceedings against the secretary of the district committee of the Amalgamated Society of Engineers (ASE) – a certain Tom Rees – under DRR 42, the Abbey Wood men went out on a one-day token strike and it appeared likely that the Woolwich men would follow.[87]

For the HO and Ministry of Munitions, this case was something of a test to see how the DRRs would hold up in the face of a strike in a controlled industry in wartime. Was, for instance, picketing legal in such a case? Earlier, the decision of the Lord Advocate was that it was not, under DRRs 42 and 48. The law officers agreed.[88] Rees was therefore arrested following an incident of picketing before mandatory arbitration had taken place. The government appeared disposed to make this a test case. The Ministry of Munitions asked the press bureau to do whatever it could to ensure that the subsequent trial received maximum publicity.[89] In March, however, proceedings against Rees were dropped, and the munitions workers agreed not to strike. Agreement had been sped by the arrival of the president of the workers' union, Robert Young, back from the fighting front with the message 'Hurry up the shells'. There had been no real loss of work. For the moment, at least, the peace with organized labour was maintained.[90]

More worrisome, altogether, was the Sheffield engineers' strike of November 1916. This strike has often been taken to be nothing less than a turning-point in the history of British labour,[91] the reason being that the strike occurred despite the wishes of the union leadership and regardless of the fact that agreement had been reached on all issues. The strike was, in theory, sparked by the attempt of the authorities to call to service a skilled man (Leonard Hargreaves) who held a union exemption card. In short order, the government backed down, Hargreaves was released and the right of the union to grant exemptions reaffirmed. This did not prevent the rank and file, led by their shop stewards, from walking out anyway.[92] The strike has therefore been taken to indicate that war accentuated and created grievances that had developed among at least one type of worker to the point that the rank and file might not, if conditions were wrong, accept union discipline. Their grievances had grown to the point where they were directed against the system rather than piecemeal. It was no longer some aspect of the workplace but the way in which the war was being conducted on the home front that was the problem. If this is a correct reading of what happened at Sheffield, the wildcat strike of 1916 was a dangerous development indeed. It was not a good sign, furthermore, that the strikers were only brought back to work following explicit promises from the government that conscription would not mean unrestricted manpower compulsion, only two weeks before the final decision was made (on 30 November 1916) to implement compulsion in principle. The strikers had extracted political not workplace concessions, from the government rather than their employers; and the violation of these promises was already on the government's agenda. It was no very happy augury either that during the strike and afterwards engineers began to flow into the NCF, which they had hitherto ignored.[93] The association of labour unrest with anti-war dissent through anti-compulsion appeared to be well in train, as Morel had predicted from the beginning. Nor was it a happy coincidence, finally, that many of the most prominent shop stewards who led the strikes would later go on to become founding members of the British Communist Party – their programme, therefore, was not only against the system and political, but total.[94] Not only was Morel being proved correct, but, it appeared, Lenin as well.

These strikes were, finally, only the first foreshadowing of a type of dissent which would become dangerous throughout the course of the following year. It was a type of disaffection all the more worrying, since, by its nature, it could not help but involve a greater and more critical mass, have an impact upon Britain's performance in the war, and build upon prewar cleavages. If principled dissent capitalized upon the class question as aggravated by the war and given a boost by opposition to conscription and the way it was being imposed, then an implicitly, perhaps explicitly, revolutionary (and certainly war-losing) situation might develop. While it was the intention of very few British dissenters to produce outright revolution, most were aware that the wind was beginning to blow in their direction. Morel, for instance, encouraged by the strikes of 1916, hoped that finally, a critical mass in the labour movement could be brought over to the UDC. He looked to the ever more militant 'Triple Alliance' (miners, railwaymen, transport workers), in particular, to provide such a mass.[95] His perception was acute. Labour, led by the Triple Alliance, was moving towards the UDC, pulled, in large measure, by the militant shop stewards. If the association ever became complete, Morel would have produced, in effect, the new radical coalition for which he had been hankering from the outbreak of war. The question, of course, was whether the workers led by their stewards would have been willing to stop at Morel's limited agenda.

The official history of the Ministry of Munitions summarized the situation on the home front at the end of 1916 as follows:

Thus while the policy of the Government was moving rapidly towards a comprehensive scheme of industrial compulsion, certain craft unions had secured the privilege of exempting their members from military service ... This privilege was emphasised by the decision to withdraw from all semi-skilled munitions workers their legal certificate of exemption from military service ... In these circumstances the industrial situation at home was hardly less menacing than the military situation abroad.[96]

If the situation on the home front in the winter of 1916–17 was not, perhaps, desperate, it certainly gave no grounds for absolute confidence. It would require, it was obvious, careful handling, if Britain's capacity to continue with the war were to be preserved.

By the end of 1916, most of the elements of an effective repression were present, as were the ingredients of a dangerous dissent. What was lacking in both was system and the will to construct it, though these were beginning to develop. While the government was as able as Morel to judge the trend of the times,[97] it was not until the advent of the Lloyd George total-war administration that an effective, unified, systematic government response began to emerge. Before we can consider the activities and policies of the Lloyd George government, however, we must first explore the shape of the ugly social–political divide which

FIGURE 1: MATURE DISSENT, DECEMBER 1916

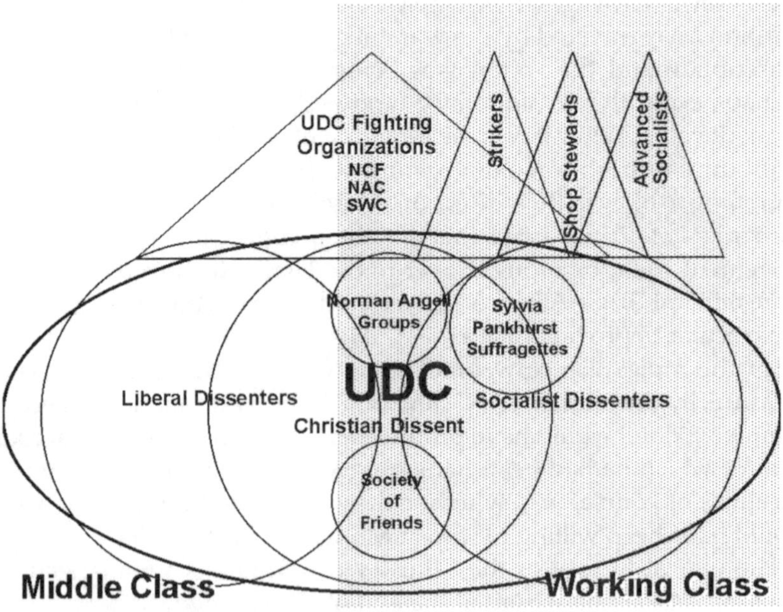

was developing during 1916, and which would prove to be a principal factor affecting both the way in which dissent developed and was dealt with in the last years of the war.

NOTES

1. PRO HO 45 10782/278537, Anti-Conscription 1915–1916, file 81, Chief Constable South Shields Borough to HO, 21 January 1916.
2. Ibid., file 92, Chief Constable Surrey to HO, 25 January 1916.
3. Ibid., file 75, Chief Constable Liverpool to HO, 18 January 1916; file 70, Chief Constable Cardiff to HO, 17 January 1916; file 90, Chief Constable Nottingham to HO, 25 January 1916.
4. Ibid., file 57, Chief Constable Southend on Sea to HO, 11 January 1916.
5. Ibid., file 90, Chief Constable Nottingham to HO, 25 January 1916.
6. Ibid., file 86, Sir E. E. Blake to HO, 24 January 1916. Some sense of the scale of the leaflet campaign can be gained from the HO files. For example, Clifford, it appears, had printed 2.5 million copies of the leaflet 'Conscription' alone.
7. Ibid., file 82, GEO to HO, 22 January 1916.
8. De Groot, *Blighty*, p. 148.
9. PRO 30/69/1159, NAC to MacDonald, 16 May 1916.
10. See, for example, PRO HO 45 10782/278537, file 88, Sir Joseph Slaton Bart, MP, to HO, 22 January 1916.
11. He had been assured, like McKenna and Simon before him, that the Prime Minister's policies continued to be designed to ward off rather than bring on manpower controls.
12. HLRO, Samuel Papers A/46, Samuel to Runciman, 28 December 1915.
13. Lord Samuel, *Memoirs* (London: Faber & Faber, 1945), p. 114. For Samuel as Home Secretary, see also B. Wasserstein, *Herbert Samuel, a Political Life* (Oxford: Clarendon, 1992), pp. 177–97.
14. Samuel, *Memoirs*, p. 114.
15. See, for instance, his correspondence and papers at the HLRO.
16. Lloyd George, *War Memoirs*, Vol. I, p. 640.
17. Example: HLRO, Samuel Papers, A/46, Samuel to Runciman, 28 December 1915:

    I hope you will not think me offensive if I send you a line earnestly appealing to you not to leave the government. The only thing that would justify resignation would be, I think, a conviction that, on grounds of fundamental principle, compulsory service ought never to be established in this country, and that view you do not hold. The question of the number of men that the country can afford to spare from industry does not arise at this juncture, for it is plain that the Prime Minister's pledge would prevent us from securing for the army, unless the question of the single men is dealt with, more men than about a third of the total, who can admittedly be spared.

18. Swartz, *The Union of Democratic Control*, p. 121.
19. In consideration of attempted communications with foreigners the policy of the Asquith governments was 'not to use the powers of the Executive to prevent people advocating negotiations for peace, inconsistent with the national purpose through such advocacy'. PRO HO 139/23/96, Part 2, File 23, Samuel to Troup, 20 October 1916. This was hardly a ringing endorsement for censorship.
20. PRO HO 139/11, Case 8695, 4 March 1916.

21. PRO HO 139/23/96, Part 2, File 23, Samuel to Troup, 20 October 1916.

22. PRO HO 139/11, Case 3636 (USA), 1 April 1916 (Shaw); Case 10119 (USA), 21 October 1916 (Russell).

23. PRO HO 139/23/96, Part 2, File 23, Samuel to Troup, 20 October 1916. For warning to, and reaction of, Morel's Glasgow publisher see Troup minute, 1 November 1916.

24. PRO HO 139/23/96, Part 2, File 21, Samuel to Asquith, 5 October 1916.

25. PRO HO/21/84, File 16, WO to Solicitor General, 1915; and Buchan to McKenna, 28 February 1915. The effect of the amendments was that 'where the military authorities ... think a case is one that does not call for Military trial and Military punishment, the Civil authorities will be at liberty to act'.

26. See, for example, correspondence relative to the activities of the chief constable of Glamorgan in PRO HO 45/10743/263275/274, WO to HO, 26 November 1916; summarized in Swartz, *The Union of Democratic Control*, p. 122.

27. Swartz, *The Union of Democratic Control*, p. 123. While Cave considered prosecuting Morel, the HO considered this difficult since Morel continued to focus on war aims, rather than war conduct. DORA could only have been made to apply if the government were prepared to issue, at this time, a statement of its war aims. It was not. For the moment, no prosecution followed. Swartz, *Union of Democratic Control*, p. 129.

28. PRO HO 45 10782/278537, file 74, Metropolitan Police, Special Branch, to Home Secretary, 6 June 1916.

29. PRO HO 25/10742/263275/202, 21 November 1916.

30. PRO HO 45 10804/308532, file 81, Samuel minute.

31. Ibid., file 88, Sir Joseph Slaton to HO, 22 January 1916, Minute 26 January. See also file 77, Report on Mr Clifford and Mr Massingham, 17 January 1916, Samuel minute.

32. Ibid., file 86, Sir E. Blake to HO, 24 January, Samuel minute, 26 January 1916.

33. E. S. Pankhurst, *The Home Front*, p. 301.

34. Ibid., p. 329.

35. PRO HO 25/10742/263275/202, Director of Public Prosecutions, W. Jackson, to HO, 15 June 1916.

36. D. Mitchell, *Women on the Warpath*, pp. 341–2.

37. Ibid., p. 333.

38. PRO 30/69/1159, MacDonald to Johnson, 27 June 1916.

39. PRO HO 45 10782/278537; see also HO 144/314670 for Russell's police file. For the text of the offending pamphlet, see pp. 79–81. See also Wasserstein, *Herbert Samuel*, pp. 191–6.

40. See MUH, Volume 805, 'Legal Actions: The Everett Case', Morgan Jones to Russell, undated 1916, and, F. W. Pethick Lawrence, 'The Liberties of the Subject', Peace and Freedom Leaflet No. 2, undated, 1916.

41. MUH, Russell Papers, Lt.-Col. Alich Russell to Bertrand Russell, 31 August 1916. The proximate cause was an annoying, and dangerous series of meetings Russell had conducted in south Wales in the early summer. See Chapter 7 below.

42. B. Russell, *Autobiography of Bertrand Russell*, Vol. II, p. 33.

43. See MUH, Russell Papers, Volume 710, M15 to Russell, 11 September 1916.

44. MUH, Russell Papers, Russell to Cockerill, 12 September 1916.

45. MUH, Russell Papers, Volume 410, Cockerill to Russell, 2 October 1916.

46. MUH, Russell Papers, Volume 710, Cockerill to Russell, 13 September 1916. Russell proposed to travel within a prohibited area to give lectures on topical questions or a general nature. Cockerill returned:

    Such topics as 'the sphere of compulsion in good government' and 'the limits of allegiance to the state' would in particular seem to require very careful handling if they are not to be mistaken for propaganda of the type which it is desired ... [to stop] ... until after the conclusion of hostilities.

See also Cockerill to Russell, 22 September 1916.

47. For Russell's refusal see MUH, Russell Papers, Volume 710, Russell to Cockerill, 15 September 1916 and Russell to Cockerill, 9 October 1916; for the army's response, see Cockerill to Russell, 12 October 1916. See also Volume 410, Russell to Lt.-Col. Russell, 5 September 1916, Lt.-Col. Russell to Russell, 11 September 1916 and Russell to Lt.-Col. Russell, 1 December 1916. Russell had wanted to deliver a set of lectures in Glasgow. In the end, they were delivered by proxy by Robert Smillie. *Collected Works of Bertrand Russell* (New York: Routledge, 1995), Vol. XIV, p. 224.
48. MUH, Russell Papers, Volume 410, Russell to Cockerill, 7 September 1916: 'The natural inference to be drawn from such a prohibition is that in the eyes of the authorities there is some reason to suppose me a person likely to seek and use dishonourably information which might be valuable to the enemy.'
49. MUH, Russell Papers, Russell to Cockerill, 12 October 1916.
50. Russell, *Autobiography*, Vol. II, letter Cecil Spring Rice to President of Harvard, 8 June 1916.
51. R. Gathorne-Hardy (ed.), *Ottoline at Garsington* (London: Faber & Faber, 1974), p. 111.
52. CCC, Fenner Brockway papers.
53. PRO 30/69/1162, Allen to MacDonald, 27 December 1917; 11 June 1918. See also Marwick, *Deluge*, p. 82.
54. Mitchell, *Women on the Warpath*, pp. 331–46. If the Russell Papers (MUH) are any guide, Catherine Marshall, especially, was an indefatigable collaborator with the NCF – so much so, in fact, that Clifford Allen continually warned Russell to monitor her work, so worried was he that she would do herself irreparable damage.
55. PRO HO 10801/307402, 655 W. 923, Stuart Nicholson to HO, 27 May 1916. Underlined passage underscored in red in original.
56. PRO HO 45 10801/307402, file 75, Raid on Offices of National Council Against Conscription, 23 June 1916.
57. PRO 30/69/1159, MacDonald to Johnson, 27 June 1916.
58. PRO HO 45 10804/308532, file 14, Meeting Peace Negotiations Committee, 6 October 1916.
59. PRO HO 45 10804/308532, file 67, Mr Trevelyan, 1 January 1916.
60. Ibid., file 83, Anti-Conscription Speeches delivered in Finsbury Park, report of Sgt William Lange, Acting Superintendent, 23 January 1916.
61. Ibid., file 83, Anti-Conscription Speeches delivered in Finsbury Park, report of Sgt William Lange, Acting Superintendent, 23 January 1916.
62. PRO 30/69/1160, 'Trafalgar Square Peace Demonstration, Easter Sunday, April 23, 1916', 4 April 1916.
63. LSE, Morel Papers, Morel F6/9, *Morning Post*, letter from W. Faulkner, 17 April 1916.
64. LSE, Morel Papers, Morel F6/9, *Morning Post*, 18 April 1916.
65. Williams, *Home Fronts*, p. 116; Pankhurst, *The Home Front*, pp. 304–7.
66. PRO HO 45 10810/311932, Prohibition of Public Meetings, file 6, Grimsby Borough Chief Constable to HO, 17 May 1916, Samuel Minute 18 May 1916. Regulation 9A was an amendment to DORA under Order in Council, which specified that:

> Where there is reason to apprehend that the holding of a meeting in a public place will give rise to grave disorder and will thereby cause undue demands to be made upon the police or military forces, it shall be lawful for a Secretary of State, or for any mayor magistrate or chief officer of policy who is duly authorized for the purpose by a Secretary of State, or for two or more of such persons so authorized, to make an order prohibiting the holding of the meeting.

As above, Order in Council, 19 April 1916.
67. Ibid., letter 19 May.
68. Ibid., Horsham District Council to HO, 5 June 1916.
69. PRO HO 45 10810/311932, Barrow-in-Furness Borough Council to HO, 27 June 1916.
70. PRO HO 139/23/96, Part 2, File 21, Samuel to Asquith, 5 October 1916.
71. PRO HO 45 10814/312987, Mr and Mrs Snowden. Pacifist Activities 1916–1918, file 1, Snowden to HBS, 18 May 1916.
72. Ibid., file 3, 26 June 1916; file 4, 27 June 1916.
73. Ibid.
74. Ibid.
75. Swartz, *The Union of Democratic Control*, p. 149.
76. PRO HO 45 10814/312987, file 3, 26 June 1916; file 4, 27 June 1916.
77. Snowden, *An Autobiography*, Vol. I, pp. 425–6.
78. PRO HO 45/10814/312987/8, Ward to Asquith, 30 November 1916.
79. Snowden, *Autobiography*, Vol. I, pp. 417–18.
80. PRO HO 144 1459/316786, Charles Trevelyan, Pacifist Activities 1918, file 30, June 1916.
81. PRO HO 144 1459/316786, file 22, December 1916.
82. PRO 30/69/1160, *The Citizen*, 10 November 1916.
83. PRO HO 144, 1459/316786, file 3, Ambassador in Washington to HO, 2 January 1917.
84. Correspondence contained in PRO 30/69, PRO 30/69/736, 737, 738.
85. H. Pelling, *A History of British Trade Unionism* (London: Macmillan, 1963), p. 151.
86. See, HO 10785/290314, Rulings of Munitions Tribunals 1915–1919, file 4, Munitions of War Act, 19 November 1915; file 2, Munitions Tribunal Rules 1915, August 1915.
87. PRO HO 45 10804/308532, Picketing of Munitions Workers, 1916, file 2, 21 February 1916.
88. Ibid., file 1, Woolwich, possibility of a strike, February 1916.
89. PRO HO 139/25/104, Part 2, File 18, Ministry of Munitions to Press Bureau, 17 February 1917.
90. PRO HO 45 10804/308532, file 3, March 1916.
91. Wrigley, *David Lloyd George*, p. 166.
92. Ibid., p. 171.
93. Ibid., p. 182.
94. C. Wrigley, 'Trade Unions and Politics in the First World War', in B. Pimlott (ed.), *Trade Unions in British Politics* (London: Longman, 1982), p. 72.
95. Wrigley, *David Lloyd George*, p. 179.
96. Official History, Ministry of Munitions (London, HMSO), Vol. VI, Part I, p. 44.
97. See, for example, BLO, Milner Papers, Vol. 128, folio 6, 'Note on Strike Movement by W.M.L.', 15 December 1916.

5

A Society Turning Against Itself

B Y THE autumn of 1916, with anti-conscriptionist and other dissenting forces in disarray, their leadership in or on its way to prison, their publications confiscated, the great dissenting campaign projected for the summer stillborn, the ILP and the UDC leadership closely monitored, and organized labour quieted if not quiescent, it appeared that HMG was well on the way to final victory in its war on the home front. The illusion did not last for long. The problem, as always, was simply the fact of total war itself. Also by autumn 1916, much of the most effective dissenting propaganda had moved beyond the abstract to the concrete. As the cost of the war increased, and as the home front was reorganized to pay it, it was almost enough for the dissenters simply to recount fact to damn the whole enterprise. The battle against dissent was becoming more and more a fight against the truth, or, at least, against one reading of what the truth signified.

In October 1916, for instance, MacDonald criticized government policy in an article in *UDC*, the UDC's official journal, entitled 'The Great Push'. What had the Battle of the Somme established, he wondered, that had not been known for some time? The Germans could not win the war, but it still remained to be seen whether the Allies could, and at what cost. The attempt to achieve absolute victory without consideration for the cost could, potentially, destroy victor and vanquished alike.

> Our people have believed [in absolute victory]. Without in any way visualising its military possibilities, absolutely blind to its political consequences, they have made up their minds to wait for it in the belief that it would settle something. It will settle nothing except this. It will prove that if the warring nations care to go on fighting, the combination of military and economic power possessed by the Allies will in a few years exhaust Germany. But the victors – except, perhaps, Russia – will themselves be ruined. 'We shall fight to the last man and the last shilling' is not figurative language, though it is meant to be. It is literal.

It is our last man who will survive and our last shilling as capital upon which to begin anew his struggle for existence.[1]

'Mr Lloyd George', F. W. Pethick-Lawrence continued the charge, 'says the war ought to go on until we have given Germany the knockout blow. The UDC says that the war ought not to go on one day after the reasonable objects for which the Allies are fighting can be obtained.'[2] Bertrand Russell, in an open letter to the President of the United States written at this time and widely published in the United States, appealed to Wilson to arbitrate peace out of common humanity. The verdict of the war, he wrote, had demonstrated that neither side could win. The Germans, having won the most, were most willing to make peace. The Allies would never consider peace until, in two or three years, the balance had been corrected. The war would end, he said, with negotiations which would leave to each side what it had won in battle. Meanwhile, Europe would be devastated.[3] Ramsay MacDonald was correct. Mrs Emmeline Pethick-Lawrence was only being reasonable. Bertrand Russell was saying nothing that could not be found in the strategic appreciations produced by the General Staff. None of these dissenters was saying anything much more than Lord Lansdowne, the Conservative elder statesman, was publicly – and notoriously – saying himself. Indeed, it was a sign of the times that MacDonald offered to serve under Lord Lansdowne if he could produce a coalition, peace government.[4] Given the hideous cost of the war and the fact that, in the aftermath of the Battle of the Somme, victory no longer appeared either easy or near, people were inclined to listen not only to Lansdowne, but also to Ramsay MacDonald and the others.

There was another rationale, however, which could not be accommodated with that of the dissenters. This was how the government and its supporters – many of them as passionate in their support of the war as the dissenters were in their opposition – in interpreting the same facts arrived at entirely opposite conclusions. Perhaps it was true that the Germans could not win the war, and that further fighting would only lead to continued, terrible loss, ultimately producing a peace scarcely better than defeat. How to make peace, however, given that the Allies had been almost universally defeated to this point in the war? What if the Germans were not willing (as they were to demonstrate in December 1916 that they were not) to concede a reasonable peace, based on the *status quo ante*? What alternative existed then? Would not negotiation be surrender? What would be the long-term consequences of such a policy? They were unlikely to be very happy. Both positions were reasonable; both were easily maintained. Both were passionately held. They were, however, entirely irreconcilable.

Quickly, a new stridency became visible within British society on both sides of the patriot–dissenter divide, and thus within the government as it sought to apply conscription, deal with dissent and ensure civil peace. In the end, 'continental conscription' came to imply in practice the same suppression of dissent as on the Continent. In the more stringent conditions after 1916 the dissenters had much to say, and HMG was, quite simply, less inclined to be tolerant. Meanwhile, the patriots were still ready, and ever more willing, to do work the authorities continued to eschew.

It is time to consider who the patriots were. Indeed, it is probably past that time, given that the patriots have already been identified as one of the central mechanisms by which dissent was contained in wartime Britain. As has been suggested, a 'patriot' in wartime Britain was someone willing to employ violence on the home front to silence dissent and maintain national cohesion in a war which was a fight to the finish. In the main, patriot bands were composed of members of the working and middle classes to whom the national emergency was far more important than any generalized class interest, perhaps described better as those for whom victory in the war was often taken to be exactly a class interest. It appeared to the patriots that defeat might follow from tolerance of anti-war dissent of any kind. It was in 1916 that patriot organization began to become effective. It was also the year in which it became apparent that the government could either identify itself with the patriots, or fall victim to their charge that its vacillation, as exemplified in part by its mishandling of dissent, was losing the war. In the end, Asquith was unwilling to march to the patriot drum. By this point in the war, he was 'heartily sick of it' all, had lost a son at the battle front, personally disapproved of much of what his government was already doing – accepting conscription only because his own party would have nothing less – and was inclined to believe that Lord Lansdowne was right.[5] Asquith remained in power, in large measure, to keep his enemies out.[6] This was not a programme likely to make for success. The Lloyd George government came to power in December 1916 on a straightforward patriot platform.

Who, more particularly, were the patriots? What was making them, by 1916, such a powerful, even dangerous, force? Many patriots were simply middle-class people, driven nearly frantic by the war and the prospect of defeat, committed to victory at whatever cost, confused by the social transformation effected by the war, and horrified at the politicization of elements of the working class which the war had produced. Why members of the middle class should disapprove of anti-war movements is less understandable than their abhorrence of a dissent which consciously, and obviously, sought to amplify and utilize ambient inter-class conflict for its own purposes. As dissent began during 1915–16 to redirect its energies into organizing a mass rather than elite movement it became much less acceptable to those whom such a disgruntled mass seemed to threaten. To speak on principles to an educated audience in Cambridge was one thing. To attempt to turn the reaction against compulsion into anti-war dissent, into socialist activity, and therefore into a potential revolution, in Glasgow, east London, or south Wales was quite another, and quite extraordinarily provocative in a Britain which had experienced more than its share of potentially dangerous inter-class conflict in the prewar years.[7]

Middle-class dislike of dissent, however, was not unique. Sections of the working class abhorred anti-war dissent. This phenomenon, working-class patriotism, was perhaps most notable in the Midlands – especially in Birmingham – and London. These were areas in which the working class had long been known for its chauvinism. While most evident in these places, working-class patriotism for most of the war and in most of Britain was the majority reaction.

For many British working men – among them prominent prewar ILP members and trade unionists – as we have seen, the fight against German militarism was often taken to be exactly a social war, though conducted on an international level. To do anything to damage the national war effort was not only national but class betrayal. Ramsay MacDonald and his comrades, for the patriotic working class, were not only traitors, but doubly damned traitors.

There was, of course, much more to working-class patriotism than chauvinism or apprehension of class interest. Calculation of personal interest helped to determine whether a working man became a patriot or a dissenter probably at least as much as conviction. The burden of the war plainly did not fall equally on all sections of the working class, or on all classes in British society. Disparate effects produced a discordant response. For one thing, sections of the working class were particularly favoured in that the government viewed their civilian occupations as more important than any service at the front might be. Not only were these less likely to serve, but they were most likely actually to benefit from the war in the form of receiving substantial wage hikes. The Admiralty, from 1914, had been 'badging' its essential workers. The army and the Ministry of Munitions quickly followed suit. In some trades – engineering for instance – badging was a jealously guarded union prerogative. Workers so privileged, quite plainly, had far more to lose from industrial compulsion or withdrawal of exemption than did members of occupational groups considered non-essential to the war effort. It is the case, for instance, that while 69 per cent of government employees and 64 per cent of those engaged in commerce ultimately served, only 16 per cent of dockers, 18 per cent of railworkers, 24 per cent of miners and 25 per cent of metal workers ever donned uniform.[8] The reaction of members of these various occupation groups was apt to be disparate. The interest of the privileged was to limit their direct participation in the war, the interest of the others to spread the burden. Working-class opposition to the war generally developed in direct relation to the success of an occupation's members in avoiding direct knowledge of the front. By 1917, for instance, with a gnawing man-power shortage at the front, and an obvious government desire to solve it by thorough-going debadging and industrial compulsion, fully 81 per cent of the membership of the ASE and 53 per cent of miners had come to oppose government policy. These were among those specific groups within the working class which had benefited most from exemption and which stood to lose most by the extension of conscription, and most over all (as skilled and semi-skilled workers) if, to accelerate the move-ment of able men to the front, production processes were streamlined so that skilled men were not required at home.[9] It is a fact, as well, that by one means or another, the resisters achieved considerable success in opposing the policy of HMG. Lloyd George never did manage to introduce effective industrial compulsion. In October 1916, when the manpower drought began, there were 1.4 million badged workers. In October 1918, after two more years of total war, and following drastic attempts to rationalize production so as to permit thinning out, the number of exempted men, far from decreasing, had nearly doubled, to 2.3 million.[10] This is hardly what we would expect, and is a testament to the political power possessed by organized and militantly self-interested groups of particularly favoured workers. For those privileged, exemp-tion was a right to be defended. Exemption was a policy, however, which those less fortunately placed might be expected to resent. The less powerful or essential found themselves on their way to the front in greater and greater disproportion. The question for these, of course, was who they should blame. Was the fact that the burden of the war fell disproportionately on their shoulders a simple and inevitable product of a questionable war, or the result of social distortions pro-duced by selfish special interests led, many asserted, by traitors?

Whether or not an occupation was judged essential to the war effort could have other almost equally dramatic consequences. Wages tended to rise or fall, relative to other groups, depending on whether the war increased the demand for a particular trade. This was particularly the case since, in the absence of effective industrial compulsion, the only way available to the government to encourage skilled workers to relocate to where they were most urgently required was to increase wages. The result? The purchasing power of the salaries received by government employees, for instance, steadily declined through the war, and lost the most ground relatively compared, for example, with the wages of metal workers who did rather well out of the war. When we take into account that white-collar employees had historically considered themselves superior to even the most skilled artisans, loss of purchasing power represented for them a real blow to calculations of personal status. For many, this was plainly wrong – an inversion of the natural order – and productive of intense discontent. Similarly, unions of exempted workers grew by mighty leaps. Associations of the unprotected dwindled as their members left for the trenches. It was unlikely to be only the profiteers F. H. Keeling had in mind when he wrote in 1916 that, '[b]roadly speaking, the English either volunteer for this hell or else sit down and grow fat on big money at home. The contrast between the fates is too great.'[11]

To postulate a divide within the working class between the essential and the expendable and therefore privileged dissenter and challenged patriot, is overly simple. Though there is some validity in such a model, there was much more to it than this. For one thing, we must not forget that chauvinism ran deep in *all* sections of the working class, and an inconsistent response to the war both in the individual and in the aggregate became nearly the rule. For a working man to support the war but oppose conscription was not at all rare. It was not uncommon, going further, for miners to volunteer for the war, be sent home as essential, militantly oppose any notion of industrial compulsion at home, and then willingly return to the front when required. Not only was there not absolute contiguity between those who opposed the war, those who opposed conscription, and those who opposed compulsion, but calculations of interest were highly personal, and could be affected by any number of confounding variables.

One such variable was the increasing dilution of the labour force. Though generally resented and feared, this also confused the response of even skilled exempted workers, while often setting the interests of these apart from those of the lower social strata which dilution bene-fited. 'Dilution', of course, referred to the practice of streamlining industrial practice – thus freeing able men for the trenches while increasing production – by bringing in unskilled workers and setting them to work machines set by those skilled men who were retained. On the one hand, skilled workers in occupations substantially diluted had much more to lose by a continuation of the war than unskilled workers, who, after all, were moving into occupations from which they had hitherto been excluded. Dilution meant for the skilled ultimate vulnerability to debadging, declining unions, fears that craft privileges would not be restored after the war and, once again, real loss of status, relative to social levels hitherto considered inferior; however, retained, exempted workers did extremely well out of the war. For the unskilled, on the other hand, the war quite plainly served as a social accelerator. Since the machine tenders were generally paid by the piece, they sometimes received better pay than their skilled workplace superiors paid an hourly rate, however inflated. On the other hand, unlike the retained, skilled men, the unskilled were drawn from sections of the population truly vulnerable to conscription of all sorts. Another variable still: whole categories of new war workers – women, for instance – were joining the industrial labour force, and moving into types of non-traditional labour, precisely from patriotic motives.

The question was still more complex. Even total protection from dilution was no guarantee that dissent would not emerge in a particular workplace. Workers at naval dockyards, for instance, never had to worry much about being replaced by machines and their tenders. On the other hand, they were so specialized and essential, and therefore so hedged in by restrictions, that they were unable to benefit from the wage hikes they might have expected had they been able to transport their skills. These often found themselves in the situation that less highly skilled workers, in less tightly controlled establishments, were doing much better. For dockyard workers, therefore, absolute security implied wages falling behind those received by other, less controlled and hitherto less favoured groups. While these workers were not exposed to conscription, had near absolute job tenure, and little to fear from dilution, they tended to be among the most discontented and militant of British workmen. At the other end of the spectrum were the dockers. Among the most disadvantaged of Britain's workers before the war, their response was almost uniformly patriotic. Why not? Casual work done by non-unionized navvies became permanent, essential war work within a newly unionized workplace. Wages rose rapidly, and substantially. Not only were unions recognized, but they received considerable, even remarkable prerogatives, while docks became closed shops. What was there about the war that a docker would dislike?

Other powerful variables were age and gender. The interests of young men were not necessarily those of older workers, the very young or women. These had simply less personal interest in opposing conscription than those vulnerable to it. Discrimination of response by age and gender existed not only within all occupational groups, but also between them. Some occupational groups were simply composed to a much greater degree than others of young, militarily useful men. An occupation dominated by the very old, the very young or women was unlikely to feel very threatened by conscription. There is little evidence of domestic servants, for instance, actively opposing either the war or conscription. Those women moving into heavy industry by autumn 1915 were not typically new workers. They came to the factories from more poorly paid, less stable workplaces, often dislocated by the war. High wages and job security were new for them. There is little evidence that they voluntarily withdrew from industry in 1918, but considerable evidence that they were assailed by the unions throughout the war.[12] What was there about the war or controlled workplaces for these women to fear? What was there about union militancy that they would like? The miners, on the other hand, were famous for their opposition to compulsion of all kinds, and this was in part because they were a veritable (and under-utilized, from the perspective of those less fortunately placed) cornucopia of active, young men. With so much at stake is it difficult to see why the miners, more than most, feared manpower compulsion? The correlation between age, gender, resultant vulnerability to service, and therefore dissent, was not, once again, absolute. Prewar police forces, for instance, were mainly composed of young men, with preference going to army reservists. No occupational group served overseas in greater disproportion, yet few were as frantically patriotic. As with white-collar and government workers there seems to have existed some point at which the degree of vulnerability became so acute that the particular interest of an occupation became the imposition of a general obligation to serve rather than the protection of particular privilege.

What does all of this mean? It means that to generalize about the wartime perceptions and politics of the 'working class' is often to forget that workers reacted in a highly individual manner to the challenge and cost of war. Still, some generalizations are possible. We might expect, for instance, that government workers would be far more apt than railwaymen to support the war, conscription and compulsion. We might expect, by extension, that government workers were far more likely to be wartime patriots than railwaymen. We might expect that a skilled worker, the wages of whom did not increase apace with prices and whose long-term prospects were threatened by the war – a worker in the royal arsenal for instance – would be apt to be much more militant than an unskilled machine tender who was doing better than ever before. We might believe that a young miner was more likely to dissent than a young woman, previously a servant now an armaments worker, following the WSPU's injunction to win the vote through war service.

All of these suppositions would be correct. Beyond all such generalizations, however, the most important lesson to be learned for our purposes is that the working-class response was very various, and that the pressure of the war served less to consolidate a common opposition to the war than to accentuate internal divides to the point where violence, not simply against an intransigent working class, but between various elements of a fractured working class, became common.

Examples of how extreme this working class divide could become came later in the war, when local TUCs and unions began to split into patriotic and pacifist wings. Such splits exemplify the tensions existing at this stratum of society, throughout Britain, all through the war. In Liverpool, for instance, organized labour's response to the war was confused from the beginning. While Liverpool certainly contained convinced dissenters, it also produced rather more than its share of notable patriots. One of these was James Sexton, leader of the National Union of Dock Labourers (NUDL). Despite the fact that he was the son of a Fenian father, with more than sufficient cause for labour radicalism – he had worked for ten years as a casual labourer on the docks, been permanently disfigured by an accident in 1882, and first came to local prominence as the leader of the unemployed workers' movement – from the beginning of the war Sexton left no one in any doubt that it was his intention to support the war effort to the utmost. On 7 August 1914, three days after the declaration of war, he led the NUDL in promising to 'spare no effort in assisting the government' at this time of crisis.[13] In short order, more than a quarter of the NUDL's membership was in service, despite the fact that dock work was a certified occupation. Many of those remaining were enlisted in special dock volunteer corps. These require some explanation.

In 1915, Lord Derby in association with the NUDL announced a scheme by which special NUDL dockers' battalions would be formed. The men would receive a uniform, be placed under military–union discipline, and work wherever in the country they were required. Lord Derby would be the commandant. Roland Williams, from the Liverpool labour exchange, would be adjutant. Sexton himself would serve as an unpaid staff officer. The union would provide NCOs. Keefe and McKibbon, presidents, and O'Hara, a vice-president, acted as sergeants. So successful was the experiment that 1,000 men presented themselves for the 350 positions in the 1st Battalion. In March 1917 a 2nd Battalion was formed on Merseyside, with other battalions formed elsewhere in the country. Meanwhile, Mersey dockworkers were withdrawn from the army into National Transport Battalions in 1916.[14] Many others members, not selected for service with the dockers' battalions, served in the Volunteer Force (VF); Britain's First World War equivalent of the Home Guard. The union strongly encouraged all of these activities.

Still further, the NUDL response to conscription was quite at variance to those of many other trade unions. Not only was it not opposed, but the NUDL formed a committee voluntarily to weed out dockworkers whose work did not justify their retention at home. Sexton himself took a seat on the local military service tribunal.[15] With the Lloyd George government came further responsibility and closer ties to the state. Sexton, with a group of other patriotic trade unionists – Tillett, Gosling, Williamson and Bevin – was appointed to the Port and Transit Executive Committee.[16] In 1917, Sexton accepted a CBE for his war work.

Needless to say, local labour dissenters were less than happy with this state of affairs.[17] From the beginning, a dissenting faction in the local TUC, led by Fred Hoey, worked to indict, expel and otherwise discomfit the patriots. In March 1916 the TUC, with Hoey leading the charge, moved to condemn Sexton's war work, while Sexton's deputy, Thomas Dunford, virulently defended his chief.[18] Tit for tat: a year later, when the local ILP and BSP united with the TUC to sponsor a meeting in Sheil Park welcoming the Russian revolution, the NUDL ostentatiously dissociated itself.[19] Shortly thereafter Sexton walked out of the Labour group in the city council. His enemies responded by tabling a resolution calling for the expulsion of the NUDL from the Liverpool TUC. Before this blow could be landed, the NUDL struck itself. Dunford withdrew the union from the TUC, taking with him the membership of the Dock, Wharf and Riverside General Labourers' Union (DWRGLU: later the Workers' Union), the National Amalgamated Seamen's and Firemen's Union (NASFU), the National Amalgamated Union of Labour (NAUL) and the stewards' union, along with the carters, enginemen, cranemen and members of the farrier's society into an alternate TUC. Since these were Liverpool's most powerful unions, with a combined membership of 55,000 men, Sexton and the patriots had essentially launched a counter-coup which expelled the dissenters. This had been done, one of his deputies, George Milligan, explained, to preserve the TUC as a working men's association outside politics.[20]

Another example of a TUC split came in Birmingham in 1918. The first sign that in Birmingham there was anything but a uniform labour reaction to war came not in 1918, but in the summer of 1915 when a TUC committee, formed to care for Belgian refugees, split against itself. One section was adamant that any means necessary be employed to ensure victory. The other was opposed to conscription at least, and inclined to follow the ILP peace faction's line. Kesterton, the president of this committee, John Beard and Julie Varley, who were members, were all later prominent in the local patriot movement. Kneeshaw, the secretary, was later a conspicuous leader of local dissent.[21]

With the failure of the National Register Act and the advent of the Derby Scheme later in 1915, the split widened into a chasm. The Birmingham TUC broke into conscriptionist and anti-conscriptionist groups. Throughout 1916, Kneeshaw was active in the anti-conscription campaign. Meanwhile, John Beard had not only joined the volunteers and taken to attending meetings of the TUC in uniform,[22] but had resigned from the ILP.[23] Charles Duncan, a comrade of Beard's in the DWRGLU, was by this time a perennial speaker at recruiting meetings.[24] So successful were the local patriots that Birmingham not only met, but exceeded its Derby quota. Nevertheless, the dissenters succeeded in passing through the local TUC – by 55 votes to 30 with 40 abstentions – a vote of protest against what was viewed as government betrayal in implementing conscription regardless. Beard, Kesterton and three other members of the TUC responded, in turn, by accepting service on the local appeals board. By doing so they had, like Sexton, crossed their Rubicon.[25] A dissenter-controlled local labour press thereafter routinely savaged them as blacklegs, government stooges and bought men.

A year later it was the dissenters' turn to go too far. In January 1917, one of them, F. W. Rudland, narrowly emerged victorious in a contest for control of the Birmingham TUC (by 63 votes to 54), and in 1918 led the conference in voting for a resolution demanding a negotiated peace. If Rudland was only acting in accordance with the current line of the ILP leadership, he had nevertheless gone far too far for the patriots. Led by the secretary of the conference, Kesterton, and Beard, the brassworkers, the members of the DWRGLU, the musicians and the coal workers resigned their membership of the Birmingham TUC.[26] What was their grievance? As in Liverpool, Birmingham's working men patriots disagreed not only with the dissenters' opposition to the war but also to their supposed improper use of trade union organizations to serve political purposes.[27] The dissenters had forgotten what trade unionism was about, and were seeking to use the movement as a lever calculated to shift the entire political system. For this it had not been intended. There was a widespread belief, for instance, and not only in Birmingham, that the dissenters, associated with the more militant working-class elements, were plotting not only treachery in the war but revolution at home, and were prepared to pay the price of a 'German' peace for it.[28] Furthermore, it was charged, the leadership of the trade union movement, often pacifist by conviction, used its union credentials to pretend that it spoke for a much larger constituency than was in fact the case, and that voting procedures at conferences were manipulated to ensure majority dissenting votes.[29] Who were the dissenters in Birmingham? According to the brassworkers' leader, they were not real trade unionists but a few individuals, mostly of military age, 'supported by agents of the pacifists', bolstering in turn leaders out of touch with the true rank and file.[30] Sexton's opinion was similar. Did the UDC and the MacDonald wing of the ILP speak for the working class? Did union leaders associated with MacDonald speak for their membership? The answer from large sections of the working class was a resounding 'NO!'. If there was a 'rank and file' movement of the left, therefore, the patriots were very largely an even more convinced rank and file movement of the right.[31]

Elsewhere prewar turf battles between unions competing for the same membership could become wartime dissenter–patriot splits. On the Clyde, for instance, Emanuel Shinwell had been seeking to build his Seafarers' Union (SU) into an alternative to John Havelock Wilson's powerful NASFU, which he suspected of working with management. At least initially Shinwell was not against the war; indeed, he attempted to enlist in the Royal Navy on the war's outbreak.[32] As the NASFU began to obtain exceptional favours from the government, Shinwell's radicalism increased, as did the patriotic NASFU's hatred. By 1916, so far had the breach developed that Shinwell would not visit his Broomielaw offices for fear of Wilson's goons. Further, he could not go to Liverpool at all to visit SU lodges there. Earlier, NASFU activists had set fire to his offices, with Shinwell inside, and tried to throw him back in as he ran to escape the blaze. Shinwell was, however, not a man to back down from a fight. He responded to violence with violence, not only against his NASFU enemies, but their government allies.[33] Throughout 1916, John McGovern, Shinwell's goon, attacked and disrupted Wilson's prowar NASFU meetings.[34] Wilson and his allies in Neil Jamieson's Scottish Patriotic Federation, struck in turn – on one occasion, a 90-minute brawl resulted. Ultimately the police arrived on the scene and arrested 30 of the rioters – all Shinwell's men, though it was his meeting that had been disrupted. Jamieson shortly thereafter summoned Shinwell himself to appear for assault. Shinwell was released as obviously not guilty. The presiding magistrate was careful to note, however, that personally he was in sympathy with the police and the patriots. In Glasgow, the authorities were obviously not entirely objective in what had begun as essentially a conflict between rival unions.[35] Shinwell, in response, was ever more openly and violently associated with dissent.

Eventually the conflict between the SU and the NASFU deepened to become a factor in national, labour politics. Personal and union disputes had become a factor in the patriot–dissenter divide. At the Leeds conference, for instance, Captain Tupper (NASFU) denounced Shinwell and his friends for being in league with the 'devil Kaiser'. Shinwell responded by moving the expulsion of Tupper, Wilson and the NASFU from the TUC. Tupper and Wilson responded in turn by getting Shinwell summoned before a manpower tribunal, which withdrew his exemption and ordered him to report to the army. Only the personal intervention of Arthur Henderson prevented Shinwell from going the way of Allen and Brockway.[36] Once again, Shinwell was reminded that in pursuing his inter-union fight he was running against the authorities who were in collusion with his enemies. By the time of the Leeds conference, however, Shinwell had gone about as far as he could go in reaction. Had there been a British Lenin in the latter war years Shinwell would certainly have been a Bolshevik.[37]

Under the pressure of war, individual unions could also split, though it often takes a careful reading of union histories to find the fault lines. At the beginning of the war, for instance, both the organising secretary (brother Lawrence Russell) and general secretary (brother H. A. Bywater) of the London Busworkers' Union joined the army. The president, brother 'Tich' Smith, remained at home, acting for the absentees. Meanwhile, the Busworkers' Union anti-war membership formed a vigilance committee to force upon the leadership 'progressive change' through 'inner-union struggle'.[38] While the membership of the union burgeoned – by 1918, 90 per cent of all busworkers had joined – relations with the government quickly turned sour. The great grievance was that the government refused to classify cabbies and busworkers as essential labour. Men were called up. The union was left with little power to combat dilution. Particularly resented was the employment of female bus drivers. When Bywater, by now a sergeant, returned from the front to commence recruiting activities in London, a state of 'open warfare' quickly developed within the union.[39]

In May 1916 a meeting heavily attended by cabbies, but poorly by the more numerous and far more radical bus drivers, re-elected Bywater and Russell. The vigilance committee was horrified. What followed was a rank and file revolt which split the union. In June, Bywater and Russell's leave of absence for the war was withdrawn, and 'Tich' Smith immediately resigned. In November, at a meeting dominated this time by busworkers, 'Tich' Smith was re-elected president, Bywater and Russell convincingly ousted, and the offices of general secretary and organizing secretary eliminated altogether.[40] In this union, a patriot–dissenter split had produced dominance by the dissenters. It is symptomatic of Britain at this time, however, that the greater union family with which the Busworkers' Union was affiliated (the Workers' Union) was dominated by known patriots. One of these, Ernest Bevin, would not forget and would use the opportunity presented by an unauthorized strike in 1937 ('the coronation strike') to discipline and purge the union.[41]

If the dissenters were capable of building an organization, so were the patriots. A significant characteristic of this organization was the way in which it was designed to link both middle- and working-class responses. Like the dissenting movement, moreover, the patriots made good use of pre-existing movements and associations to reinforce the structure. The resulting edifice, rather similar to the German Fatherland Front, emerging about the same time, bore more than a few resemblances in doctrine, practice and form to postwar Fascism. Perhaps it would have become a fascist party if conditions following the war had favoured its continued existence.

From the patriotic elements in the labour movement we see emerging already in 1915 the British Workers' National League (BWNL) led by Victor Fisher and A. M. Thompson, and including, rather strangely, the Fabian H. G. Wells as a vice-president.[42] Fisher, like Wells, had been a Fabian, but had moved on to the Social Democratic Federation and the British Socialist Party (BSP). In 1914, he, with the remainder of the BSP's leadership (Harry Hyndman and Ben Tillett, for instance) had resigned from the party due to the pacifism of its rank and file membership, which they deplored.[43] There was nothing particularly strange about this passage of the Marxists to a patriotic rather than a dissenting position. Marxists, after all, are not pacifists. They are absolutely willing to support a war effort provided that it is seen as progressive. For Hyndman and the other leading British Marxists, there was never any question that a victory for Britain and France would be a victory for progress.[44] Moreover, like Mussolini, Fisher and the others quickly came to the conclusion that opposition to the war would bring the socialists lasting odium, while uncompromising patriotism might give them an audience which had hitherto eluded them. According to A. M. Thompson, one of its more prominent wartime rightists, the breach occurred for no other purpose than to 'save British Socialism from public discredit and execration'.[45] Following the purge of remaining patriots from its ranks, in April 1916, the BSP moved to a straightforward anti-war course.[46] Hyndman went on to form the National Socialist party, and Fisher, at least initially, assembled something he called the Socialist National Defence Committee (SNDC) which was the seed from which the BWNL grew.[47]

The purpose of the organization was to win the war as a class interest by consolidating a divided society into a more potent whole. The BWNL was

> formed by groups of British Socialists in the Summer of 1915 ... to free the Socialist movement in this country from the stigma of Anti-nationalism which it was incurring through the policies and methods of the Independent Labour Party and kindred organisations, and to emphasise the fact that a belief in collectivist economics does not entail anti-national sentiments or opinions.[48]

It would not seek to accentuate national cleavages, but to heal them: 'to enlist all British citizens, and especially the working classes, on behalf of a broad national policy'.[49] 'Fellow citizens!', a BWNL leaflet began:

> The ultimate internationalism cannot be brought about by the pious resolutions of little sects of visionaries; it can only be realised by the complete vindication of national rights, and bonds of agreement between independent and mutually respecting nations.
> The most solid basis of such an international understanding is the integrity of the British Empire.[50]

And how to preserve the Empire? First of all, Britain must be defended against the 'sweated labour of our present enemies'. Ranks had to be closed against Germany autocracy and its soldier-slaves – the international enemy of both the international, and more particularly the British, working class. In the grand social consolidation which would follow the war, and which the war would produce, agriculture must be revived, education would be reformed, and the institutions of the state would be democratized.[51] What was to be done in the meantime? The BWNL intended to consolidate national labour and to organize support behind individual members of parliament, particularly of the Labour persuasion, dedicated to victory in the war. It would, as well, wage war on waste, inefficiency, fraud and profiteering.

One of the more convinced trade unionists attracted by the BWNL, and who worked closely with it throughout the war, was Ben Tillett, the combative founder of the DWRGLU. His passage to the right was typical. Before the war Tillett had been, seemingly, a convinced Marxist and violent syndicalist. A closer reading of his period statements, however, reveals that he was also a chauvinist, monarchist and imperialist. In himself, therefore, Tillett embodied the central ideological paradox of the British working class: Alf Garnet as ever was.[52] Initially, Tillett was inclined to oppose the war; he took part in Keir Hardie's anti-war demonstration in Trafalgar Square on 2 August 1914. On the outbreak, he summoned his docker supporters and convinced them to pass an anti-war resolution which he then posted to the leaders of the triple alliance. His motivation, it seems, was to stop the war by starting a general strike.[53] Very quickly, however, this anti-war resolve began to melt. Tillett could neither fail to notice nor afford to ignore the awakening chauvinistic convictions of his followers: convictions he shared. His transformation from syndicalist to patriot firebrand had commenced: '[t]he nationalist groundswell [had] touched a deeper chord in him than Marx ever reached'.[54] By the end of the year he had offered his services to Lloyd George, who placed him in touch with H. J. Tennant at the WO. Shortly thereafter, Tillett was in France at government expense. There he was confronted with evidence of German atrocities, and acquainted with British and French soldiers. He was entirely converted. 'What I have seen', he confessed in April 1915, 'has convinced me that henceforth [we] ...have only one business – the war.'[55] 'Here', he thundered to survivors of the fighting at Ypres, 'is the greatest war England has ever known ... she fights for the liberty of the world.'[56]

Arriving back in the UK, Tillett commenced a whirlwind speaking tour in which he addressed 40 different audiences in the first three weeks following his return, and over the next 16 months, 600 different meetings.[57] His speeches were as violently pro-war and anti-dissent as they had once been pro-general strike, and anti-plutocracy. In one speech, in July 1915, confronted by anti-war hecklers, Tillett 'goaded them, he lashed and slashed them and gashed them with flaying scorn, he mocked them, he reviled them, he laughed at them' – until, that is, the hecklers were ejected by the soldiers acting as stewards.[58] By April 1915, he had joined the SNDC. From the beginning, he co-operated closely with the BWNL. Tillett was not alone. Many other labour leaders of the patriot persuasion – some we have seen, some we will see – worked closely with the BWNL. When the facts are considered without prejudice, H. A. Clegg's claim that the BWNL had little power in the unions looks simply bizarre.[59]

Perhaps it might seem odd – perhaps not – but from these beginnings, the BWNL was steadily drawn into a Milnerite orbit. Lord Milner was very interested in the League, and in the end was not only involved in this agitation but largely responsible for organizing it. Milner's was powerful patronage. He was influential in the Unionist group, had substantial backers and powerful collaborators in industry, was considered the best administrative brain in Britain, and was to become the second most important man in the Lloyd George government.[60] How to account for Lord Milner's interest?

The advocacy of a socially inclusive, imperialist–statist–nationalist–

protectionist – rather than a socialist – platform by the BWNL was certainly something which could be expected to interest Milner. He had long advocated similar policies, and had tried to work for them before the war through the Liberal Party, and then the Unionists, and unofficially through, for instance, the Co-efficient Club, a dining club which brought together social imperialists of all political colorations.[61] The coincidence between the Milnerite and BWNL programme did not stop there. Milner had been a principal leader of the prewar national service agitation. Ben Tillett and Hyndman, for their part, had constantly agitated that the Labour Party include in its platform a call for a citizens' army. An army composed of conscripted workers was less apt, they believed, to be a tool of repression on the home front.[62] Tillett had opposed naval armaments before the war. His rationale in doing so, however, was very close to the Milnerite position. 'Breadnoughts', he considered, were simply more important than 'dreadnoughts'. If it was a choice of one or the other, then it had to be remembered that '[t]he international fighting machines are in home and industry'.[63] There was precious little difference, in effect, between socialism as Hyndman and Tillett understood it, and Milner's social imperialism. In addition to coincidence of policy there was also a shared feeling of urgency. Milner's early war work – organizing food, and working as a coal expert – had strengthened his conviction that some drastic, new departure was an urgent necessity; by 1916 he considered this to be necessary not only if the empire were to be preserved over time but if Britain were even to survive the immediate demands of the war. Nothing short of the whole Milner programme, and nothing but the whole programme, he considered, would now suffice to stave off starvation and chronic industrial conflict at home. The war, of course, would be lost incidentally.[64] From 1916, similarly, the Socialist Nationalists were convinced that a new departure was required if Britain were to prevail in the war and avoid revolution.[65] If the UDC were necessarily destroyed as an obstacle to the application of the joint programme, that would be all to the good. A platform more opposed to Milner's own deepest inclination could hardly be imagined than that which MacDonald, Trevelyan, Snowden and Morel had put together.[66] For their part, Fisher, Tillett, Hyndman and the rest positively loathed the dissenters.

Milner could already answer for the adherence of many of the Unionists to his programme. Milner had worked with some Liberals, particularly those of the Rosebery persuasion and Lloyd George of course, and was prepared to work with them again. To produce the required shift in national policies, however, a fusion of like-minded elites was not enough. Milner needed a mass movement capable of swinging the working class behind him; powerful enough, in any case, to paralyse opposition to the imposition of his agenda. Moreover, the BWNL, Milner believed, had the makings of a mass, campaigning organization which could be used in ways and for purposes for which the traditional parties were unsuitable. It could become a means of directly 'counter-acting the deliberate agitation of mischief makers'.[67] These, in any case, were the ways in which Milner's association with the BWNL was sold to his political ally, Lloyd George. To make sure that Lloyd George was apprised of this opportunity, Milner introduced Fisher to friends who had gone on to work for Lloyd George – most particularly to Waldorf Astor and Christopher Addison.[68] Fisher, the BWNL leader, did not hesitate. He was willing, and waiting for the BWNL to be used in this fashion. If Morel and the other troublemakers were to be successfully opposed, somebody was going to have to get dirty. Fisher had no inhibitions here. He was quite prepared to use the BWNL to 'counter-mine' the UDC.[69]

There were precedents for this type of activity. This was not the first time that Milner had looked outside the parliamentary system to find support for his policies. Like Morel, he had fruitful experience with prewar pressure groups. One of the more important of these had been the National Service League (NSL), within which he had played a role similar to that of Morel in the Congo Reform League. Also like Morel, Milner was quite willing to use prewar groupings for wartime advantage – rolling them over into new organizations directed to an immediate war purpose. Since the outbreak of war the NSL had been looking for an heir. Its platform by this time had been overtaken by events. It had always sought a working-class constituency, without much luck.[70] Might the NSL still not become, if combined with the BWNL, Milner considered, the nucleus of a new type of political organization? If the BWNL would provide the mass, and the brawn, the NSL would add resources, brains, respectability, connections, an apparatus and a programme. Might the NSL not provide focus and direction for a new, potentially greater organization, the BWNL? Milner thought it might.[71] Already, by October 1915 Milner was plainly intrigued. Might it not be a good idea, he suggested to his collaborator in the NSL, Lord Willoughby de Broke, for the radical conservatives to seek an alliance with patriotic labour? Should the NSL not see 'whether there might be some permanent basis of agreement between them and men like you and me, whom they do not regard as party men of the ordinary type?'[72] Willoughby and Milner's other die-hard collaborators in the NSL were inclined to think that there might be something in what Milner was suggesting.

Through the NSL Milner set out to take control of the BWNL, and through the BWNL of the patriotic working-class movement as a whole – the basis, Milner hoped, of a permanent political synthesis. Negotiations commenced. By August 1916 agreement between the NSL and the BWNL had been reached. A joint conference agreed on a postwar programme, which would include mandatory enrolment in both the cadets and the Territorial Force (TF) and compulsory service in the Territorial Reserves until the age of 30.[73] Ultimately, the full BWNL platform included, in addition:

1. The continuation of the war to a victorious conclusion.
2. Rejection of class hostility in favour of reconciliation.
3. Public ownership of key industries.
4. Adequate defences.
5. Agricultural autarchy.
6. Educational reform.
7. Democratic federation within Britain.
8. Imperial federation with the Dominions.
9. Trade protection.

The influence of Milner was palpable. The NSL had found its heir. The BWNL had swallowed the whole Milnerite prescription.[74] In exchange for ideological predominance, Milner passed off to the BWNL the assets of the NSL and acted as BWNL bagman for the duration of the war. He was excellently suited for this position. In addition to the NSL, Milner also had connections with the British Empire Producers Organization, the British Sugar Growers Association and other organizations with deep pockets interested, particularly, in agricultural autarchy and empire protection.[75] They were prepared to pay to support a patriotic organization willing to fight, if necessary, for their interests, particularly if such an organization bore Milner's seal of approval. Milner could give the BWNL even more than this. Another bequest of the NSL to the BWNL and to the patriots in general was a type of professional political organizer skilled in the arts of rabble-rousing and not afraid of violence. Some of these we will meet shortly. They were not a nice breed. And finally, Lord Milner could virtually guarantee to the BWNL a sympathetic hearing in the mainstream, respectable press, in part because the editor of *The Times*, Geoffrey Dawson, was one of his most convinced disciples,[76] and in part, as well, because the press lords were friends and collaborators from before the war.

While Milner had done most of this for himself, he did not wait long for the approval of his party. In November 1917, Bonar Law approved the association of the Unionists with the BWNL. He saluted the new organization as 'the section of Labour which is national and imperialistic ... the section of Labour which recognises that for all classes, employer and employed, production is the one thing to be aimed at',[77] that section of labour, in short, which if it continued to spread might kill British socialism in its crib, assist in mobilizing the home front, and produce a new synthesis capable of keeping the Unionist group in power for a very long time.

Patriot consolidation continued. During the war the BWNL co-operated with, and essentially absorbed, two other similar organizations: the National Alliance of Employers and Employed (NAEE), and the associated Industrial League for the Improvements of Relations between Employers and Employed (ILIREE). The NAEE was a federation of 13 patriotic trade unions, sitting with 25 employers' organizations, designed to encourage mutual understanding. The principal trade union leaders associated with the NAEE were William Appleton (Laceworkers' Union and GFTU), James Brownlie (ASE), W. J. Davis (Brassworkers), Ben Tillett (DWRGLU) and J. Havelock Wilson (NASFU) – all prominent patriots and powers in the TUC. The ILIREE aimed to encourage mutual comprehension by bringing people from different backgrounds into friendly association, while conducting educational propaganda. For our purposes both of these can be considered affiliates of the BWNL.[78]

Whatever we might think of it today, the BWNL was certainly successful during the war. Its propaganda was effective and mixed patriotism with soft-sell, inclusive socialism – 'Britain has been good enough to fight for; it must be made good enough to live in for all Britons'.[79] From the beginning the BWNL exercised power within the labour movement out of keeping with its surface strength. At least five Labour members of parliament were associated with the organization: J. F. Green, John Hodge, G. H. Roberts, James O'Grady and Stephen Walsh. Hodge and Roberts went on to serve in the Lloyd George government.[80] Eventually the BWNL grew to 150 branches, organizing 100 mass meetings a week. Meanwhile, it published two popular dailies of its own – the *British Citizen and Empire Worker* and the *Clarion*. In 1917 it began adopting parliamentary candidates, and during the coupon election which followed the war returned ten MPs.[81] The UDC, by contrast, contained 10,000 members at its 1917 peak, the NCF never more than 15,000.[82] The BSP, following its 1916 purge of patriots, mustered only 6,435 members; the ILP, through the middle war years, saw the number of its branches decline from 600 to 500, while its membership fell to 35,000 – the circulation, oddly enough, of the *British Citizen and Empire Worker*.[83]

Some idea of the final patriot programme can be gained from debates in the House of Commons where the League MPs were anything but shrinking violets. Another good source for this type of labour critique can be found in the records of TUC conferences, not from BWNL members of course – many of these left the ILP and even the TUC on joining the BWNL[84] – but in the positions adopted by leaders of the unions in which patriots appear to have been in sufficient strength to gain the leadership. Most important here, of course, were John Henson and J. Havelock Wilson's NASFU – the union solidly convinced, its leaders fanatical patriots – and the DWRGLU led by Ben Tillett, James Sexton and Ernest Bevin. Tillett, as we have seen, was SNDC and BWNL. Sexton was a simple patriot. Bevin, on the other hand, was no jingoist and remained sceptical, in particular, of the diplomacy which had led to the outbreak of the war. He considered, however, that victory and the unity of the labour movement were more important that scoring partisan points by pacifism.[85] As for the membership of these unions, merchant seamen, of course, were virtually servicemen during the war, and dockers who formed the backbone of the DWRGLU were among Britain's most convinced patriots.

Speaking against the possibility of a negotiated peace, in 1917, Henson expressed himself in these immoderate terms:

> If you came into our Trade Union Office – Thomas, MacDonald or anyone else – and listened to the stories of the men, who, after being torpedoed four, five or six times, have willingly gone back to sea to bring the food to every man who is sitting in this congress, you would not ask us to meet our enemies around a friendly table … The 6,000 drowned men who lie at the bottom of the sea, with their sightless eyes staring at us in our dreams, are a reminder of the foul deeds that have been committed by the Germans, and these victims of barbarous brutality make mute but affective appeal to us, their friends and survivors, to reject with scorn the suggestion that we should meet the countrymen of those who have thus requited the faithfulness of our comrades to the highest traditions of the sea.[86]

Supporting the sailors, Ben Tillett expressed his belief 'that the leaders of the Labour movement in Germany are brutal and bloody murderers like the rest of them' – unworthy of special consideration, incapable of making any just peace, and just as culpable as the Kaiser and his generals. So much for peace by negotiation, and the international solidarity of the working class.[87]

Aside from the disruption of the TUC caused by the adherence of certain trade unions to the patriot line – and therefore the failure of Morel's attempt to align the TUC with the ILP and the UDC – growing working-class patriotism began, as well, to produce a growing mass of convinced, and violent, supporters of government policy. By the end of 1916 the NASFU, in particular, was difficult to separate from the BWNL, and its members were very prominent in increasingly violent patriot disturbances in the latter war years. John Havelock Wilson ultimately developed into a veritable demon of dissenting labour, being indicted, along with the BWNL, for producing the debacle in Birmingham.[88] Even the Clydeside radical John McGovern, spoke of Wilson with respect, as a worthy and crafty foe, who was prepared to use violence – no faint praise from one equally convinced and unconstrained by inhibitions. Other local leaders, activities and links of the seamen to the BWNL in at least one British port (Cardiff) we shall see shortly. It was the association of the BWNL with powerful unions and convinced leaders, by and large, which made it a potent and dangerous foe of dissenting labour, and a significant factor on the British home front.

When all the pieces were added together, the Milnerite–NSL–BWNL combine made a rather interesting, and frightening, synthesis. Given its reactionary – sometimes nearly hysterical – message, the violent nature of much of its membership, its acceptance of a corporatist social model, and its militaristic, chauvinistic programme, it is not difficult to see the BWNL as a proto-fascist organization. Even its name suggests this. Perhaps it owed its wartime success to the fact that total war produces societies and politics which are by their nature total. Perhaps, as well, the various causes which ultimately gave rise to Fascism on the continent, existing in Britain as well, could be expected to produce a similar result. It is fortunate, in this regard, that when peace returned and hysteria abated, Britain remembered the principles in defence of which the war was waged in the first place. The BWNL faded and disappeared quickly after 1918. For the duration, however, Milner could not have asked for better.

Another of the more independent, uncompromisingly pro-war organizations in British society, rather surprisingly, was the mainstream Women's Social and Political Union (WSPU), Mrs Emmeline Pankhurst's suffragettes from whom her daughter Sylvia's anti-war suffragettes had split. While Emmeline Pankhurst remained a potent figurehead within the movement, by 1915 effective control had passed to her equally patriotic daughter Christabel.[89] In 1914 the WSPU had suspended its activities for the duration. In 1915, it swung into action again, at least initially, to combat Sylvia's heresies, in particular, the idea of a 'stop the war' women's congress which would bring women from both sides together.[90] Shortly thereafter, convinced by Lloyd George that the participation of women in the workplace was essential, the WSPU began to use its organization and influence to buttress production.[91] In July 1915 the Pankhursts went one better than Lloyd George and organized the first of their monster pro-war rallies in London: a suffragette parade two miles long accompanied by 90 bands, drawing the attention of 60,000 Londoners.[92] When a partisan of Sylvia's, Miss Annie Bell, attempted to disrupt a WSPU meeting shortly thereafter, she was shouted down as 'pro-German', and denied entry to the next meeting. When she attempted to resist she was expelled by the stewards, arrested by the police, charged with obstruction and imprisoned.[93]

The message of the WSPU was clear. A victory for Germany would be a disastrous defeat for women's rights. 'A woman's deepest instincts and her reason', Christabel thundered in April 1915, 'tell her that Prussia stands for all that is deadly to woman spirit in the world. We will not be Prussianised!'[94] There was, as well, a danger that the war effort would be subverted from inside by 'that vague cosmopolitanism which is detached from love of one's country'.[95] Yesterday's friend, Ramsay MacDonald, was now a 'complete fraud': 'the flunky and toady and tool of the kaiser' as was Asquith before the war.[96] To combat Prussianism, Christabel taught, women must be willing to go even into the firing line. To combat subversion, they must work for a new, internal *ralliement* beyond class and gender.[97] Against Sylvia, she proposed not the abolition of bourgeoisie privilege, but that of the proletariat.[98]

Sylvia did not remain the WSPU's only *bête noire*. The suffragettes were insistent that there was a distinction between their country's cause in the war, and the government of the day, which, by its inefficiency, was jeopardizing hopes of victory.[99] So inflexible and violent of language was the WSPU that the government, in the Asquith years, considered suppressing the organization on several occasions; neither for its suffragette activities, nor of course for opposing the war, but for so violently criticizing the government for not waging the war with sufficient vigour and wisdom. Particularly obnoxious to the government was the hysterical tone of the personal attacks contained in the suffragette journal, *Britannia*. Even today many of these remain shocking. At the time, the anti-government tirades of *Britannia*, launched in support of the war, made the most fearsome condemnations of the UDC look like praise.

In December 1915 this paper was seized, as we have seen, for an attack on Sir Edward Grey libellous in tone and intent. The offending article, written by Christabel, began 'Against treachery, even the Son of God was helpless'. It continued:

> Judas at the British Foreign Office has worked to frustrate the glorious Serbs. The cold, premeditated long-calculated treachery of Sir Edward Grey might, indeed almost make Judas of old time blush.[100]

Rather offensive stuff indeed. Christabel was unrepentant. 'We are not surprised', the next issue began, 'that Sir Eyre Crowe and the Foreign Office should desire the disappearance of *Britannia*, the most outspoken, most persistent and most damaging of their critics. BUT BRITANNIA RECANTS NOTHING AND REITERATES EVERYTHING.'[101]

A year later the issue of 8 December 1916 came in for particular censure for an attack on Sir William Robertson (CIGS), carried under the headline 'ROBERTSON BETRAYS THE EMPIRE'. The offending article (not least offensive to Robertson himself who brought it to the attention of the authorities) began by once again blaming Sir Edward Grey for his mishandling of diplomacy in 1915. It moved on to indict Robertson, 'who', it said, 'is simply the military tool of Lords Grey and Haldane, and as such is the author of the military disasters in the Balkans, [HE] MUST GO'.

The political and military leadership was not alone in its incompetence and treachery. The FO, in its entirety, was utterly rotten,

> corrupted as it is by Germanism, German blood, German and pro-enemy ties and sympathies [it] must be CLEARED OUT and its whole staff replaced. There are no really sound and vigorous British Patriots in the foreign office at present, for such would long ago have left that nest of traitors of their own accord.

Grey, Cecil and Crowe in particular – 'connected with Germany both by birth and marriage' – were going to have to be eliminated.[102] Mrs Pankhurst, Fox and Kenney, this issue concluded, were scheduled to address a meeting at Queen's Hall the following Wednesday to inform the public of just how inefficiently the government was waging the war. Whether the HO bothered to stop this meeting is unknown; it is unlikely, since Lloyd George had just come to power.

Almost immediately the WSPU's tone changed. Perhaps Mrs Pankhurst remembered that, unlike Asquith and Grey, Lloyd George had always been a friend of the suffragettes. As we have seen she was in correspondence with him, in any case, from 1915 at least. More probably, she was simply impressed with his more aggressive handling of the war. Even more possible still, with the equation 'citizen equals soldier' having been made with conscription, Mrs Pankhurst saw that the suffragettes were far more likely to get the vote by supporting the war than by opposing it.[103] This was the belief not only of Mrs Pankhurst but of as old-school a Tory as Lord Selbourne, who considered that in extending the franchise to soldiers the government had made the error of equating the vote with war service. How to deny it, then, to war workers, however unskilled, whatever their gender?[104] Whatever the cause, the relationship between the Pankhursts and Lloyd George became very close. Lloyd George, *Britannia* wrote in 1917, was 'of the greatest possible value in the present crisis. Its [the WSPU's] members would, if necessary, lay down their lives to protect his.'[105]

While the WSPU remained critical of government weakness, it now focused primarily on buttressing the war effort, while the suffragettes themselves rushed to don khaki. By 1917, the WSPU was redoubling its efforts to buttress the home front and had come to view this as its special war vocation. Mrs Pankhurst had travelled to Russia in summer 1917 at the behest of the government. In September she had fled, one step ahead of the Bolshevik uprising, after having received warnings from her friend Tomas Masaryk, the Czechoslovak leader. She returned to Britain determined that there would be, if she could help it, no repetition of the Bolshevik revolution there.[106] She saw potential Bolsheviks everywhere: everywhere she and Christabel worked to stop them. In November 1917, the WSPU renamed itself the Women's Party. In its 12-point programme, only the last three dealt with traditional suffragette issues. The first plank in the platform was that the war be waged as a fight to the finish with Germany, the second that vigorous measures were required at home to ensure victory.[107] The Women's Party was not slow in translating talk into action. Almost immediately it commenced

> a vigorous 'Industrial Campaign' in the munitions areas with the object of stimulating feeling against those who ferment [*sic*] among Munitions Workers and against the Pacifist intrigues. The Union is doing good work on the Clyde, at Sheffield, Newcastle, south Wales and in the London areas ...[108]

Because of their gender, suffragettes could work in areas where no other patriotic agitator would be safe. Mrs Pankhurst's supporters used this fact to maximum advantage. So reliable had the WSPU come to seem – so patriotic, in effect, as the term was then understood – that by 1918 it was being indicated in memorandums prepared by patriotic labour organizations (these brought to the attention of Ramsay MacDonald) as reliable in *every* eventuality.[109]

Holding all of these organizations together, of course – as with the dissenters, was the fact of previous membership in existing societies, and a common source of funding. The NSL, the Navy League, the Tariff Reform League, the Territorial Army and the volunteer movement seem to have provided the organizational and membership base upon which many patriot organizations were founded. These were the patriot equivalents of the London Peace Society, or the Norman Angell movement. The equivalent of Norman Angell himself was, of course, Lord Milner, whose ideas were held in common by most of the patriot organizations. Gladstone's place in the dissenting pantheon was occupied by Joseph Chamberlain in that of the patriots.

Another factor was money, in this case provided not by the Quakers, but by the press lords. The rather understandable suspicion that the press lords were keeping the patriots in the field against them had developed among the dissenting leadership as early as 1915, following the first outbursts of patriot violence. Northcliffe, Chesterton, Blumenfeld and other 'patriots of that stamp', it appeared at least to Trevelyan, were already working in association against dissent.[110] Even some Unionists suspected a conspiracy. 'We know', Walter Long wrote to Sir George Cave later in the war, 'that Milner and Beaverbrook are the power behind the throne. Do we care for our own sakes to wait till these gentlemen decide that the time has come to drive us out?'[111] Another influential Unionist, Austen Chamberlain, hated the press lords and attempted, on several occasions, to raise his party against them, if only to prevent the total compromise of Lloyd George and Lord Milner, their associates.[112] If the press–Milnerite–patriot combine was useful against the dissenters, might it not also seek to shift, or dominate the Unionist agenda?

While such relationships were always informal, and therefore, liable, at times, to strain and rupture, the essential unity of policy between the various elements in the patriot amalgam remained. While, for instance, a nasty breach could occur between Milner and Northcliffe later in the war, following a press attack on Milner, this was personal not policy, and based on disagreements regarding immediate rather than ultimate intention.[113] Essential unity of policy ensured that all remained throughout the war at least travelling on the same road, if not always together.

In some cases, as with Quaker support for foreign policy dissent, the connection preceded the war. The press lords had long supported the Unionists, the Milnerite faction and the NSL, for instance, as did the other protectionist producers' clubs, associated with Milner. Connections between the press proprietors also dated from before the war – existing not only between, for instance, the press lords themselves, but also between these and others who would become notable, indeed notorious, patriots during the war. Horatio Bottomley, as we will see, was one of the more violently patriotic journalists of the war. He was also, before the war and after, in chronic trouble with the legal authorities and with creditors. In 1911 Lord Beaverbrook had already considered bailing him out (as a fellow traveller on the road to Empire) during one of his periodic scrapes with the law. In the end, however, Beaverbrook decided to await Bottomley's vindication in the courts before committing himself.[114] The 1911 correspondence ended, however, with Beaverbrook expressing his sympathy, and promising to subscribe £1,000 to help solve Bottomley's financial problems once the dust had settled.[115] Perhaps he only did so to discourage Bottomley from making good his implicit threat to return to the Liberal fold if disappointed.[116] Bottomley, quite obviously, was for sale. Did Beaverbrook or Northcliffe buy him either before or during the war? Something, in any case, was not quite right about Bottomley, even during the early war years. In September 1915 a Liberal lawyer, appalled by the tone of Bottomley's journalism, offered to disclose to MacDonald information relating to Bottomley's financial situation as editor of *John Bull*, calculated to silence him once and for all.[117] It is interesting to speculate what the nature of this information might have been. It could not have been that Bottomley was a bankrupt and a fraud; these things were already widely known.

Rather along the same line, Beaverbrook was also, through Oliver Locker-Lampson (another press proprietor with whom Beaverbrook had and was to maintain strong ties of friendship and collaboration,[118] and who was to be the Ministry of Information's man in south Russia in 1918, as commander of an RNAS armoured car squadron[119]) associated with yet another patriot trail-blazer, Cecil Chesterton, to whose prewar legal defence fund Beaverbrook was asked to subscribe.[120] Through Locker-Lampson, Beaverbrook gained a link to the HO in the form of his brother George, by December 1916 the Unionist MP for Salisbury (1910–18) and parliamentary private secretary to Sir George Cave, then Home Secretary.

If the press barons were indeed tied, in some fashion, to the more irresponsible patriotic publishers, then something like an implicit differentiation of function emerges. Beaverbrook and Northcliffe would go only so far in their editorial line, and never so far that they began to lose credibility with the great mass of the population in the centre. Chesterton–Bottomley, on the other hand, would be free to sling mud, consolidating the more violent and least discriminating of the patriots to the general cause. For instance, Bottomley's attacks on MacDonald for his illegitimacy in 1915 appear to have provoked widespread disgust even among people who disliked ILP politics.[121]

Even the King made no bones of the fact that Bottomley's editorial line sickened him.[122] Others, of course, were not so fastidious. The press lords never went so far; and yet the attack was made, without the essential unity of the patriot position having been compromised.

In any case, rather more important, of course, were the prewar links established between the Unionist die-hards, the Milnerites and the press lords. With the *Daily Express*, in particular, relations with political fellow-travellers appear to have been close. In the Blumenfeld collection there is a considerable and friendly correspondence, lasting throughout the war with Lord Carson. There is also evidence that, at the time of the prewar Ulster crisis, Blumenfeld was co-ordinating his line with that of Lord Milner.[123] Given the similarity in the political prescription advocated by both the proprietor and editor of the *Daily Express* with the thinking of the die-hards and Milnerites, it would be strange if such close association ended with the outbreak of war.

Once again, such links and the perception of an essential unity of interest were not unique to Beaverbrook and Blumenfeld. Northcliffe (like Beaverbrook a minister in the Lloyd George government) was willing to use his newspapers to support the government agenda when he agreed with it, to attempt to shift government thinking when he did not, and was prepared to give a lead himself when this was lacking. He was from early on a Lloyd George supporter.[124] This did not always mean that he followed Lloyd George's political line. At times, realizing the political restraints under which the government worked, he was willing to go where, he felt, the government would have gone itself had it been able. In spring 1917, for instance, we find him wiring Beaverbrook that with recruiting falling off, and with no lead coming from the government, it was necessary for the press lords themselves to provide direction to the nation. They would have to run a publicity campaign, he thought, to support the government, and if all went well the government and the other papers would take up this cause.[125]

There were, as well, several pre-existent links between the press and labour's nationalist wing, and again with Chesterton and Bottomley. Sympathetic press coverage for the BWNL, for one thing, followed rather naturally from the fact that Victor Fisher appeared to be intent upon realizing the Northcliffe–Beaverbrook dream of 'Unionist working man's candidates', essentially the co-option of organized labour into an imperialist–protectionist–Unionist bloc. It is interesting to note, as well, that Locker-Lampson had been the prewar secretary of the Unionist Working Men's Candidates Fighting Fund and had duelled with Beaverbrook for control of the *Daily Express* in 1912, both determined to use this paper to fight this fight.[126] Rather interestingly as well, in the light of future events, it was Locker-Lampson, through the Fighting Fund, who, as we have seen, organized financial support for Chesterton's defence during his prewar trial for libel; not very surprisingly, it was to Beaverbrook that he turned.[127] Less surprisingly, since it had been Beaverbrook's intention from the beginning to agitate for a new political synthesis, to push imperial issues, and since he had acquired the *Daily Express* for this purpose, from the outbreak of war he was advocating the formation of a new coalition of forces based on the old Unionist group in order to carry his agenda. 'There can', he wrote in December 1914, 'never be a continuation of political parties on the old lines'[128] – rather odd sentiments to be expressed by a man generally remembered as the best friend of the Unionist leader, Bonar Law.

Much of this, the association of patriotic labour with the Milnerites, with the Tory die-hards, with the Lloyd George populists, with the press lords and with the patriotic suffragettes, and the galloping consolidation of their programmes, had been anticipated before the war. The motive had been to create a new, national, party capable of cutting through party-political differences to deal adequately with the problems of the day. The resulting solution would bear a rather complete resemblance to Chamberlain's social imperialism: a new, more just and efficient empire, constructed on a reformed Britain, capable of maintaining itself against potential enemies far into the future.

Following various preliminary shocks – Chamberlain, Liberal imperialism, the National Efficiency movement, the co-efficients club, and so on – an attempt was made in 1910 to bring together under the leadership of the then Chancellor of the Exchequer, the charismatic Lloyd George, exactly the coalition of forces evident in the patriot movement during the war and to implement something like the patriot fusion programme of 1916. While the attempt failed, it constituted a dress rehearsal for the patriot synthesis of the latter war years. From 1910, it has been asserted, Lloyd George, growing increasingly disenchanted with pure, unrefined Gladstonian Liberalism of the Simon–Samuel–Asquith variety, was hankering to become a 'second Joseph Chamberlain' – to produce a new synthesis within British political life, and to lead it in a vigorous attempt to find a 'national' solution to Britain's problems.[129] Many who would later become associated with Lloyd George in wartime government conspired with him in this early period: Churchill and Addison among the Liberals; the Milnerites, Austen Chamberlain and F. E. Smith among the Unionists; and the Fabians. Other important figures, themselves difficult to place politically – Rosebery, Curzon and Balfour, for instance – were sympathetic.[130] The war was to give Lloyd George his chance to attempt to realize this dream.

Note that by 1916 Lloyd George was not the only one biding his time, and was not the first off the mark, as the patriot reaction appeared to be producing exactly the type of social realignment favourable to the realization of this idea. The possibility that the Unionist group might be reconstructed with a powerful working man's component through association with the BWNL, appears to have become confounded with a Unionist conspiracy to use the war not only to hijack labour, but to produce a popular consensus behind long-term Chamberlainite and Milnerite ideas.[131] Asquith would be expelled, the unity of Labour and Liberal parties shattered, and a fundamental reworking of Britain accomplished. The major mover of this conspiracy was not the leader of the Conservative Party – Bonar Law – but Sir Edward Carson, the intransigent leader of the Ulster wing of the party.[132] In the months before Lloyd George took power, rumour among the Unionists appears to have been that Carson was on the verge of establishing a dictatorship himself, ruling in co-operation with Lloyd George and Churchill, at the head of a cabal of malcontents from all parties.[133] Something of a dress rehearsal appears to have been attempted shortly before Lloyd George came to power, when Carson led Tory back-benchers in attacking the government's proposal to permit citizens of neutral states to buy captured German property in Africa.[134] When Lloyd George turned against Asquith, in December 1916, he did not simply co-opt, but also pre-empted this coup. Indeed, when a Unionist committee composed of Austen Chamberlain, Robert Cecil, Walter Long and Lord Curzon came to see Bonar Law to inform him that he must support Lloyd George, Bonar Law was convinced, at least initially, that they were there to oust him from the leadership of the Conservative Party, prior to leading a revolt against Asquith.[135]

It was, by and large, the dream of the Unionists – though he shared it – which Lloyd George was attempting to realize following the cabinet coup of December, from which he, rather than Carson, emerged Prime Minister. If Lloyd George was the ultimate beneficiary of this coup, however, that should not be taken to mean that he was solely, or even mainly, responsible for organizing or orchestrating it. Indeed, it would have been nearly impossible for him to do so, since the political force employed was, in the majority, Unionist. Lloyd George did not act alone. Rather, the change in government occurred when Carson, Lloyd George and Northcliffe combined to force Asquith from power. Silent partners in this combination were Lord Milner – linked to the conspirators by his disciple Geoffrey Dawson, editor of *The Times*, and an associate, therefore, of both the press lords and Lloyd George – and the indispensable go-between, Beaverbrook.[136]

Nor did the coalescence of the Lloyd George government mean that all Unionists were content to let the Welsh Wizard attempt to realize their programme. The arrival of Lloyd George did not quiet Carson. Lloyd George had only narrowly edged out the Unionists. His policies were not always so resolute as those Carson would have preferred – particularly regarding Ireland, and conscription. In the end the balance had tipped in favour of Lloyd George mainly because he had fewer enemies and more friends in more parties than Carson; because those who disliked Lloyd George hated Asquith more; and because Labour proved more friendly to Lloyd George, as a populist, than to Carson. Bonar Law, the Conservative Party leader, put himself out of the running; he did not want the job, and could not, in any case, bring either Labour or the Liberals (without Asquith) into a coalition government.[137] Milner, while respected for his intellectual prowess and programmatic clarity, had little taste for politics and no party following.[138] Defeated and disgruntled, Carson, unlike many of his colleagues, was initially kept out of the government, and was therefore able to indulge a considerable talent and taste for intrigue. Indeed, his ultimate inclusion in the government, and in the war cabinet, followed almost directly from his many machinations. Lloyd George sought to absorb what he could not silence.[139]

In the government, rather significantly for our purposes, Carson continued to agitate for the hard line, and became one of the associates of Lloyd George most concerned with dissent on the home front. Carson plainly saw danger ahead. 'The present temper of the people', he wrote early in 1917, 'is a fruitful source for propaganda on the part of the Union of Democratic Control and we see around us sedition openly preached without any action being taken.'[140] Part of the answer, he considered, was counter-propaganda directed at the home front by the government. In 1916 this seemed a little much. By 1917, both the government and perceptions had changed, and Carson quickly came to exercise general supervision over those government organizations engaged in domestic propaganda. In this capacity, he was the man who would be responsible for putting the National War Aims Committee (NWAC) on a sound footing, as part of this greater effort.[141]

Still this was not enough. There was at least one attempt to follow the ousting of Asquith with the fall of Lloyd George, largely due to what was seen as his half-hearted approach to the Ireland issue and at home. Walter Long and H. A. Gwynne, proprietor of the *Morning Post*, charged that the Unionists were betraying Ulster by co-operating with the slippery Lloyd George. Long, Lord Selbourne and Lord Lansdowne very nearly split from the government and from the Tory party on the question of Ireland.[142] The only way to deal with that troubled province, they believed, was to impose conscription as an internal discipline, and crush the perceived Irish–German conspiracy 'with an unsparing hand'. For Lloyd George's more flexible policy they had no sympathy whatsoever. What if, through coalition, the Unionist faction lost its own soul?[143] By July 1917, at least a faction in the Conservative Party, led officially by Henry Page Croft, but actually by Carson, was attempting to produce a new party – the National Party to Promote Reform, Union and Defence – from the Lloyd George synthesis, excluding the premier. This was not an attempt by backbench Unionists to pull the party out of coalition, but an attempt to produce a new amalgamation. The Unionists, the rebels charged, had conspired to produce a coalition which was a 'mockery of the true spirit of the nation'.[144] The Lloyd George government was just not patriotic enough. The idea of a National Party – like the idea of a coalition government – was not new. Even before the war Page Croft had attempted to form a new, imperial party: the Imperial Mission: a Milnerite–Imperialist fusion, with chapters in the dominions, unified behind Chamberlainite principles. The Imperial Mission, however, had been a failure, after which Unionist malcontents had focused on taking control of the Conservative Party.[145] Their agitation was suspended at the outbreak of war; not least because the most convinced Unionist dissenters, including Henry Page Croft, were quickly on their way to the front.[146] In essence, the National Party of 1916 was a continuation of this earlier agitation. The first meeting of the new party took place in the Tariff Reform League's London offices. The list of those attending reads like a roll call of the prewar die-hards. Lords Ampthill, Willoughby de Broke, Ebury, Leconfield, Clifford of Chudleigh, Northesk, the Duke of Somerset and the Bathursts were leading members.[147] Despite considerable press attention, particularly from the *Morning Post* and the *National Register*, this scheme never appears to have got off the ground. Despite a lot of talk about forging a link to the working man, Henry Page Croft, at least, does not appear to have had much of an idea of how exactly to go about doing it.[148]

Why did the Unionist die-hards fail? Why did all of the Unionist wartime scheming not result in what might be thought to be its logical conclusion – a militant, patriot, Unionist synthesis ruling in tandem with the armed services, Milnerites and the press lords? For one thing, this was not a party conspiracy. It remained for the duration of the war *sub rosa*, and while it involved influential Unionists, the Conservative Party itself was not implicated. Bonar Law, its leader, would probably have preferred that the conspiracy against Asquith not proceed, and would certainly not acquiesce in a repetition of this coup to topple Lloyd George. It was not simply, as Lord Selbourne believed, that Bonar Law was no leader.[149] Law sincerely believed that the Lloyd George government was the best alternative, for the country and for his party. Before the summer of 1918, if then, he wanted nothing to do with any new party policies or men, most particularly policies or men directed against his own leadership. A new political constellation could be expected to dissolve not only the Liberal and Labour, but the Conservative Party as well. As for the new National Party, Law considered it a mistake. It would

> do nothing but harm. It is not really a national party in any sense as its supporters are all coming from our Party and is just another form of a feeling of unrest which is one of the greatest dangers we have to face in connection with the prosecution of the war.[150]

A Unionist attempt to create a new party to impose, during war, the Chamberlain vision would represent a return to sectarian politics which could only be divisive and dangerous. From a party perspective as well, masterly inactivity seemed the best policy. If the Tories were content to wait and let Lloyd George have his innings, a unified Conservative Party would face fractured Liberal and Labour Parties after the war.[151] If it were not unified, then the alternative to a Lloyd George-led national government, Law believed (probably correctly), was not a Unionist new party but martial law, which he (unlike Carson and perhaps Milner) viewed as certainly dangerous and likely to damage rather than further Britain's prospects in the war.[152] Therefore, while Lloyd George's government was certainly a 'dictatorship' based upon a patriot synthesis organized by the Unionists, Bonar Law was resigned to back him to the 'fullest extent' as the best hope of victory,[153] and because, if Lloyd George were allowed to monopolize wartime headlines, he would certainly ride the postwar tigers.

Carson and Croft failed, finally, because Lloyd George succeeded. Lloyd George was simply more effective at consolidating the various patriot strands. By early 1917 Lloyd George was busy weaving all of the various schemes and agendas into a greater scheme still: Lloyd George's own new party, arrayed behind a new doctrine which he was calling 'Nationalist Socialism'. It was essentially a restatement of the principles with which he was increasingly associated after 1910, and a party formed from those elements and actors with whom he already had a history of co-operation. This will be dealt with later, in Chapter 7. Let it suffice, for the moment, to say that Lloyd George more than any rode

FIGURE 2: BRITISH SOCIETY, 1917

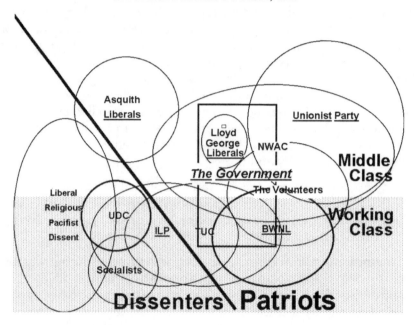

the patriot wave. He was its most passionate, convinced and popular leader. He, like Milner, was coming to look to the patriots to provide the mass to permit a basic reworking of British national life. The path to this glorious future, however, lay through present endurance and victory in the war. A few broken heads and lost liberties seemed to many, including Lloyd George, a small price to pay for a new Britain.[154]

It is apparent, therefore, that by 1916, British society was quite simply beginning to turn against itself. Those who opposed the war were looking to correct the greater social disequilibriums which were held responsible for the outbreak of the conflict in the first place, or, at least, to redirect dissension arising from social inequality into anti-war dissent. Those who identified with the war effort were calling upon the government ever more stridently to protect the nation from internal enemies, while insisting that a new, more inclusive society would follow from common wartime experience. Tolerance of divergent political opinions began to disappear. A situation of ever-increasing social–political polarization began to develop through 1916, worsening daily until the end of the war. The poles, in this case, were constituted by, on the one hand, the dissenters, aligned with those elements of organized labour most likely to oppose the expansion of the war's demands, and increasingly, therefore, the war itself; and, on the other, the patriotic labour–Unionist–press lords–Lloyd George synthesis, at the head of a powerful and convinced patriot amalgam which included a militant, organized and confrontational working-class component. Under Asquith the government attempted to mute the confrontation. In December 1916, of course, the Lloyd George group became the government.

NOTES

1. PRO 30/69/1041, 'The Great Push', *UDC* (October 1916), Vol. 1, no. 12.
2. PRO 30/69/1041, UDC, (October 1916), Vol. 1, no. 12.
3. Russell, *Autobiography*, Vol. II, pp. 28–31.
4. Lord Newton, *Lansdowne: A Biography* (London: Macmillan, 1929), pp. 474–5.
5. Ibid., p. 412. The loss of Raymond Asquith was personally devastating. As for many of the most pessimistic British leaders – indeed, like Lansdowne himself – the loss of a son was the anteroom to personal despair, and could not but affect performance and perceptions.
6. S. Koss, *Asquith* (London: Penguin, 1976), p. 214. See also D. French, '"A One-Man Show?", Civil-Military Relations During the First World War', in P. Smith (ed.), *Government and the Armed Forces in Britain* (London: Hambledon Press, 1996), pp. 86–7.
7. Remember, in this regard, the picture of class relations provided by Orwell in *The Road to Wigan Pier*, pp. 126–38. In his Edwardian boyhood, as a member of the 'lower upper middle class', Orwell learned to view the working class as essentially a different species by turns comical and threatening, but always disgusting. It was exactly the 'lower upper middle class' which appears to have provided much of the mass in patriot mobs. Orwell himself writes of participating in street battles, as a student, against working-class children in 1916–17.
8. P. Dewey, 'Military Recruiting and the British Labour Force During the First World War', *History Journal*, 27, 1 (1984), pp. 199–224.
9. C. Wrigley, *David Lloyd George*, p. 220.
10. Dewey, 'Military Recruiting', pp. 199–224.
11. Marwick, *The Deluge*, p. 218.
12. G. Braybon, *Women Workers in the First World War* (London: Croom Hall, 1981), pp. 46–9. The only union friendly to women was the Workers' Union, which considered them part of its target audience. Women's participation in this union grew from 3,000 in 1914 to 80,000 in 1918. Elsewhere, women were refused membership of unions, where the unions did not actively discriminate against them. Ultimately, 4,808,000 women were in the workforce, up from 3,276,000 in 1914.
13. E. Taplin, *The Dockers' Union: A Study of the National Union of Dock Labourers* (Leicester: Leicester University Press, 1985), pp. 125–7.
14. Ibid. Wages in these battalions were considerably higher than dockworkers were used to receiving. This may well account for their popularity. Before the war, dockers had typically made 5s 9d per day for shipmen and 4s 6d for porters. During the war, this rose to 9s a day for shipmen and 8s 4d for porters. By May 1917, dockers were guaranteed 44 shillings a week, for 51 hours' work. In the dockers' battalions, in addition to food, clothing and quarters, workers received 35 shillings a week with an additional 7 shillings army pay. Corporals received, over and above this, 1s 8d and sergeants 2s 4d. Once again, why would a docker dislike the war?
15. Ibid., pp. 125–7.

16. J. Schneer, *Ben Tillett* (London: Croom Helm, 1982), p. 191.
17. See, for example, J. Davies, *The Prime Minister's Secretariat 1916–1920* (Newport: R. H. Johns, 1951), p. 163.
18. Taplin, *The Dockers' Union*, p. 135.
19. Ibid.
20. Ibid., p. 136. Most of these unions, of course, were either associated with NUDL or Tillett's DWRGLU. Others were associated with the militant seamen of the NASFU – Cotter, of the stewards' union, in particular, being powerfully influenced by the fanatically patriotic leader of the NASFU, J. H. Wilson.
21. J. Corbett, *The Birmingham Trade Council, 1866–1966* (London: Lawrence & Wishart, 1966), p. 110.
22. R. Hyman, *The Workers' Union* (Oxford: Clarendon Press, 1971), p. 82.
23. Corbett, *The Birmingham Trade Council*, p. 110.
24. Hyman, *The Workers' Union*, p. 82.
25. Corbett, *The Birmingham Trade Council*, p. 113.
26. Ibid., p. 114.
27. B. Waites, *A Class Society at War: England 1914–1918* (New York: Berg, 1987), pp. 191–2.
28. See, for example, LSE, MacDonald Papers, J8 Vol. VI, 'Memorandum L.U. No. 4, "The Rank and File Movement"', 14 September 1918.
29. This appears, for instance, to have been a burden of the charge levelled against J. H. Thomas, Smillie and the president of the Blackpool conference, by Ernest Bevin, Ben Tillett and J. Havelock Wilson. See *Report of the Proceedings at the 49th Annual Trade Union Conference, September 3–8 1917*, pp. 82–4.
30. Corbett, *The Birmingham Trade Council*, p. 114.
31. This critique may have followed, in part, from the divorce which took place at about this time between rank and file members and leadership. In Victorian Britain, union leaders had been workers temporarily seconded from their work, to which they would return. In the Edwardian period, with the gradual development of a professional union leadership – a process accelerated by the galloping expansion of unions during the war – this ceased absolutely to be the case. H. Clegg, *Trade Union Officers* (London: Basil Blackwell, 1961), pp. 211, 217–18.
32. Slowe, *Manny Shinwell*, p. 49.
33. Ibid., pp. 62–6.
34. McGovern, *Neither Fear Nor Favour*, pp. 46–50.
35. Slowe, *Manny Shinwell*, pp. 67–8.
36. Ibid., p. 70.
37. Ibid., p. 71.
38. K. Fuller, *Radical Aristocrats: London Busworkers from the 1880s to the 1980s* (London: Lawrence & Wishart, 1985), pp. 39, 48.
39. Ibid., p. 39.
40. Ibid., p. 50.
41. Ibid., p. 39.
42. BWNL Organization: A. M. Thompson, chairman; Victor Fisher, hon. secretary; Charles Duncan, John Hodge, James O'Grady, C. B. Stanton, Stephen Walsh, H. G. Wells, A. Wilkie, vice-presidents. Wells, at least during 1917, looked for national regeneration from the war, and like most Fabians did not necessarily disapprove of conscription, while disapproving profoundly of many dissenters. He believed that Norman and Cannan, for instance, based their objection on hate rather than love; he believed MacDonald and Morel to be 'thoroughly dishonest'. See Russell, *Autobiography*, Vol. II, p. 72, Wells to Miles Malleson, 1916.
43. A. Gollin, *Proconsul in Politics* (London: Anthony Blond, 1964), p. 546.

44. Shaw, 'War, Peace and British Marxism', pp. 53–6.
45. C. Brand, *British Labour's Rise to Power* (Stanford: Hoover War Library, 1941), p. 77.
46. Shaw, 'War, Peace and British Marxism', p. 56.
47. Brand, *British Labour's Rise to Power*, pp. 74–6. The Socialist National Defence Committee executive comprised Victor Fisher (secretary), Dan Irving (BSP), John Burgess (ILP), Stuart Headlam (Fabian Society), Robert Bletchford (Socialist), H. G. Wells (Fabian Society). See also De Groot, *Blighty*, pp. 151–2.
48. LSE, MacDonald Papers, J8 Vol. VI, 'Memorandum L.U. No. 4, "The Rank and File Movement"', 14 September 1918.
49. BLO, Milner Papers, Milner 44, National Service League to Milner, 18 April 1916, enclosing article from *Morning Post*.
50. Ibid.
51. BLO, Milner Papers, NSL to Milner, 18 April 1916.
52. Schneer, *Ben Tillett*, pp. 149–78.
53. Ibid., pp. 179–81.
54. Ibid., p. 181.
55. Ibid., p. 185.
56. Ibid., p. 185.
57. Ibid., p. 187.
58. Ibid., p. 192.
59. H. Clegg, *A History of British Trade Unionism since 1889* (Oxford: Clarendon, 1985), Vol. II, p. 231.
60. J. Wrench, *Alfred Lord Milner: The Man of No Illusions* (London: Eyre & Spottiswoode, 1958), p. 319; V. Halperin, *Lord Milner and the Empire* (London: Odhams, 1952), p. 158.
61. R. Scully, *The Origins of the Lloyd George Coalition* (Princeton: Princeton University Press, 1975), pp. 172–210; G. R. Searle, *The Quest for National Efficiency* (London: Ashfield, 1971), pp. 54–106. Many of the members of the co-efficient club were later to become prominent in the Lloyd George administration; others, on the other hand, in dissent.
62. Schneer, *Ben Tillett*, p. 178. Tillett's wartime recruiting work was designed to produce exactly that: a citizen's army. Tillett's comment when his prewar agitation failed: 'So the flapdoodle of hysterical goody goody peace is accepted.' For Hyndman, see also Shaw, 'War, Peace and British Marxism', p. 54.
63. Schneer, *Ben Tillett*, p. 177.
64. See BLO, Milner Papers, especially Milner 44.
65. See, for example, Schneer, *Ben Tillett*, p. 189. Fear of revolution, Schneer tells us, was Tillett's 'constant preoccupation'.
66. Gollin, *Proconsul in Politics*, p. 547.
67. BLIO, Curzon Papers, F 112/113, Milner to Curzon, 2 August 1917. See also C. Wrigley, *Lloyd George*, p. 7.
68. Gollin, *Proconsul in Politics*, pp. 543–5.
69. Ibid.
70. The NSL, the Navy League and the Tariff Reform League were all, in part, attempts to link the working class to the Unionists. While the NSL, in particular, became quite powerful, none succeeded to the satisfaction of its makers. The membership of all remained conservative, Anglican and middle class. See, for example, A. Summers, 'The Character of Edwardian Nationalism: Three Popular Leagues', in P. Kennedy and A. Nicholls (eds), *Nationalist and Racialist Movements in Britain and Germany Before 1914* (London: Macmillan, 1981), pp. 68–87.
71. BLO, Milner Papers, see, for instance, Milner 44 and 45/1.
72. G. Phillips, *The Diehards: Aristocratic Society and Politics in Edwardian England*

(Cambridge, MA: Harvard University Press, 1979), p. 155.

73. BLO, Milner Papers, Milner 44, 'Report of a Meeting of Joint Conference of a Sub-Committee of the National Service League and the British Worker's National League, Which Took Place on August 23rd 1916, at 3.p.m.'.

74. LSE, MacDonald Papers, J8 Vol. VI, 'Memorandum L.U. No. 4, "The Rank and File Movement"', 14 September 1918.

75. See, for correspondence with such organizations, BLO Milner papers.

76. Gollin, *Proconsul in Politics*, p. 545.

77. Wrigley, *Lloyd George*, p. 7.

78. LSE, MacDonald Papers, J8 Vol. VI, 'Memorandum L.U. No. 4, "The Rank and File Movement"', 14 September 1918. For NAEE, see also Schneer, *Ben Tillett*, p. 189; and Clegg, *A History of the British Trade Unionism*, Vol. II, p. 231.

79. BLO, Milner Papers, Milner 44, NSL to Milner, 18 April 1916.

80. Brand, *British Labour's Rise to Power*, p. 76. Just as MacDonald, etc., were ordinary members of the NCF, these were ordinary members of the SNDC and later of the BWNL.

81. C. Cook, *Sources in British Political History, 1900–1951* (London: Macmillan, 1975), Vol. I, pp. 31–2. See also R. Douglas, 'The National Democratic Party and the British Workers League', *Historical Journal*, 15 (1972), p. 536.

82. Cline, *E. D. Morel*, p. 102; Ceadel, *Pacifism in Britain*, pp. 33, 35. Considerably more was claimed for the UDC. Its 300 affiliated organizations claimed to represent 650,000 persons. Such claims, given the fractured nature of British society at this time, need to be treated carefully.

83. De Groot, *Blighty*, pp. 151–2.

84. Two we have already seen: Beard and Duncan, in Birmingham, later became BWNL after having left the UDC and ILP. They remained, however, members of the General Workers' Union. Another example we will see shortly: the BWNL vice-president, C. B. Stanton, was a prewar ILP and miners' organizer.

85. A. Bullock, *The Life and Times of Ernest Bevin* (London: Heinemann, 1960), pp. 47–8.

86. *Report of the Proceedings at the 49th Annual Trade Union Conference, September 3–8 1917*, p. 81.

87. Ibid., p. 84.

88. Corbett, *The Birmingham Trade Council*, p. 115.

89. Christabel's patriotism was influenced by her sojourn in France as editor of *The Suffragette* during the immediately prewar years, and by her 1913 religious conversion, Mitchell, *Women on the Warpath*, p. 47. In contrast, in August 1914, Sylvia was in Dublin covering the 'Bachelors Walk Massacre' for *Dreadnought*, and had been Keir Hardie's lover for some time, Winslow, *Sylvia Pankhurst*, p. 75. Each believed that the other had sold out everything their family and the suffragette movement had stood for.

90. Sylvia Pankhurst, *The Home Front*, p. 149. In the event, this congress took place, but failed without Mrs Pankhurst's help. Originally the ELFS had wanted to send 200 delegates. McKenna agreed to grant passports to 20 'women of discretion'. The infighting that followed was damaging. Eventually, three women did travel over-seas. The ELFS, however, experienced a heavy loss of membership, and refounded itself as the WSF, the WIL being founded at this time as well, De Groot, *Blighty*, pp. 146–7.

91. Mitchell, *Women on the Warpath*, pp. 58–60.

92. Ibid., p. 60.

93. Ibid., p. 50.

94. Ibid., p. 54.

95. Ibid., p. 48.

96. Ibid., p. 72.
97. Ibid., p. 48.
98. Ibid., p. 77.
99. Ibid., p. 53.
100. PRO HO 139/23/96, Part 2, File 9, *Britannia*, 17 December 1915, Vol. V, no. 10.
101. Mitchell, *Women on the Warpath*, p. 60.
102. PRO FO 800/197, Robertson to Cecil, 22 December 1916, forwarding copy of *Britannia*, edition 8, December 1916. It is an open question whether Robertson found it more offensive to be labelled at 'traitor' and 'pro-German', or credited with fathering the Salonika expedition!
103. S. Grayzel, 'The Outward and Visible Signs of Her Patriotism: Women, Uniforms and National Service During the World War', *Twentieth Century Britain*, 18, 2 (1997), pp. 145–64.
104. G. Boyce (ed.), *The Crisis of British Unionism: Lord Selbourne's Domestic Political Papers* (London: THP, 1987), Selbourne to Salisbury, 25 August 1916.
105. Mitchell, *Women on the Warpath*, p. 64.
106. Ibid., pp. 66–70.
107. The 12 points the Women's Party demanded: (i) a fight to the finish against Germany; (ii) vigorous measures at home; (iii) the purge of enemy aliens and persons of foreign blood from HMG; (iv) the destruction of the Austro-Hungarian Empire; (v) the postwar maintenance of the Grand Alliance; (vi) the retention of national powers in any League of Nations; (vii) and (ix) essentially a corporatist industrial reformation; (viii) the rejection of home rule for Ireland; (x) the realignment of the workplace; (xi) the reform of education; and (xii) a vigorous housing programme, Mitchell, *Women on the Warpath*, p. 76.
108. LSE, MacDonald Papers, J8 Vol. VI, 'Memorandum L.U. No. 4, "The Rank and File Movement"', 14 September 1918.
109. Ibid.
110. BLO, Ponsonby Papers, Trevelyan to Robertson, 26 July 1915.
111. BL, Cave Papers, Cave 62497, Long to Cave, 4 August 1918.
112. UB, Austen Chamberlain Papers, AC 5/7/5, Chamberlain to Milner, Carson and Curzon, 21 and 22 February 1918. See also C. Petrie, *The Life and Letters of the Right Honourable Sir Austen Chamberlain* (London: Cassell, 1940), pp. 105–6.
113. Gollin, *Proconsul in Politics*, p. 545.
114. See HLRO, Beaverbrook, BBK 1/2: Bottomley to Beaverbrook, 24 May 1911 and 4 July 1911; Beaverbrook to Bottomley, 15 July 1911. For Bottomley, see below, Chapter 6.
115. HLRO, Beaverbrook Papers, BBK B/1/2, Beaverbrook to Bottomley, 15 July 1911.
116. HLRO, Beaverbrook papers, BBK B/1/2, Bottomley to FE Smith, 22 May 1911. Bottomley:

> ... I am convinced that so long as the present party system lasts and so long as the Liberals are an ominium gatherem of cranks and faddists I shall find myself instinctively more in sympathy with your friends than with them ... [needs to get £20–25,000 to extricate himself from city affairs. Wants Unionist shareholders for this purpose. And in return] I cannot help thinking that the active sympathy of a journal with a circulation approximating a million weekly and the support of an independent member of the House with a large following in the country as President of the biggest League in existence, is an item worthy of consideration. [If money not forthcoming, will have to do something else] ... It will, however, be a horrible blow to me if such arrangements should in any way have the effect of handicapping me in my instinctive hostility to the hideous and fortuitous

concourse of fanatics who at present constitute the Government party in the House.

117. See, for example, PRO 30/69/1159, E. Bell to MacDonald, 3 September 1915.

118. Locker-Lampson was owner, in his own right, of the *Peterborough Standard*, the *Huntingdonshire Post* and the *Empire Review*, and competitor, at least initially, for the *Daily Express*.

119. PRO ADM 116/3934B, 'Anglo-Russian Armoured Cars'.

120. HLRO, Beaverbrook, BBK/B/9, Locker-Lampson to Beaverbrook, 23 May 1913 and 28 May 1913.

121. See, for example, PRO 30/69/1159, E. Bell to MacDonald, 3 September 1915; H. Russell to MacDonald, 2 September 1915. Excerpt, Russell to MacDonald:

> I deplore your attitude over the war and, having no axe to grind or party to uphold, I consider some of your public utterances worthy of repression by the State. Nevertheless, I hasten to express to you my very great sympathy with you on this occasion of a public attack upon you by reason of your birth. I venture to think that all right-thinking men and women will feel as I do, although for one reason or another they may not feel able to write and tell you so.

Another example, Anonymous to MacDonald, 1915:

> For your villainy and treason you ought to be shot and I would gladly do my country service by shooting you. I hate you and your vile opinions – as much as Bottomley does. But the assault he made on you last week was the meanest, rottenest, low down dog's dirty action that ever disgraced journalism EVER! (Marquand, *Ramsay MacDonald*, p. 91.)

122. D. Judd, *George V* (London: Weidenfeld & Nicolson, 1973), pp. 129–30.

123. For instance, HLRO, Blumenfeld Papers, Milner 1, Milner to Blumenfeld, 2 March 1914.

124. Clark, *Northcliffe in History*, p. 112.

125. HLRO, Beaverbrook papers, C/261, Northcliffe to Beaverbrook, 22 May (?) 1917.

126. HLRO, Beaverbrook Papers, BBK/B/4, Locker-Lampson to Beaverbrook, 23 May, 11 and 19 December 1911, 11 June 1912. Beaverbrook's friendship with Locker-Lampson seems, in part, to have derived from this contest. Locker-Lampson had, apparently, assembled the money to buy the paper, but stood down in favour of Beaverbrook.

127. HLRO, Beaverbrook, BBK/B/9, Locker-Lampson to Beaverbrook, 23 May 1913 and 28 May 1913.

128. HLRO, Beaverbrook Papers, BBK/B/9, Beaverbrook to Edge, 8 December 1914.

129. See, for instance, Scully, *The Origins of the Lloyd George Coalition*; Searle, *The Quest for National Efficiency*, pp. 171–204.

130. See, for instance, Scully, *The Origins of the Lloyd George Coalition*, pp. 172–210; Searle, *The Quest for National Efficiency*, pp. 173–9.

131. See, for example, HLRO, Beaverbrook Papers, BBK C203, Gratton Doyle to Law, 6 June 1916.

132. For Carson's intrigues with Sir Henry Wilson and other disgruntled Unionists, see B. Millman, 'Sir Henry Wilson's Mischief: Field Marshal Sir Henry Wilson's rise to power 1916–1918', *Journal of Canadian History* (Jan. 1996).

133. R. Self (ed.), *The Austen Chamberlain Diary Letters* (Cambridge: Cambridge University Press, 1995), Chamberlain to Ida, 20 October and 4 November 1917. See also, S. Koss, *Asquith* (London: Penguin, 1976), pp. 214–15; Jenkins, *Asquith*, pp. 417–20.

134. Wilson, *The Political Diaries of C. P. Scott*, entries for November 1916; A. Chamberlain, *Down the Years* (London: Cassell, 1935), pp. 113–14.

135. Chamberlain, *Down the Years*, p. 127; C. Petrie, *The Life and Letters of the Right Honourable Sir Austen Chamberlain*, p. 60.

136. HLRO, Beaverbrook Papers, BBK C/261, various. See also R. Blake, *The Unknown Prime Minister: The Life and Times of Andrew Bonar Law, 1858–1923* (London: Eyre & Spottiswoode, 1955), p. 295; Lord Beaverbrook, *Men and Power 1917–1918* (London: Hutchinson, 1956) and *Politicians and the War* (London: Thorton Butterworth, 1928).

137. Newton, *Lansdowne*, p. 455. The King asked first Bonar Law to form a government, in December 1916. His half-hearted attempts were not, however, sufficient to convince anybody to come in with him.

138. See, for example, Wilson, *The Political Diaries of C. P. Scott*, diary entry for 19–21 April 1917, p. 278.

139. The invitation to Carson to join the war cabinet (HLRO, Lloyd George Papers, F/6/2/35, Lloyd George to Carson, 6 July 1917) followed almost immediately from a Carson communication to Lloyd George in which he acquainted him with the state of grass-roots Unionist dissatisfaction (F/6/2/34, Carson to Lloyd George, 22 June 1917).

140. HLRO, Lloyd George Papers, F/6/2/34, Carson to Lloyd George, 22 June 1917.

141. For the NWAC see Chapter 9 below.

142. J. Kendle, *Walter Long, Ireland and the Union 1905–1920* (Montreal: McGill Queen's, 1992), pp. 106–19.

143. Ibid., p. 166.

144. Phillips, *The Diehards*, p. 156. For Carson's involvement, see Koss, *Asquith*, pp. 214–15.

145. L. Witherall, *Rebel on the Right: Henry Page Croft and the Crisis of British Conservatism* (Newark, NJ: University of Delaware Press, 1997), pp. 165–213.

146. Ibid., p. 207. Page Croft served 22 months at the front.

147. Phillips, *The Diehards*, p. 155.

148. G. R. Searle, *Country before Party: Coalition and the Idea of 'National Government' in Modern Britain, 1885–1985* (London: Longman, 1995), p. 108. See also Millman, 'Henry Wilson's Mischief'.

149. Boyce, *The Crisis of British Unionism*, 1916 Memorandum, p. 188. Bonar Law, Selbourne believed, was no leader but straight. Lloyd George, meanwhile, was not straight but a leader.

150. HLRO, Bonar Law Papers, 84/6/124, Bonar Law to Wrightson, 15 September 1917.

151. HLRO, Bonar Law Papers, 84/6/133, Bonar Law to Lord Lansdowne, 30 November 1917, for example. By August 1918, however, Ulster was beginning to appear increasingly in Bonar Law's correspondence, and the possibility of a postwar election, run on sectarian, party lines, was being mooted. See Bonar Law Papers, 84/7.

152. HLRO, Beaverbrook Papers, C 203, Law Speech 13 April 1916.

153. HLRO, Bonar Law Papers, 84/6/23, Bonar Law to Walter Long, 27 December 1916.

154. H. Taylor, *The Strange Case of Bonar Law* (London: Stanley Paul, 1932), p. 225; and A. Clark (ed.), *A Good Innings: The Private Papers of Viscount Lee of Farnham* (London: John Murray, 1974), diary entry for 6 December 1916, p. 162. For Miller, see Searle, *The Question for National Efficiency*, pp. 168–9.

6

The Battle of Cory Hall:
'By Any Means Necessary Short of Murder'

BEFORE DISCUSSING the ways in which the Lloyd George government attempted to deal with dissent, it is important to consider more fully what the polarization of British national life, apparent by 1916, could mean at a local level. Some examples of patriot activity we have already seen. The most famous example of what could happen when dissenters met patriots head-on, at a time and place of social dislocation, came in Cardiff, a nine-day wonder in November 1916, since forgotten, during which dissenters and patriots battled in the streets following an attempt by dissenters to hold a meeting directed at a local trade union audience. While violence between patriots and dissenters was already endemic, the Battle of Cory Hall is of particular interest because of a number of characteristics which set it apart. Considering what these were is also a useful review before we proceed.

It was certainly significant, for instance, that the Battle of Cory Hall occurred in November 1916, just as the casualties experienced on the Somme were making further industrial realignment, even compulsion, likely. The manpower problems which followed the Somme gave the dissenters an issue with broad social appeal. It also undermined the fragile Asquith coalition, and paved the way to power of Lloyd George and his Unionist allies a month later. Tactically, in November 1916 the UDC was busy trying to organize the working-class, trade union reaction behind its programme, attempting, in particular, to marry the bumptious 'Triple Alliance' to dissent. UDC activities among the south Wales miners, in autumn 1916, were part of this plan.[1] Ultimately, the failure in Cardiff put paid to the effort to consolidate dissent into a combination capable, in 1916, of shifting the national agenda. The social–political balance revealed in Cardiff is significant, moreover, in understanding the reasons for the emergence of a Lloyd George-led, patriotic, nationalist–socialist coalition in December.

For our purposes, of greater immediate interest, perhaps, is the identity of the local actors and the social context in which the battle was played out. Cardiff and its surrounding region, if the accepted version of the left is correct, was just such a place where we might expect a unified working-class response to have occurred. Social divisions were marked. The miners and seamen of the region were socially and politically conscious and combative. Keir Hardie, the father of the ILP, sat as Labour MP for Merthyr Tydfil between 1900 and his death in 1915. Lloyd George, at least initially, a radical, nationalist populist, although from north Wales, was a power in the land. The prewar Tonypandy disturbances and the first great strike of the war – the south Wales miners' strike of 1915 – had been local disturbances.[2] Looking ahead, Aneurin Bevan, at this time a very young man, was already politically active and far more radical than he was later. If, therefore, no uniform class response was possible in Cardiff, it is likely that no uniform working-class reaction to the war was ever possible anywhere. This is not only a retrospective judgement. It was the common sense of the day. Throughout the war the region was closely watched both by the government and the dissenters. If first conscription, and then the idea of broader restructuring and compulsion were tolerated here, then they would, most considered, be tolerated everywhere.[3] If they were successfully opposed here, following the unification by the dissenters of the working-class response, then a rough ride might lie ahead nationwide.

Far from finding in south Wales a unified anti-war response flowing from a heightened class consciousness, even a cursory examination of what transpired in Cardiff indicates not simply a polarized society, but a splintered working-class reaction to the war. It is quickly evident that most of the patriot rioters – perhaps in even greater proportion than the dissenters – were working people, making common cause with their bosses against individuals whom they believed to be enemies of the nation. Nevertheless, the considerable interest demonstrated by at least some of the miners in the ILP–UDC message must be taken as a demonstration, once again, that if the working class was not uniformly dissenting, neither was everyone convinced that victory at whatever the cost was equally the interest of all.

So what happened in Cardiff? Quite simply, a dissenting meeting convened under the aegis of the National Council for Civil Liberties (NCCL) by a local ILP leader and miners' agent, James Winstone, at which J. H. Thomas (the railwaymen's leader and Labour MP) and Ramsay MacDonald were scheduled to speak, was broken up with considerable violence by a mob led by Cardiff's leading citizens, including local trade union leaders and an ILP MP, while the police looked on. It is probably important to say, at the outset, that what happened in

Cardiff had been brewing for some time, was all the more violent for this fact, and was typical of the type of personal and political conflicts which were leading, by 1916, to virtually unbridgeable patriot–pacifist chasms even in predominantly working-class areas. The Cardiff region did not suddenly become split in 1916; it had been split for some time. The war accentuated cleavages.

The predominant political force in the city of Cardiff, in the years prior to the war, had been the Cory family (hence Cory Hall) – a family of ship and colliery owners, of whom, in 1916, two members were sitting in the House. Sir Clifford Cory was chairman of the Cory Brothers Colliers, a Justice of the Peace (JP) and deputy Lord Lieutenant and High Sheriff of Glamorganshire, MP for St Ives, Cornwall, in 1906–24, and a supporter of Lloyd George. His brother, Sir James Herbert Cory, was a shipowner, a JP and likewise deputy Lord Lieutenant, elected as a Conservative MP for Cardiff in November 1915. Aside from the Cory brothers, the leading establishment figure was David Alfred Thomas (baron, January 1916, and later viscount Rhondda of Llanwern: hereafter 'Rhondda'), senior partner in Thomas and Davey Coal Shippers, a JP and deputy Lord Lieutenant; later he was food commissioner in the Lloyd George government. Rhondda represented Merthyr Tydfil as a Liberal MP from 1888 until he transferred to Cardiff. In 1910, he retired from politics until his translation to the House of Lords. The Corys and Rhondda were the bosses. Quite plainly, they owned Cardiff and its environs both economically and politically, and, in the immediately prewar years and the wartime period, their domination had been growing as concentration and combination continued. Already, most of the coalfields were in the hands of five combines – Rhondda's Cambrian combine and Cory's being two of the largest. At this time, A. Hutt tells us, to 'journey in South Wales [was] not to journey from one county, or one valley to the next, but to travel from territory to territory of one or other of these combines'.[4] With outright control of one-quarter of south Wales coal production, and a hand in much of the rest, Rhondda especially was a power to be reckoned with.[5] His Cambrian coalfields, moreover, had been the epicentre of the Tonypandy disturbances.[6] Naturally, the owners and the 'better sort' viewed the anti-war agitation as unpatriotic. As dissenting agitation steadily grew to implicate existing, and widening, class and labour disputes, dissent began to look more and more socially and politically dangerous – even, in potential, revolutionary. In Cardiff, as elsewhere, dislike gave way to steady and ever more active opposition.

Against the bosses was arrayed organized labour – the coal miners of the valleys, the seamen and dockers of the port, and the iron and steel workers of Ebbw Vale, Tredegar, Merthyr and Pontypool. The opposition of these to the established order was all the more complete since the coal and steel industries in the region had grown up so quickly in the last half of the nineteenth century that they had created small towns without any amenities, built on slag heaps, and big towns that were 'sinks of vice'.[7] The population of the Rhondda Valley, for instance, had grown from perhaps 1,000 persons in 1850 to 152,781 in 1911. The population of the valleys was, moreover, entirely distinct from that of the towns, and the owners. The miners and steelworkers, in large measure, were drawn from the rural Welsh population, distinct in ethnicity, religion and language from the town population, gentry and established clergy – 'the enemies without'.[8] A powerful, and very diffuse trade union structure, superimposed upon the local chapel movement, reinforced local identities and provided the framework for powerful local, working-class loyalties.[9] To make matters worse, the fractured nature of Welsh geography, which encouraged isolation, had allowed very advanced notions to develop in the minds, in particular, of younger workers. Ultimately, these notions were encouraged, and inculcated through a vigorous system of independent schools, necessary, in any case, owing to the prevalent religious nonconformity of the region. Twenty-one of 30 members of the miners' committee called to discuss union reform, in the years prior to the war, for instance, were products of the Plebs League schools. Notable local agitators graduated from these to attend, not Oxford or Cambridge, but the Central Labour College.[10] Cultural distinctiveness, therefore, made the acceptance of divergent and advanced ideas easier, and encouraged the creation of local self-help education systems which, by the immediately prewar period, were beginning to make such ideas universal. Moreover, unlike many miners, Welsh miners tended to be home owners, which made them voters even before 1919 – politically active voters, it might be added.[11]

The result? A social–industrial situation characterized by yawning, obvious and ugly divides, and which was commonly interpreted by reference to political ideas much less compromising, better thought out, and more firmly held than those typical in the working class as a whole. Aneurin Bevan was later to write of the downright revolutionary fervour which underlay labour politics in south Wales in his youth.[12] In the years just before the war, this fervour had produced powerful unrest, expressed in ugly labour disturbances which made south Wales the most turbulent region in a generally stormy time. In 1908, while the rest of the country had experienced a swing to the Liberals, Labour in Wales had remained strong, and the SWMF had voted overwhelmingly for affiliation to the Labour Party.[13] The years 1910–12 had seen constant disruption. In 1911 members of the SWMF had shocked their less convinced brethren in Durham, Northumberland and north Staffordshire by their militancy. Welshmen were, the MFGB was informed, touring the country preaching a syndicalist general strike. Could they not somehow be restrained?[14] By 1914, Noah Ablet, the Marxist author of *The Miner's Next Step*, was agitating for nothing less than a seven-hour day and eight shillings an hour minimum wage.[15] These were very advanced notions for 1914. Ablet was willing to achieve them by means equally advanced.

Until his death in 1915, a leader of the miners nationally and the local Labour MP for Merthyr Tydfil in the coal belt was the venerable Keir Hardie, the founder of the ILP. Prominent among his collaborators were two miners' organizers, Charles Butt Stanton and James Winstone. Both of these men had been among the new generation of radical leaders which had come to the fore of the local Labour movement following the retirement of gradualist, Lib-Lab William 'Mabon' Abraham from the leadership of the SWMF in 1912. Where Mabon had insisted that 'half a loaf is better than none', Stanton, Winstone and their fellows insisted that 'we are demanding the whole bakehouse'.[16] Winstone had been notable as a resolute industrial/political leader. Stanton, the Aberdare miners' agent and, after 1912, a SWMF delegate to the MFGB, on the other hand, had been the quintessential young man in a hurry, noted for his fiery and uncompromising approach. He had no time for gradualism. '[T]he faint hearted, over-cautious, creeping, crawling, cowardly set who pose as leaders but do not lead', he insisted, 'are responsible for the rotten conditions of things today.'[17] When, in 1910, the mine owners had threatened violence, Stanton had threatened them in turn with 'fighting brigades' which would return blow for blow.[18] Before the war he had been one of the most convinced syndicalists in south Wales.[19] 'Before the war', Stanton was later to tell the House of Commons, 'I was a fighting man, and I did something more than the honourable Member for Derby [J. H. Thomas] did. I had the full confidence of my men [then], and I could have it today.'[20] Both Stanton and Winstone, of course, were members of the ILP.

The war, as might be expected, accentuated the gap between workers and owners, town and country. It also split the ILP, separated the miners and steelworkers from the seamen, and divided the miners against themselves. To existing social splits were added cleavages within the working class which were all too apparent by November 1916. It was inevitable that the seamen would tend to the patriotic position. They were, after all, members of what was essentially a fighting service. The seamen, moreover, were less exposed to the radicalism of ASE members – men beside whom many miners lived in the valley towns. But neither were the miners a united whole. It is true that the war hardly calmed tensions in the pit towns. The strike of 1915 was almost repeated in 1916; became, thereafter, a situation of almost permanently incipient strike.[21] It should be remembered, once again, that industrial disputes, however angry, were not always directed against the fact of war. While some might insist that the time had come for peace and a change in the system, others reacting to the same set of problems, equally adamantly, could advocate a change of government, and more efficient prosecution of the war.

There were other sources of division. While Welsh workers might dislike their bosses, they also identified strongly with the victimized nations of the First World War. The war, Lloyd George asserted, was not being fought for further imperial aggrandizement, but on behalf of the 'little five-foot-five nations' – like Wales, he need not have added.[22] This aspect of the war was, perhaps, the source of the highly uncompromising and belligerent tone adopted by Welsh divines. In Wales, of course, chapels were not only religious, but social, political and national institutions.

The ideological split in Wales, moreover, overlay a splintering of local labour radicalism, already under way. In the years immediately prior to the war, Welsh radicals had won important victories: most particularly land reform, and the disestablishment in Wales of the Church of England. Before the war, national and class agendas had coalesced. By 1914, they were beginning to pull apart. The national ILP line was that class issues must be predominant, and that Welsh nationalism was little better than a parochial distraction, something which went without remark. Many workers were not so certain. Mabonist Liberalism – Liberalism combined with a gradualist Labour agenda mixed with Welsh nationalism – was still very powerful.[23] Lloyd George was Wales's favourite son: a Welsh radical with a populist agenda become Prime Minister, who was surrounded by other Welshmen, and who kept a Welsh household at 10 Downing Street.[24] His annual pilgrimage to the national *eisteddfod* was known throughout Wales as 'Lloyd George's day'.[25] Ultimately the split between radicals and Mabonists would lead to the foundation of Plaid Genedlaethol Cymru in 1925. In the war years this split was already incipient. In the 1910 election, for instance, Ben Tillett, a BSP import, had been swamped in Swansea city, while even in a Labour stronghold like Merthyr Tydfil Keir Hardie had run second to Edgar Jones – a local nationalist and a Baptist clergyman.[26] In 1913, the Liberals had attempted a local counter-offensive in Merthyr, running a second candidate – T. Artemus Jones, a product of the nationalist movement – and had nearly unseated Hardie.[27] Just as the squires and mine owners seemed to be members of a foreign oligarchy, so Keir Hardie and his supporters were seen as foreign interlopers, attempting to foist an internationalist agenda upon a movement which had always focused in part on national regeneration.[28] In many respects, Mabonists were often closer to Rhondda than to Keir Hardie, to Lloyd George than to Ramsay MacDonald. As D. A. Thomas, after all, Rhondda had been a radical, a nationalist and a founder of Cymru Ffydd.[29] For members of the Plaid tendency, support for the war effort did not necessarily appear to be inconsistent with either Welsh nationalism or class interest.

From the beginning, the ideological response of Welsh workers, even those in categories most likely to favour dissent, was plainly confused by conflicting motives. Strike they might, but miners were not slow to volunteer to fight in the national cause. In the first year of the war, nationally miners led the way in rates of enlistment. By July 1915, one-quarter had enlisted. Some of the highest rates of enlistment, even within this highly patriotic category, were registered in Glamorgan-shire. Wales, as a whole, ultimately achieved the highest rate of partici-pation in the war of any constituent part of the United Kingdom.[30] Political strikes and enlistment: these were symptoms of a growing divide. While radicalism remained a feature of local political life, working-class patriotism of a particularly virulent variety was evident from the beginning.[31]

In south Wales, as in Birmingham and Liverpool, the division of the working class into feuding patriotic and dissenting factions was formalized. When Keir Hardie died, in September 1915, a by-election followed. Since Merthyr Tydfil was a two-seat constituency, in which one seat was held by a Liberal and the other by Labour (Keir Hardie), the contest that ensued occurred almost entirely between competing branches of the ILP. What should have been an administrative process quickly became a bitter struggle between Winstone and Stanton. In a very nasty contest for nomination, both sides flung charges of corruption and treachery. Both miners' factions were just 'not playing the game'. Cards were not being checked. Boys were being allowed to vote. Branches were saying that they would not be bound by the general verdict.[32] Which side was held to be more guilty of corruption depended upon the personal political position of the commentator.

Meanwhile, the national leadership of the miners' union fell to Robert Smillie, a convinced dissenter. The war, Smillie considered, was an unmitigated disaster. Conscription was the beginning of total compulsion, which would not be removed after the war and was, therefore, an evil which would have to be fought.[33] Some miners certainly agreed. Once again, however, the views of Smillie were not universally shared. Many miners had already volunteered, and many of these were ultimately returned from the front to the pits as essential labour. Here they constituted a significant patriotic leaven. The presidency of the SWMF, after the retirement of Mabon, had gone to William Brace, the miners' agent for Monmouthshire and an MP. A radical, and the leader of a very combative section of a combative union, he was also a convinced patriot who had already taken office in the government as the parliamentary under-secretary at the Home Office – a position he would hold until 1918.[34] By 1916, Mabon himself had joined the BWNL.[35]

In the end, Winstone received the nod to stand as the official ILP candidate, following a narrow victory over Stanton. Winstone continued to toe the cautious line established by the leadership of the ILP's peace faction. If not exactly anti-war, or revolutionary in any sense of the word,[36] Winstone was definitely anti-conscriptionist and pro-UDC.[37] Stanton, meanwhile, was a fully engaged patriot. On 6 August 1914, he had shown his cards when he led a patriot mob in an attack on Keir Hardie in his constituency office.[38] On its formation, he accepted office as a vice-president of the BWNL. By 1915, his partisanship had become so violent that even Max Blumenfeld was accustomed to floating his correspondence past members of the government prior to publication in the *Daily Express*, censoring what did not pass muster as too inflammatory.[39] Despite his defeat, he ran in the by-election as an 'unofficial' ILP candidate. It was a sign of the disarray in Labour ranks, however, that Stanton rather than Winstone was the candidate officially backed by the Labour Party national executive.[40] Although big guns were rolled out in support of Winstone – J. H. Thomas and the Bradford Labour leader, and then chairman of the ILP, Fred Jowett – in the contest that followed Stanton was returned as ILP member for Merthyr Tydfil by a majority of 4,000 votes, with support from the government parties and the BWNL.[41] Opposing as he did the most important planks in the ILP wartime platform, it is probably closer to the truth to see Stanton, by this time, as an angry and resentful independent much closer to Lloyd George than to Ramsay MacDonald, or even Arthur Henderson. So he is remembered, in any case, in Labour histories.[42]

The Merthyr Tydfil by-election was noted for its mud-slinging, hateful character. Stanton's campaign literature was particularly violent, and became increasingly so. One of his pamphlets, 'What Mr Winstone's Party and Supporters have Said on the War', began by instancing anti-war statements of leading Labour politicians, continued through 'What the Germans think of Mr Winstone's Party' (counting on it to produce revolution) and ended by declaring that 'Every vote for Winstone is a Vote for Germany'.[43] Another pamphlet, 'Put Your Patriotism First and Vote for Stanton', is worth citing at length, to illustrate the temper of the campaign.

Put Your Patriotism First and Vote for Stanton

Electors! Read This Before You Vote

Mr James Winstone, the official Labour Candidate for the Merthyr vacancy, professes to be a loyal supporter of the War. He denies having said or done anything against recruiting. The following facts are worth recalling to the memory of Mr Winstone [specific charges abbreviated in what follows]:

1. Winstone was the official nominee of the ILP and the ILP was 'pro-German', as exemplified best by its opposition to recruiting.

2. Winstone was a member of Pontypool branch of the party which had passed anti-war resolutions. He supported Keir Hardie and Ramsay MacDonald in their opposition to the war.

3. Winstone had presided at an ILP meeting at Pontypool, at which Mr Walton Newbold had given a lecture entitled 'The Russian Menace'. Newbold had since been indicted for interfering with the ammunition supply from the US.

4. Winstone had been active in supporting ILP resolutions at party conferences.

In the face of the above facts [the handbill concluded], how can Mr Winstone claim to be a supporter of the War? If he were, the ILP would not be so anxious for his election at Merthyr.[44]

It was, as has been said, an ugly contest. In the end, Stanton won election, very probably because he slung more mud, obtained more and more powerful outside support, and because the miners were themselves split Winstone–Stanton/UDC–BWNL. Nationally, Lord Milner and Mabon considered the election a 'historic turning point', marking the shift of labour from a dissenting to a patriotic position.[45] The horrified dissenters reacted by consolidating their control on the local party machine. While Stanton had been elected as an ILP candidate, the local Labour Party association quickly made itself notorious by being the only one to vote against continued participation in the coalition government.[46]

It is important to note that in the political pattern developing locally during 1916–17 Merthyr Tydfil was hardly unique. Stanton's election was part and product of a nationwide movement. ILP candidates who stood on a dissenting platform in by-elections were universally defeated. Meanwhile, by manipulating voting procedures, dissenters gained control of local party machines and moved them to ever-greater levels of opposition. A case very similar to that of Merthyr Tydfil, for example, developed a few months later in North Salford, at the height of the so-called 'swing to the left'. Here Ben Tillett was convincingly elected on a violently patriotic platform. Though Tillett was officially a Labour Party candidate, and would ultimately become the PLP government whip, the vote which elected him was organized by the local Unionists (his election was warmly welcomed, he was told, in the Carlton Club), the NSP and BWNL. While Hyndman and J. Havelock Wilson supported him, the only Labour man willing to speak on a Tillett platform was James O'Grady. Of course O'Grady, while a Labour MP, was also a leading member of the BWNL. Meanwhile Tillett's opponents seized control of the local Labour Party – using it to pursue an agenda directly opposite to Tillett's at the Nottingham party conference in June 1917.[47] Similarly, Churchill, compelled to submit himself for re-election in the summer prior to re-entering the cabinet, was convincingly re-elected in Dundee. This was by no means, however, the clear-cut vindication of government policy it seemed. Churchill had prevailed because he received support from all the government parties, and because he retained the personal political loyalty of Dundee's substantial Irish and Catholic population. Already, however, loyalties were beginning to shift. Edwin Scrymegour, Churchill's opponent, hitherto best known as a temperance advocate, was in the process of reinventing himself as a labour and peace crusader. The Irish and Catholics were already wavering.[48] The only member of the UDC convincingly re-elected at this time was Arthur Henderson, who re-fought his seat prior to entering the Lloyd George coalition. Participation in the national government, however, was hardly consistent with the dissenting programme.[49] A splintered, increasingly polarized working-class political response was the rule and the patriots were almost everywhere in the ascendant.

In any case, in Cardiff an unpleasant political situation became a still more disagreeable labour situation rather quickly. The miners, as we have seen, had long been in a state of almost chronic unrest which did not end with the commencement of hostilities. They were now divided against themselves. Moreover, the patriot wing of the miners' movement was aligned, through the BWNL, with the seamen of the city, and of course, ultimately with the Liberal and Unionist owners. The seamen and Stantonite miners were a patriot mob waiting to be assembled, indeed, were looking for an excuse to assemble. Workplace grievances, accentuated by the war, were producing calls for industrial action. Given that one of the most dangerous grievances was looming compulsion, existing ILP–UDC policy, and the identity of the miners' leadership, any strike would almost certainly take a political and anti-war direction. The bosses could be counted upon to resist such pressure as dangerous, even perhaps implicitly revolutionary. The situation in south Wales, in 1916, was volatile indeed. When, therefore, a year after his defeat, James Winstone announced that an NCCL meeting would be held in Cory Hall, at which J. H. Thomas and prominent dissenters would speak, this was taken to represent not simply another dissenting meeting. It was also viewed, implicitly, as a class challenge, a national danger, and a gauntlet flung at Stanton's feet. It was not a gauntlet which he failed to pick up.

Whatever Morel might have hoped to accomplish in 1916, the Cory Hall meeting may have been intended as no provocation at all. The UDC did indeed intend to stir the pot in south Wales, but the Cardiff meeting was probably not associated with this campaign at all. Charles Trevelyan had spoken at Merthyr on a UDC platform only a few months before and there had been no trouble. Bertrand Russell, similarly, had conducted a series of 'wonderful' NCF meetings in the summer of 1916 – at Briton Ferry, Merthyr Tydfil and Cardiff – without meeting any local obstruction.[50] Trevelyan was one of the principal leaders of dissent nationally, and was not a man inclined to pull his punches. Russell was both UDC and NCF and utterly opposed to the war and to conscription. If anybody was in Wales to foment trouble, it was probably Russell.[51] The meeting scheduled for November 1916 was not a UDC meeting. It was NCCL – not quite the same thing – even though this body had already been identified by local opponents as a 'pro-German' conclave.[52] Moreover, the keynote speaker in Cardiff on this occasion was J. H. Thomas. He was not a very convincing dissenter. Thomas was in Cardiff in November not to stop the war, but to head off a wildcat strike by south Wales railworkers which appeared to be in the offing.[53] He was there, as well, to deal with the miners. Increasing compulsion had meant that exemptions were being cancelled. Particularly obnoxious was the case of one miner, the father of five children, who had been called to the colours.[54] In both capacities, Thomas was acting as the agent of Sir William Robertson, the CIGS, rather than of E. D. Morel.[55] Robertson had appealed to Thomas in September to defuse the local labour situation in order to prevent strikes which might well become national. Thomas was in Cardiff, therefore, not to further, but to defeat Morel's purpose.

Why then was Thomas appearing on a dissenting platform? While neither anti-war nor anti-government (he had already spoken to over 100 recruiting meetings), Thomas was, however, anti-conscription; not necessarily, however, because he had moral objections. Thomas believed that peace at home could only be preserved if conscription did not necessarily involve mandatory, government-controlled workplace realignment, and ultimately, universal labour compulsion. Since it would, there could be no conscription, since disruption at home would mean defeat. At the meeting in Cardiff, he was to speak in support of the motion: 'That this conference holds that military compulsion has already involved industrial compulsion, and endangered industrial conditions, and demands that this invasion of the rights of labour at once cease, and that guarantees be given for its non-recurrence.'[56] This was hardly a ringing call for opposition to the government; less still, incitement to class, or anti-war violence.

Once again, however, Morel and the UDC were attempting to manipulate the volatile mixture in south Wales for their own purposes. Recall that Morel was looking to construct a coalition between the UDC, the Labour Party and the 'Triple Alliance'. Trevelyan and Russell meetings in south Wales, in particular, were part of this campaign, and south Wales was judged particularly ripe for the picking.[57] The patriot leadership was as alive to potentialities in the region.

Mrs Pankhurst, for instance, had identified south Wales as a government sore spot even in 1915, and had brought her fears to the attention of Lloyd George. If Lloyd George had been inclined not to take too pessimistic a view in 1915, this was not the case in 1916. The Thomas meeting was scheduled to take place at a time when relations with labour were touchy throughout Britain. The Sheffield engineering strike exploded two days later. Morel's grand coalition of dissent appeared about to be born.[58] It may be, perhaps, that the Cardiff meeting provoked such a violent response, not because of what its organisers meant it to accomplish, but because its timing seemed to suggest that another agenda altogether was being followed.

Whether there was ever a danger that trouble in the Midlands might combine with trouble in Wales, or that Morel's scheme might work, Thomas's motion was never put. Whatever Thomas intended to accomplish, Stanton appears to have decided, from the beginning, to stop the meeting from taking place. Not only would he not tolerate dissent in his bailiwick, but neither was he inclined to back down before what looked very like a personal challenge. 'If I have my way', Thomas later quoted Stanton to the House of Commons as saying to his supporters,

> they will never hold the meeting in the Cory Hall. If the police are there to interfere let them. If I have a following I am prepared to prevent these people getting inside the doors by all means short of murder.[59]

As Stanton did not bother to correct or deny Thomas's charge, but rather gloried in it, we can safely presume that this was a true statement of his intention from the beginning.

Notification that the Thomas meeting was to be held was followed almost immediately by advertisements for a counter-demonstration. Headlines in local newspapers blared: 'Britons Beware!!! Great Patriotic Citizens Demonstration', and 'PEACE PLOTTERS. AN AMAZING AGENDA FOR CARDIFF CONCLAVE'. An open letter was carried in the local press (the *Western Mail* and the *South Wales Daily News*) from one Captain Atherley Jones, organizing secretary and later chairman of the British Empire Union, a one-time NSL organizer, failed recruiting officer and semi-professional rabble-rouser of a type inherited by the BWNL from the NSL.[60] 'It may interest you readers to know', it began,

> although I have been up to London last week and placed the whole facts before different Departments, it has not yet been decided to prohibit the holding of the Peace Conference at Cory Hall, Cardiff, on Saturday, the 11th November, at 2.30 p.m. Consequently a counter-demonstration has been arranged and will take place in Cardiff on Friday the 10th November 1916, at 7.30 p.m.[61]

A committee chaired by Major-General Sir Ivor Herbert, the Lord Lieutenant of Monmouthshire and 'a pillar of non-conformist radical-ism',[62] was organized to co-ordinate the patriot response.[63] It included most of Cardiff's most prominent citizens – the Corys, Rhondda – combined with its most convinced patriots – the BWNL and other patriot leaders, the Stanton miners' and seamen's representatives. This committee operated, moreover, under the implicit authority of Lloyd George. 'My dear Sir Ivor Herbert', Lloyd George had written,

> You have my best wishes for the success of your meeting. We all realise the many calls the country has made on the men of south Wales and how well they have responded. On the battlefield, in the coalfield, and in their many industries they have alike done good work, and all of us realise, I hope, how great are the efforts that are needed from our industries as well as from our armies.
>
> Wales is deservedly proud of her sons. They have carried her flag

high: they have enhanced the reputation of our race, and, I am sure that the people of Wales will respond to every call that will be made on them.

But let us not forget that no great work is done without great labour; no great cause carried to triumph without great sacrifice. The immediate future may call for increased efforts and greater sacrifices and we must all be prepared to bear them.

No faint-hearted nation and no feeble-hearted person ever achieved any great purpose. The spirit of a people is measured by the fortitude with which they face difficulties, and the people of Wales have never been tried and found wanting.[64]

This was hardly an incitement to riot. It was sufficient, nevertheless, to cloak the meeting with an aura of governmental authority.

Lord Rhondda's message, read to the meeting by Captain Atherley Jones, was more inflammatory. 'I very much regret that I cannot be with you this evening', Rhondda began,

for the resolution to be proposed at the meeting has my hearty concurrence. I wish we could infuse a dash of Cromwell into the Cabinet. The Government are, in my mind, showing far too much lenience toward both the peace prattlers and the conscientious objectors. I should like to have them in hand myself for a few hours. We may, however, regard with contempt the insignificant number of those who want to discuss peace conditions at this time, and with even greater contempt the half-baked intelligence that suggests the discussion. I have strong objections myself, as all decent persons must have, to taking life, but I have a darned sight stronger objection to the other fellow taking mine. We were forced reluctantly into this struggle, but being in we mean to win.

We were fighting for peace and for such conditions as will ensure, as far as it is humanly possible to do so, peace for our time; but we know that it is idle to talk of peace until we have given the Huns a thorough thrashing. They can have peace as soon as they are prepared to accept our terms.

What the peace prattlers want is a patched up peace, which would mean armed neutrality, with huge standing armies in every country in Europe, and render vain all the sacrifices we have made. To that sort of peace no sane man will consent.[65]

The reception accorded to the speech of Ben Davies, the Pontypridd miners' agent, and an ally of Stanton, indicated the populist agenda of the local patriot movement. '[T]he danger to the country was not altogether outside', he concluded.

> There was danger within. There was the danger of apathy, the danger of Government weakness, the danger of a premature peace. [There was danger of profiteering.] I notice ... that not many of you applaud that ... I don't know whether we shall lose the British Empire in this war and find it in Lord Rhondda's pocket (loud laughter). I was surprised this week to find that he is putting the German Empire in as well.[66]

Another popular speaker, and Stanton friend, was the BWNL chairman, Victor Fisher, who, like Davies, was careful to indict profiteering as a scarcely smaller threat to the war effort than pacifism. For the moment, however, Ramsay MacDonald was a greater threat than Lord Rhondda.

Having heard the messages and speeches, the committee decided to stop the meeting, at whatever cost, by whatever means were necessary. Given Stanton's existing determination, it is likely that there would have been an attempt to do so in any case.

The dissenters, apprehending trouble, placed their hopes in government forbearance and police protection. Ivor Thomas, the local organizer of the NCCL, wrote to Ramsay MacDonald shortly before the meeting was scheduled to take place. '[Captain] Atherley Jones and his "gang"', he informed MacDonald,

> are very busy, with the aid of the 'Daily Express', 'Morning Post', 'Western Mail' and a couple of other papers. They have tried to get the authorities to prohibit the conference. I think they have failed. Their move is to organise a counter demonstration to be held the night before our conference – you know the object – Do you think we could claim police protection against organised hooliganism?[67]

In the event, something more than simple 'hooliganism' occurred, while both the police and the HO proved particularly ineffectual at maintaining the public peace. They did indeed know the patriot 'object', and, by 1916, had come to employ it implicitly to silence dissent. Neither the police nor the HO, however, expected that events would develop to the degree that they did in Cardiff. Given the inflammatory social–political situation in south Wales, it is unlikely that anybody could have done much to prevent what transpired. There was at least one attempt, however, to ensure that events did not get too far out of hand. The HO, apprehending danger from the scheduled counter-demonstration, had considered prohibiting either one, the other, or both meetings.[68] In the end the counter-demonstrators were forbidden to approach within a quarter of a mile of Cory Hall, where the dissenters were to meet.[69] The Cardiff police were directed to try to keep patriots and dissenters apart, and a police reporter was detailed to take minutes of Ramsay MacDonald's speech.[70] Events would show how insufficient these dispositions were.

Faced with intimidation, the dissenters, with some misgiving, continued preparations for their meeting. James Cory, on behalf of the patriots, made one last attempt to induce Samuel to prohibit the meeting.[71] When this didn't work, the patriots determined on more direct action. Stanton had pledged, after all, to do whatever was necessary to ensure that the meeting did not take place. The morning of the day of the scheduled meeting (11 November), the patriot committee sent a message to the Home Secretary, Samuel. 'As you have not seen fit', it went,

> to prohibit the pacifist meeting to be held to-day at 2.30 p.m., the seamen of the port are taking the matter into their own hands, and you must accept full responsibility for what will undoubtedly occur if the meeting is held. We absolutely refuse to be held responsible.[72]

A national leader of the NASFU and BWNL, Captain E. Tupper, signed this message. The fact that Tupper was on the ground gives some indication that at least the powerful NASFU considered that something special was happening in Cardiff. Tupper was J. Havelock Wilson's hard man, always in place to supervise those aspects of union business which Wilson considered required special handling.

That afternoon, while the dissenters began to gather, the advertised counter-demonstration took place at a nearby Congregational church under the auspices of the British Empire Union (Atherley Jones) and the BWNL (Stanton and Fisher). Invited, as well, were members of local chapters of the seamen's union and of other friendly trade union organizations and women's groups from across south Wales.[73] Having been harangued by the scheduled speakers – including the Earl of Plymouth, the Earl of Dunraven, Rhondda, Lord Merthyr and, of course, Stanton and Jones – the patriots set out to break up the meeting. They were led by a band of miners, ex-soldiers carrying a banner inscribed with the motto of the Welsh Fusiliers, 'Better Death than Dishonour'. Meanwhile, outside the hall itself, angry seamen crying 'dirty tykes' and 'rotten shirkers' were confronting dissenters. Later, as the meeting commenced, 'pro-British' orators took up position outside to speak to a growing crowd. These speakers more closely reflected the feelings of the patriot mob than did the more temperate message of

Lloyd George or even that of Rhondda. 'Our boys are fighting and dying for the infernal curs and traitors inside', one speaker cried:

> Are you going to stand for this? 'NO!' ... Is Cardiff going to be disgraced in the eyes of the British Empire and its Allies? 'NO!' ... The miserable blighters are entrenching themselves behind women and children whom they have taken into the hall with them. The poor kiddies and the women are not to blame.[74]

Victor Fisher, on hand outside the hall, charged the dissenting delegates with being 'dastards and cowards, some of whom ... were the paid agents of the enemy, and ... traitors not only to their country but to civilization'.[75]

Even before Stanton's parade arrived, 900 dissenters found themselves besieged by 1,500 patriots. The patriots, by and large, were composed of Stanton's miners and the seamen of the port. Those inside were representatives of 290 trade union branches, 37 trade councils, 100 peace organizations, 13 religious bodies, 16 co-operatives and 29 women's organizations.[76]

As the crowd in front of Cory Hall worked itself into a lather, the counter-demonstration marchers appeared. Having paused for a moment at the quarter-mile limit they were led on by Stanton and Captain Tupper. According to the *Daily Express*, at the quarter-mile limit Tupper cried to the crowd, 'Who'll follow Stanton and myself to Cory Hall? It's not the first time I've had to go against the police!'. The crowd had answered, enthusiastically, 'We will!'.[77] A few minutes later the marchers arriving cheering and singing outside Cory Hall.[78] Once the parade had arrived and been united with the crowd of patriots already assembled, the violence began. Singing 'God Save the King', and with cries of 'To hell with the Kaiser', 'Get into Khaki' and 'No Peace. Down with the Traitors!', the marchers broke through the police barricade and rushed Cory Hall. They were led, apparently, by a man carrying a Belgian flag, and by a sergeant major who had lost an arm at Ypres.[79] The besieged dissenters attempted to bar the doors and keep up their spirits by singing *The Red Flag*. Ramsay MacDonald, seeing which way the wind was blowing, appears to have slipped out of the back door – his disappearance later described as 'sleuthy' by an unsympathetic *Western Mail*[80] – and escaped injury and insult. Once the doors gave way, however, and the mob entered the building, neither J. H. Thomas nor the chairman of the meeting, Winstone, were so lucky. Thomas tried to quiet the rioters. Stanton, however, having first cautioned his patriots to take care of the women – who had fainted – refused Thomas's offer to parley and ordered his men to 'Clear the Germans out'. From there,

Stanton proceeded to the speaker's platform where he struggled with his enemy, Winstone.[81] Both Thomas and Winstone, having suffered considerable insult and abuse, were eventually led away by police – the while being pelted by mud and tomatoes and subjected to cries of 'traitor' and 'coward'.[82] The patriots, having taken possession of the hall, listened to a series of speeches from prominent local citizens. Their meeting ended with the passing of a resolution calling 'on the Government to use all the resources of the nation in a relentless prosecution of the war'.[83] Such, in brief, was the Battle of Cory Hall.

The chief constable of Cardiff, as might be expected, faced some criticism for his handling of the affair – the most outrageous patriot excess yet. His defence, however, was hard to fault. With much of his force enlisted in the army, he had only 150 constables available for street duty. While there were 1,183 special constables in Cardiff, he had thought it unwise to call them out, as he considered it likely that, given the nature of the duty that would be required of them, they would be less than reliable. It was, he thought, too much to expect of even the best disciplined policemen that they should stop what they conceived to be a patriotic demonstration in order to protect another which they deemed little short of treasonous. It is important to keep in mind as well, that by the autumn of 1916 special constables were generally older, retired policemen (aged 50–60), or members of the VF available for such duty.[84] Retired men were unlikely to be up to the duty. Volunteers were unlikely to be disinterested. A considerable number of volunteers, moreover, appear to have enlisted as special constables during the early war spy scares – as, for instance, that with which the war began, and that which followed the publication in 1915 of John Buchan's *The Thirty-Nine Steps*. Few of these were likely to have much appetite for facing an angry mob of patriots.[85] There was very little the HO could say. This was a dilemma which it could not resolve itself: how to protect dissenters and prevent disturbances if the only method of doing so was the prohibition of meetings held in support of the war effort?[86] Was such a policy even wise? Furthermore, the chief constable was correct: how to restrain anything with the nature of the force available to him?

Nor was public opinion any firmly set rock upon which to anchor government policy. Indeed, in general, both the public – if the press is any guide – and the House of Commons were more censorious of the meeting dispersed than of the rioters who scattered it. On 14 November, J. H. Thomas, back in London, opened debate on the question in the House by asking the Home Secretary for an explanation of the police failure to protect the meeting he was to have addressed. Did he, Thomas wanted to know, propose to take any action to prevent a repetition of what had been, in effect, 'incitement to riot ... and thus preserve the right to meet in public to discuss questions of national importance'.[87] A good question, but the temper of the time was illustrated better by Colonel Craig, who, before Thomas had spoken, asked the Speaker, in making a motion for adjournment, whether he could 'suggest the best way in which this House can express its thanks to the hon. Member for Merthyr Tydfil [i.e. Stanton] for breaking up [this] pro-German meeting'.[88] Major-General Sir Ivor Herbert – powerfully implicated in the disturbances himself – demanded of the Home Secretary whether he had been informed before the event that the dissenters were about to convene a 'meeting calculated to offend public feeling and provoke the breach of the peace that actually occurred'.[89] Stanton, entirely unrepentant, promised more of the same if further dissenting meetings were allowed to take place. 'I would like to ask you, Mr Speaker', he said,

> whether you are aware of what has appeared in the Press that they threaten us in Merthyr with another of their pro-German meetings, and whether you are aware that we will not tolerate it, whatever the consequences? Also whether you are aware that we are not going to be hounded out of what we believe to be our rights as Britishers by a crowd of pro-Germans, who, if they come to Merthyr, will be dealt with whether you deal with them or no?[90]

The Home Secretary, Samuel, could do little but reiterate the government's position. The chief constable, he said, had not apprehended grave disorder. He believed that he could prevent the two demonstrations from mixing. The gentlemen organizing the patriot counter-demonstration had promised that they would depend entirely upon legal and constitutional methods of stopping the meeting, and had written to this effect to the chief constable. A week later, when it became clear that a grave disturbance was in the offing, the chief constable had attempted to prohibit the Cory Hall meeting under provision of Defence of the Realm Regulation 9A, but, while it was considered that the Cory Hall meeting would certainly 'give offence to the great majority of the population of Cardiff ... its objects were not in themselves illegal'.[91] In the future, therefore, the

> Government does not propose to use the powers of the Defence of the Realm Acts to interfere, so far as it can be avoided, with the expression of opinions on matters of policy. Even if some disorder results when a small minority places itself in open opposition to the sentiments of the nation at large, that is preferable, so long as the disorder is not of a

grave character, to the minority being able to assert that the Government uses its power to suppress meetings by force of law and to prevent views attacking the Government's policy from being expressed. On a careful review of all the considerations, on the one hand, and on the other, I thought it inadvisable to prohibit the holding of the conference.[92]

In short, dissenters were free to make public their opposition to the war; and the patriots were equally free to beat them up. The government, meanwhile, was constrained to do nothing.

Thomas was not mollified. This was mob rule, he asserted, and there would certainly be a repetition, given especially that the dissenters had indeed announced their intention of holding another conference at Merthyr Tydfil, while Stanton had just announced his intention of breaking it up. Government indecision, in effect, amounted to complicity with the patriots. This made a mockery of HMG's assertion that it was fighting for democratic freedoms.[93] Ramsay MacDonald spoke in the same vein – his speech interrupted, many times, by the heckling of Stanton and his friends.[94]

If Thomas and MacDonald were angry, Stanton was scarcely coherent, so enraged was he by what had transpired. He is worth quoting at length because he was so typical of this leadership of this branch of the labour movement, at this juncture in the war. 'What the Cardiff people did', he warned,

is what the people of Merthyr Tydfil are going to do. Seeing that they [the dissenters] have failed in Cardiff – and they did fail splendidly and magnificently – we in Merthyr Tydfil have been threatened with a meeting ... then there will be trouble again ... I am not going to tolerate these people coming into our midst, poisoning the minds of our people and creating all the mischief they possibly can. There is a much greater danger and menace than some people would realise ... Is it the business of the Government to stand by and back up a crowd of traitors [Honourable Members: 'Oh! Oh!'] – absolute traitors to our Flag, to our country, as against the men who have fought for that Flag, who have their sons at the front, and who are doing all they can to try to win this war? ... [I]t is not for me to say, I can prove that they are having money from Germany – there is German money shifting around. I can judge by the hoardings, and by the money that is being spent, and it does not come out of the sixpence or shillings of the delegates who paid to get in there ... We want to be loyal citizens and to play the game, whatever we may have been, but we ask the House to believe that we were only actuated by the most honest motives as

Britishers. We want to win the War, and we believe these people were treacherous in what they were doing, and we went there at any risk to put an end to it, and none of us are sorry.[95]

If it came to it, then Stanton was prepared to go to jail; both he and Captain Tupper were of like mind, and both had been in prison before for their union activities. They were going to stop dissenting meetings wherever they took place, by whatever means necessary, and despite the consequences.

There was little for Samuel to do, faced as he was with an unmoveable object and an unstoppable force, but further equivocate. He pleaded for understanding and forbearance from the patriots. The real question, he asserted, was 'whether … in these circumstances the Government can do more harm or good to the national cause by using the powers of the law, by using the powers of the gaoler, to suppress the expression of the opinion of this minority'. If suppressed, would dissent not be driven underground, and there 'assume a formidableness that it has not yet attained and is not likely to attain', provided that everyone were free to see just how insignificant was this species of opinion.[96] But, on the other hand, Samuel continued, how and why should the HO protect the holders of unpopular opinions from the consequences of their unwisdom? Protecting Ramsay MacDonald in Stanton country was rather like protecting a Jesuit in Shankhill. 'As to the future', he finished,

we must judge each case, as we do now, on its merits. It is impossible for me to guarantee in all cases and at all times, especially as the police forces are so depleted owing to the War, that every pacifist meeting shall remain undisturbed.[97]

The only way to do that would be to request military assistance. No Home Secretary liked calling in the army; particularly when

our Army is fighting against a foreign enemy, to bring in a military force in order to protect pacifist meetings against interruption is clearly a course which it is utterly impossible for any Home Secretary to adopt. Subject to that qualification, the Home Office and the police author-ities will do their best within the measure of their powers to prevent mob law, and to secure that freedom of speech which even in time of War the Government of this country has, however, tried to maintain.[98]

Neither the patriots nor the dissenters were much impressed by Samuel's reassertion of a policy which strove, at least, to be relatively even-handed – at a minimum to avoid open commitment to either side;

in the meantime, of course, furthering the government agenda. Doing nothing, after all, was implicitly to support the patriots as the more violent side in the dispute. Neither side was willing to let the matter stop here. With something rather more than impudence, Stanton continued to call upon the HO to provide protection for patriotic meetings, then being broken up, he charged, by pacifist gangs – 'organized bands of independent labour persons, syndicalists, pro-Hun and anti-British peace advocates'.[99] Samuel minuted privately that there was nothing for him to do here, since it seemed hardly credible that patriots required police protection. Samuel's disbelief is probably understandable.

The attitude of the House of Commons was substantially that of the press: predominantly supportive of the patriots, rather than sympathetic to the dissenters. This is not surprising, given the fact that much of the national press was controlled by the press lords (the Northcliffe–Rothermere combine, and Beaverbrook especially) – themselves convinced patriots, and already implicated in inciting domestic violence against dissent. *The Times* considered it a 'pity when people are forced to take the law into their own hands', and thought that 'the Government must realize that there is still a limit to human endurance'.[100] The *Daily Express* considered the riot 'a natural result of a gratuitous affront', and carried its coverage under the headline 'PEACE CRANKS ROUTED. Cardiff's Lesson to the Friends of Germany. Mr Winstone pelted with Tomatoes'.[101] The *Daily Mail*, similarly, covered the story under the rubric: 'THE FLIGHT OF MR. RAMSAY MACDONALD. FIRST TO BOLT'.[102]

Of all the major newspapers, only the independent *Daily News* and *Manchester Guardian* were censorious of the patriot excesses. Of course the proprietor of the *Daily News* was the prominent Quaker, George Cadbury, while a staunch Liberal, C. P. Scott, ran the *Manchester Guardian*. Their disapproval was to be expected. Stanton, the *News* reported, at a meeting the day before the riot, had exhorted 'his approving audience "to stop these men by any means short of murder"'. 'He appears', it continued, 'to have been permitted to carry his threat into execution with singularly little opposition.'[103] The *Guardian* considered the whole episode 'A Discreditable Affair'.[104] It was 'deplorable', both thought, that a breach of the peace could be advertised in advance and permitted to go ahead. This was also, by and large, the line taken by the local *South Wales Daily News*: '[t]he best reply to pacifism is to oppose it with the truth in free and fearless discussion. In every such encounter it will be routed in the future as in the past'.[105] At the time, of course, many were not inclined to be even as tolerant as this.

The last mention of the incident in HO files came in December, when the chief constable of Cardiff forwarded to Samuel a copy of a handbill, widely distributed, appealing for subscriptions to meet the cost of the counter-demonstration.[106] The handbill was probably the same one which Atherley Jones, with almost unbelievable impertinence, had already despatched to Ramsay MacDonald. 'Please don't put this letter in the wastepaper basket. Do me the justice of at least reading it, and sending me any reply you think fit.' Attached, of course, was an appeal for money, the counter-demonstration having cost over £100, and only £23 having been raised by subscription.[107] Ramsay's MacDonald's reply (if any) has not survived in his correspondence.

The public hostile, the press and the House of Commons unsympathetic, the dissenters could do little more than attempt to put their case before the only sympathetic audience they could find, at public meetings of like-minded individuals, growing increasingly shrill if only in the effort to be heard. The day after the battle of Cory Hall, MacDonald ended a speech at such a meeting:

> But still there were circumstances which made it impossible to hold the conference yesterday. There are certain people and certain things that are so loathsome to men who have any self-respect and common decency, that when the former appear the latter prefer to go. At this moment, when the best of our land are giving their lives for what they believe to be the liberty of the country – that those should be championed by a man who reeled and staggered to that conference [Stanton] – (shame) – is one of the most insulting and disgraceful things ever thrown in the teeth of the British Army (shame).[108]

'That conference', MacDonald promised, 'is to be held. (Applause.) Those resolutions are to be passed, and the speeches that were not delivered yesterday are only postponed for a week or two and will not suffer by the postponement'.[109] MacDonald, hitherto an advocate of conciliation, steadily began to become more intransigent, it having become clear that there was little tolerance coming from the other side in the debate, and still less desire for compromise. For his part, old J. H. Thomas, a supporter of the war, was left wondering how he could continue to advocate quiet on the home front, in the interest of the war effort, when things like the battle of Cory Hall were allowed to happen.[110] It was a sign of his confusion that even while tremendously angry as he undoubtedly was, Thomas still played a crucial part in bringing Lloyd George to power and would certainly have served with him if invited to join the War Cabinet.[111] The general pattern was that dissent, having begot the patriot reaction, was itself consolidated and pushed to greater, more active, confrontational, and total dissent by reaction. It is good that the war ended before this process reached its logical conclusion either with civil war, or the total victory of either tendency, concentrated during the process of opposition.

Whether we consider the battle of Cory Hall a discreditable affair, best forgotten, or the inevitable product of a society splintering under the great pressure produced by total war, it certainly illustrates that the shape assumed by British society during the Great War was rather more complex than that often portrayed. In south Wales, in November 1916, we do not find either a split developing along an existing social fault line, or national solidarity renewed by the war. Both of these views are too simplistic. We see instead a situation in which not only were classes turning against one another, as the war affected them differently, but a working class which, in particular, reacted diversely to a stimulus productive of very different effects, interpreted in different ways. This picture, rather than either simplified image, is the one which emerges most clearly when actual events on the home front are examined for what they were. To consider the battle of Cory Hall and the wartime Cardiff in which it took place, is to step away from easy answers. To consider wartime Britain, made up, after all of thousands of such local systems, each in part unique, is certainly to get no closer. To deny or invalidate diversity, however, is certainly to present an inaccurate picture of the truth.

MacDonald and Samuel were not the only ones shocked by what had happened at Cory Hall. In the aftermath of Cardiff, the willingness of local authorities to permit dissenting meetings to proceed declined still further. The level of violence which had been seen at Cardiff, moreover, increased local willingness to take police cautions at full value. Occasionally, a police official, acting on his own, would prohibit dissenting meetings altogether in order to avoid the development of Cardiff-style violence on his beat. At Ilkeston, for instance, Superintendent Charles Walker prohibited a peace meeting scheduled for the end of November on the grounds that it was certain to lead to violence. The HO, while doubting that he had grounds for doing so, approved his action and judged that he had probably acted in good faith.[112] In good faith or not, his fears were certainly well grounded. Where halls were not denied, or where police prohibitions were not enforced, violence was virtually inevitable.

In February 1917, for example, a meeting at Stockton-on-Tees, in support of the Peace by Negotiations by-election candidate, Edward Backhouse, at which Charles Trevelyan was scheduled to speak, was broken up by a 'very hostile' crowd which ended by 'storming the platform and breaking up the meeting'.[113] A meeting in Hull at which

Snowden was to speak was broken up by a group of sailors led by a Methodist minister before it could even begin.[114] About the same time, the 'Herald' speeches in Finsbury Park in London came under constant attack. They continued, however, despite demands from the local populous that they be stopped outright by police prohibition. Why should they be stopped, the HO wondered, when they were regularly attended by members of the CID, and were never allowed to amount to much in any case?[115]

It was not just meetings which patriots found annoying. Tolerance for dissenting publications was declining. About the same time that the public was pushing to end open-air anti-war meetings, Major Hunt, in the House of Commons, demanded an assurance from the Prime Minister that all anti-patriotic literature (i.e. all literature calling for an inconclusive peace) would be seized and destroyed and proceedings instituted against those involved in its production and dissemination. Samuel, still Home Secretary, was unable to give him such an assurance.[116]

At this low ebb in Allied fortunes, the government was plainly at a loss as to how to handle the pressure coming from both sides. The Asquith government never did find a way of dealing with the divide that was beginning to emerge in British society. It had learned to tolerate the patriots for what they could do. By November 1916, however, they were becoming dangerous, and growing increasingly critical of the government for what was taken to be its weak handling of the war, best exemplified, perhaps, by its unwillingness to act vigorously at home. The tool, in short, was becoming master. From December 1916, the Lloyd George government wrestled with the same problem. Initially, on the home front, while it was characterized by a more aggressive style and composed of more bellicose ministers, it had few more productive ideas than that of its predecessor – to look elsewhere while problems were settled on the streets. It learned quickly. It was during the Lloyd George period that the various elements in the practice of suppression were systematized and given official sanction, albeit in a covert form.

NOTES

1. Wrigley, *David Lloyd George*, pp. 179–81.
2. See, for instance, J. M. Winter, *Socialism and the Challenge of War: Ideas and Politics in Britain* (London: Routledge & Kegan Paul, 1974), p. 208; Arnot, *The Miners*, pp. 164–70; K. O. Morgan, 'Peace Movements in Wales', *Welsh History Review*, X, 1 (1988); A. O'Brien, 'Patriotism on Trial: The Strike of the South Wales Miners, July 1915', *Welsh Historical Review*, 30 (1984).

3. Adams and Poirier, *The Conscription Controversy*, p. 132.
4. D. Egan, 'A Cult of Their Own?: Syndicalism and the Miners' Next Step', in A. Campbell, N. Fishman and D. Howell (eds), *Miners, Unions and Politics 1910–1947* (Aldershot: Scolar Press, 1996), p. 20.
5. Lord Rhondda, *This Was My World* (London: Macmillan, 1933), p. 199.
6. Williams, 'The Hope of the British Proletariat', p. 133.
7. HLRO, Lloyd George Papers, F 4/2/10, 'Barnes Memorandum of Interview with Mr D. Lleufer Thomas, Chairman of the Wales Commission of Enquiry into Industrial Unrest', 20 August 1917. See also Williams, 'The Hope of the British Proletariat', p. 133.
8. D. Gilbert, *Class, Community and Collective Action* (Oxford: Clarendon, 1992), p. 67. See also P. Morgan and P. Thomas, *Wales: the Shaping of a Nation* (Newton Abbot: David & Charles, 1984), p. 141; K. Morgan, *Rebirth of a Nation: Wales 1880–1980* (Oxford: Clarendon, 1981), pp. 124–6.
9. See, for example, Francis and Smith, *The Fed*, pp. 12–14, 41.
10. Gilbert, *Class, Community and Collective Action*, p. 80; Williams, 'The Hope of the British Proletariat', p. 125; Morgan and Thomas, *Wales*, p. 144.
11. Gilbert, *Class, Community and Collective Action*, p. 80.
12. Simpson, *Labour*, p. 68. See also M. Foot, *Aneurin Bevan*, Vol. I (London: MacGibbon & Kee, 1962), pp. 32–5; V. Brome, *Aneurin Bevan* (London: Longman, 1953). For radicalism in Wales, in general, see G. Jones, *Modern Wales* (Cambridge: Cambridge University Press, 1984), pp. 226–44.
13. Morgan, *Rebirth of a Nation*, p. 137.
14. Clegg, *A History of British Trade Unionism*, Vol. II, p. 47. Kenneth Morgan makes the strange claim, on the other hand, that 'Above all, Edwardian Wales was a land of relative peace', *Rebirth of a Nation*, p. 137.
15. Jones, *Modern Wales*, p. 255.
16. Williams, 'The Hope of the British Proletariat', p. 125; Francis and Smith, *The Fed*, pp. 18–22.
17. Williams, 'The Hope of the British Proletariat', p. 124. Stanton had been 'considered to be a near revolutionary' in the period before the war, Morgan, *Rebirth of a Nation*, p. 144.
18. Morgan, *Rebirth of a Nation*, p. 148.
19. Gilbert, *Class, Community and Collective Action*, pp. 76–7; Clegg, *A History of British Trade Unionism*, Vol. II, p. 45.
20. Commons Debates, 87, 14 November 1916, cols. 718–19, 721–2.
21. Arnot, *The Miners*, p. 170.
22. Morgan, *Rebirth of a Nation*, p. 160.
23. Morgan and Thomas, *Wales*, p. 144; G. Jones, *Modern Wales*, p. 249; and, K. Morgan, *Rebirth of a Nation*, p. 145.
24. Jones, *Modern Wales*, p. 256. Support for Lloyd George, Jones tells us, was 'whole-hearted' throughout the war. In the 1918 coupon election, waged in Wales as a test of Lloyd George's personal popularity, coalition Liberals won 25 of 36 Welsh seats, with Labour victorious in ten.
25. Morgan, *Rebirth of a Nation*, p. 137.
26. Ibid., p. 144.
27. Ibid., p. 144.
28. Morgan and Thomas, *Wales*, p. 146. Welsh radicals had already demonstrated dislike of any form of internationalism. Sometimes this took the form of outright pro-British chauvinism. In the riots before the war the property of Jewish landlords had been a particular focus of attack, Morgan, *Rebirth of a Nation*, p. 148.
29. Jones, *Modern Wales*, p. 249. Similarly, his daughter (later the Viscountess Rhondda)

had been a radical, prewar suffragette. During the war, however, she worked for her father and the government – ultimately serving as head of the women's section of the Ministry of National Service. S. M. Eoff, *Viscountess Rhondda: Egalitarian Feminist* (Cleveland: Ohio State University Press, 1991), pp. 34–63.

30. J. M. Winter, *The Great War and the British People* (Basingstoke: Macmillan, 1986), p. 35; Morgan, *Rebirth of a Nation*, p. 160.
31. Morgan, *Rebirth of a Nation*, p. 166.
32. PRO 30/69/1159, Merthyr Tydfil Association to MacDonald, 20 October 1915.
33. Winter, *Socialism and the Challenge of War*, p. 209.
34. Williams, 'The Hope of the British Proletariat', p. 125; Clegg, *A History of British Trade Unionism*, Vol. II, bibliographical appendix.
35. Morgan, *Rebirth of a Nation*, p. 165.
36. In January 1916, Winstone, with many other leading dissenters, signed a petition addressed to Sir John Simon, asking him to move into open opposition to lead the fight against dissent. Simon had just resigned from the government on the issue of conscription. He was hardly a revolutionary firebrand. BLO, Simon Papers, Simon 52, circular letter to Simon, 11 January 1916. On the other hand, Winstone had addressed recruiting meetings, and already had a son at the front, Morgan, *Rebirth of a Nation*, p. 173.
37. PRO 30/69/1159, Winstone's speech accepting nomination at Merthyr Tydfil.
38. Morgan, *Rebirth of a Nation*, p. 165.
39. Example: HLRO, Blumenfeld Papers, Ce.1, Robert Cecil to Blumenfeld, 28 January 1916. 'I have received your letter of the 26th and am very much obliged to you for having kindly let me see the letter which Mr Stanton has sent to you for publication in the 'Daily Express'. // The reproduction of so fiery a letter in your paper would not, I think, be in the public interest'.
40. Morgan, *Rebirth of a Nation*, p. 173.
41. Adams and Poirier, *The Conscription Controversy*, p. 132.
42. So he is remembered, in any case, in Labour history. Carl Brand refers to him, though not by name, as 'an independent pro-war Labour man with unofficial Unionist and Liberal backing', Brand, *British Labour's Rise to Power*, p. 49.
43. PRO 30/69/1159, 'What Mr Winstone's Party and Supporters Have Said on the War', November 1915.
44. PRO 30/69/1159, 'Put Your Patriotism First and Vote for Stanton'.
45. Morgan, *Rebirth of a Nation*, p. 173.
46. Brand, *British Labour's Rise to Power*, p. 37.
47. Ibid., p. 49; Schneer, *Ben Tillett*, p. 193. Ellis, however, was a good catch. Not only was he the president of the ASFU, but he had been a member of the parliamentary committee of the TUC (1889–98, and again in 1918–19) and an MP (1892–95; and again, 1918–22), Clegg, *A History of British Trade Unionism*, Vol. II, biographical appendix.
48. W. M. Walker, *Juteopolis: Dundee and Its Textile Workers* (Edinburgh: Scottish Academic Press, 1979), pp. 379–80, 450–2.
49. Brand, *British Labour's Rise to Power*, p. 32.
50. Morgan, *Rebirth of a Nation*, p. 163. This was the trip which, however, earned him the animosity of General Cockerill, and swiftly resulted in the restriction of his movements. See Chapter 3, and MUH, Russell Papers, volume 710, Russell note, 5 September 1916.
51. MUH, Vol. 410, Clifford Allen to Bertrand Russell, 27 June 1916.
52. PRO 30 30/69/1160, Atherley Jones Circular, 16 November 1916.
53. P. Bagwell, *The Railwaymen* (London: George Allen & Unwin, 1963), p. 352.
54. Commons Debates, 87, 14 November 1916, col. 711.

55. Commons Debates, 87, 14 November 1916, col. 717; Bagwell, *The Railwaymen*, p. 356. Present at the September meeting between Thomas and Robertson were the Minister of Munitions, the President of the Board of Trade and the Minister of Labour.
56. Commons Debates, 87, 14 November 1916, col. 711.
57. Wrigley, *David Lloyd George*, p. 181.
58. Ibid.
59. Commons Debates, 87, 14 November, col. 715.
60. PRO 30/69/1160, 'The Career of W. H. Atherley Jones'.
61. Carried in *Western Mail* and *South Wales Daily News* on 30 and 31 October 1916.
62. Morgan, *Rebirth of a Nation*, p. 162.
63. *Western Mail*, 9 November 1916. The advertisement for the counter-demonstration called upon citizens of Cardiff to 'COME IN YOUR THOUSANDS AND PROVE THAT YOU ARE TRUE BRITISHERS'; also, Commons Debates, 87, 14 November 1916, col. 715.
64. PRO 30/69/1251, *New Wales Daily News*, 11 November 1916.
65. Ibid.
66. Ibid.
67. PRO 30/69/1251, Thomas to MacDonald, October 1916.
68. PRO HO 45 10810/311932, Samuel to Cardiff Chief Constable, 10 November 1916.
69. *Daily Mail*, 13 November 1916.
70. PRO HO 45 10810/311932, Cardiff Police to HO, 9 November 1916.
71. PRO HO 45 10810/311932, file 19, Public Meeting at Cardiff, 9 November 1916.
72. *The Times*, 13 November 1916.
73. PRO HO 45 10810/311932, file 19, Cardiff Police to Samuel, 9 November 1916.
74. Ibid., file 19.
75. PRO 30/69/1251, *New Wales Daily News*, 11 November 1916.
76. PRO 30/69/1251, *The Pioneer*, 18 November 1916.
77. *Daily Express*, 16 November 1916.
78. *Daily Mail*, 13 November 1916.
79. PRO HO 45 10810/311932, file 19; *The Times*, 13 November 1916; *Daily Express* 13 November 1916; *Daily News*, 13 November 1916.
80. *Western Mail*, 13 November 1916.
81. *Daily Express*, 16 November 1916.
82. PRO HO 45 10810/311932, file 19. See also file 20, Cardiff Chief Constable to Samuel, 13 November 1916.
83. *The Times*, 13 November 1916.
84. PRO WO 161/107, 'VF: Organisation and Administration', 'Memorandum on Volunteer Force', 12 October 1916. Volunteers available for duty as special constables were designated 'Section P', and a list of names maintained. See also, for police reserve, PRO MEPO 5/118, Special Reserve.
85. C. Dakers, *The Countryside at War* (London: Constable, 1987), p. 119.
86. PRO HO 45 10810/311932, file 20.
87. Commons Debates, 87, Session 7 November to 23 November 1916, 14 November, col. 593.
88. PRO HO 45 10810/311932, file 26, November 1916. Commons Debates, 1916, 87, 14 November, col. 593.
89. Commons Debates, 1916, 87, 14 November, col. 593.
90. Ibid., col. 594; also col. 596.
91. Ibid., col. 595.
92. Ibid., col. 596.
93. Ibid., col. 596.
94. Ibid., cols. 731–9.

95. Ibid., cols. 721–6.
96. Ibid., cols. 740–6.
97. Ibid.
98. Ibid.
99. PRO HO 45 10743/263275, file 261, 1 November 1916.
100. *The Times*, 13 November 1916.
101. *Daily Express*, 13 November 1916. The dissenters were denounced, variously, as the Kaiser's 'agents', his 'friends' and his 'dupes'. The UDC was stigmatized as 'U(nter) D(eutsches) C(ontrol)'. Those attending, the *Daily Express* continued, were 'chiefly pasty-faced, weedy lads who could be picked out of the crowd as conscientious objectors'.
102. *Daily Mail*, 13 November 1916. Its coverage continued that upon the approach of the counter-demonstrators, a white and shaking MacDonald 'was off the platform in an instant and through a side door, of which he had apparently made earlier acquaintance'.
103. *Daily News*, 13 November 1916.
104. *Manchester Guardian*, 13 November 1916.
105. *South Wales Daily News*, 13 November 1916.
106. PRO HO 45 10810/311932, file 29, Chief Constable Cardiff to HO, 4 December 1916. For public reaction, see also, file 32, 7 December 1916.
107. PRO 30/69/1160, Atherley Jones to MacDonald, 16 November 1916.
108. *Aberaman Leader*, 18 November 1916.
109. *Aberaman Leader*, 18 November 1916. The conference was ultimately held, but only because Samuel, by his personal intervention, was able to convince Stanton to allow it to take place. Pankhurst, *The Home Front*, p. 418.
110. Commons Debates, 88, 14 November 1916, col. 720.
111. Bagwell, *The Railwaymen*, p. 356; Davies, *The Prime Minister's Secretariat*, p. 19. On 8 December 1916, Thomas offered to serve in the government as Minister of Labour provided that he received a seat in the War Cabinet. When this was not possible, the offer lapsed.
112. PRO HO 45 10810/311932, file 33, 18 December 1916.
113. *The Times*, 3 March 1917.
114. Snowden, *Autobiography*, p. 419.
115. PRO HO 45 10743/263275, file 249, 25 September 1917.
116. PRO HO 45 10743/263275, file 256, 18 October 1917.

7

The Lloyd George Solution

A S MIGHT be expected, the very fact of the Lloyd George government accentuated the divide between patriots and dissenters. For many dissenters the Lloyd George government was a war-loving dictatorship. The hatred of the dissenters would probably have to be accepted. It was to the patriots that the new administration looked for support – those people who, according to Lord Curzon, were 'not merely willing to be led, but ... almost asking to be driven'.[1] To these Lloyd George promised total measures consistent with total war. Asquith had almost flinched at conscription: Lloyd George, the patriots were assured, would implement even total labour compulsion if that were necessary for victory.[2] And yet, for the patriots, the new Lloyd George coalition did not seem to be much of an improvement on the despised 'Squiff' administration, at least in the early months while it was finding its feet. If anything, the strategic situation became more dire. Lloyd George came in with a flood of promises to improve the manpower situation. The result? The lacklustre tenure of Neville Chamberlain as manpower controller – a period of fewer men and galloping exemptions.[3] Nor did the government move quickly and decisively against dissent. That it was going to have to find some solution was obvious in the aftermath of Cory Hall.

Exaggerated expectations on all sides were not Lloyd George's only problem. During his first months in office, the nature of dissent was changing quickly, and, from his perspective, entirely for the worse. Two factors were principally responsible: the galloping association in wartime of those with workplace and social grievances, and the example of the Russian revolution. The former, by the end of 1917, had produced something like an embryo revolutionary amalgam. The second accelerated the movement of this amalgam towards dissociation from the war as a first step. Each of these processes was, of course, affected by the other. Each, and the response produced by the Lloyd George government, will be considered serially in what follows.

One factor encouraging the unification of dissent was the way in which Lloyd George had come to power. The problem was that Asquith, bitter at Lloyd George's betrayal, refused to support the new government. Lloyd George became premier in undisguised alliance, even dependence upon, the Unionists. Asquith, like McKenna and Simon, refused to use his independence to reassemble an opposition party in the House. Thereafter he presided over a dwindling and ineffective rump of party stalwarts. Lloyd George, meanwhile, had been compromised as a viable Liberal leader. One half of the Liberal Party had reduced itself to impotence: the other steadily began to betray everything Gladstonian Liberalism stood for. Effectively, the great Liberal Party had committed suicide. Until this time it was the Liberal Party which had been the primary focus of radicalism and, as such, the focus of dissenting hopes. From December 1916, those who opposed the war – whatever their prewar political coloration might have been – quickly began to defect to the ILP. That the Labour Party became the vehicle through which radicalism found expression was the primary reason that it, rather than the Liberal Party, emerged as one of the parties which dominated the peace.[4] For our purposes, however, the most important consequence of Liberal disarray was the growing unity of dissent. Increasingly dissent = UDC = ILP. It was at about this juncture, for instance, that Gilbert Cannan (NAC), Herbert Dunnico (Peace Society) and Leonard Woolf (Fabian Society) entered the ILP.[5] They had been followed by the end of the war by Morel and Ponsonby, and shortly after the war, by Trevelyan,[6] Russell and Angell; a bitter Morel – just released from prison – moved from his position that to associate the UDC with any one party was to make a mistake,[7] to the position seemingly being espoused by Russell from 1916 – that dissent implied membership of the UDC, involved necessarily affiliation with the ILP.[8] This was a dangerous development.

Meanwhile dissent was becoming steadily more effective and radical. This was, in part, because of the defection of the less convinced. The more squeamish dissenters, through the latter war years, dropped from view as dissent began necessarily to involve conspiracy and the acceptance of violence: the first because open, effective operation was ever more difficult, the second if only in answer to the patriots. If dissent was finding effective responses to the nature of the suppression employed, it also was coming to imply opposition to the government, and perhaps to the existing order. Moreover, as dissent began to move away from its Christian roots towards the socialist critique, government and social inhibitions against direct action, even pre-emption, began to drop away. The process was reinforced.

Sometimes the rarefied dissent which resulted from this process took dangerous forms. Within the trade unions, for instance, the rank and file movement had come to be strongly influenced by agitators who were less anti-war in principle than anti-war because syndicalist. The war, for these dissenters, was not a crime but an opportunity. From the second general conference of the rank and file movement, on 3–4 March 1917, the syndicalists were working less to gain satisfaction for labour grievances than to find an excuse for a general strike which they would use to further an advanced political agenda.[9] Quickly this programme began to associate itself with anti-war dissent. The ILP, UDC and the fighting organizations were penetrated and began to tack in this direction. This, again, was a dangerous development, and hardly what Morel had in mind when he began to associate class and workplace with anti-war dissent in 1914. The tool was beginning to become the master.

While anti-war dissent gained coherence and virulence, the man-power question grew more urgent and productive of a popular audience. As the Battle of the Somme gave way to Arras, to the Third Battle of Ypres, Britain's manpower situation became desperate. Despite the Allies' best efforts, the Germans had gone from victory to victory. Britain's allies were failing. The strength of the British Expeditionary Force peaked in 1917, and it would thereafter inevitably decline unless there were some radical departure in policy. Conscription had been introduced in 1916. To many it seemed essential that complete control of labour be introduced so that the domestic work force could be efficiently 'thinned out'. Unfortunately for Lloyd George, the Asquith government had always promised that total controls would not be essential. The dissenters had always insisted, on the other hand, that conscription would necessarily lead to compulsion. In reneging on its promises, the government proved the dissenters right in this instance. But the dissenters, as we have seen, had not stopped there. The government would use compulsion, they warned, to break the unions and reduce the working class to new dependence and misery. Were they right in this also? To many it seemed so. The movement to broader manpower controls accelerated the linkage of large sections of organized labour to dissent and encouraged the development of an amalgam which was implicitly revolutionary.

By spring 1917 the compulsion debate had produced a rash of political strikes, particularly in the engineering trades, which, for a time, appeared to presage the type of domestic discontent which had just brought Russia down. The crux of the problem was that the promises of 1916, within four months of being made, were totally obsolete. The government, remember, had promised during the Sheffield ASE strikes not to touch the union-controlled exemption card scheme. In March

1917 the government attempted to cancel the union scheme and to substitute a government-controlled Schedule of Protected Occupations.[10] Despite last-minute agreement with the ASE leadership, by May 1917, 200,000 men were on strike and ultimately 1.5 million working days were lost.

In April, the HO informed chief constables that it had received intelligence which suggested that a movement was afoot to organize labour involved in munitions production, at a level obviously more than local, in order to create unrest in this vulnerable economic sector.[11] The engineers, it was feared, were no longer protesting against conditions of work. Led by their shop stewards, they were organizing revolution. In response, chief constables were instructed at this time to watch for, and gather evidence of, revolutionary organization in industry, and to report on all meetings of workers, speeches and anything else suggesting 'dissatisfaction with working conditions' – breakdown of arrangements for paying, transporting, housing or feeding workers, and so on. In effect, they were to infiltrate labour organizations and spy. 'Black lists' of suspect individuals (those who were to be pre-emptively arrested in the event of a substantial industrial disturbance) were prepared, and distributed, though these lists themselves are not now available.[12]

Even so, the strikers were only brought back to work following the arrest of 15 shop stewards on 9 May. Another seven were arrested ten days later. The men chosen for arrest had obviously been selected with an eye to deterrent effect. The fact that the government knew, by this time, exactly whom to arrest attests to the efficiency of police activities in April. Of the first nine arrested, two each were snapped up in Manchester, London, Sheffield and Coventry, with the ninth being jailed in Leicester.[13] With further arrests prepared the promise was wrung from the government by George Barnes (himself an engineer) that those already arrested would be released if work resumed.[14] An important thing to note about these arrests is that they occurred without warrant, DRR 14 being invoked to permit pre-emptive arrest. This was the only time in wartime Britain that the government went so far. The Cabinet was persuaded to countenance such drastic action because it believed that a national, general strike was in the offing.[15]

A lasting legacy of the May strikes was the creation of the Commission on Industrial Unrest, under George Barnes. In theory it was intended to identify and settle grievances before they led to industrial action.[16] In the end, with a network of local commissions and integral police liaison, the Commission became yet another domestic surveillance and intelligence sharing mechanism as well.

About the time Lloyd George came to power, therefore, Britain entered the danger period of the war on the home front. 1915 had seen the effective unification of the dissenting leadership, and the creation of skeleton organizations. 1916 had seen a critique developed, and issues and methods identified. In 1917 force and mass were to flow into the forms constructed. Grievances accentuated by the war, as Morel had predicted, were producing a discontent which was being channelled into support for anti-war activity – if not always those activities of which Morel would have approved. Not only did dissent appear, it actually was much more effective. 'We are today', the prominent Quaker C. R. Buxton noted in May 1917,

> no longer the preachers of a desperately unpopular doctrine. A year ago we were treated with contempt, as a negligible minority. To-day we have become strong enough to be feared and ... tomorrow, we shall be resisted but we shall be a formidable fighting force, not capable of being suppressed ...[17]

Even commentators outside the government could see that the coalescence of dissent represented a new, and much more dangerous, threat. 'Above all', C. P. Scott wrote in his diary somewhat later,

> it [is] necessary to disassociate the extreme anti-war movement of a small minority from the industrial issue with which it [is] at present combined and through which it [is] liable to derive altogether fictitious strength.[18]

This was an assessment with which the Lloyd George government would have agreed, and a process that it had been assembled to combat.

The new government met the challenge, in part, by a far more sympathetic and astute handling of labour issues. Palliation of discontent – dealing with problems before they could become the cause of political dissent – was always Lloyd George's favourite method.

One of the more universal of working-class grievances was easily dealt with. It was that with the war in its third year nobody had yet bothered to explain what Britain was fighting for. Early in 1916, the bumptious MFGB had sponsored and narrowly passed through the TUC a demand for the reconstitution of a joint board for foreign policy with the Labour Party, excluding the government-friendly General Federation of Trade Unions (GFTU) in order to press the government on this issue. The TUC, as a whole, supported the proposal for tactical rather than for ideological reasons. This procedure would give it greater leverage in the Labour Party, and might allow it to restrain the dissenters. Smillie's aim, however, was to give the UDC platform the imprint of the TUC.[19]

Lloyd George recognized a political danger when he saw one. If war aims were important to the workers, then Lloyd George would work to convince them that the war was being fought for aims with which they could sympathize. Might this not take the sting from MacDonald's charge that the war was being fought to put France in Syria, Italy in Dalmatia and Russia at the Straits, with the enormous residual, of course, accruing to Britain?[20] Might it not, as well, pre-empt the proclamation of the US position, particularly any call for a negotiated peace? Throughout 1917, Lloyd George tested the waters. The war, he informed C. P. Scott in March 1917, was being waged to achieve three things: the elimination of militarism, the establishment of democratic governments, and the 'destruction of the barbarous domination of the Turk' – principles sufficiently exalted to gladden Liberal hearts.[21] Two days before Wilson proclaimed his 'Fourteen Points' Lloyd George made a major statement before a TUC audience at Caxton Hall, Westminster. Lloyd George considered this the 'most important speech [he had] yet made'.[22] The war was being fought to defend democracy and the rights of small nations, to end war by eliminating militarism, and to produce a more equitable system at home, not to obtain any squalid territorial revision. It speaks for the purpose of the exercise, of course, that Lloyd George chose a TUC forum for this major policy pronouncement. It is certainly significant as well that Lloyd George's line was virtually identical to the war aims recently adopted by the TUC/Labour Party joint committee, and bore almost no relation to the war aims being produced by the cabinet committees looking into the question.[23] Lloyd George's speech was much more a palliation of dissent than a statement of British policy. It worked. Lloyd George's war aims were immediately acclaimed by Labour.[24]

Lloyd George did not stop here. The vision of the postwar world being related to combatant Britain was also recast in order to give ammunition to patriotic labour. It was better still if some elements of the Lloyd George vision were actually anticipated during the war. Soft-pedalling industrial compulsion, and ensuring the passing of the Representation of the People Act in 1918 were probably the most important things Lloyd George actually did during the war to consolidate labour behind the national cause. The second, particularly, was no small thing.[25] The idea, of course, was to make an increasingly class-based anti-war critique simply irrelevant to British realities. If that were not possible, then Lloyd George could still hope to prevent a coalescence of labour opposition against the government. Labour patriots, in effect, if no longer effortlessly dominant, were nonetheless, active, convinced, missionary and combative.

Lloyd George was also vigilant to ensure the loyalty of patriotic labour because he planned to use the volatile conditions produced by the war to remake British politics, and afterwards, Britain itself. This plan was not without powerful wartime implications. Incidentally, of course, Lloyd George would consolidate his own hold on power. In 1916, he was a man without a party. He would not endure long if this remained so. He might have attempted to capture the Liberal Party from Asquith. Lloyd George, however, considered the party to be quite plainly 'moribund'. Its ideas, like its leaders, were survivors from a previous age.[26] He had no option, therefore, but to construct a party machine of his own. If he failed, he would remain a prisoner of the Unionists, used for the war, and then cast off.[27] From the time he took power Lloyd George set out to hijack the Unionist faction. He hoped that it, like the Labour and Liberal parties, might be shattered by the war and its active elements worked into a new political structure designed to supersede the old parties, and render irrelevant the partisan and class conflicts of the past. Such a structure, he hoped, would be competent to settle the urgent questions of the day and reorganize the country on sounder bases for the future. He and the few Liberals around him would provide executive direction. The Unionists would provide organization, money and parliamentary mass. A popular element, however, was essential if the new party were to fly. Lloyd George was always attempting to draw his Labour collaborators (Henderson and then Barnes and their PLP colleagues) into formal association. There was as well the BWNL – by the end of 1917, the instrument of Lloyd George.[28] Could these be brought together, separated from their dissenting comrades, and permanently associated within the new party? Lloyd George hoped that would be possible.

For his association and policies, Lloyd George has sometimes been accused, as Premier, of betraying the liberal, radical and populist principles which had guided his conduct prior to the war. While it was certainly true that Lloyd George as Prime Minister was hardly the radical of 1900, it is also true that the times had changed. Moreover, it was Lloyd George's practice more than his principles which had changed. If he had parted company with Liberalism, he was no less a committed populist and radical. He had always been attracted to the idea of national efficiency, and if some other principles were sacrificed on this altar then so be it.[29] It is not necessary to be tolerant, liberal or even democratic in order to be populist and radical. National efficiency is not inconsistent with populism; indeed, in the British context it was almost inconceivable without it. The career of Joseph Chamberlain had already indicated that it is possible to be as populist and radical at one end of the political spectrum as at the other. Lloyd George had simply made the same journey. It is probably true as well that by 1917 Lloyd George had few real choices. The perceptive Lord Esher considered that, having been brought to power to wage the war more vigorously, Lloyd George would have to do whatever had to be done to implement his programmes or go the way of Asquith, probably taking Britain's chances for victory with him. Lloyd George would have to rule like Cromwell if he were not to see every effort nullified and every chance lost.[30] If Lloyd George shrank from the challenge someone else (Carson) would unite the patriots and do the job. As Bonar Law realized, that might well mean civil war or martial law. In turning outside Britain to wage the war more effectively, moreover, it is probable that Lloyd George had already embarked on a course which would require greater ruthlessness at home. Tightened control, even repression at home is inherent in total war. 'Whoever wants to defend it [civilization] from external challenges faces a dilemma', Erzensberger quite correctly observes. 'The more fiercely civilization defends itself against an external threat and puts up barriers around itself, the less, in the end, it has left to defend.'[31]

The Lloyd George coalition government was constructed in such a manner as to provide both method and message. What would the new Britain look like? Look at the government. What were the particulars of Lloyd George's 'Nationalism–Socialism' programme? Look to the government, its nature and policies. There Nationalism–Socialism was foreshadowed.

The corporatist nature of the new line was immediately apparent. Businessmen, for instance, were brought in to take control of government agencies it was thought their prior experience would most perfectly fit them to lead. Labour representatives sat in the government because it was considered necessary and fitting that a balance be maintained. Charged by Bonar Law with introducing unqualified men to important offices, Lloyd George responded:

> They are not Ministers because they are the most suitable men, but because they represent a large class, who should have a voice in the government of the country.[32]

There were six Labour Party members of the Lloyd George government, one of whom (Arthur Henderson, and then George Barnes) was in the War Cabinet.[33]

The press was one of the more important business 'corporations' with

FIGURE 3: MATURE LLOYD GEORGE SYSTEM, 1917

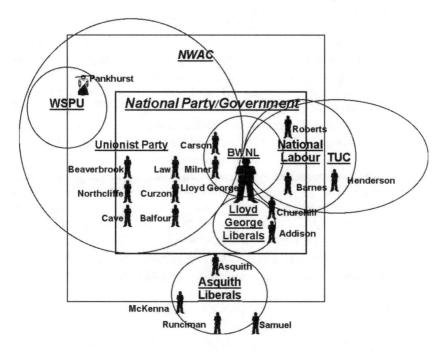

which Lloyd George was determined to remain on good terms. It is entirely significant that Rothermere, Northcliffe and Beaverbrook served in his administration, two of them in publicity ministries. The co-option of the press lords would ensure, if nothing else, that the new vision was implemented amidst a wave of favourable publicity. Meanwhile (a major consideration for Lloyd George) they would work for, rather than against, the new vision.[34] Lloyd George looked to the press lords, and particularly to his friend, the ever helpful Lord Beaverbrook, to fund his new party.[35] The inclusion of the press lords ultimately meant as well the colonization of the propaganda apparatus of state by convinced patriots, who came to office with policies and associates of their own, which ultimately began to find expression through official channels.

The shape of the economic future, should the new party gel, could be seen in the wartime statist–corporatist approach to questions of production and labour, already apparent in the constitution and policies of the Lloyd George coalition, from the activities of the government during the war, and from the many ruminations indulged in by Lloyd George and his associates regarding 'reconstruction'. While the ultimate picture remained a little hazy, 'Nationalism–Socialism' was

Lloyd George's own term for the policy he was following, and around which he hoped to construct the postwar world.[36]

More important for our purposes, the shape of the political future was also previewed in the way in which Lloyd George handled dissent. Of course, it was always his greatest purpose to satisfy dissenters by acknowledging such of their grievances as were justified. If this did not work, then a political *ralliement* might. Failing these methods, and for those who could be expected to ignore Lloyd George's call, there was always increased repression. Having determined to shift British politics in a patriotic direction, and with revolution predicted by the authorities and feared by many of the Prime Minister's colleagues, 'slowly and unselfconsciously', we are told, 'the Lloyd George Coalition began to make itself a counter-revolutionary government'.[37] The policies adopted by the Lloyd George government which validate such a harsh judgement, we will see soon enough. There was nothing, however, particularly 'slow' or 'unselfconscious' about what Lloyd George was doing. On the contrary, after some initial hesitation, Lloyd George moved quickly, in a direction foreshadowed some years before the war.

The Lloyd George government, therefore, was a patriot synthesis anticipated before the war and projected to last into the peace. For our purposes, it was not just what the Lloyd George coalition did, but also what the whole represented that is significant. Not the least effective way in which Lloyd George combated the growth of a dissent seeking to capitalize upon class conflict was to oppose it with a vertical, corporatist reorganization of the social, economic and political nation, accomplished through explicit appeals to patriotism as an integrating force beyond class and particular interest. Once again, as with so much in the latter years of the First World War, this was a foretaste of the interwar fascist response.

In the new government, faced with an augmented and more coherent threat, there was a new Home Secretary, Sir George Cave. Samuel, like most of Asquith's friends, had refused to serve under Lloyd George, though it appears that Lloyd George had asked him to continue. Samuel ultimately would have had to part company with a government not at all to his taste.[38] Austen Chamberlain appears to have been sounded out for the job, but turned it down. Half the job, he considered, was routine (and therefore boring), while the remainder was police work, which Chamberlain considered repellent.[39] Asquith's Attorney General, Sir George Cave, was the next choice because he was a hard worker, and because he did not share Chamberlain's rather fine sensibilities. Cave was a man in sympathy with Lloyd George's immediate war requirement, if not with his long-term political goals.[40] He was a man, moreover, who had already demonstrated the inclination to follow a much more restrictive policy towards dissent than had prevailed hitherto. Cave had no particular liking for the job either, and entered the government only on the understanding that as soon as the home front stabilized, he would return to the law. His lack of enthusiasm, however, did not derive from moral or ideological scruples, but from professional ambition. Cave's greatest aspiration was not cabinet rank, but a high legal sinecure. A year after taking office, in February 1918, Cave attempted to leave the HO so that he could take office as Master of the Rolls, following the retirement of Lord Cozens-Hardy. Almost immediately, Cave reconsidered, withdrew his resignation, and wrote to inform Lloyd George of the reasons for his change of mind. When he had taken office, he informed the Prime Minister, Russia was still in the war,

> and it appeared just possible that by the close of the year the end of the war would be in sight; ... but things have changed; the war promises to be long and difficult and there may be trouble at home.[41]

Cave stayed on to ensure exactly that 'trouble at home' did not become defeat in the war; the while taking on the burden of government work in the House of Commons – the passage of wartime prohibition, the Representation of People Act, Ireland, and so on.[42] In the main, however, he remained Home Secretary for the remainder of the war for precisely the purpose of ensuring home security. If Lloyd George would have to be Cromwell, Cave was resigned to being his Colonel Pryde.

From December 1916, the HO brake which had been effective during the tenure of McKenna and Simon, and which had begun to fail with Samuel, gave way almost altogether under Cave. In fact, in the future, the HO would become an accelerator of suppression. Hereafter it led where it had followed. Unlike his predecessors, Cave was a constant advocate of restrictive policies. The attitude he adopted towards the question of patriot violence, for instance, was so unco-operative that Herbert Morrison, ILP and just commencing his career in the London Labour Party, was left to conclude that his stance was, by its nature, 'an encouragement of the use of mob violence against unpopular minorities'.[43] Morrison's opinion should be given some weight. He was, after all, to go on to be Britain's Home Secretary during the Second World War. It is probable, by this time, that increased direct attack on dissent was necessary if it were to be contained. Palliation of grievances, while certainly effective, was still failing to prevent dissent from becoming stronger and more radical. A strategy of social–political *ralliement* produced a patriot party. It could not stop dissent. While the Samuel period had seen episodic attacks on dissenters and their organizations, under Cave attacks became systematic. The offensive against dissent was possible because the consolidation of patriot strands by Lloyd George mobilized exactly the working consensus for increased repression which was always a prerequisite before any accentuation of the war against dissent was practical.

Under Cave the HO intensified its attack on the production and dissemination of pacifist literature and worked to impose tighter censorship of all kinds. It also worked to co-ordinate its programme more closely with those of other agencies alive by now to the dissenting danger. There was, as well, increased police surveillance, which almost certainly derived as much from the change in government as from the increase in dissenting activity. The same month that Lloyd George came to power on a policy of prosecuting the war with greater vigour, and Cave took over at the HO, we note, for instance, that much greater police attention came to be directed at Russell, Snowden and Trevelyan. This connection was not simply correlational.

We note, as well, that from this time police agents appear to have been operating widely, attempting to identify and penetrate suspect organizations of all kinds. The Ministry of Munitions had been monitoring working-class dissent since winter 1916. Detectives were seconded from the CID for this purpose. The aim was to be 'in a position to know at once against whom action should be taken in the event of strikes, which interfere with the output of munitions'. Sites of special interest were, hardly surprisingly: Glasgow, Liverpool, Manchester, Nottingham, Barrow, Birmingham, Leicester, Wolverhampton and Cardiff.[44] Other agencies were in this game, or wanted to be – the Ministry of Labour and probably military and naval intelligence. In 1917, however, surveillance was systematized and became a police responsibility. Under Assistant Commissioner Basil Thomson a special office of the CID was established: the predecessor of the postwar Special Branch. Its later, similar activities against postwar communist organizations are much better documented.[45] The police were becoming increasingly active in their own right, partly because they were genuinely concerned, but also because they did not believe that industrial and social surveillance could safely be delegated to other agencies. HMG could expect a rough ride, Thomson warned, if it were ever discovered that soldiers were spying on workmen.[46] The generals were, he considered, full of 'ignorant alarmism' concerning dissenting activities and simply could not be trusted to manage something so subtle as industrial surveillance.[47] By the end of the war, Thomson's office had expanded from 112 to 700 policemen. Denied a role in domestic surveillance it might have been, but MI5 still expanded from three detectives and seven clerks in 1914 to 850 employees in 1918.[48] There is, sadly, little surviving evidence of wartime domestic surveillance operations. Two examples will suffice here.

In spring 1917, one police agent, Alec Gordon, pretending to be a member of the IWW, managed to penetrate a family circle of dissenters which seemingly was bent on the assassination of Lloyd George. All they lacked was a suitable triggerman. Alec Gordon, ready to oblige, introduced into the conspiracy his boss, Herbert Booth, who played the part of a desperado apparently well enough to convince. The arrest, trial and imprisonment of the family Wheeldon followed in March.[49] All in all, it was a rather comic opera episode, included in the biography of Lord Birkenhead (in 1917, the Solicitor General) by his son as a curiosity. What is most interesting about this story, however, is not that the police were in this game, but that they were in it at such a low level. The Wheeldon family was hardly so large or obvious a dissenting organization as the UDC. That policemen were able to snap them up – indeed, were trying to penetrate dissenting organizations at this level – suggests plain good luck, a very comprehensive apparatus of internal surveillance or, as Pat Barker might suggest, considerable reliance on the testimony of informers and *agents provocateurs*.[50] The latter two, given what we have seen, and will see, were more likely.

Occasionally there were comedies, revealing for what they tell us not only about the degree of official paranoia, but also, once again, about the scale and effectiveness of the measures employed against dissent. In 1917, a meeting of the SWC was called. Greatest secrecy was enjoined. Two members turned up, both women. Each nominated the other for one of the offices which had to be filled. Both, hardly surprisingly, were elected. Each encouraged the other to hold fast and avoid discouragement. Both, it turned out, were police spies. Where were the other SWC members? Probably in prison or frightened off. As Roger Geary indicates, it would be interesting to know how many other dissenting organizations by 1917 had been effectively destroyed and were being run as police shams, attractive mainly to other police spies.[51]

Once again, it was not only the police who were taking action against dissent. There was a new spirit of co-operation in the government as a whole. In April 1917, at a meeting attended by representatives of the HO, WO, Ministry of Munitions, Ministry of Labour, Admiralty Shipyard Labour Department and National Service Department, the decision was made to institute 'systematic surveillance of the working class'. All of these agencies would pool information which would then be collated by the HO and a summary sent to all participating organizations.[52] This arrangement was probably essential if MEPO's predominant role in intelligence gathering were to be preserved, and other organizations prevented from using their own intelligence assets against the domestic enemy.

Perhaps the inclusion of the Admiralty Shipyard Labour Department here requires some little explanation. Through HM dockyards, the Admiralty was a large-scale employer of skilled labour. As such, it resisted all attempts to bring its practice into line with other industries. Its workers were not only tied to their jobs (as war essential), but underpaid by comparison with those engaged elsewhere because the Admiralty refused to change its scheme of job classification. For instance, a driller making 24 shillings a week with the navy would make six shillings and sixpence a day with a civilian contractor. Hardly surprisingly, the Admiralty was a constant target for labour agitation. Throughout the war, the Admiralty waged a constant turf battle with the Ministry of Munitions and the Ministry of Labour in particular, winning its point (that it was special and could organize its workers according to its own rules), but ultimately facing chronic labour unrest among its own workforce. It could only be expected, therefore, that naval intelligence would play a prominent role in monitoring industrial unrest (particularly in port cities), that the Admiralty was included here, and that the navy's general attitude towards organized labour was not only sceptical, but downright hostile – rather more so than that of the army.[53]

Most important, of course, was the development of a system of suppression from the disparate elements which various agencies had produced to this point. For the first time, we can speak of a unified government policy towards dissent. The HO worked first to co-ordinate its censorship policy with that of the army. The general line, agreed with the WO, was that while there was nothing illegal about advising people to declare themselves COs, it was illegal to advocate refusing to obey the law – which in practice meant recommending refusal to serve.[54] To say anything publicly against conscription, or any other settled government policy for that matter,[55] placed a dissenter in imminent danger of prosecution. Meanwhile the DRRs were reaching rather comprehensive proportions. They were directed ever more pointedly against dissent. As judgement followed judgement precedents emerged, loopholes disappeared, and censorship, in particular, became ever more absolute. The change of attitude was marked. Inhibitions were gone. Utility was now the only consideration. As early as October 1914 Lloyd George had warned Bertrand Russell that he would prosecute a reprint of the Sermon on the Mount if it interfered with production.[56] The intervening years had done nothing to soften the new premier's attitude. Cave's thinking was similar.

The usual procedure, by this time, was to invoke DRR 27 against opponents of the war. This dealt with expression of ideas that were false, likely to produce disaffection, interfere with military successes or prejudice relations with foreign powers. Where this could not be made to apply, there was always DRR 42 which concerned anything likely to cause mutiny, sedition, or disaffection among soldiers, or anything likely to interfere with war work, or impede prosecution of the war. When either DRR 27 or 42 had been breached, and printed material was involved, DRR 51 placed in the hands of any competent military, naval or police authority the power to seize copies of printed material, or plant used to print such materials, while initiating further action against the authors.[57] When none of this could be made to work – for public meetings, for instance – there was always the old standby: DRR 9A, which we have already seen in operation. Public expression of certain opinions could be prohibited on the grounds that they were apt to produce unrest.

While the military, navy or police could order materials to be seized, all were agreed by this point that action directly against those in contravention of DRRs, while legally as much a matter for military as for civil courts, would continue to be carried out through the agency of the civil police and civilian judiciary so as not to unsettle British sensibilities unduly. It was now understood that in taking action, the HO would be careful to consider the requirements of the other agencies. The charge of militarism, therefore, was to be kept in check by an informal system in which the HO remained the only obvious actor in the suppression of dissent. The army would return to the shadows. Meanwhile dissent would be more vigorously dealt with.

Military censorship was to be similarly disguised. Some things the army could do by itself without producing any enormous public outcry. Bureau MI7a (press bureau), for instance, could issue reporters with ID cards to ensure that authorities would have no doubt as to the identity of those judged to be responsible journalists.[58] Censors could stop dissenting publications – including almost anything put out by the National Labour Press, and everything carrying the UDC imprint – from leaving the country through the mail. The *Call*, the *Herald*, *Solidarity*, *Satire*, the *Woolwich Sentinel* and *UDC* were stopped as a matter of course. At the front, regimental censors could stop all unsuitable materials from reaching soldiers; particularly those felt to be most susceptible – recent conscripts from the north of England especially.[59] Communication between soldiers, and by soldiers with home, could be strictly monitored, as could the correspondence of identified dissenters with anybody. Confidential notices could 'be issued to the Press from time to time indicating to editors subjects to be avoided or treated with extreme caution and items of news, prospective and retrospective, which should not be mentioned at all'.[60]

All of these were powerful elements of wartime censorship. The last method, however, was particularly astute. It was effective and could be employed against anybody concerning anything, but did not violate the existing policy of voluntary compliance with the press bureau. It did not coerce; it simply suggested possible recourse to coercive machinery if a suggestion were not obeyed. Moreover, publishers were not allowed even to indicate that a matter of concern had been placed off limits by the press bureau, so that the existence of this mechanism was unknown to the public as would be, given compliance, the news the press bureau was seeking to suppress. Since this was an administrative method dependent upon voluntary compliance, the authorities were never compelled to justify exactly why a given subject had been placed off limits. It was a method subtle yet effective, and tailor-made for British scruples.

An example of a cautionary notice is this one received by Ramsay MacDonald on 5 January 1918.

> I have been asked by the Directors of the Official Press Bureau to send to you the following confidential notice (not for publication or communication) for your guidance:
>
> An Official report of the proceedings of the meeting of Minister and Labour Representatives held on Thursday at the Central Hall, Westminster, will be issued very shortly. The Press are requested not to publish any statement which purports to give information beyond the official report. No reference should be made to any suggestion that the Government is about to issue a statement of war aims or a calculation of numbers of men now on Military Service with estimates of what further numbers might be supplied by any given means. It is of National importance that these subjects should be avoided at the present time whether in regard to the meeting in question or otherwise.[61]

Increasingly it was domestic news that was prohibited. In 1917, for instance, the press bureau, at the instance of the Ministry of Munitions, prohibited several times the publication of news of incipient or actual strikes.[62] When a caution was unlikely to suffice, the censors could issue warnings that prosecution would probably follow from the continuance of a given editorial line. The assertion that Britain had 'stabbed Germany in the back' by declaring war while Germany was pleading for neutrality in exchange for a German guarantee of France and

Belgium, and that Britain had ever since the beginning of the war been 'deceived by its ministers',[63] was met with the hair-raising warning:

> The statements are false in every particular and it is my duty to warn you that any newspaper that lends itself to the publication of matter such as this at the present moment, incurs the grave risk of prosecution and punishment. I am willing to assume in your favour on this occasion that the full gravity of what has appeared has escaped your notice, but if after this letter any similar statements are published no such presumption will be made.[64]

By 1917, censorship had increased in scope as well as scale. During the last years of the war, censorship expanded to cover types of literature hitherto exempt (leaflets, broadsheets and billboards). Cave was the moving spirit here. Similarly, mail could now be opened 'if there were any ground for suspecting the agency of spies' – which was a rather nice way of saying whenever the military censors chose.[65] By 1918, 4,000–5,000 censors were busy opening mail alone.[66] MI7a continued to monitor the domestic press for articles of a hostile nature (the labour press, in particular, with growing attention). MI7b (5), by

FIGURE 4: CENSORSHIP, 1917

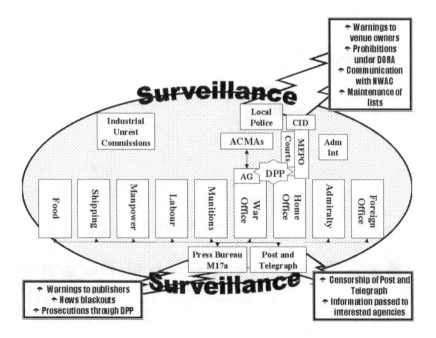

November 1917, was getting into the act as well, monitoring for the last year of the war 550 newspapers a week. Its staff of 15 combed all the London papers, 30 provincial papers, all the weeklies, all the labour and pacifist papers, all the religious press and 70 provincial weeklies.[67] Items noted by these agencies which appeared to be in contravention of DRRs were referred to MI6 (1), on to the DMI (Macdonogh), and through the Treasury Solicitor to the DPP for action.[68]

While this does not appear to be much of a change from the system existing under Samuel, it was different in two important respects. First, the military authorities were distanced from the legal process. And, secondly, the HO was able to exercise greater influence. This return to constitutional practice was permitted by the services because Cave was much more accommodating than his predecessors. Simon and Samuel were seldom consulted because the answer would always be 'no'. Cave's answer would always be 'yes' unless he had sound political grounds for taking a specific case under advisement. Ultimately Cave, and the government, retained power to facilitate or stop any repressive action. Thus, although the opinion that counted was military opinion effective action could not be taken except through the agency of a willing HO and following a political judgement that prosecution was unlikely to backfire. Here Lloyd George himself (Asquith's 'foolometer':

FIGURE 5: JUSTICE AND DISSENT, 1917

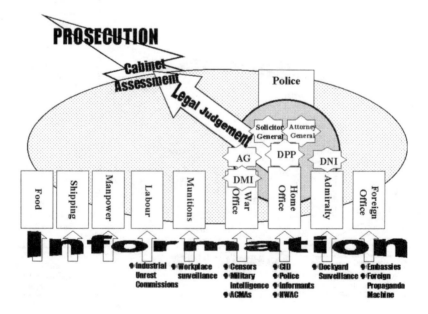

a man who knew instinctively what the common people were thinking, being common himself) was invaluable, as were first Henderson, and then Barnes, for their insight as to just what would be tolerated and what would not.

An example follows. In January 1917 Cave was convinced that prosecution of the *Labour Leader* and the *Tribunal* would be possible for actions in contravention of DRR 27. Other agencies concurred. Both of these papers had gone far beyond advocating peace or criticizing the government and were beginning to advocate civil disobedience.[69] Lloyd George consulted Henderson. The best course, he ultimately replied to Cave's request for permission to proceed, would be to wait. Henderson was then engaged in attempting to win over the Labour Party at its Manchester annual meeting, and this item on the greater agenda might be jeopardized if any heavy-handed actions were taken before he had been successful.[70] Cave was brought to agree. The best course would be to wait, harass and collect evidence.[71] An accounting could wait. This, of course, was simple wisdom and an example of the type of forbearance derived from political acumen which saw Britain successfully though the war without uncontained, potentially war-losing situations developing on the home front.

Nevertheless, under this new dispensation convictions for writing and distributing seditious literature began to become much more commonplace, as did the prosecution of dissenting leaders – at least, that is, leaders of the second tier. The first-tier, political leadership of dissent – Snowden, Trevelyan and MacDonald for instance – was protected by parliamentary immunity. The authorities were only too aware of the fact that the prosecution of a serving MP, even when subversive intent could be proved, was a far more serious affair, likely to have significant consequences, than the silencing of a mere organizer. While the second-tier and membership during 1917 were exposed to furious assault, touching the political leadership, for the moment, remained taboo.

An example of the official tolerance of leading dissenters is the case of Philip Snowden, who had moved from a position of anti-conscription to more straightforward anti-war agitation. By the winter of 1916–17 he was speaking on whatever platform he could find, arguing that Britain was fighting, quite plainly, no longer for itself but for Russia, and that an immediate negotiated peace was the only rational course.[72] In summer 1917, Snowden was still beating the Russian drum. By this time it was a different drum. In a speech to a meeting of the ILP at Woolwich on 30 July, he spoke of the situation in Russia. Britain should, he said, 'follow Russia'. The 'Revolution', he disclosed to his listeners, 'is coming'.[73] His wife, taking the podium, declared herself against the National Anthem. She 'wanted to know the reason why she should pray for the King', she said, 'just because he was the son of his father' – 'a declaration', according to the police, 'which evoked considerable enthusiasm'.[74] In the army and navy, she informed her audience, unions were being formed and soldiers were refusing to obey orders. Fortunately for the HO this was much more alarming than true. While it thought that certain of the statements of both Snowden and his wife were actionable, it would not permit prosecution. Ramsay MacDonald notwithstanding, Snowden was at this time probably the most active and prominent peace agitator in the country. The HO under Cave, as under McKenna, Simon and Samuel, was unwilling to make martyrs – at least martyrs likely to have a large and sympathetic following. Had Snowden not been an MP, however, both he and his wife would quickly have found themselves doing time for sedition.

To all rules there are exceptions. Once during the Lloyd George period, parliamentary immunity was violated. As with the application of DRR 14 to ASE strike-leaders, this was a precedent without a recurrence. On 15 November 1917, the police raided the offices of the NCF and struck, as well, at the homes of Arnold Lupton MP, and a Mr Zusman, associated with the NCF. At the Lupton home they were searching in particular for copies of the pamphlets 'Every Day at the Present Time', and 'What Are We Fighting For?', which had been unconditionally censored by the authorities in October.[75] Lupton's crime? These pamphlets noted, quite correctly, that each day of war was costing Britain 1,000 lives and £8,000,000. The only alternative to peace, Lupton had written, was a continued haemorrhage of blood, and eventual bankruptcy.[76] Confronted by Lupton's wife, the investigating officer, Chief Inspector Parker, informed her that the raid was being carried out under DRR 51 on the grounds that there was suspicion that the house contained subversive literature. Most frighteningly, 150 letters from serving soldiers asking for copies of Lupton's pamphlets were also found. This time, however, the disgruntled policemen did not find enough evidence to justify prosecution.

Another raid on the Luptons, on 3 December, was more successful and netted the police copies of the pamphlet 'The War', which had already cost Lupton a £200 fine (with costs) in November 1916, and of his newer effort 'Every Day at the Present Time'. They also found, most damagingly, a copy of a letter requesting help in obtaining a listed job for a dissenter in order to keep him out of the army. In the opinion of the WO legal branch, this evidence was more than sufficient to obtain a conviction under DORA.[77] The WO was right. Lupton was convicted.

It would have been strange if he were not. By this time, conviction for the distribution of material considered prejudicial to recruiting normally depended upon the presentation of military evidence. The WO having decided that there were grounds for prosecution, it would be asked, as an authority, if there were grounds for conviction. The WO always agreed with itself. On 2 and 16 February 1918 Lupton was arraigned. The most damaging evidence against him, perhaps not in law, but in the minds of his jurors, was the discovery in his rooms of letters from German prisoners of war thanking him for literature sent to them.[78] Lupton's trial judge, in his summing-up, professed himself satisfied 'that the whole intent of the pamphlet [i.e. "Every Day at the Present Time"] was mischievous and calculated to cause disaffection'. 'The suggestions in it', he thought, 'were certainly seditious, dangerous to the State, and prejudicial to recruiting.'[79] He ordered Lupton to be imprisoned, in a division two institution, for six months under the Newspaper and Printers Act of 1869. Lupton's appeal to be placed under a lighter regime was dismissed with costs. 'I don't think', Lupton's judge concluded after rejecting his appeal, 'a more wicked pamphlet throughout, from beginning to end, could be conceived.'[80]

The limits of HMG's patience can be better illustrated by reference to the cases of Angell, Morel and Russell – all prominent certainly, but all organization men unprotected by parliamentary immunity, and therefore goads no longer to be tolerated. Moreover, as organization men, they were crucial to the dissenting cause. To remove them from circulation would wreak powerful damage on dissent without producing the same sort of outcry as could be expected to follow the arrest of the parliamentary dissenters. A rather effective form of attack.

Hitherto HMG had considered Angell to be too well known and respected to touch. Like Snowden, however, by the winter of 1916–17 Angell was advocating a much more comprehensive, even revolutionary protest. He was also a public advocate of continued American neutrality. By January 1917, Angell was habitually speaking, MI5 complained, as if he 'had no nationality'.[81] About the time the Lloyd George government came to power, Angell proposed to go on a lecture tour of the United States. When this came to the attention of the press, it went wild. The *Daily Express* screamed 'STABBING IN THE BACK', and, 'MEAN INNUENDO. HUN'S GOSPEL' on 1 January, and later, on 17 July, 'PRO GERMAN THEORIES IN ENGLISH GUISE'.[82] The HO decided to refuse him a passport. 'This is not the time', it was judged, 'when we can afford to take any risk.'[83] The censorship of Angell went further. In May, an article he had written for the *New Republic* was censored absolutely. Bonar Law, the Unionist leader of the House, defended this action 'on the grounds that it contained certain statements which, in the circumstances existing at the time, were considered prejudicial to the public interest'.[84] It is doubtful that the House of Commons would have accepted this explanation a year earlier, and more doubtful still that it would have been offered.

There was a rash of arrests. Bertrand Russell was arrested for violating DORA by sending material outside the country for publication. Worse, this material had contained what appeared to be attacks on British Allies. 'The American garrison', Russell had written,

> which will by that time be occupying England and France, whether or no they will prove efficient against the Germans, will no doubt be capable of intimidating strikers – an occupation to which the American Army is accustomed when at home.[85]

For this offence Russell was fined. When portions of this pamphlet were reprinted in the *Tribunal*, in January 1918, Russell faced his third prosecution, and first imprisonment. By the end of the war he had, in addition, been relieved of his lectureship, and refused a passport to take up a new position in the United States.[86]

Morel, the moving spirit behind the UDC, was jailed for evasion of censorship. The moving spirit behind the arrest of Morel was Lord Robert Cecil (at the FO) who brought Morel's actions to the attention of the HO – streamlined co-ordination between government agencies, once again, the order of the day.[87] Morel had been, until this time, yet another organizer too significant to act against. That had changed. The arrest of Morel was simply part of a greater campaign being waged against the UDC which saw its operations ever more tightly circumscribed though not forbidden. In 1915, Morel had been permitted to despatch printed materials overseas, provided it had been cleared through censors.[88] A year later, the WO was finding it necessary to have Morel's mail intercepted, and searched for 'matter which might have been used by the enemy for the purpose of his propaganda'.[89] Moreover, Morel was informed, the UDC would henceforth be stopped by the Post Office and turned over to the WO for destruction if any attempt were made to export it.[90] When Trevelyan sought clarification, he received none.[91] It was simply reiterated time and again that the UDC could not be sent overseas.[92] Persistence in questioning ultimately provoked the suspension of the UDC's licence to send printed material of any kind overseas.[93]

Morel's conviction followed from his frustration. Seeking to evade this restriction, it appears that he arranged to have two of his publications hand-carried to neutral Switzerland. Letters from the carrier (Ethel

Sidgwick) to Morel were intercepted by Lieutenant Featherstone, a military censor, and passed through the military authorities to the HO. Sidgwick's part of the correspondence leave little doubt about her actions. Morel's replies suggested complicity, enough, at least, to convince Lieutenant-Colonel Russell (CMA) to issue a warrant for the search of Morel's office and premises. The resulting raids garnered letters which appeared to confirm that Morel had conspired to smuggle UDC literature through Mrs Sidgwick to Romain Roland in Switzerland. One letter to Mrs Sidgwick, in particular, included the telling phrase '[p]erhaps you can smuggle some across', in reference to Morel's forbidden pamphlet, 'Tzardom's Part in the War'. While Morel always maintained his innocence,[94] given the evidence he appeared to be in obvious contravention of DRR 24B (by which it was a crime to export, without a permit, any literature from the UK), and of DRR 48 (conspiring to do the same). Morel was refused bail twice and subjected to a long period on remand, though the crime was only a misdemeanour. The result of the trial was six months in the second division at Pentonville, and more importantly, a corresponding abatement of UDC activity during the period of his imprisonment (September 1917–February 1918).[95]

Morel having been committed to prison, Cave refused to place him in a division where life would have been easier, despite a succession of appeals during Morel's time in jail.[96] Nor would Cave do anything to ameliorate the circumstances of Morel's imprisonment. There would be no extra books, unless approved by the commissioner, no pamphlets whatsoever and anything sent became the property of the prison library. He could have one photograph. It could not be a group portrait. There would be no extra visits, food, clothing, or letters. Only once did Cave relent. Ultimately he permitted Morel's wife an extra visit, once a fortnight. That was all.[97]

Morel emerged from prison, six months later, to find himself the focus of a savage slander campaign. He was, for instance, being described in the House of Lords, by Lord Denbigh, a die-hard speaker for the NWAC and VF organizer, as no Englishman at all, but rather as a 'very dubious Frenchman'.[98] In the *Nineteenth Century and After*, Morel was openly accused of being in German pay and 'working with the sanction and approval of the German Foreign Office'.[99] In the *Evening Standard*, Morel was being characterized as nothing less than the 'Generalissimo of Defeatism'. 'Morel, in short,' the article began,

> grasped the idea of a single front and unity of command long before the Allies did. He organized under a single direction all the divers

forces hostile to the war and favourable to a German peace – the Quakers, the doctrinaire Liberals of the Ponsonby type, the Syndicalists and social rebels, the bitter fanatics like Mr Snowden and intriguers like Ramsay MacDonald ...

The Union of Democratic Control, the Independent Labour Party, the No Conscription League, the Fellowship of Reconciliation, the Quaker Conventicle and the Syndicalist lodge were all mobilized by the same master mind. 'Morel' has never shown any interest in Labour, religion, Liberalism, or democracy as such; but he became vividly interested in them all when they could be used for the purpose of weakening the national will.[100]

All highly offensive stuff certainly, and just the type of material which might by itself have led even an old liberal like E. D. Morel to shift into a more advanced type of opposition. On the other hand, Morel emerged from prison an ILP hero. Denounced in the patriot press, he was lionized by Glasgow militants as a martyr for dissent.[101] While Morel himself always insisted that he had become a socialist from conviction,[102] the 'system' had certainly done little to endear itself to him in 1917–18.[103]

As we might expect, the smaller fry were not even so lucky. In May 1917, for example, eight men were fined £100, with £10 costs each, or 61 days' imprisonment, for publishing a leaflet judged to be seditious on military evidence, entitled 'Repeal the [Military Service] Act'.[104] A year earlier it probably would have passed without comment as a statement of political opinion. The leaflet did not advocate evasion, simply repeal. Samuel had promised never to take action against expression of opinion on topical issues. Mr R. C. Wallhead, a full-time propagandist for the ILP, was jailed in January 1918 for asserting that men conscripted during the war, would be retained with the colours afterward to help police the peace.[105] This was, of course, as the experience of many would demonstrate, a simple statement of fact.

Meanwhile, the old methods of suggestion, pressure and intimidation continued to function. It was not just the leadership and the membership of dissenting organizations who came under attack. Venues, proposed conferences, propaganda distribution systems and meetings likely to give a forum to dissent were watched, and on some occasions, action was taken. Patriots gangs continued to rampage.

From Newcastle upon Tyne, for instance, came the report that the local YWCA was distributing pacifist literature. Charged with this by the local police, the general secretary – a Miss Cox – denied it and indicated the local chapter of WIL as the likely culprit. She promised to deny them facilities in the future.[106] Nothing absolutely against the law, however, had been done here. In Llandrindod Wells, an FOR meeting was broken up by the deacons of the chapel in which it was being held when it took an anti-war direction. The organizers, they assured the police when they inquired, had gained access to the chapel under false pretences.[107] In the House – broaching the subject of the 'Herald' speeches again – a Mr Pennefather asked Cave if he was aware of a subversive meeting recently held at Finsbury Park. He called upon the government to pledge itself to deny the use of public parks for 'any purposes calculated to assist the enemy', and to cease tolerating the 'preaching of sedition in public parks'.[108] This was too much even for Cave. The patriot insistence on action continued to be greater, even, than the resolution of the Lloyd George government. Still nothing was done out of keeping with the state of general public opinion.

While the old methods continued to be employed, the fact of shortages and control, brought on by war, began to provide new weapons in the war against dissent. For instance, paper shortages, caused by the increased demand produced by the war and the lack of shipping, became endemic by 1917. Imports of newsprint were something like one-quarter of what they had been before the war (2,000 tons imported in 1917 compared with 8,000 tons in 1914). Available stocks were divided up between consumers on the basis of ratios of prewar circulation. By its nature, this system favoured the patriotic Beaverbrook–Northcliffe combine over the dissenting press because of their larger prewar sales. No allowance was made for expansion of circulation. Tom Bell, the chairman of the BSP, claimed in April 1918 that the circulation of the *Socialist* had tripled in the course of the war.[109] If this was the case, then three times as many papers were being printed with less than one-quarter of the prewar paper allotment. Furthermore, given their broader range of contacts and greater financial resources, the press lords were in a much better position than the opposition to obtain extra newsprint. In spring 1917, for instance, Lord Northcliffe persuaded Associated Press to give him access to a huge amount of paper, which he proceeded to divide up among his friends. Beaverbrook, of course, got some (1,000 tons). It is unlikely that Clifford Allen and Tom Bell were numbered among the elect.[110] Beaverbrook, for one, was certainly aware that this form of censorship existed. As Minister of Information, in 1918 he justified government tolerance of some dissenting publications, by simply noting the difficulty faced by the dissenters in obtaining paper to publish anything.[111] Seeking to employ this form of censorship more fully, Beaverbrook suggested to Lloyd George that it might be a rather good idea to give the Ministry of Information full control over the supply of newsprint so that it could reward papers for war work and punish them for opposition. Whether he succeeded in gaining a news-print monopoly is not known.[112] For other organizations involved in the propaganda fight against dissent – MI7b and the NWAC for instance – such constraints were not even an issue, since they received their supply straight from HMSO. In comparison, the National Labour Press was by April 1918 reduced to making appeals for waste paper; the paper shortage by this time was so extreme that even the publication of a four-page newspaper was becoming unsustainable.[113] Its publications, it has been asserted, were simply 'casualties of the war'.

Conscription too was proving a useful tool for silencing dissent, particularly when deliberately employed as such following depart-mental collusion. How this might work had already been fore-shadowed in 1916 when one of the more vocal and annoying of the dissenters, C. H. Norman (NCF, NAC, SWC, UDC, ILP, IWW), fell foul of registration and ended up in prison. Norman, whom we last saw attempting to get his article 'Why the War Should Be Stopped' pub-lished, finally succeeded in spring 1916, when *New Age* took it. Prosecution for breach of DORA was considered by the HO, but since Norman was already in jail for refusing to register, the AG advised that it would be better to let the army deal with him. The military authorities would certainly jail him. If, on the other hand, civil proceedings were begun, Norman would have an excuse not to join the army, while his ultimate conviction would remain uncertain. Good thinking, consid-ered the press bureau and the DPP: let the army jail him.[114] It did.

As we have seen, Norman was followed quickly into jail by his friends from the NCF, Clifford Allen and Fenner Brockway, both effectively taken out of circulation for the duration. Already in trouble with the censors, both were among the first to be called up. No absolute exemp-tion was granted to either. When both espoused the 'absolutist' position (no participation whatsoever in the war, or war work; no compromise short of unconditional conscientious objection),[115] both were tried and imprisoned. Allen's trial, in particular, Snowden considered to be a 'comic travesty of justice'.[116] Five other leading members of the NCF (Aylmer Rose, the secretary, along with Ralf Cranmer, George Coles, George Parrin and James Arthur Tristram) were snapped up at this time for ignoring their call-up.[117]

By the time Lloyd George came to the premiership, with full con-scription being applied, this tool became one of almost general utility. It is possible that it was being applied as such with the concurrence of the government. Even the dissenters could see that Asquith, Samuel and Walter Long (at the local government board) were trying to be fair to those whose conscience would not permit them to participate in the war; it was the army and the local appeals boards which used conscription as a scourge for dissent.[118] No one, on the other hand, ever claimed that Lloyd George and Cave were interested in dealing leniently with COs – especially those with a political objection. Indeed, it would be hard to maintain any such claim, given the notoriously hard line consistently advocated by Lloyd George himself. Absolutists, according to Lloyd George, did not deserve 'the slightest consideration', and he would make it his job, he promised, 'to [make] the lot of that class a very hard one'.[119]

We can get some notion of the scale on which conscription was being used as an automatic mechanism for the suppression of dissent from the increase in the number of dissenters tried and the sentence they received. In the records of the Department of the Judge Advocate General (JAG) survive daily returns of COs tried, with the sentence awarded by a court martial. In summer 1916, with Asquith in office and conscription new, it was normal for 20 to 30 COs to be tried by the army each day.[120] The usual sentence was 56 to 112 days' detention. Elements of fairness still survived. The cases of a group of COs sentenced at Weymouth, for example, were reviewed and overturned, on the grounds that

> there was no evidence before the Court about the time and place of parade referred to in the particulars of the charge in each case had been appointed by the Commanding Officer of the accused
> ... the fact that the accused were defaulters was not properly proved as laid down in King's Regulations
> ... and further that it is unusual for a Court to award as it has done in these cases a heavier sentence to an accused who had elected trial than might have been awarded by his Commanding Officer.

The result was 'the conviction of these cases should be quashed and the accused relieved from all consequences of this trial'.[121]

If, on the other hand, the army tried to be fair, it could also be brutal. During the time that trial and punishment of COs remained an army prerogative, conscription was a spur to dissent rather than an inhibitor. The reason was the harsh way in which the army dealt with resistors. For instance, three brothers Walker – Frederick, Charles and Harry – and a friend, Llywelyn Hughes were called up together in 1916. All appealed. All were offered alternative service. All refused. All were arrested, frogmarched to Mill Hill jail, put into khaki forcibly, and transferred to Chatham lower barracks. Here, for refusing drill, they were forced onto the square and beaten into various drill positions until they collapsed. For refusing physical training, they were dragged through exercise. For refusing to eat, all were forcibly fed.[122] Going even further, in May 1916, three groups of conscientious objectors who were deemed to have enlisted in the Non-Combatant Corps (one of them, unfortunately appears to have been a Walker brother) were actually sent to France. For refusing orders while on active duty, they were tried by court martial, and 34 of them were sentenced to death.[123] Even the Church of England was appalled. No less a luminary than the Archbishop of Canterbury, seconded by the Bishop of Oxford, led the charge in the House of Lords.[124] High-ranking delegations – and not only of dissenters – began to appear in ministerial anterooms.[125] Dissent, frayed by the pressures of the past year, began to reconsolidate against what was considered a manifest abuse of power.[126] The army, on behalf of the government, had plainly gone too far. The sentences were commuted to ten years' military imprisonment.[127] Ultimately it was decided to place COs in HO, rather than military, custody.[128]

By winter 1916–17, with full conscription being more ruthlessly applied, the normal number of dissenters sentenced by courts martial doubled to 40 to 60 cases daily, with a corresponding increase in sentences. COs actually in the army could now expect to be detained for 112 days. Absolutists faced imprisonment with hard labour for two years.[129] Nor, by this time, do we read of any more reprieves. Marwick characterizes the fact that objectors, by the end of 1916, were being tried in court rather than court martial, and imprisoned rather than detained as a victory for the NCF.[130] Given the fact that the incidence of trial and conviction, and the total length of time spent in prison had doubled, this was a pyrrhic victory at best. Lloyd George certainly never thought that two years imprisonment with hard labour, often following a period of detention, was doing anybody any favours.[131] In all, according to Snowden's figures, there were something like 16,000 men who claimed conscientious objection to military service. This may have been the tip of the iceberg, since he apparently received more than 30,000 letters from persons aggrieved by the way in which the system had functioned in their case. Of these, 1,543 were 'absolutists'.[132] By February 1917, 3,025 COs were in jail, though 2,297 of them were nearing the end of their sentence.[133] Ultimately, something like 5,000 COs spent time in prison, and two of them appear to have died of pneumonia during their time behind bars.[134] All of the 'absolutists', moreover, were not only imprisoned, but disenfranchised for five years under the Franchise Act of 1917.[135]

Now, since a regime had been established under which only those dissenters were tried who refused not only military but also alternative service,[136] the conscription net was calculated, by its nature, to catch only hard-core dissenting fish, and to provide a very fine mesh for these. It was also designed to drive a wedge between religious and political objections.[137] The wedge went in all the easier since religious dissenters were less radical than their socialist comrades. At bottom, not a few were 'patriots' who simply disapproved of mandatory military service. It is probable, as well, that many were also growing uneasy at the extent to which their objection was becoming confused with, and absorbed within, the political, socialist critique.[138] Many, in short, were looking for a reason to jump the dissenting ship. The government was quick to oblige them by providing one. If the surviving records of the Middlesex Manpower Appeals Tribunals are anything to go by, persons refusing combatant service because of well-defined religious objection – Baptists,[139] members of the Salvation Army,[140] Quakers of however recent vintage,[141] even followers of Tolstoy[142] – were generally treated with kid gloves, as were those who came under their protection.[143] Once the danger of compulsory military service was removed, Christian dissent declined markedly.

In a similar fashion, by November 1917 a regime was adopted by which COs who were ill would be released as convalescent army reservists, and absolutists could be released provided they were willing to accept a royal pardon. The moving force behind this amelioration in conditions was not the NCF, but no less a figure than Lord Alfred Milner.[144] Since NCF absolutists would not accept pardons (they considered they had done nothing wrong), those pardoned tended to be well-connected religious objectors like Milner's godson, Steven Hobhouse. A way was opened for those who wanted to take it. For those who did not, there was always cat and mouse: they remained in the army, but did not die in prison. When they had recovered, they were recalled to the colours and reimprisoned. Hobhouse went free. Allen was in and out of prison, and in any case out of circulation. Brockway was in, and then out since nearly dead. J. Scott Duckers (ILP, UDC, SWC), called up in April 1917, was still in prison in December 1920, serving his time with hard labour.[145]

Meanwhile, another propaganda advantage was won. If religious objection were granted, if work of national importance was almost always offered as alternative service, and if anyone could be released simply by asking to go, then did it not follow that the absolutists in prison must certainly be political cranks and fanatical religious sectarians? To many it seemed so.[146] Did these not deserve the harshest sort of treatment? Only a few more would have disagreed. In October 1917, Lord William Cecil, the Anglican Bishop of Exeter, proposed that all religious objectors should be granted unconditional exemption.

Political objectors, on the other hand, deserved special treatment. They should be gathered, he proposed, in those areas most likely to be bombed.[147] There was nothing exceptional about that. Cecil was an Anglican bishop. A sign that the policy as applied was working exactly to drive a wedge between religious and political dissent, however, came shortly thereafter when the *Manchester Guardian* – a Liberal paper friendly to dissent – supported the proposal. 'We have no sympathy whatsoever', it wrote, 'with people who call on their conscience to help them in their refusal to defend their country.'[148]

For political COs there was more ruthless treatment. Allowance had been made in law for the possibility of absolute exemption for reasons of political principle. In practice, however, political objections were scarcely considered as grounds for even conditional exemption. The fate of a conscript who announced that his objection to military service derived from the teaching of the ILP,[149] or a socialist who considered war service of any kind 'revolting to the whole of my feelings, my views, my hopes, and to my faith for the future of humanity',[150] was unlikely to be much happier than that of the man working for the Royal Small Arms Factory (!), who wanted unconditional exemption on the grounds of conscientious objection.[151] The board which heard Clifford Allen's appeal, for instance, not only did not grant him absolute exemption, it doubted that he had a conscientious objection at all. Allen's trial judge shared these doubts. Allen, of course, was perhaps the most utterly convinced objector in Britain.

Meanwhile, conscription provided yet another opportunity for the army and the police to interfere with dissenting activities and meetings. Not all men called up were content to take their chances with the tribunals. By 1918, a considerable number, in fact, appear to have been in hiding. To find them, raids became common. On one occasion in November 1916, for instance, a meeting of the Herald League at Holborn Hall was invaded by police and soldiers searching for absentees. In the end, four men were led away. In the process, of course, the meeting was disrupted. Such disturbances, according to the testimony of Sylvia Pankhurst, were common in the latter war years.[152]

In 1917, therefore, if dissent was growing in size, scope and effectiveness, the government response was keeping pace. A prime minister of profoundly populist inclinations was energetically attempting to settle grievances before they could become political dissent. The consolidation of patriotic tendencies into the Lloyd George whole ensured not only an adequate power base for the premier, but the maintenance of a working consensus for more comprehensive policing of the home front, while itself serving to split the potential dissenting audience. At the HO, a new home secretary, no longer restrained by liberal inhibitions, was organizing the system which had begun to appear in the Samuel period. Where suppression of dissent had been episodic, it began to become far more systematic. While it might produce dissent, conscription proved to be a mighty weapon in HMG's hands. Other elements of war government which could be used similarly at home we will see in what follows.

As always, however, what the government had found was less the antidote to dissent than the cure for the dissent of a year previous. HMG was always obliged to play catch-up, for reasons we have seen. The Lloyd George government was no different. While it was acting with greater vigour and effectiveness against dissent, developments during 1917 were beginning to produce a type of dissent against which new powers would be required and still more inhibitions would need to be jettisoned. Meanwhile, events in Europe, by providing an example to British dissenters, were increasing the association of dissent with existing grievances, and providing both a programme and vehicles through which it could be expressed.

NOTES

1. House of Lords Debates, 1916, Volume XXIII, column 922.
2. See PRO CAB 17/56; see also Adams and Poirier, *The Conscription Controversy*, pp. 176–7.
3. See K. Grieves, *The Politics of Manpower 1914–1918* (Manchester: Manchester University Press, 1988), pp. 90–114. Grieves: 'Chamberlain was utterly dependent on the manipulation of patriotic goodwill at a time when war weariness was the dominant response to the continuation of the conflict' (p. 205).
4. Catherine Cline has argued that convergence of foreign policy positions between Labour and Liberal dissenters facilitated the conversion of the latter (*E. D. Morel*, pp. 113–14). This is certainly true. Similarity of views, however, could have worked the other way and during prewar Lib-Lab co-operation had tended to do so. It was the Liberal Party's wartime disarray which tipped the balance in favour of the Labour Party.
5. Swartz, *The Union of Democratic Control*, p. 100.
6. Morris, *C. P. Trevelyan*, p. 140. Trevelyan ran as an independent in the coupon election, but had pledged himself, long before this, to 'work with the men he agreed with'.
7. Swartz, *The Union of Democratic Control*, pp. 102–3. Trevelyan and Morel both considered that overt association with the ILP, in particular, would make the position of Liberal members of the UDC intolerable. See LSE, Morel Papers, Morel F6/4, Morel Minute, with Trevelyan Note, 9 July 1915.
8. Swartz, *The Union of Democratic Control*, pp. 99–100.
9. Wrigley, *David Lloyd George*, p. 190.
10. Ibid., p. 183. The Industrial Unrest Committee of the TUC also listed real grievances – poor housing, food shortages and continued belief that profiteers were making

money from general misery – in addition to hatred of conscription as causes of the May strikes. *Report of the Proceedings at the 49th Annual Trade Union Conference, September 3–8 1917*, p. 84.

11. PRO HO 144/1470, Precautions at Munitions Centres, file 1046/p, 12 April 1917.
12. Ibid.
13. Thomson, *The Scene Changes*, entry for 17 May 1917, p. 369.
14. Wrigley, *David Lloyd George*, p. 196.
15. Thomson, *The Scene Changes*, diary entries for period 5–7 May 1917, pp. 365–6. See also entries through to 18 May for later developments.
16. See PRO CAB 17/56; see also Adams and Poirier, *The Conscription Controversy*, p. 203.
17. K. G. Robbins, *The Abolition of War* (Cardiff: University of Wales Press, 1976), pp. 309–10.
18. Wilson, *The Political Diaries of C. P. Scott*, diary entry for 3–5 February 1918.
19. H. Pelling, *A History of British Trade Unionism* (London: Macmillan, 1963), pp. 157–8. It is not surprising that the GFTU was friendly to the government. Its chairman, W. A. Appelton (Laceworkers' Union), was a notorious patriot.
20. For Ramsay MacDonald as leader of the No-Annexations debate, see, PRO 30/69/1041, *UDC*, Vol. II, no. 8 (June 1917).
21. Wilson, *The Political Diaries of C. P. Scott*, diary entry for 15–16 March 1917, pp. 267–8.
22. K. O. Morgan (ed.), *Lloyd George's Family Letters 1885–1936* (Cardiff: University of Wales Press, 1973), letter 5 January 1918. See also for the Lloyd George war aims, Marwick, *The Deluge*, pp. 216–17; and Lloyd George's own pamphlets 'When Will the War End', and 'The Allied War Aims'.
23. Webb, *The History of Trade Unionism*, p. 695; Clegg, *A History of British Trade Unionism*, Vol. II, p. 233.
24. K. Middlemas (ed.), *Whitehall Diary* (London: Oxford University Press, 1967), T. Jones diary entry for 7 January 1918, p. 43.
25. 'The extremists in the Labour camp', George Barnes, Lloyd George's most faithful Labour collaborator, wrote, 'are always declaiming against the Labour Party's association with what they call the Capitalists; meaning thereby the coalition Government [but] … it has passed more legislation [friendly to Labour] in two years, than has been done by any previous government in two decades' (HLRO, Lloyd George Papers, F/4/3/32, Barnes to Davies, 29 August 1918).
26. Searle, *Country Before Party*, p. 108; Morgan, *The Age of Lloyd George* (London: George Allen & Unwin, 1971); Lord Riddell, *War Diary* (London: Nicholson & Watson, 1933).
27. Searle, *Country Before Party*, pp. 101, 108.
28. Ibid., p. 106.
29. K. O. Morgan, 'Lloyd George and Germany', *Historical Journal*, Vol. 39, no. 3 (1996), pp. 755–65; Searle, *Country Before Party*, p. 108.
30. Wrigley, *David Lloyd George*, p. 183.
31. H. M. Erzensberger, *Civil Wars* (New York: New Press, 1995), p. 138.
32. K. Middlemas, *Politics in Industrial Society: The Experience of the British System Since 1911* (London: A. Deutsch, 1979), p. 151; Wrigley, *David Lloyd George*, p. 177.
33. Initial Labour representation in the coalition government was: Henderson (War Cabinet), John Hodge (Ministry of Labour), George Barnes (Pensions), William Brace (Under-Secretary at the Home Office), George Roberts (Parliamentary Under-Secretary at the Board of Trade), and James Parker (a Junior Lord of the Treasury), with George Wardle the House leader for coalition Labour. Hodge and Roberts were doing double duty here; they represented, as well, the BWNL.
34. HLRO, Lloyd George Papers, F 21/2/13, F. Guest to Lloyd George, 1918. See also Marwick, *The Deluge*, pp. 212–14; Wilson, *The Political Diaries of C. P. Scott*, diary

entry for 4 March 1918.

35. Morgan, *The Age of Lloyd George*, p. 71.

36. Riddell, *War Diary*, p. 309.

37. J. Turner, *British Politics and the Great War* (New Haven, CT: Yale University Press, 1992).

38. Sir Herbert Samuel, *Memoirs* (London: Faber & Faber, 1945), pp. 124–6.

39. Self, *The Austen Chamberlain Diary Letters*, Chamberlain to Ida, 20 October and 4 November 1917.

40. His closest political friend appears to have been Walter Long, the robustly Tory Colonial Secretary, who disliked both Lloyd George and those Unionists who conspired with him.

41. BL, Cave Papers, Cave 62497, Cave to Lloyd George, 2 February 1918; C. Mallet, *Lord Cave: A Memoir* (London: John Murray, 1931), p. 206. Had Cave left the government, one suggested replacement was Brace, the miners' leader, put forward by Barnes as a useful counter to Henderson (who had left the government) and equally as likely to unite his men behind the government by giving labour a 'bigger show'. HLRO, Lloyd George Papers, F/4/2/20, Barnes to Lloyd George, 20 February 1918.

42. See Mallet, *Lord Cave*.

43. PRO 30/69/1162, Herbert Morrison to Lloyd George, 25 September 1918.

44. PRO HO 144/1470, CID to Troup, 4 December 1916

45. Geary, *Policing Industrial Disputes*, p. 59. In May 1919, without a break, Thomson's bureau became the Special Branch, responsible for gathering domestic intelligence regarding subversive organizations.

46. Thomson, *The Scene Changes*, diary entry for 2 December 1916, p. 355.

47. Ibid., diary entry for 5 April 1917, p. 360.

48. Thurlow, *The Secret State*, p. 49.

49. Lord Birkenhead, *Frederick Eden Earl of Birkenhead* (London: Thorton Butterworth, 1935) pp. 80–3; Wiltsher, *Most Dangerous Women*, p. 197; Mitchell, *Women on the Warpath*, pp. 339–41.

50. Pat Barker's novel, *The Eye in the Door* (London: Plume, 1993), is based in large measure on the Wheeldon case.

51. Thomson, *The Scene Changes*, p. 314; Geary, *Policing Industrial Disputes*, p. 59.

52. PRO CAB 24/13, GT 733, 'Labour Intelligence', 15 April 1917; PRO HO 144 1484/349684, 'Proceedings Against Strikers, Report of Strikes, Labour Unrest, and Sabotage', April 1917. See also Waites, *A Class Society at War*, p. 183n; Morgan, *Conflict and Order*, p. 66.

53. See, for instance, PRO ADM 1/8482/46, *Committee of Trade Union Congress. Interview at the Admiralty*, particularly: 'Report of an Interview Granted to a Deputation from the Trades Union Congress on 16 February 1916'; ADM 1/8525/140, *Shipyard Labour*, particularly: Director of Priority Section (Sir Lyndon Macassey) to First Lord, 1 January 1917; ADM 1/8523/125, *Munitions of War Act*, particularly: 'Notes of a Meeting Held in the Financial Secretary's Room at the Admiralty, 19 October 1917', 'Munition of War Amendments (November 1917) and Analysis', Addison to War Cabinet GT 2691, 20 November 1917, WC GT 2656, November 1917, and R. R. Scott Minute, 20 May 1918.

54. PRO HO 45 10801/307402, Anti-Conscription Movement, Agitation 1916–1917, file 4, Secretary of State minute, and Army Council to GOCs (enclosed).

55. Consider, for instance, the case of Margaret Ashton, a WPC activist, prosecuted for advocating refusal to buy war bonds. Wiltsher, *Most Dangerous Women*, p. 197.

56. MUH, Russell Papers, Volume 710, Cockerill to Russell with Russell note, 6 October 1914.

57. This was a mighty inhibitor, and a considerable innovation. Previously, if something were judged actionable, publishers stood to lose only the actionable material. Under DRR 51, they could lose their presses and type. They could also, under DORA, face direct prosecution themselves.

58. PRO INF 4/1B.

59. BLIO, Chelmsford Papers, MSS Eur E 264/4, No. 19a, Secretary of State to Viceroy, 28 Feb 1918, summarizing memo by MI, WO with opinion HO and Scotland Yard. This is an interesting communication, essentially a 'how-to' from the government to India, on how to institute censorship, and concerning what organizations and publications from the UK were to be treated with greatest care.

60. PRO INF 4/1B.

61. PRO 30/69/1162, E. Robbins to MacDonald, 5 January 1918.

62. Examples: PRO HO 139/25/104, Part 3, File 71a, 'Engineers Strike at Liverpool', Press Bureau to Press, 23 February 1917:

> We understand that a general strike of engineers is contemplated at Liverpool and it is particularly requested that nothing may be published which might tend to encourage the workmen concerned otherwise than in the direction of an uninterrupted continuance of work.

Also, PRO HO 139/25/104, Part 4, File 75, Ministry of Munitions to Press Bureau, 7 May 1917. Attempt being made to organize engineers for strike against loss of exemption:

> The Minister is of the opinion that any mention of these strikes, or the probability of them, in the Press, might be likely to encourage their occurrence, and he would be glad, therefore, if you would be good enough to take steps to provide against any information of this character appearing in the Press.

63. PRO HO 139/23/96, Press Bureau to *MidCumberland & North Westmoreland Herald*, 19 February 1915.

64. Ibid.

65. Mallet, *Lord Cave*, pp. 202–4.

66. Ibid., p. 204, has 4,000. Cockerill, the censor in chief, on the other hand, has 5,000 in PRO HO 139/21/84, Part 17.

67. PRO INF 4/1B.

68. Ibid.

69. HLRO, Lloyd George Papers, F/6/4/2, Cave to Lloyd George, 12 January 1917.

70. HLRO, Lloyd George Papers, F/6/4/3, Lloyd George to Cave, 15 January 1917. Similarly, Henderson always advised Lloyd George that any attempt to crush the radical press would be 'highly inflammatory' and totally undermine his position with Labour. Leventhal, *Arthur Henderson*, p. 63.

71. HLRO, Lloyd George Papers, F/6/4/7, Cave to Lloyd George, 15 January 1917.

72. PRO HO 45 10814/312987, file 2, 26 June 1916 (reporting a speech at Merthyr Tydfil on 25 June, transcript enclosed); file 9, CID to HO, 1 December 1916 (reporting a speech at Coventry 26 November, transcript enclosed); file 8, Lincoln Local Committee of the Peace by Negotiations Committee, 30 November 1916 (transcript of speech enclosed); file 9, Swansea Borough Chief Constable to HO, 4 December 1916 (transcript of speech from shorthand record enclosed); and file 10, Snowden speeches, 2, 3 December at Clydach and Briton Ferry (transcript enclosed).

73. Ibid., file 12, 31 July 1917.

74. Ibid. The Snowdens' statements are reflective of a dangerous, and excited time. By the end of the war, both of the Snowdens were notorious and fiery anti-Bolsheviks. See, for instance, Russell's account of the Snowdens on their visit to Russia in 1920,

Russell, *Autobiography*, Vol. II, p. 102 etc.

75. PRO HO 139/23/96, Part 2, File 22, 12 October 1916.

76. PRO HO 144 1459/316284, Sedition. Arnold Lupton. MP Sleaford 1916–1918, file 7A ('Every Day at the Present Time'); file 4 ('What Are We Fighting For?'); and file 7, 'Raid on Residence', 16 November 1916.

77. Ibid., file 9, M.I.7a to HO, 3 December 1917.

78. *Manchester Guardian*, 17 April 1918.

79. *The Times*, 18 February 1918. See also HO 144/316284, file 10 for trial transcripts.

80. PRO HO 144 1459/316284, file 12, Proceedings by Director of Public Prosecutions, 22 April 1918.

81. PRO HO 45 10834/328752, Norman Angell, file 2, Mr Norman Angell's Visit to the United States of America, 26 January 1917.

82. *Daily Express*, 1 and 26 January 1917. On 17 July, Cecil Chesterton, reviewing his book for the *Daily Express*, judged his opinions 'not only false, but a loathsome insult to humanity'.

83. PRO HO 45 10834/328752, Norman Angell, file 2, Mr Norman Angell's Visit to the United States of America, 26 January 1917.

84. Ibid., file 3, 7 May 1917.

85. Snowden, *Autobiography*, p. 423.

86. Williams, *Home Fronts*, p. 70. The prohibition on movement to the United States was probably a mistake. Russell wanted to go to Harvard to teach mathematics. In October 1916, Francis Younghusband appealed to General Cockerill to let him go. Teaching duties, he thought, would leave Russell with little time to cause trouble (MUH, Vol. 710, Bertrand Russell to Cockerill, 5 October 1916). On the other hand, Russell's fines do not appear to have been much of a problem. A fine in July 1916, for instance, was ultimately paid by well-wishers who oversubscribed the fund several times. Russell's goods, seized as security, were returned, and excess money turned over to the NCF. See MUH, Vol. 710, Philip Morrell to Russell, 21 July 1916.

87. H. Cecil, 'Lord Robert Cecil and the League of Nations During the First World War', in P. Liddle (ed.), *Home Fires and Foreign Fields: British Social and Military Experience in the First World War* (London: Brassey's, 1985), p. 69. The FO had begun to monitor the foreign press to ascertain the effectiveness of the blockade. Chamberlain had been responsible for the blockade, initially. By the time of Morel's arrest he was parliamentary under-secretary. As always, during the battle against dissent, control of any kind could be re-deployed domestically. See Lord Cecil of Chelwood, *All the Way* (London: Hodder & Stoughton, 1944), p. 137.

88. LSE, Morel Papers, Morel F6/8, WO to Morel, 12 November 1915.

89. LSE, Morel Papers, Morel F6/8, WO to Morel, 16 November 1916.

90. Ibid.

91. LSE, Morel Papers, Morel F6/8, Trevelyan to WO, 20 November 1916.

92. Ibid.

93. LSE, Morel Papers, Morel F6/8, WO to UDC, 8 June 1918.

94. See, for instance, LSE Morel Papers, Morel F1/5, 'Memorandum by E. D. Morel on Rex v. E. D. Morel', March 1918. For Morel's trial see, as well, Cline, *E. D. Morel*, pp. 112–15.

95. Swartz, *The Union of Democratic Control*, pp. 178–9. See also for the trial, LSE, Morel Papers, Morel F1/3-5, 'Trial 1918'; particularly, F1/3, 'Transcript of a Trial at Bow, 1 & 4 September 1917'; F1/4, 'Morel vs. Rex'; Snowden, *Autobiography*, pp. 423–4. Morel's imprisonment was the proximate cause for the raid on the NCF offices, and the Lupton and Zusman homes, due to their known association with Morel.

96. See, for example, LSE, Morel Papers, Morel F1/4, letters to Cave, 18 September 1917; Morel F1/5, Cave to Trevelyan 19 December 1917; Cave to Ponsonby, 18 January 1918.

97. LSE, Morel Papers, Morel F1/5, Ponsonby to Mrs Morel, 1 November 1917; Cave to Ponsonby, 20 November 1917; HO to Mrs Morel, 30 November 1917 etc.

98. LSE, Morel Papers, Morel F6/6, Morel to the Earl of Denbigh, 9 May 1918. House of Lords Debates, 8 May 1918.

99. LSE, Morel Papers, Morel F6/6, Morel to the Editor, 2 May 1918. *Nineteenth Century and After*, 83, 494 (April 1918), enclosed.

100. LSE, Morel Papers, Morel F6/6, 'A Londoner's Diary', *Evening Standard*, 24 May 1918. Morel of course protested that none of this was true, and due to the nature of the UDC was able to disavow membership of almost everything. His letter to the paper was followed by others from most of the organizations named indicating that Morel had never been a member.

101. Cline, *E. D. Morel*, pp. 113–14.

102. LSE, Morel Papers, Morel F6/7, Morel to Mrs Snowden, undated.

103. Morel's principal contemporary biographer maintains that Morel gravitated to the Labour Party following his realization that it was the only party that adhered to the foreign policy line he had long advocated (Cline, *E. D. Morel*, p. 106). Morel, she tells us, was never really a socialist. He simply believed that the ILP was the only organized force willing to change the way in which Britain conducted its affairs (pp. 107–8). While there may be some truth in this thesis, it also seems probable that there were more immediate causes for Morel's conversion. Surely his movement to the ILP owed much to his arrest, his experience in prison, and to the public calumny which greeted him upon release. The state made it obvious in a way that could not be denied that it was his enemy. Morel, like Shinwell, came to espouse a more radical position in response.

104. PRO HO 45 10801/307402, Anti-Conscription Movement, Agitation 1916–1917, file 54a, May 1917. Those fined were: Edward Grubb, Archibald Brockway, William Joseph Chamberlain, Walter Henry Ayles, Alfred Brown, John Fletcher, Morgan Jones and Leyton Richards. In addition, henceforth, police files were kept on Brockway and Jones.

105. Snowden, *Autobiography*, p. 426.

106. PRO HO 144/1470, file 254, Chief Constable, Newcastle upon Tyne to HO, 12 October 1917.

107. Ibid., file 263, 12 November 1917.

108. Ibid., file 270, November 1917.

109. PRO HO 139/23/96, Part 2, File 34.

110. HLRO, Beaverbrook Papers, C/261, Beaverbrook to Northcliffe, 2 March 1917.

111. House of Lords Debates, 8 May 1918.

112. HLRO, Lloyd George Papers, F/4/5/20, Beaverbrook to Lloyd George, 3 June 1918.

113. PRO 30/69/1162, E. Whiteley to MacDonald, 16 April 1918.

114. PRO HO 139/23/96, Press Bureau to Stephenson, 27 March 19167; Matthews (DPP) to Press Bureau, 22 April 1916.

115. See MUH, Russell Papers, Volume 410, 'Alternative Service' (Clifford Allen), May 1916. For Allen's continued truculence, see, for example, Clifford Allen to NCF, 31 May 1917.

116. Snowden, *Autobiography*, p. 405. For the transcript of Allen's trial, see MUH, 410.046849, 'The Case of Mr Clifford Allen'.

117. See *Daily Express*, 10 June 1916; *The Times*, 15 and 25 June 1916.

118. Local appeals boards, Snowden notes, were often packed with men who had been prominent recruiters, and who had been selected from party lists. They were not, therefore, men very willing to give dissenters much of a hearing. We have already seen, as well, how a defining feature of patriot labour leaders was their willingness to serve on appeals boards. Snowden, *Autobiography*, p. 403.

119. See, for instance, House of Commons Debates, 26 July 1916. For Lloyd George's thinking on compulsion, see PRO CAB 17/56; also Adams and Poirier, *The Conscription Controversy*, pp. 176–7.
120. For example, PRO WO 83: ADJA for JAG to AG, 26 June indicates 22 objectors being tried with sentences ranging from 56 days' imprisonment, to two years' imprisonment with hard labour. ADJA for JAG to AG, 27 June, lists 28 men, sentences ranging from 28 days' to 112 days' imprisonment. ADJA for JAG to AG, 28 June, indicates that 34 men were tried and sentenced to two years' imprisonment.
121. PRO WO 83, JAG to Secretary of State, 30 June 1916.
122. PRO MH 47, letter of Isaac Goss to review board, case M1890, 12 June 1916, enclosing letter from Hughes to Goss 22 May 1916, letter of unnamed soldier to Goss (undated), and letter of Walker brothers to sister, May 1916. Not all absolutists were dealt with so harshly. Morgan Jones, a friend of Bertrand Russell, was held at the depot of the Welsh Regiment, and had nothing really to complain about except the food, which he found appallingly bad. MUH, volume 805, Morgan Jones to Russell, undated 1916.
123. See MUH, volume 535, Catherine Marshall circular letter, 14 July 1916; 'Are COs going to be shot?', NCF pamphlet, undated 1916. See also Marwick, *The Deluge*.
124. House of Lords Debates, no. 21, 4 May 1916, cols. 904–13; Wilkinson, *The Church of England*, p. 50.
125. See, for example, MUH, Russell Papers, Philip Morrell to Bertrand Russell, undated 1916.
126. The Society of Friends, the NCF and the FOR united to wage a joint campaign against this element of conscription. MUH, Russell Papers, Vol. 535, Russell to Branch Secretaries NCF, 4 July 1916, and 'Report IV Arrests', 9 May 1916.
127. Marwick, *The Deluge*, p. 81. Marwick's source is J. W. Graham who was the principal of Manchester University and a member of the Liverpool Labour Party and the UDC – therefore, hardly an objective source. In France, their crime was given greater significance, as the objectors would then be judged to be on foreign service.
128. PRO WO 123/58 (1916): AO 179/1916: X – Offences against Discipline. –

  1. With reference to paragraph 583 (xi) of the King's Regulations, where an offence against discipline has been committed and the accused soldier represents that the offence was the result of conscientious objection to military service, imprisonment and not detention should be awarded.
  2. A soldier who is sentenced to imprisonment for an offence against discipline, which was represented by the soldier at his trial to have been the result of conscientious objection to military service, will be committed to the nearest public prison ...

129. PRO WO 83, JAG to AG, 5 December 1916, and JAG to AG 30 January 1917.
130. Marwick, *The Deluge*, p. 81.
131. Wilson, *The Political Diaries of C. P. Scott*, various.
132. Snowden, *Autobiography*, p. 410. Snowden's figures probably derived from those compiled by the Conscientious Objectors' Information Bureau. If so, they are certainly understated, as only 125 men are listed as 'objectors who evaded the draft'. Pankhurst, *The Home Front*, p. 367.
133. Mallet, *Lord Cave*, p. 188.
134. Ibid., p. 204. Snowden's figure is much larger, and seems to have influenced the subsequent historical account, though it appears to have been derived from wartime dissenting propaganda. Snowden, *Autobiography*, p. 410. Marwick, closer to Mallet, has 16,000 conscientious objectors, of whom something like 6,000 ultimately did time in prison, and of whom 70 died in, or as a result of prison.

Marwick, *The Deluge*, pp. 83–4; the figures are again derived from J. W. Graham. Sylvia Pankhurst also lists a far larger number of objectors who died from their experience but does not give a source, Pankhurst, *The Home Front*, pp. 364–7. Higher figures are repeated, for instance, in Mitchell, *Women on the Warpath*, p. 337, who has 71 conscientious objectors dying.

135. Snowden, *Autobiography*, p. 411.
136. Examples of those exempted if they found employment of war value: PRO MH 47, Case of Leo Richard Riocreux, Case 39 (to find work with special constabulary); Case of Francis Albert Simmonds, Case S376, November 1917 (refused not only military service, but service with Red Cross; conditionally exempted).
137. Nigel Young, for instance, believes that the idea of alternative service was developed explicitly to satisfy the requirements of religious dissent. Young, 'War Resistance and the British Peace Movement since 1914', pp. 31–2.
138. Quakers, in particular, appear to have been exercised by this danger. See Ceadel, *Pacifism in Britain 1914–1945*, p. 25.
139. PRO MH 47, Case of Archibald Montague Mather, M2908, February 1917.
140. PRO MH 47, Case of Edgar Raillons Parker, January 1917.
141. PRO MH 47, Case of Alexander Sim, M1213, June 1916. Maurice Gregory, Minister, Society of Friends to Middlesex Appeals Tribunal, June 1916:

> As a minister of long-standing in the Society of Friends, and Clerk to the Elders for eight years of the Westminster and Longford Monthly meeting of the same society, it gives me great pleasure to say that, if it will help you in your application for exemption from military service, you are quite at liberty to mention to the local Tribunal the fact that you consulted me in March 1915, as to the tenets and practices of the Society of Friends.
>
> I have full recollection how that upon my brief explanation of the views of the Friends you stated your intention of seeking membership in the Society if, after twelve months consideration and prayer, you felt led to do so.
>
> I am further glad to know that after the twelve months study of the Book of Discipline and Practice you are as I believe, most genuinely convinced of the Holy Spirit that you should seek membership in our society, and that you are now an attender at the Ealing meeting.

142. PRO MH 47, Case of Arthur Herbert Gates, M 452, April 1916 (allowed to work with YMCA).
143. PRO MH 47, Case of Dr Rosslyn Earp, May 1917 (desired by Society of Friends for work with Friends War Victims' Relief Committee); case of S. T. Wallis, July 1918 (required for work with War Victims Relief Committee); case of Clement Edward Russell, M673, May 1916 (required for Friends Ambulance Unit).
144. *Collected Works of Bertrand Russell*, Vol. XIV, pp. 345–6.
145. PRO HO 45 10808/311118, John Scott Duckers. Arrest Under Military Services Act.
146. The perception that dissenters were prigs, sectarians and fanatics seems to have had lasting implications for the Labour Party. Orwell indicates it as a primary inhibition keeping many, otherwise sympathetic persons, from becoming socialist in the interwar period. 'If only', he wrote in *The Road to Wigan Pier*, 'the sandals and the pistachio-coloured shirts could be put in a pile and burnt, and every vegetarian, teetotaller and creeping Jesus sent home to Welwyn Garden City to do his yoga exercises quietly!' (p. 221). 'The ordinary man may not flinch from a dictatorship of the proletariat, if you offer it tactfully; offer him a dictatorship of the prigs, and he gets ready to fight' (p. 182). There is some suggestion that Clifford Allen ultimately came to see that the NCF had made a tremendous tactical mistake in refusing all co-operation. See, for example, De Groot, *Blighty*, p. 156.

147. Wilkinson, *The Church of England*, pp. 49–50. For the dissenters' reaction, see 'A Valuable Suggestion by the Bishop of Exeter', *Collected Works of Bertrand Russell*, Vol. XIV, pp. 334–5.

148. Wilkinson, *The Church of England*, p. 50. Although C. P. Scott, the editor, was no friend of conscription, an enemy to compulsion, and inclined always to favour tolerance for COs, he was also a friend of Lloyd George, and his dislike of conscription was based on his religious rather than political principles.

149. PRO MH 47, Case of William Herbert Hoy, 29 November 1917. Judgement of tribunal: 'The man's objection to Military Service is purely political and does not amount to a Conscientious objection and to the taking of life and everything designed to assist in the war within true intent and meaning of the Military Services Act' (Central Decision 55).

150. PRO MH 47, Case of James Henley Winship, M641, May 1916.

151. PRO MH 47, Case of Frederick John Maer, M29, March 1916. Note to file: 'This man is earning his living making *Rifles* but says he is a conscientious objector'.

152. Pankhurst, *The Home Front*, pp. 399–400.

8

Leeds, Stockholm and After

IF THE social–political situation in Britain was not dangerous enough, there was as well the enormous fillip for discontent of all kinds provided by the first Russian Revolution in March 1917. For all dissenters (and most Britons) this revolution, whatever its implications for the war, seemed to be a signal victory for liberty. Clifford Allen celebrated the thrilling news coming out of Russia by leading his fellow absolutists in a boycott of prison work which earned them a corresponding hardening of the conditions in which they were held.[1] The editor of the *Manchester Guardian*, C. P. Scott, no radical, hailed the revolution as 'a wonderful and glorious event'.[2] Even H. G. Wells – a vice-president of the BWNL after all – enraptured by the news coming out of Russia, advocated the abolition of the monarchy in *The Times*.[3] For dissenters, the revolution was a doubly favourable event in that it was also a clear sign that the war could not long continue. Dissent, throughout 1917, waxed in strength and confidence. Already, on 31 March 1917, George Lansbury's Anglo-Russian-Democratic Alliance (a new organization) arranged a mass meeting of friends of the Russian revolution in Albert Hall. Nearly 12,000 people attended, with 5,000 being turned away at the door. Lansbury used the opportunity to sound the tocsin for a negotiated peace. This was the first time since 1915 that a large, public rally of dissenters had been successfully staged in London.[4] It was obvious that 17,000 people could not readily be intimidated even by patriot gangs. If patriot coercion were employed on the scale that would be required, then this was not civil disturbance but something like civil war. It was equally unlikely that a press blackout would stop the news of this success from spreading.[5] It was less likely still that the government could simply prohibit events so large that they must reflect a significant shift in public opinion. The example of the revolution was the more dangerous because that faction most interested in peace (the Bolshevik party) was also most determined upon violent social upheaval. From the beginning, the Bolsheviks were a power in the soviets and used these to attempt to end what they viewed as a purposeless war to begin a very purposeful revolution. Some in Britain sympathized with, and were prepared to assist this programme. Before the October revolution many more heeded the line coming from the soviets, if only to further the cause of peace. Not only, therefore, did the revolution encourage dissent as a whole, but it continued the process by which dissent emerged in an ever more coherent and extreme form with a powerful social–political component.

In the process, of course, the Russian revolution increased political polarization in Britain. While dissenters celebrated the event, the failure of even an autocratic ally led to little rejoicing in patriotic circles, H. G. Wells notwithstanding. Rather, it produced a sense of desperation productive in turn of hysteria. Moreover, many government leaders doubted that the spring revolution was an auspicious event even for Russia. Milner, Curzon and Henderson quickly recorded their belief that it was apt to pave the way for another revolution, state collapse, and social disintegration.[6] Many patriots began to fear that a repetition in Britain was distinctly possible. 'The state of affairs is very bad', the normally phlegmatic Lord Derby (War Minister) wrote to General Haig (Commander BEF) as early as May 1917, '[and] there is no doubt that the Russian revolution has created an unrest which is revolutionary and dangerous.'[7] The Russian factor became even more divisive following the October revolution, an event absolutely abhorrent to British conservatives, and taken as a sign of the way things were likely to shape at home if dissent were not effectively contained. Dissenters were no longer simply 'pro-Germans', but potential Lenins.

One of the first illustrations of how things would be in the future came when a peace meeting in Leeds, scheduled to commemorate the Russian revolution and to coincide with an ILP national congress, was forbidden outright by police authority.[8] It was questionable that the police had the power to do this. Certainly there was no precedent. Previously, HMG had consistently attempted to restrain such over-zealous behaviour by local authorities. Forbidding a party conference would be a new departure, which could not but be provoking.

Some associates of Lloyd George, at this juncture in the war, believed that absolute prohibition was less dangerous than permitting the conference to proceed. Pre-emption, these considered, was now essential. Lord Milner, for instance, advised by Victor Fisher, harassed Lloyd George mercilessly to stop the conference.[9] Was it not the avowed intention of the convenors (Jowett, Lansbury, Smillie, Snowden and MacDonald) to start a process 'to do for this country what the Russian Revolution has accomplished for Russia'?[10] What more evidence did the government require that revolution was now the aim, and a policy in keeping with the nature of the new threat an urgent requirement? For the moment, however, to forbid a party conference was to go too far. Following a political clamour, which produced a government back-down, the ILP conference went forward from 3 June 1917.[11] The War Cabinet considered that while the conference would certainly take on a 'revolutionary character', prohibition would be impolitic. Soldiers, of course, were to be prohibited from attending in order to prevent the inevitable treachery which would flow from the conference infecting the services. The conference itself could not be stopped.[12]

The Leeds conference, for our purposes, is a useful barometer. Until the Leeds conference, patriots had consistently outnumbered dis-senters at trade union and Labour Party conferences. A Labour Party conference at Manchester, in January 1917, had ended with the resolution passed with a majority of more than five to one (1,637,000 to 302,000) that Britain had to persevere in the war until Germany had been utterly defeated. An even greater proportion, nearly six to one (1,849,000 to 307,000), voted for participation in coalition.[13] George Lansbury had concluded from this performance that 'the [Labour] Party [was] hopeless' for the purpose of carrying dissent because of its TUC and patriot majorities.[14] At the Leeds conference, however, the proportions were reversed. Nearly two to one, delegates voted for a negotiated peace. The dissenters, for the first time, were ascendant despite the best attempts of Bevin, Tupper and their flag-draped supporters.[15]

We should note, of course, that this did not mean that the dissenters were now a majority of the working class as a whole, although that has sometimes been the claim.[16] At Leeds, the ILP and BSP – both grossly over-represented, and with the BSP recently purged of the last of its patriotic membership – formed a short-lived united socialist council. This enabled them to set the agenda to a much greater extent than was warranted.[17] Meanwhile Philip Snowden had replaced the more cautious Fred Jowett as chairman of the ILP.[18] Doctrinal differences were forgotten as dissenting leaderships united against the war. An ebullient, convinced, missionary left dragged the more powerful TUC behind it. But still, how could the united ILP–BSP, a minority within the Labour party and its affiliates, be considered competent to speak for the working class as an entirety – particularly given the fact that many prewar members had simply abandoned both parties for the BWNL? Moreover, no sooner did the conference end then there were second thoughts in the TUC. Labour leaders, by their nature, did not approve of socialist sectarians. Keir Hardie might have approved of the policy Leeds produced: he would have been appalled by how it was produced.

Apprised of what Robert Williams, the Transport Workers' organizer, had been up to at Leeds, the virulently patriotic James Sexton flayed him at union meetings. Leeds, Sexton shouted, was 'the most bogus, the most dishonest, the most corrupt conference ever conceived'.[19] Sexton, of course, was only speaking for his dockers. The climb-down from Leeds began almost as soon as the conference was over.

Nevertheless, 'Leeds angered and frightened people', MacDonald wrote, 'because it revealed how widespread and confident was the popular peace movement for liberty and peace'.[20] It did reveal, in any case, that dissent was becoming united, and establishing a place for itself on the far left, and that it was capable of influencing considerable numbers of the less convinced to give it a hearing. Leeds meant, potentially, that dissent might well obtain a political vehicle, where it had been a minority tendency within all parties before. 'Hitherto', Trevelyan exulted in *The Nation*,

> the British Labour Party has played a secondary part as a force of discontent driving Governments to progressive courses. It has now become a directing force, stepping in to divert the world from imitating the old patterns. More important to shape a new course.[21]

Bertrand Russell, then chairman of the NCF, excited by the turn events had taken, began to distance himself from his early war connections. For the following year, he worked heart and soul for the Labour Party, seeing in revolution, or the threat of revolution, the only way of bringing the government to its senses and Britain out of the war.[22]

With the example of the Russian revolution before them and with the Labour Party wavering, the dissenting line became ever more fundamental, political and explicitly socialist. At Leeds, the accolades heaped upon revolutionary Russia by leaders hitherto not known for their Marxism – Sylvia Pankhurst, Macdonald and Snowden, for instance – were so extravagant that the genuine Marxists (Gallacher, McManus) were left with nothing to say.[23] It was George Lansbury, a Christian Socialist, and not Red Gallacher who called for a 'complete social and industrial revolution by the organized Labour and Socialist movements'.[24] Bertrand Russell spoke movingly about the plight of Clifford Allen, and, more exceptionally, supported a resolution that workers' and soldiers' soviets be formed in Britain, following the Russian model.[25] Indeed, he went further than this: in the aftermath of Leeds, still exultant, he ordered NCF branch secretaries to send delegates to the soviet then assembling in Leeds.[26] It was the opinion of F. E. Smith and the law lords that some of the dissenters – though not Lansbury or Russell – had moved to the point where even spoken expression of their opinion was now actionable. Passages in the speeches delivered by Smillie, Mrs Montefiore, Bevan, Ammon, Robert Williamson and Fred Shaw in particular, it was considered, gave grounds for prosecution under DRR 42.[27] All the fire, outrage and excitement, of course, was probably simply a sign that the speakers did not truly understand what a revolution meant, or, more particularly, what was then happening in Russia.[28] Whatever was happening in Moscow, the police were certain, at least, that they knew what was happening in Leeds, and were careful to note it all down. What they heard in Leeds simply confirmed what they had long suspected in any case.

The Leeds conference was also important in that it occasioned an outbreak of anti-Semitic rioting aimed at the resident Jewish community.[29] While the conference proceeded, there were several incidents of stone-throwing, and shop-breaking which targeted Jews. Private Max Rosenbloom, a Jewish volunteer on leave, was hospitalized.[30] The press, rightly, deplored the incident. The only consolation the *Yorkshire Evening Post* could find was that most of those involved were juvenile hooligans. Reporting the Rosenbloom incident, the *Post* took some comfort from the fact that once the rioters had injured a soldier in uniform the rioting had quieted considerably, and a threatening crowd had formed determined to prevent other such incidents.[31] This was too much, plainly, even for the majority of the patriots. Nevertheless, further anti-Semitic rioting was reported in London in October.[32]

Why the Jews? To answer this question is also to understand the significance of the incident. In the eyes of many 'patriotic' Britons, the Jews were triply damned as aliens, as socialists (according to the popular stereotype), and finally as 'shirkers'. Jews were vulnerable to this last charge since many were recent arrivals, and it followed from their legal identity as aliens that few were allowed to enlist in the British Army. A pogrom, however muted, was simply a reaction to tensions raised from what was transpiring at the conference, and illustrated, once again, how nasty things were becoming on the home front. The Leeds riot was the first incident in a widespread, irrational anti-foreign mania continuing through to the end of the war. Every month a new focus was found – one month, the Jews, the next the Germans, then the Ukrainians, then the Germans again. What had been sporadic anti-German excess began to become a climate of universal, xenophobic dislike and distrust. Meanwhile, a new charge was being levelled against the dissenters – that they were aiding the German bomber offensive, and were therefore simply foreign agents pure and simple. Even in working-class neighbourhoods this charge could be highly inflammatory and effective. Later in 1917, for example, there was an attempt to organize a soviet in London, following from the Leeds decision. Bertrand Russell, in particular, was an enthusiastic advocate. The first meeting of the soviet, however, was advertised in the press, and patriot leaflets charged attendees with aiding and abetting the enemy. The soviet never assembled, and Russell himself was narrowly saved by the police from being murdered by women wielding boards full of nails.[33] Excesses of all kinds – rising xenophobia and violence against dissenters – were symptomatic of the near-delirium which gripped much of British society in the last bitter years of the war.

The Leeds conference, finally, was significant in that it provided a platform from which a far more ambitious programme could be expounded. It was at Leeds that the idea of a reassembled Second International arbitrating a peace over the heads of the governments was first mooted in Britain. The proposal originated with a Dutch–Scandinavian group of socialist parties, after which it was taken up by the Russian soviets. It dovetailed with a Bolshevik attempt to convene a Labour–Socialist conference to end the war and start the revolution.[34]

However attractive it might be for dissenters, a peace negotiated at a meeting of the Second International, as Ramsay MacDonald saw, was not a peace the government would like. It was obvious to him that the government hated the new order emerging in Russia. 'Our upper classes have not accepted the Russian Revolution', he advised his readers in *Free Man* even before the Bolshevik coup. 'They are for the Czar, and they dislike the new government with its democratic candour and its backbone.'[35] MacDonald, on the other hand, viewed the March revolution as an entirely positive development, and the calls for a negotiated peace coming out of Russia as a tremendous opportunity to end the war with the balance of political victory in favour of the democracies. He was certain, in any case, that the idea of a compromise peace however obtained should not be rejected out of hand.

> If the war must go on, it must go on. But labour is not sure; and, in view of the admitted need to revise terms, of the secret undertakings which are contrary to the original purpose of the war, and of the utter unreliability of the press, Labour has a right to satisfy itself that it is not being used as a mere pawn in a game of which it does not approve.[36]

So what to do? The dissenters were inclined to test the water at Stockholm, and could probably get the authorization of the Labour Party to do it. The government was sure to be opposed. The idea, quite simply, was going to have to be marketed. If the Germans could be brought to attend, MacDonald considered, then might the internal collapse of the Central Powers not come about through Stockholm?[37] This, in any case, was the argument which MacDonald attempted to make to Lloyd George.[38]

MacDonald was right about this at least: the government hated the idea. It was not up to Ramsay MacDonald to give permission to the German socialists to attend. While a collapse might well develop out of Stockholm, it was unlikely, HMG considered, to be Germany's. Moreover, Stockholm would represent a huge breach in censorship. Contact between ordinary Britons and Germans had been effectively stopped from 1915, and with Russians from the spring of 1917.[39] How to rebuild the dikes, if they were once breached? Even more than for all of these reasons, the government hated Stockholm because of the nature of the appeals coming from the soviets. Here the process was envisioned as ending, not with a discussion of issues, but in a peace negotiated despite the governments.[40] HMG was never prepared to consider this notion.

Milner, by this time probably the second-strongest member of the War Cabinet, was horrified. Even the idea of Stockholm badly shook Milner's faith in the British working class. In a private capacity he warned Cave that he had better start having all working-class meetings watched, because whether such a meeting started out as such or not it could not help but 'turn into, a pacifist and revolutionary meeting'.[41] The attendance of a British delegation at Stockholm, he thought, would be 'absolutely disastrous'. The government should do everything possible to 'discountenance [Britain's] attendance & to damn the thing generally'. If this were not done, and if labour failed to receive a strong lead, then it would bend to the Stockholm line and 'where should we be then? Frankly I feel the position will soon become untenable.' The Unionists in the government, Milner advised, were going to have to hold together on the Stockholm question and impose their will because, Milner thought, Lloyd George was insufficiently resolved to employ sufficient force to kill this thing once and for all.[42]

Carson, at this time the Cabinet minister with principal responsibility for the propaganda fight against dissent, was just as frightened. Do not wait, he advised, for the thing to blow up. Pre-empt it in common with the other allies.[43] His advice?

> I desire ... to state that I hold the very strongest view ... that the Government should give no sanction whatever to the holding of the Stockholm Conference and should as soon as possible make an announcement that it will not tolerate any delegates going from this country to meet the enemy. ... [T]o allow delegates of any party or organization to usurp the duties and functions of Government would

be fraught with the most disastrous of consequences to the future of this country.[44]

Even far away in India, political officers were worried, and hoped that if Stockholm could not be stopped there would be, at least, a powerful, official British delegation to keep the oriental delegates in line.[45] Sir Edwin Montagu, Secretary of State for India, advised the Viceroy that, in his opinion,

> The situation with regard to Labour and the Stockholm Conference is critical … I am certain of this, speaking for myself, that it is difficult to ask our soldiers to hurl themselves against the German machine-guns if we are going to countenance parleying with the enemy at the same time.[46]

About the only Cabinet Minister who appears to have retained any sense of balance was the phlegmatic Lord Derby who gave as his opinion that if Ramsay MacDonald were the British delegate, and if he restricted himself to speaking in Stockholm the way he talked in Britain, there was nothing to worry about.[47]

While other governments simply prohibited attendance from an apparent absence of other alternatives, Lloyd George was more resourceful. Placed in a room without windows and only one door, Lloyd George could normally identify three or four possible exits. He decided to manage what he was afraid to stop. He worked first to draw Stockholm's poison before encouraging others to kill it.

The first step was to attempt, through Henderson, to kill the idea that the Stockholm conference should be a forum for peace.[48] Henderson, of course, was hardly the man for the job. Initially, he had opposed Britain's entry to the war, so much did he hate the idea of alliance with Czardom. He was, moreover, secretary to the British section of the Second International.[49] In addition, he had returned from a fact-finding mission to Russia convinced that a negotiated peace was now essential, if only to give his friend Kerensky the opportunity to win the fight against the Russian extremists.[50] Not for nothing was he viewed by the Bolsheviks as a 'British Kerensky'.[51] When Henderson balked at this charge, Lloyd George attempted to convince him to work to ensure that patriotic Labour or, failing that, the TUC controlled the selection of delegates.[52] When the Labour Party voted by a strong majority, at the beginning of August, to attend the meeting, Lloyd George advised Henderson to 'chuck the Labour Party' altogether, and move over to his projected new National Party and work to consolidate labour there.[53] Had Henderson followed Lloyd George's advice he would have hopelessly fractured the Labour Party. This, of course, was the premier's purpose. Henderson, however, was too much of a party loyalist to go so far. He could plainly not go on in the government. Henderson, confused and hopelessly compromised, refused to assist Lloyd George any further and withdrew from the government.

At first there was trouble. Henderson had been popular with both dissenters and patriots. Even the patriotic TUC MPs, furious at the way in which Henderson had been treated during the 'doormat incident', thundered that this meant the end of co-operation with the government. '[A]nyone taking Henderson's place', they considered, would be nothing less than a 'blackleg'.[54] Lloyd George, always politically adept, replaced Henderson in the War Cabinet with the popular and patriotic George Barnes. George Wardle, meanwhile, became acting chairman of the PLP.[55] Through Barnes and Wardle, the government encouraged division within labour ranks, and thus ultimately deprived the Stockholm idea of much of its original force as patriots battled with dissenters for control. The issue, of course, was camouflaged. Often it seemed to be not so much dissenters versus patriots, as trade-unionists versus socialists: a fight about internal power, and not about the ultimate agenda. In such a fight, even Keir Hardie would hardly have known where to stand. In the end, Barnes and his allies (Wardle, Adamson, Tillett, Bevin, Wilson, Sexton, and so on) managed to handle the affair so that it was safe men who were nominated to attend.[56] Barnes and his faction persuaded the TUC to demand that any delegates to Stockholm would have to come either from the Labour Party or from the TUC. Those who were simply socialists, lacking affiliation, would not be acceptable.[57] In practice, this would amount to trade union domination of any delegation. And, even before such a cooked delegation would be allowed to proceed, Barnes and Albert Thomas (France's Socialist Minister of Munitions: the French equivalent of Barnes) would organize a preliminary conference of allied labour and socialist representatives in London to co-ordinate a common allied line. This line, needless to say, would be suitably patriotic.[58] Ultimately, Kerensky himself came to the assistance of Lloyd George: first with a letter to J. H. Thomas in August, and then by arriving in person after the October revolution. While Stockholm might have been a good idea in June, he thought, it was a terrible idea by August as he lost control of the soviets and the soviets lost control of the situation.[59]

With all of the confusion, equivocation, stalling, and in-fighting orchestrated by Lloyd George, his collaborators and their allies, enthusiasm for the Stockholm experiment quickly began to decline. Initially, for instance, the idea of sending a delegation to Stockholm had passed through a TUC conference with a majority of 1,846,000 votes to 550,000. By 21 August, this majority had slipped to 1,234,000 votes to 1,231,000, as the MFGB turned against the proposal.[60] This was hardly a resounding vote of support. By September, the TUC was insisting that there should be no international meetings until total allied solidarity had been ensured.[61] How to participate in any meeting of the Second International, Barnes wanted to know, when the American Federation of Labor, and the Belgian, French and Italian socialists had already said they would not attend?[62] By the end of the month, the TUC was insisting, this being the case, that it would not support participation in any international meetings prior to victory.[63] The upshot? Only now did the War Cabinet decide to prohibit Stockholm. Lloyd George had been waiting for Barnes and his friends to do their job, so that any prohibition would appear to follow from an existing Labour Party decision not to attend anyway.[64] Prohibition would appear a restraint on splitters reinforcing Labour unity, rather than an item in a programme of political or class repression.

The government's careful handling of the TUC at the time of the Stockholm question was significant for another reason. In an effort to bypass the Labour Party's unpredictable political leadership, the government had been dealing directly with the unions, the membership of which had grown by half since 1914, and some of which, by consolidation and expansion, had grown mighty indeed.[65] In aligning itself with the unions HMG ensured that, whatever happened, production, the war effort and social peace would not be seriously compromised. Lloyd George, working through Barnes and his friends, had managed to decouple the TUC from the socialists, and therefore, labour from the dissenters at a dangerous juncture, and concerning a alarming and divisive question.

What was assembled instead, on 11 October 1917, was the London conference of Trade Unions of the Entente Powers, Affiliated to the *Internationale* Secretariat. Needless to add, this was supportive of allied policy and insistent on victory. By the time this conference assembled, moreover, the NWAC was up and running and its assets were used to propagandise the delegates.[66] In January 1918, the patriots back in the saddle, the Nottingham Labour Party conference voted two to one (1,885,000 to 722,000) for continued participation in the coalition, and perseverance in the war.[67] This, of course, was hardly what the Russians had in mind when they suggested a meeting of the Second International to consider the future of the war, and a giant step back from Trevelyan's hopes of the spring.

There was better still to come. When Ramsay MacDonald announced his intention to go to Stockholm as a private citizen in order to represent the minority dissenting tendency, he was boycotted by the NASFU. When MacDonald attempted to take ship, Captain Tupper was personally on hand to prevent him from going on board. To make the NASFU action particularly poignant, the seaman delegated to send MacDonald packing was from his home town. 'We'll no carry traitors as ye on this ship' was his message to MacDonald.[68] When Henderson attempted to attend a later conference, he received the same answer from the seamen. Meanwhile, in order to underline its re-established dominance, the TUC insisted that there could be no minority positions in the British Labour Party (LP).[69] All the frustrated dissenters could do was to send messages to the Russians, through Geneva, that any British delegates who might attend international conferences did not represent the entirety of the LP. This message, rather annoyingly, was not actionable, since good care was taken to ensure that it did not go through the post or telegraph, was not committed to paper and hand-carried, and was not intended for publication in a foreign paper.[70] In the end, the Stockholm idea was a complete failure. An attempt to do better, assembling a new conference at Berne, failed as miserably. Here, the only British representation was a letter from the TUC which announced that since Germany had started the war and was waging it in a reprehensible manner, no TUC delegate could possibly sit at the same table as a German.[71]

Still, the dissenters were not without their successes, however modest. It was at this time, for instance, that the LP accepted a truly socialist platform for the first time. While worrying for the government ('socialist' was still thought to imply 'revolutionary'), this development by no means constituted a call for immediate revolution, nor was it, really, even an expression of dissent. While Ramsay MacDonald has often received the credit for the 1918 programme, the moving spirit was actually Henderson assisted by Sidney Webb. Neither Henderson nor Webb were dissenters. Henderson we have seen. He never doubted that Britain's cause was just. In 1917, for a moment, he believed that peace was in the general interest and that he could be more useful outside, than inside, the government. Webb, the Fabian and a one-time Co-efficient, looked to the war as an opportunity to be exploited.[72] He did not even disapprove of conscription provided that it was implemented fairly and rationally. In designing the LP 1918 platform, Henderson, Webb and their TUC collaborators were most interested in ensuring the unity of the party in the postwar world, while preventing a recurrence of the excessive exuberance demonstrated at Leeds by their dissenting comrades on the left.[73] They would do this by conceding principle to the left while retaining a critical mass of party power for the TUC.

Stopping Stockholm was not enough. HMG was already attempting to impose a quarantine on all non-official contacts with Russia. An example unknown is an example unheeded. The trigger was the Bolshevik attempt to contact Western dissenters, initially through the soviets and then later through Russian state machinery following the October revolution, in order to end the war and start the revolution.[74] This was far too inflammatory a message for unhampered communication.

When, for instance, Maxim Litvinov began contacting British newspapers, in the winter of 1917–18, he was censored absolutely. Newspapers (*Pioneer, Workers' Dreadnought, Call, Daily Herald, Labour Leader*) which had been following his speeches and publishing his appeals, were warned that they would not be protected simply because Litvinov was the Russian ambassador.[75] The press prohibition was natural. Litvinov's message was blatantly seditious.[76] When the *Daily Herald* failed to heed the first warning, and printed both a copy of Trotsky's appeal at Brest-Litovsk and a message from Litvinov, the Cabinet considered suppressing it absolutely. In the end, the idea was dropped. The issue had already been sold. The paper was popular, and Lloyd George considered that smashing it might do more harm than good.[77] The *Daily Herald* did, however, receive another more strongly worded warning. 'Our attention has been called to the fact', the press bureau warned,

> that you have published a document which, in the form of an appeal from Bolsheviks in Russia to British workmen, contains incitements to disaffection and civil war in this country. This document contravenes the Defence of the Realm Regulations and its publication cannot be defended on the ground that it was supplied by M. Litvinoff, supposing that to be the case.
>
> It has been decided not to take proceedings on this question, but we warn you, that the article in question must not be reproduced, and that the publication of any similar article, from whatever source it may emanate, is forbidden by law.[78]

The redoubtable George Lansbury knew a naked threat when he read one. While he promised nothing, he assured the press bureau that the matter would receive his fullest personal attention in the future.[79] Little more was heard by or about either Litvinov or the Soviet experiment in the *Daily Herald* thereafter.

A final note: the very vigour of the censors' language here was intentional. It was not only intended to scare Lansbury, but to make publication of the letter either impossible or unwise. Some dissenting publications had made a habit of passing their publications through the press bureau and publishing them with the imprint 'passed by censor', to underline their legitimacy.[80] When parts were censored, these were left blank, to indicate the fact of censorship. When letters accompanied replies from the press bureau, explaining censored parts, these too were published as a back-hand way of indicating what the government feared. How could Lansbury publish this letter? What could he gain from doing so? Tit-for-tat.

Pressure from the patriots to kill this monster by the most vigorous action was unrelenting, and increasingly hysterical. A feeling of imminent revolution began to develop. The movement of dissent, as a whole, towards a more full-blooded socialist position, particularly when signalled by the type of inflammatory language which many, like Snowden, were now accustomed to use, and the galloping consolidation of all in the ILP, did not only frighten the HO; it thoroughly alarmed the middle class as a whole – already horrified by the German bombing of London. While Snowden was addressing a working-class audience in Woolwich, Horatio Bottomley and Leo Maxse were speaking to a strictly middle-class assembly at Queen's Hall in London. Their message was as violent and uncompromising as Snowden's; it moved – little comfort to Lloyd George – in the opposite direction. While the patriots continued to be a useful tool, and an essential prop of the government, they were becoming a double-edged sword. Careful handling was going to be required if the government were not to be driven faster than it wanted to go.

For the moment, Bottomley in particular was a dangerous loose cannon, and was to remain so through the latter war years and early postwar period. By conviction, apparently, a Liberal himself, he had come to hate the Liberal Party, which he considered even in the prewar period to be 'an omnium gatherem of cranks and faddists'.[81] On whatever platform he could find, he had moved into total opposition from about 1911 – the year he led the South Hackney Liberal and Radical Federation out of the London association. Horatio Bottomley was also a well-established publisher: founder of *Financial News*; proprietor of the *Sun, Sunday Illustrated, Sunday Evening Telegram*, and *John Bull* – the last of these, attaining a circulation of nearly one million even before the war. He had also been, and was to become again, a prominent parliamentarian: Liberal MP 1906–11 for South Hackney; resigned in 1912 following his bankruptcy; re-elected for South Hackney as an independent in December 1918, and leader thereafter of the Independent parliamentary group. In short, Bottomley was a dangerous man, all the more dangerous for being popular and the more popular for being dangerous – willing to beat loudly whatever drum the populace seemed inclined to hear. In the latter war years, as we have seen, it is an open question whether he was acting for himself or whether he was a part of the greater campaign being orchestrated by the press lords.

Whatever the case, Bottomley was a thoroughly nasty piece of work. His ultimate motivation does not appear to have been patriotism at all. He was one of the great confidence men of Edwardian Britain, and most of his activities managed to net him a tidy profit. Before the war, for instance, despite his popularity, he had already earned himself a reputation as a promoter of bogus companies. In 1914, the most successful recruiter in Britain, he had earned himself £27,000 as fees for his nationally famous, patriotic lectures.[82] By 1917, he was on the watch to turn even the wartime social divide to his own benefit. The game? Apparently to make himself popular with the patriotic middle class and thereafter rich by victory bond rip-offs and bogus 'support the war' lotteries advertised in his papers. It was not until his exposure and imprisonment for seven years, in 1927, on 23 counts of fraud, that this gadfly was removed.[83] For the moment the gifts which had made him an effective con-man made him doubly dangerous. Basil Thomson, who ultimately brought Bottomley to book, summed him up as follows:

> Among the army of cheats who have battened on the credulity of their fellow-men, Bottomley stands almost alone. His blustering eloquence, whether as a speaker or a writer, was due to his quick apprehension of the temper of his audience. He had a protean gift of instinctive knowledge of what people were thinking of him. Nothing pleased him more than pitting himself against the cleverest advocates at the Bar and scoring off them. He was armed at all points with vanity, but there was one weak spot in his armour: he could not stand ridicule. It is difficult to explain how he contrived to captivate so many lawyers and others in high places except by the suggestion that the whole country had lost its judgement and its balance ...[84]

A thoroughly bad man certainly, but, in 1917–18, he was a very dangerous sounding board for fears and discontents which, unlike Bottomley's lotteries and bonds, were all too real.

The Bottomley critique was assisted by the fact that by this time feelings were running high against the government for what was thought to be its incompetent and half-hearted handling of the war. Even the energetic Cave, always vigilant to strike at opponents of the war where he saw an opportunity, was being widely criticized throughout 1918 for what was seen as his pro-German attitude. This was exemplified best by his poor taste in having a German brother-in-law.[85]

Ominously, such criticism came not just from the hysterical, but from the mainstream national press, Northcliffe as much as Bottomley inspired. So intense and dangerous did such pressure become that, by the summer of 1918, Cave moved amidst a host of detectives and bodyguards while his house was surrounded by uniformed police.[86] In 1918, Cave was recalled from The Hague (where he had been arranging for prisoner transfer), and took the chair of a new home affairs committee convened, apparently, to counter the violent anti-alien agitation which became a notable feature of British public life during the 1918 by-elections,[87] and which had been foreshadowed by the anti-Semitic rioting of the previous year. While attempting to hold the balance, the Lloyd George government was ultimately forced, in July, to call for a review of all certificates of exemption from internment under the British Nationalities, and Status of Aliens Act, 1918).[88]

If the opposition were coalescing, therefore, so also were the supporters of the war – in such a manner that made both their continued tolerance of dissent and support of even the Lloyd George government problematic. There were continued rumours that the government was on its last legs. Unionist coups were reported, plotted and attempted. The mood of the public was not good. The patriots were not entirely agreed that even Lloyd George's efforts were thorough enough, or sufficient to ensure victory. Bottomley thrived in this environment of fear and division. The meeting at Queen's Hall, for instance, ended with a resolution censorious of the government for its failures – in particular, for its perceived inability to ensure the safety of the capital against aerial bombardment.[89] Bottomley continued this line in *John Bull*. Why, he wanted to know, did the 'Government so obstinately refuse all investigation into open, obvious, palpable treachery' – particularly as the effectiveness of the German bombing made it so obvious that there were traitors in Britain, working 'a secret wireless or a secret cable between London and Berlin'.[90] There was no answer to such criticism (because it was groundless and meaningless). The criticism remained and was all the more dangerous since it derived from those elements of the population which the government had hitherto judged safe. As well, it could not but pour yet further fuel on a fire already burning too brightly. The government could not ignore this criticism, nor could it silence Bottomley. Having been assembled to wage the war in a more energetic manner, it began to act in a manner more commensurate with public feeling … at least, half of public feeling.

As always in the latter war years, the real problem was total war. By the end of 1917, Britain was subject to immense pressure. It would have been strange had old cracks not widened, and new ones appeared. The manpower question was most pressing, given the cost of the Third Battle of Ypres. There was no sign of a let-up, and precious few victories. What was the war being fought for? The government seemed unsure, despite Lloyd George's best efforts. How and when would victory come? That no one knew. In 1917 new problems emerged which increased the pressure on the home front. While demands on shipping grew, the Germans initiated unrestricted U-boat warfare. The U-boats throughout 1917 appeared poised to bring Britain to its knees. By winter 1917–18 disaster was plainly approaching. Food stocks were disappearing.[91] Amidst allegations of profiteering, the price of food had skyrocketed, far beyond rises in wages. Later in the year, Rhondda (the food controller) introduced controls and, in 1918, rationing. The quantity of available food fell precipitously as it was hoarded.[92] It was impossible to maintain supplies of traditional foodstuffs. By January–February 1918, a million people a day were queuing in London for food.[93] The government, quite simply, did not seem able to do anything right. The result? Generalized dissent, less revolutionary than angry and despairing, constituting what has been called 'a general crisis of defeatism'.[94]

The government was, if anything, hyper-aware that the war was at a turning-point and that it could no longer count upon simple, residual loyalty to see Britain through. Pessimistic appreciations of the state of the home front came from all sides. Certainly a lot of people were attending patriotic meetings, Barnes warned Lloyd George in October 1917, but

> there are, however, large numbers – the larger numbers – who have no opportunity of attending meetings but who are kept at work late and early and have been subjected to an immense strain during the last three years. On the whole, they are as yet quite sound, but at the same time, there is no use blinking the fact that the Pacifists are active amongst them, and there is a good deal of war weariness which might easily be turned into disaffection by any great reverse or untoward circumstances here at home.[95]

The pacifist press was growing. New papers were appearing. There had been an absence of military success to date (rather an understatement in the winter of 1917–18) which propaganda could no longer disguise. Fighting between the generals was working on civilian morale. Casualties, in 1917, had reached the point where they must have political impact. '[I]t is open to grave doubt in my mind', Barnes concluded, 'if we can continue our losses on the present scale without serious risk.'[96]

Barnes was not the only one who had come to believe that Britain was poised on a knife edge. Pessimistic forecasts came in from all sides.

In November, Carson forwarded to Lloyd George a memorandum prepared by a Liberal MP, labour expert, and speaker for the NWAC,[97] Dr T. J. Macnamara, in which he set out the conclusions he had reached regarding the current social situation. At the moment, he thought, the mass of people were solid. 'They want to see this thing through for their sons' sake.' Macnamara thought: 'But they are tried and tempted in more than one direction.' The ILP was dangerous as it was always ready to capitalize on grievances. In the end, its propaganda might tell, and 'is telling with an increased momentum now because the people are getting rather weary with the long continuance of the war'. The government was going to have to deal with real grievances (compulsion, rationing, profiteering and hoarding). Domestic propaganda was essential. It would give the government a more popular face while 'nail[ing] false charges to the counter'. War aims need to be defined, and popularized. 'I know of nothing which arrests the attention and compels the conviction of the working class', Macnamara concluded, 'better than do Mr. Wilson's statements.'[98] Go you, Lloyd George, and say likewise.[99] Failing the adoption of such a policy, there was no telling what direction working-class discontent might ultimately take. It might surely force Britain out of the war, but would this be all? The example of Russia was suggestive.

About the same time A. M. Thompson, an industrial expert and writer who had been working for Lord Northcliffe in the north and Midlands, penned a similarly bleak view of the state of labour unrest. In the north, he had been very 'stirred by what he had found': a weary population, susceptible to pacifist propaganda, and increasingly willing to listen to the more radical elements in the labour movement. The shop stewards' movement in particular, Thompson thought, was dangerous and active.[100]

The new Industrial Unrest Commissions were coming to a similar conclusion. While the home front remained sound, there was no telling which way things would develop in the future. Revolution, it was considered, was unlikely. A Bolshevik programme was only popular insofar as it capitalized on real grievances, of which the failure of wages to keep pace with inflation was the worst.[101] Time would tell which way the wind would blow. It could blow in any direction.

The NWAC, organized, as we shall see, not only to combat pacifism but to keep a government finger on the pulse of the nation, agreed. 'Our daily reports show', it informed the government in December 1917,

> that apart from the demand for definition of War Aims there is no weakening of public opinion on the war. There is, however, increasing

discontent in consequence of administrative acts of the various Government Departments which deal with matters closely related to the daily life of the people. It is to be feared that these things coupled with general belief as to the enormous amount of profiteering which is going on, is producing a state of mind in which anti-war propaganda secures sympathetic attention.[102]

The home front was still sound, but if not carefully managed, things could become volatile quickly.

Even the dissenters, by this time suffering under a domestic regime which had become rather harsh, were rejoicing at the change that only a few months had brought, and were beginning to sense new possibilities. 'You will find yourself, I am glad to say', Seymour Cocks informed Morel, upon his release from prison,

> in a very different world to the one you left last autumn. There has been a very great change in public feeling since then and a distinct alteration in the public temper. People are losing the illusions which blinded their eyes so long. They never talk now about 'the knock out blow' 'fighting to a finish' and 'marching to Berlin'. The opinion is rapidly spreading that the war will never be ended by military means and that a decisive blow is impossible for either side. I believe that this conviction is deepening and that it is permeating all classes ... As for the Government, that is becoming discredited on every hand and the forces of democracy seem at last to be really stirring in every country. In fact opinion is changing more rapidly than some of us realize.[103]

'He will', Ramsay MacDonald wrote to Mrs Morel,

> find an enormous change in public opinion since he began his enforced rest cure, and he will not discover that his influence has suffered in any way. I have never known such a change in the spirit of the House of Commons as has made itself manifest between the ending of the old session last week and the beginning of the new one yesterday. In fact if the Liberals were worth their salt they could have the Government down in the course of a week or two if not even more quickly than that.[104]

Fenner Brockway, released from prison in September 1917, wrote to Bertrand Russell that the change of atmosphere left him 'almost intoxicated with hope'.[105] Surely, he considered, now was the time to launch a general strike to end the war, with revolutionary feeling as high as it then stood.

Things indeed were changing quickly. But since, by winter 1917–18, the probable end to the war was typically being projected as taking place no earlier than the summer of 1919 (and more likely in 1920 or 1921), it seemed to most impossible that the war would end without profound disruption on the home front, possibly culminating in the type of 'disaffection' which worried Barnes. Whether this was a horrifying or comforting thought depended on whether one was a dissenter or a patriot. Few doubted that it was germinating.

NOTES

1. MUH, Russell Papers, Volume 410, Clifford Allen to the NCF, 31 May 1917.
2. Wilson, *The Political Diaries of C. P. Scott*, diary entry for 21 March 1917, p. 270.
3. H. Nicolson, *King George the Fifth* (London: Constable, 1952), p. 308.
4. R. Postgate, *The Life of George Lansbury* (London: Longman, 1951), p. 165.
5. Nicolson, *King George the Fifth*, pp. 307–8.
6. For Milner see Gollin, *Proconsul in Politics*, p. 552; A. Williams, *Labour and Russia* (Manchester: Manchester University Press, 1989), p. 7. For Curzon see Wilson, *The Political Diaries of C. P. Scott*, p. 280. While Henderson welcomed the revolution, he was afraid that there would ultimately be a showdown between the moderates and the radicals. He was not confident that the moderates would win. See PRO CAB 24/3, 'No. 150, Report of the Visit of the Labour Delegation to Russia, April to May 1917', May 1917; PRO CAB 24/4, 'G-152, British Mission to Russia, June and July 1917' [Henderson], 16 July 1917.
7. PRO WO 256/18, Derby to Haig, 27 May 1917.
8. PRO HO 45 10810/311932, file 35, Leeds Chief Constable to HO, May 1917.
9. Gollin, *Proconsul in Politics*, pp. 547–50.
10. Ibid.
11. PRO HO 45 10810/311932, file 40, Socialist Conference at Leeds, 3 June. See file 41 for police transcripts of the offending speeches.
12. PRO HO 139/9/36, Item 34, Labour Leeds Conference, WC 147, 25 May 1917.
13. Wrigley, *David Lloyd George*, p. 206; Brand, *British Labour's Rise to Power*, pp. 42, 89.
14. Postgate, *The Life of George Lansbury*, p. 64. Postgate's figures for the January vote were 1,850,000 to 300,000 against the *Herald* policy.
15. Waites, *A Class Society at War*, p. 191; Postgate, *The Life of George Lansbury*, pp. 169–76; Donoughue and Jones, *Herbert Morrison*, p. 40.
16. Postgate, *The Life of George Lansbury*, p. 165. With the Russian revolution, Postgate asserts, 'What had been the unpopular propaganda of a small minority became, in a greater or less degree of fervour, the conviction of the greatest portion of the thinking working class of the country'. '[G]reatest portion of the thinking working class' is far too Leninist an evasion to satisfy any non-Marxist that the dissenters even thought themselves to be in a clear majority.
17. Brand, *British Labour's Rise to Power*, p. 94. Of 1,115 delegates, the ILP sent 294 and the BSP 84, for a combined total of nearly one-third of all delegates. Given that the ILP had only 30,000 members, and that the BSP was a trace element in British politics, this was over-representation indeed.
18. Laybourne, *Philip Snowden*, pp. 69–71, 77–9. The Social Democratic Federation splintered in 1916, with the purge of the pro-war Marxists. The new Social

Democratic Party, after absorbing the left ILP, ultimately emerged as the BSP. Shaw, 'War, Peace and British Marxism', p. 56.

19. Clegg, *A History of British Trade Unionism*, Vol. II, p. 227.
20. PRO PRO 30/69/1042, *Free Man*, August 1917.
21. Morris, *C. P. Trevelyan*, p. 140.
22. For example, MUH, Russell Papers, Russell to NCF Executive Committee, 18 May 1917. See also, 'Russia Leads the Way', *Collected Works of Bertrand Russell*, Vol. XIV, p. 118 (originally published in *The Tribunal*, no. 52, 22 March 1917):

   ... as soon as there are any definite signs of Labour turning against the war, we may be sure that the Governments themselves will embark upon negotiations in order to keep the power in their own hands.

   'The International Situation: the Pope's Peace Note', *Collected Works of Bertrand Russell*, Vol. XIV, p. 295 (originally published in *The Tribunal*, no. 71, 23 August 1917).
23. Middlemas, *The Clydesiders*, p. 75. For Snowden at Leeds see Laybourn, *Philip Snowden*, pp. 77–80.
24. Schneer, *George Lansbury*, p. 145. C. B. Stanton considered that Lansbury 'ought to be shot' (p. 146).
25. Russell, *Autobiography*, Vol. II, p. 31; 'Tribute at Leeds', *Collected Works of Bertrand Russell*, Vol. XIV, p. 182.
26. MUH, Russell Papers, volume 535, Russell to NCF Branch Secretaries, June/July 1917.
27. PRO HO 45 10810/311932, file 40, Socialist Conference at Leeds, 3 June. See, file 41 for police transcripts of the offending speeches.
28. Wrigley, *David Lloyd George*, p. 198.
29. PRO HO 45 10810/311932, file 43, June 1917.
30. PRO HO 45 10810/311932, file 37, Leeds Aftermath, 4 June 1917.
31. *Yorkshire Evening Post*, 5 June 1917, and *Yorkshire Evening News*, 5 June 1917. See also PRO HO 45 10810/311932, file 46 for testimonials from Jewish organizations concerning the efficiency of the police in suppressing the riots.
32. PRO HO 45 10810/31193, file 56, October 1917.
33. Russell, *Autobiography*, Vol. II, pp. 31–2; 'Crucify Him! Crucify Him!', *Collected Works of Bertrand Russell*, Vol. XIV.
34. A. Meynell, 'The Stockholm Conference of 1917', *International Review of Social History*, Vol. V, Pts 1–2 (1960), pp. 1–25.
35. PRO PRO 30/69/1042, *Free Man*, August 1917.
36. PRO 30/69/1042, *Free Man*, September 1917.
37. PRO 30/69/1042, *Free Man*, May 1918.
38. PRO PRO 30/69/1162, MacDonald to Lloyd George, 1 January 1918.
39. PRO HO 139/9/36, file 2a, Censorship of Russian News, 5 April 1917.
40. PRO HO 139/9/36, file 2a, Censorship of Russian News, 5 April 1917, Thomas Jones (WC) to Press Bureau, 6 April 1917, and Philips to Trevelyan, 11 April 1917. The Council of Workmen's and Soldiers' Deputies, Petrograd, had recently issued an appeal to all nations, calling for a negotiated peace, and looking for labour participation at a proposed conference. Decision: stop this. Appeals of this nature should 'not be published in this country'.
41. BL, Cave Papers, Cave 62496, Milner to Cave 31 August 1917.
42. BLIO, Curzon Papers, F 112/113, Milner to Curzon, 2 August 1917.
43. HLRO, Lloyd George Papers, F/6/2/42, Carson to Lloyd George, 4 August 1917.
44. HLRO, Lloyd George Papers, F/6/2/44, Carson to Lloyd George, 8 August 1917.
45. BLIO, IOP Political and Secret, L/PS/11, file 4352, 'Stockholm Peace Congress: Attitude of Oriental Delegations', 20 October 1917.

46. BLIO, Chelmsford Papers, MSS Eur E 264/3, Montagu to Chelmsford, 21 August 1917.
47. Beaverbrook, *Men and Power*, pp. 359–60.
48. HLRO, Lloyd George Papers, F/6/2/44, Carson to Lloyd George, 8 August 1917, Lloyd George minute.
49. Wrigley, *Arthur Henderson*, pp. 70, 111–16.
50. Pelling, *A History of British Trade Unionism*, p. 157.
51. Wrigley, *Arthur Henderson*, pp. 116–18; Leventhal, *Arthur Henderson*, pp. 64–7; E. Jenkins, *From Foundry to Foreign Office* (London: Grayson & Grayson, 1933), pp. 60–66.
52. Wrigley, *David Lloyd George*, p. 208.
53. K. Middlemass, *Whitehall Diary*, T. Jones diary entry for 29 August 1917, p. 36.
54. Doormat incident: Henderson had been kept waiting outside while a Cabinet meeting was convened to discuss his behaviour. See Leventhal, *Arthur Henderson*, pp. 67–8; Wrigley, *Arthur Henderson*, p. 120.
55. Wrigley, *Arthur Henderson*, p. 117.
56. HLRO, Lloyd George Papers, F 4/2/6, Barnes to Lloyd George, 1 June 1917.
57. Wrigley, *David Lloyd George*, p. 208.
58. HLRO, Lloyd George Papers, F 4/2/8, Barnes to Lloyd George, 20 July 1917.
59. Wilson, *The Political Diaries of C. P. Scott*, diary entries of 9–11 August 1917, pp. 297–9. Lloyd George told Scott, not very convincingly that both he and Bonar Law had been in favour of Stockholm until apprised by Kerensky that it would hurt rather than help him.
60. *Report of the Proceedings at the 49th Annual Trade Union Conference, September 3–8 1917*; Wrigley, *Arthur Henderson*, p. 119.
61. *Report of the Proceedings at the 49th Annual Trade Union Conference, September 3–8 1917*, p. 84.
62. Jenkins, *From Foundry to Foreign Office*, p. 63.
63. HLRO, Lloyd George Papers, F/4/2/33, Barnes to PM, 24 September 1918.
64. HLRO, Lloyd George Papers, F/6/2/45, Lloyd George to Carson, 9 August 1917.
65. R. Basker, 'Political Myth. Ramsay MacDonald and the Labour Party', *History*, 69 (1976), pp. 46–56. See also C. Wrigley, 'Trade Unions and Politics in the First World War', in Pimlott, *Trade Unions in British Politics*, p. 69. The NUM doubled its membership in the course of the war. The Amalgamated Engineers' Union (AEU) was, in 1917, in the process of formation. The General Workers' Union was brand new, and already the biggest union in the UK.
66. PRO T 102/3.
67. Brand, *British Labour's Rise to Power*, pp. 47–8.
68. Slowe, *Manny Shinwell*, p. 69.
69. Wrigley, *Arthur Henderson*, p. 126.
70. PRO FO 800/198, Sir A. Mond to Cecil, 14 May 1917; Cecil to Sir A. Mond, 19 May 1917.
71. Wrigley, David Lloyd George, p. 217.
72. Winter, *Socialism and the Challenge of War*; Leventhal, *Arthur Henderson*, pp. 49–50.
73. R. Basker, 'Political Myth. Ramsay MacDonald and the Labour Party', *History*, 61 (1976), pp. 46–56; Winter, *Socialism and the Challenge of War*, pp. 259–63; Clegg, *A History of British Trade Unionism*, Vol. II, pp. 232–3; Wrigley, *Arthur Henderson*, pp. 120–26. Henderson especially had been horrified by Leeds. If there were ever an attempt to put Lansbury's call for the convention of British soviets into effect, he warned, he would be the first to fight against them, and the last to lay down arms. Leventhal, *Arthur Henderson*, p. 63. Henderson on the Russian Revolution: 'I think the risks of the experiment … are so great that not only might it prove a

disaster to Russia but to the allied cause'. Williams, *Labour and Russia*, p. 7.

74. R. Wade, 'Argonauts of Peace: The Soviet Delegation to Western Europe in the Summer of 1917', *Slavic Review*, 26, 3 (September 1967).

75. PRO HO 139/35/148, File 12, February 1918. Even the *Daily Express* was having problems with the censors for publishing material from official foreign sources, in this case, however, for attempting to publish official US policy papers, in seeming contradiction to Britain's own policy. PRO HO 139/35/146, File 1, *Daily Express* to Press Bureau, October 1917.

76. See, for example, J. Degras (ed.), *Soviet Documents on Foreign Policy* (Oxford: Oxford University Press, 1951), Vol. I: 'Decree on Peace Passed by the Second All-Russian Congress of Soviets of Workers', Soldiers' and Peasants' Deputies', 8 November 1917, p. 1; 'Wireless Appeal by the Council of People's Commissars to the Peoples of the Belligerent Countries to Join in the Negotiations for an Armistice', 28 November 1917, p. 11; 'Appeal from the People's Commissariat for Foreign Affairs to the Toiling, Oppressed, and Exhausted Peoples of Europe', 19 December 1917, p. 18; 'Appeal From the Council of People's Commissars to the Toiling Masses of England, America, France, Italy, and Japan on Allied Intervention in Russia', 1 August 1918, etc.

77. Middlemas, *Whitehall Diary*, T. Jones diary entry for 11 January 1918, p. 44.

78. PRO HO 139/35/148, File 12, Press Bureau to *Herald*, 12 February 1918.

79. PRO HO 139/35/148, File 12, Lansbury to Press Bureau, 16 February 1918.

80. Snowden, *Autobiography*, p. 427.

81. HLRO, Beaverbrook, BBK 1/2, Bottomley to Beaverbrook, 24 May 1911.

82. B. Thomson, *The Story of Scotland Yard*, pp. 231–7.

83. See M. Stenton, *Who's Who of British Members of Parliament* (Hassocks, Sussex: Harvest Press, 1978), Vol. III (1919–1945).

84. Thomson, *The Story of Scotland Yard*, pp. 231–7.

85. BL, Cave Papers, Cave 62497, Milner to Cave, 25 July 1918. See also Mallet, *Lord Cave*, p. 211.

86. Mallet, *Lord Cave*, pp. 18–21.

87. Ibid., p. 211.

88. Ibid., p. 212.

89. PRO HO 45 10743/263275, Pacifist Agitation, file 241, Meeting of Imperial Defence Union, CID to HO, 11 July 1917.

90. *Financial Times*, 11 July 1917.

91. A. Salter, *Allied Shipping Control* (Oxford: Oxford University Press, 1922); idem, *Memoirs of a Public Servant* (London: Faber & Faber, 1961), p. 100; idem, *Slave of the Lamp* (London: Weidenfeld & Nicolson, 1967), p. 68.

92. Wrigley, *David Lloyd George*, p. 179.

93. Rhondda, *This Was My World*, p. 210.

94. Waites, *A Class Society at War*, p. 229; French, *The Strategy of the Lloyd George Coalition*, p. 195.

95. HLRO, Lloyd George Papers, F 4/2/14, Barnes to Lloyd George, 29 October 1917. See, also: PRO MUN 5/49.

96. HLRO, Lloyd George Papers, F 4/2/14, Barnes to Lloyd George, 29 October 1917.

97. C. Playne, *Britain Holds On 1917, 1918* (London: George Allen & Unwin, 1933), p. 160.

98. HLRO, Lloyd George Papers, F/6/2/45, Carson to Lloyd George, forwarding Macnamara memorandum on working-class feeling, 28 November 1917.

99. This may well have been the reason for Lloyd George's war aims speech in Claxton in January 1918.

100. HLRO, Lloyd George Papers, F 41/7/35, Northcliffe to Lloyd George, 17 December

      1917.
101. Desmarais, 'Lloyd George and the Development of the British Government's Strike
      Breaking Organisation', p. 3.
102. PRO T 102/18, 'Report up to 8th December 1918'.
103. LSE, Morel Papers, Morel F1/5, F. Seymour Cocks to Morel, 3 February 1918.
104. LSE, Morel Papers, Morel F1/5, MacDonald to Mrs. Morel, 12 February 1918.
105. MUH, Russell Papers, Vol. 410, Fenner Brockway to Russell, 7 September 1917.

9

The National War Aims Committee

IN JUNE 1917, leading members in the government – Lloyd George, Bonar Law, Barnes – came together with Asquith to form the executive committee of a new organization, the National War Aims Committee (NWAC). This organization, officially unofficial, was designed precisely to ensure that discontents, all too evident by this time in the war, resolved themselves into renewed resolution rather than dissent. The purpose of the organization was counter-mobilizational. It furthered, therefore, both the requirements of the day and the political purposes of Lloyd George. It also had a secret, repressive agenda. The NWAC was the closest thing to a formalization of Lloyd George's projected National Party to emerge during the course of the war. The NWAC, however, remains mysterious. It has been a peripheral concern in books about other things. Even the official histories of organizations with which it worked closely – the Ministry of Information or the press bureau for instance – are silent except insofar as they perpetuate wartime turf and budget battles. There is a general consensus, however, that whatever it may have been, the very fact of the NWAC indicated just how serious the government perceived conditions on the home front to be. The NWAC derived from the atmosphere of fear which followed the Leeds conference and Stockholm agitation, most particularly, from the pessimistic way in which police and political authorities interpreted these.[1] It indicated, quite simply, a loss of government confidence and therefore of inhibitions.

What did the NWAC do? Propaganda was one of its roles, as the name of the organization would suggest. To this point, HMG had benefited from the freelance, domestic propaganda produced by the press lords and other agencies without having to sully unduly its own liberal principles. By 1917 silent collusion was no longer a viable strategy. The requirement for counter-mobilization was now imperative. Propaganda directed at the home audience, particularly that type of propaganda which crossed the line separating white from black, was the responsibility of the NWAC. Similarly, freelance patriot mobs had been good enough for Cory Hall. They were not sufficient for the Albert Hall.[2] Silently but effectively in the latter war years the government began to organize the patriots on a local and national level. Like domestic propaganda, this was a policy departure, inconsistent with liberal inhibitions. Like propaganda, therefore, this function fell to the NWAC. It could use state assets, and could be counted upon to follow direction. On the other hand, it remained sufficiently distanced from the government for its activities to be plausibly disavowed. The fiction could be preserved that there had been no fundamental change of policy or attitude. The formation and operation of the NWAC, therefore, had considerable implications for the maintenance of civil liberties in Britain. It must be taken as a sign both of government resolution and desperation, although not to the point where Liberal inhibitions entirely disappeared. Nevertheless, the social–political role adopted by the NWAC is revealing of the long-term intentions of Lloyd George and his collaborators.

The NWAC derived from a near consensus in the Lloyd George government that more vigorous action on the home front was essential if Britain were to see the war through and avoid the fate of Russia. The notion quickly developed that the government needed to innovate. Perhaps, for instance, it could motivate through propaganda if only to put off the day when it must extort compliance by force and fear. John Buchan, responsible for foreign propaganda, was particularly concerned. By the spring of 1917, he had come to believe that something big, and something soon, was going to have to be done to combat what he perceived to be rapidly growing pessimism. At least systematic propaganda directed at the home front, he considered, was now essential. The press lords, if occasionally inspired, could no longer be left to act without direction. The government itself was going to have to take on this new role. 'In the present state of popular feeling', Buchan wrote to Lloyd George in May 1917,

> I am very strongly of [the] opinion that it is necessary to do a considerable amount of propaganda in Britain itself. The papers are small in size [due to the paper shortage], and owing to the almost entire cessation of public speaking, one of the best means of informing the country is in abeyance. At the same time, the need was never greater for instruction and encouragement. I am anxious to be allowed to organize various lines of direct propaganda in this country, and, in particular, a series of lectures and addresses in all the chief centres.[3]

Working men, he thought, should be sent to the front, and MPs organized for public speaking engagements.

What might be achieved by a personal appeal to patriotism, coming from a respected speaker, had been demonstrated by no other than King George V. Faced with what appeared to be a crumbling home front, the King swung into action in the winter of 1916, despite the misgivings of a government in the first throes of panic. Having been briefed both by his ministers and Scotland Yard,[4] George V departed for a journey though his troubled realm, making tours of disaffected regions. He visited Lancashire at the request of Lord Derby,[5] before proceeding to Glasgow and the north of England. His meetings were a spectacular success. Even Red Gallacher confessed that he was a royalist the day the King appeared alone before a working-class audience in Glasgow. For the remainder of the war, King George worked hard to ensure that labour unrest would not take an unconstitutional direction.[6] No less an authority than Assistant Commissioner Basil Thomson believed that the King's actions were the principal factor in reducing tensions and ensuring continued loyalty during the critical time when the Lloyd George government was just finding its feet.[7]

Buchan's idea was good. Obviously domestic propaganda worked, but it was going to have to be organized. The King was only one man, and not everybody shared his charisma. It was the general perception in the government, however, that domestic propaganda was not a job for Buchan, who would be acting in his official capacity. Not only would this be a considerable departure which might well backfire, but propaganda produced by a government agency to popularize government policy would lack credibility. The solution was the NWAC, which would take on this work, co-ordinating its activities with the government, but which would remain neither subordinated nor obviously associated with any official agency. It would have the backing and the resources of the government at its disposal. The appearance of objectivity would, however, be retained. Meanwhile, something of a fig leaf would remain to cover liberal principles.

The idea of such an structure was not new. Lloyd George had been experimenting for some time past but had not hitherto found an instrument sufficient to his purposes. He had founded, already, the National Patriotic Organization, of which he was the honorary president, with Lords Rosebery and Balfour as vice-presidents.[8] He was also the honorary patron of the Entente Peoples' Alliance, which he did not actually found, but of which he was head by 1918.[9] Ultimately, Lloyd George rolled both of these organizations into the NWAC. If the NWAC was likely to be less directly effective (as more obviously government) it was apt to have greater overall impact as better funded and supported than any purely voluntary society.[10] It is probably safe to say, therefore, that Lloyd George was the guiding political light of the NWAC and that he envisioned it from the beginning as filling the place which these other organizations had failed to occupy.

In organization, the NWAC looked nothing like a department of state. It looked like the UDC, to which it was obviously intended as antidote. In purpose, as well, the NWAC was similar to the UDC. The UDC, remember, was designed to be the general staff of dissent: mobilizing other organizations against the war, while preserving itself for the peace. The NWAC, similarly, hoped to consolidate and organize the patriots into a network capable of winning the war on the home front without being overtly implicated itself. Restraint was necessary, not only to distance the government from any excesses, but because the NWAC was also the public face of Lloyd George's new party. In September 1917 the NWAC began contacting local people and organizations which it believed to be likely to collaborate.[11]

The attempt to consolidate all the various patriot strands behind the war and the government worked. From the onset, the NWAC was strong in both the Liberal Party and the Unionist grouping. What may appear odd today, however, is that the patriotic labour element in the organization was at least as strong. Relations with the BWNL which, as an affiliated organization, had a war aims committee of its own, were closer still. By itself the NWAC ensured, therefore, that at least Milner's minimum criteria were met. If the NWAC could never, by this time, consolidate the entire labour movement to the war, it could still help to generate sufficient enthusiasm to prevent any unified anti-war labour front.

An example of how this could work at the local level is as follows. In August 1917, the town council of Huddersfield attempted to decouple labour from the NWAC by publishing the membership of the local committee omitting labour members. These plainly decided that their duty to their NWAC partners came before labour solidarity. J. S. Armitage, the local TUC secretary, a patriot, and a member of the committee, resigned his post to make his disapproval public.[12] In the process, of course, working class unity in Huddersfield was shattered, and the possibility of a unified anti-war response destroyed. Further still, when local labour movements felt uneasy about the NWAC, they often sought guidance from the national Labour Party. This, a government party, having been co-opted into the NWAC from the beginning, would move quickly to quiet their fears.[13] Patriotism, once again, was being placed against working-class solidarity to divide and confuse.

The NWAC differed most markedly from the UDC in the degree of its professionalism, and, obviously, in the extent of its ties to the state.

The leadership of the NWAC was political and drawn from all parliamentary parties in an effort to keep the organization non-partisan, and perhaps also to ensure that all parties were equally implicated in what the NWAC was doing. Lloyd George, Asquith, Law and Barnes were joint presidents. The chairman of the new organization was F. E. Guest, the chief government whip, while the vice-chairmen were R. A Sanders, a Tory whip, and Lieutenant-Colonel Sir H. Greenwood, Coalition Labour whip.[14]

In addition to the professional politicians, in 1918 the NWAC national committee alone employed 46 full-time staff, two of whom were paid more than £1,000 a year, and six of whom were paid more than £500.[15] Total cost for NWAC national headquarters alone was £260 monthly – divided equally between salaries and printing costs.[16] Locally, the NWAC maintained, as well, a rather large force of ad hoc propagandists, writers, and professional rabble-rousers. Local costs, for the six months ending March 1918, averaged £12,528 for a borough, and £13,680 for a rural constituency. The NWAC operated in 468 constituencies.[17] Speakers, during this time, had been subsidized to a global total of £33,120 (two speakers per constituency at an average cost of £12 a week). Twenty-three of these speakers were full-time professionals, making anywhere from £1 1s. to £2 2s. daily.[18] Demonstrations and conferences had been arranged, and subsidized. Publicity had cost £8,015. Cost of pamphlets, newspapers, cinemas, postcards, cigarette cards, and coloured posters, etc., had come to £42,405 total.[19] A rather more comprehensive arrangement, altogether, than the ramshackle UDC – dependent in 1914, as in 1918, on the enthusiasm of its volunteers.

Where did the money come from? The charge has been made that the NWAC was funded from Secret Service funds.[20] This was never the case. The parties initially funded the NWAC in common. Its London City and Midland bank statements still exist. Like the UDC, NWAC was not originally very rich. In October 1917, Carson, having been directed by the government to work with the organization, announced that the government was going to come up with the money to put the committee on a sound footing.[21] The committee, hardly surprisingly, agreed unanimously to this proposal 'in view of the impossibility of financing the work of the committee from private subscriptions or Party funds'.[22] When NWAC's accounts were closed out, on 29 January 1918, a balance remained of about £2,000.[23] Ultimately – rather strangely for a non-government organization – the NWAC was almost totally funded by the Treasury, the Paymaster General handling its accounts directly as if it were an official department of state.[24] Paper, printing and supplies came from HMSO. The Department of Works arranged rent and coal.[25]

In the year and a half of the NWAC's existence, it received something like £1.2 million in subsidy or services from government sources.[26] Its total expenses, however, were certainly higher. In addition to government money, the NWAC continued to receive favours and donations. Moreover, certain of its activities were business successes (photographic exhibitions and travelling cinemas, for instance) and profits were rolled back into operations.[27] Where was the Secret Service here?

The NWAC was initially party political (if non-partisan) and, by January 1918, funded almost entirely by the state. Through both incarnations, it was essentially a government–non-government–patriot synthesis, in which professionals organized amateurs to support pro-government activities.

The official function of the NWAC was 'to assist the country during the ensuing months of strain to resist insidious influences of an unpatriotic character'.[28] Its public purpose was to organize support for the war, chiefly by organizing public meetings at which government policy could be explained. Often NWAC meetings were enlivened by patriotic entertainment. The wartime hiatus on public speaking, remember, was one of the great deficiencies identified by Buchan. Sweet has indicated that nearly 900 meetings were eventually organized, many in dissenting strongholds.[29] While this figure is impressive, it is a considerable understatement of NWAC activity. In the period 4 August–10 October 1917 alone the NWAC organized 3,192 meetings. In 1918, the NWAC Meetings Department arranged 3,959 meetings between April and October 1918 – a positive orgy of meetings occurring nation-wide in the summer of 1918, with widespread commemorations of American Independence Day (in recognition of America's entry to the war), Bastille Day (in a demonstration of solidarity with France) and the anniversary of the outbreak of the war.[30] Sweet's estimate of 900, therefore, probably represents less than a tithe of the total number of meetings arranged by the NWAC during its 14 months of existence.

Sometimes NWAC meetings could be rather spectacular affairs. The NWAC would provide the money and book the talent. Local affiliates would assist in getting out the crowd. Civic authorities, very often, would co-operate in the provision of facilities and other assistance.[31] Major NWAC meetings generally took place over a weekend, and were designed to enliven as much as to enlighten. Meetings often began with picnics and patriotic entertainment (singsongs, music and films). Some time in the early evening a popular speaker would address the crowd expressing support for the war, often taking for his point of departure some current issue or event which had caught popular attention. The speech, when it came, was not viewed as an imposition for which the rest had been payment, but a climax to which the rest had been building.

A good speech was something Edwardian Britain had much loved. As public men were forced to devote all of their time to official duties, Britain fell silent – except insofar as the dissenters gained access to public platforms. If Snowden, Trevelyan and MacDonald were the only nationally known speakers working the crowd, it is little wonder that the public perception began to move in their direction. The NWAC quickly moved to present the government's case. A roster of speakers was created of those willing to speak from its platforms. When time allowed, Churchill, Balfour and Milner were willing, and always good draws.

In some areas of the country, however, neither Churchill, Balfour nor Milner could be expected, by 1917, to play very well. This did not mean that such areas were entirely hostile to the NWAC message. Indeed, the extensive correspondence carried on by the NWAC with trade unions, labour organizations, and church groups appealing for speakers and literature would suggest that it was highly popular with at least a section of the working class.[32] It was simply the case that many working-class audiences, by 1917, would be more receptive to the NWAC message if it were expounded through someone working men trusted implicitly. Here, every attempt was made to produce a speaker who, by his nature, would be more sympathetic to the target audience. It had taken the UDC two years to learn this lesson. The NWAC operated with this level of sophistication from the beginning.

There were other areas still in which, by 1917, a labour speaker was essential if the NWAC message was to be put across at all. While it considered that a 'crusade' among working men was essential, after surveying industrial areas in December 1917, Admiralty Intelligence passed on to the NWAC a list of hard cases for special consideration. In Newcastle, it was thought, 'thoroughly good men' were required or they would do 'more harm than good'. In Birmingham, it was essential to focus propaganda on workers in the workplace. Weary armaments shift workers could not be expected to make any special effort to attend NWAC fetes. Most London workers, the Admiralty considered, were fine provided that a speaker was 'someone of their own class coming to have a word with them'. In Barrow, the Admiralty's own shipyard workers were simply impossible. No listed speaker would work here, and attempts at making propaganda would simply be inflammatory. In Hull, the men were willing to down tools at any time, and meetings were urgently required. In Bristol, the situation was not good, but was being taken in hand by the locally ascendant patriotic labour movement which wanted speakers. In Southampton, speakers could be useful to improve a situation which was not yet irretrievable. In Liverpool speakers capable of dealing with heckling could do good work. Since Glasgow was an ILP stronghold, political or trade union speakers were not advisable; Navy League speakers, it was thought, might still receive a favourable welcome.[33] Whether the estimates of local working-class feeling were accurate or not, the list and the analysis were typical of the subtle way in which home propaganda was applied.

For tough or very tough audiences, Wedgwood Benn, a consistent supporter of the committee, was likely to receive a better reception than Milner, Balfour or Churchill.[34] He was willing, and spoke often from an NWAC platform. Other useful speakers for the hard cases could come from the Federation of Women's Institutes, the Navy League, the unions (leaders of the DWRGLU or NASFU were usually good bets) or the British Empire Producers League – these organizations were suggested to the NWAC by Admiralty Intelligence.[35] War heroes, of course, were popular with any audience at any time.

Even better, as practice would demonstrate, were Americans and dominion speakers, brought over by the NWAC, who could invoke not only international labour but allied and imperial solidarity. Billy Hughes, the Australian Prime Minister, and the first Labour premier in the Empire, was very popular and was given a hearing by even the toughest audiences.[36] His allegiance to allied policy was never in doubt. Clarence Darrow, the famous fighter for labour causes in the United States, was an NWAC speaker. He could go where few others could, and could be counted upon to toe the NWAC line. Despite his prewar reputation for radicalism, Darrow had been speaking in the United States for some time past in support of the war.[37] Another of the more successful American speakers was Sam Gompers (founder of the American Federation of Labor) brought over to the UK by his friend, George Barnes, and shepherded around the country by another Barnes friend, Captain Sanders of the NASFU. Gompers could, of course, be expected to advocate a suitably patriotic and anti-syndicalist line, given his long struggle, back in the United States, with the pacifist and syndicalist IWW.[38] Even the militant Glasgow working class was prepared to listen to Gompers or Darrow. Their message? Victory in the war against German militarism was an essential, and international labour concern. *Nothing* must be done to jeopardize it. Gompers's meetings, in particular, were great successes, and he was highly influential in British labour circles in the latter war years. Considerations of allied harmony were decisive, for instance, in convincing the TUC to abandon the Stockholm idea. At the Blackpool meeting at which it was finally decided that allied consensus must precede any international socialist meeting, a message from Gompers was read aloud immediately after another invitation from the Russians. 'The righteous cause for which we are engaged in the world struggle', Gompers began,

> must be triumphant, for it is writ in the skies that the end of autocracy is near at hand, and the world will be made safe and better for Labour, justice, freedom and democracy.[39]

The Derby TUC conference, similarly, carefully handled by Barnes and influenced by Gompers, was induced to pass a resolution that Germany must be absolutely defeated *before* there could be any reconvention of the Second International.[40]

Less exalted NWAC speakers were not left to guess at the organization's message. They were minutely briefed. They were not placed before an audience simply to sound off, or beat a party drum. Their pitch had to be consistent with that of the NWAC. They were, the national committee informed them, always to keep the following factors in mind:

1. The objective of NWAC propaganda was 'to keep before our nation both the causes which have led to this world war and the vital importance to human life and liberty of continuing the struggle until the evil forces which originated this terrible conflict are destroyed forever'.

2. The NWAC 'knows no party and does not support or oppose any party'.

3. Speeches must be confined to an exposition of war aims, as defined by the government.

4. Speakers could not 'make any attack upon political opponents and must not refer to any questions of ordinary party controversy'.

5. If resolutions were called for, they must take the format: 'That this meeting thanks (insert name) for his address, and records its inflexible determination to do all in its power to assist in carrying on the war to a victorious conclusion, so that Liberty and Justice may be established and permanent peace secured'.[41]

The emphasis, therefore, was to be maintained fully upon the war. The purpose of the NWAC was to remain mobilizational, rather than informational. In the process, it was hoped, a new national unity beyond class would be formed. Ultimately, of course, this unity would become the driving force behind the political synthesis which Lloyd

George hoped would come out of the war in order to re-establish Britain on a firmer footing in the postwar world.

A good example of an NWAC speech was delivered by Winston Churchill at the corn exchange in Bedford, on 10 December 1917. The text survives in the papers of the Chartwell Trust. Churchill began on a sobering note. The war, he admitted, was not going well.

> The country is in danger as it has not been since the battle of the Marne saved Paris, and the battles of Ypres and Yser saved the Channel ports. The cause of the Allies is now in danger. The future of the British Empire, and of democracy, and of civilization hang, and will continue to hang for a considerable period, in a balance and an anxious suspense.[42]

Despite calls for a definition of war aims, he continued, the majority of people knew exactly what Britain was fighting for (democracy, civilization, etc.). Russia had been undermined, not by German arms, but (a word to the wise) by German intrigue. The war could not end before Prussian militarism had been destroyed, war criminals punished, and Germany placed in a position in which it could no longer threaten the peace. Territorial gain was not even an issue. Certainly, no one was dying to put the French in Syria, or to make Palestine British. President Wilson's 14 points had meant nothing more, and he had spoken for all the allies. The war was ideological, and represented the conflict between the aspirations of the allies and the brutality of the Germans. Defeat, or even a negotiated peace without victory, would mean more than the loss of territory. It would mean the failure of allied ideals.

The great danger of the day, however, was not Prussian militarism, but defeatism at home.

> It is not military danger which is most prominent in our minds; it is the danger that the people of this country might be tempted by some specious peace terms that would leave Germany stronger than before. I am afraid there are some people who go about saying 'restate your war aims', when what they really mean is 'make friends with the Victorious Huns'. They ask – 'what are we fighting for?' when they really mean 'Let us leave off fighting'. Be on your guard in your homes, in your streets, in your workshops, in your public places, against this deadly danger. Peace with Prussian militarism now would mean that we should have to put up with defeat, and defeat to-day would mean ruin tomorrow.
>
> We hear a lot of the Pacifist tendencies said to be so rife in this country. I represent myself a great democratic electorate, and a few

months ago we heard of this talk being indulged in vehemently and even violently in the streets, but when the electorate came to deal with the matter they swept it away as it deserved [cheers]. The British people do not mean to put up with anything but the legitimate and righteous aims with which they entered upon the war, and if such an issue as this were seriously raised it could only be decided by the nation as a whole [cheers]. I cannot see that there would be the slightest risk or danger in submitting that question for the free decision of the nation as a whole.[43]

Industrial action was a threat, Churchill conceded, though neither so widespread nor dangerous as the dissenting press would lead one to believe. Despite perils present, victory was certain. The entry into the war of the United States made victory inevitable, but only if Britain could hold together for another year. What did American involvement mean? Not only the victory of Anglo-American idealism, but the consolidation of the English-speaking peoples into one great bloc – suitable compensation for all sacrifices. All would be lost, however, if Britain shrank from duty. '[U]nless', Churchill concluded, 'the British race, unless we inhabitants of this small island'

can bear during the greater part of next year the main weight and burden of the war on land upon our shoulders, and unless at the same time we can keep the submarine choked down under the sea, there can be no American aid; there can be no deliverance, no victory … Is this, I ask you, not the greatest responsibility ever laid upon any nation of men? Is it not the most splendid opportunity ever offered to any nation of men? Is it not the climax to which all English history has led us, in which all the work of all our heroes and worthies of the past and present time finds its consummation?[44]

The speech, while not Churchill's best, was nevertheless highly effective and very well received.

Speeches were not the whole story. The nation was flooded with NWAC propaganda. Some of it was produced in collaboration with MI7b (foreign propaganda). Some of it was directly inspired by the government, with Carson seemingly the conduit for communication at this level. In November 1917, for example, the government (i.e. Lloyd George) passed to the NWAC through Carson a copy of a confidential WO paper on the situation in war theatres. The memorandum had obviously been produced with the domestic audience in mind. Carson was used because he was an 'authoritative source'. The NWAC was employed to spread the news because it was not government. The ultimate press product would look more like an authoritative leak of confidential material (and therefore objective truth) than official propaganda.[45] The procedure was typical of the sophisticated NWAC approach and, while old news today, was cutting-edge in 1917.

The tone of this particular memorandum is enlightening in what it reveals about government fears, as well as the purpose of the NWAC. Much of it dealt with the situation in Italy, where, it was asserted, the front had collapsed because of a general failure to support the war effort. National cohesion had been undermined by pacifist propaganda. Mackensen (a much feared German commander) had not been there. The Italians had not been outnumbered. Their allies had not betrayed them. Rather, a small number of Italians had 'become infected by treasonable intrigue and refused to fight', and these had carried their comrades with them. The situation was not irredeemable. 'Although this is a serious misfortune, it is far from being a decisive success for the enemy and there is no cause for depression.' The moral of the story? Even a few who listened to pacifists could undermine the war effort. And, despite what might be heard from Italy, it remained sound and the war was far from over. This was a rather effective way to relate what was a half-truth at best.[46]

NWAC was nothing if not innovative in its choice of media. Popular media would make the dissemination of populist propaganda all that much easier. NWAC photographic exhibitions were immensely popular, as were its travelling cinemas. By 1918, the organization was putting out two 150-foot shorts a week, which, shown by ten mobile cinemas, were reaching 140–150,000 persons a week in out-of-the-way places.[47] When people who saw NWAC shorts in theatres or elsewhere are added, this meant that the NWAC was reaching something like six million people weekly. Beaverbrook, as Minister of Information, hoped that the audience would ultimately grow to 12 million weekly.[48] He had already been responsible for pioneering film, photograph and art propaganda in Canada, as the London agent for the Canadian army.

Another way in which support for the war was consolidated, was through trade union tours of the front conducted by the NWAC in co-ordination with the FO, the WO and the Ministry of Labour. Co-operation between agencies was, once again, characteristic of the Lloyd George approach. This was one of Carson's brainwaves. The idea was to identify reliable workers, particularly in vulnerable or crucial industries, choose from among them by ballot, and send those chosen to tour the fighting front in France as guests of the government, compensation being paid for time off work. The idea was a good one. We have already seen how a similar tour had ended the possibility of a major strike, that of the Amalgamated Engineers in the Spring of 1916. By 1918, 300 workers were being sent to France each week. Two parties daily of 25 men each left Waterloo station. After a passage to Calais, the party would travel St Omer–Souche–Vimy–Arras–Doullens–Albert–Peronne–Amiens and then back to Boulogne and home. It was expected that those selected would share their experiences with their workmates, and convince them that their contribution was essential to the winning of the war.[49] By May 1918, 1,000 working men had been sent to France.[50] Many of them appear to have begun applying for NWAC literature for distribution to their workmates upon return.[51] The example of a Mr E. Green was not exceptional: a worker at the Portsmouth dockyard, he had attempted to volunteer many times for service in France, but had been prohibited from leaving his work. Having been selected by the Admiralty to represent his shop, he departed with a party of workers for the standard NWAC tour. He had been deeply impressed, and was determined to do whatever he could to share his experience with his fellows. Shortly after having returned, we find him writing to the NWAC requesting the use of slide lantern equipment for the speaking engagements he had lined up back in Portsmouth.[52]

Similarly, the NWAC encouraged trade unionists serving at the front to write to their lodges, and sped the letters home. Sometimes such letters appear to have been effective at restraining industrial action. An example: a letter sent from a railwayman at the front to his union's local branch when it seemed that a rail strike was pending, in the Autumn of 1917.

> Perhaps those who have not been out here scarcely realize the disastrous effects a railway strike would have, and that by the stoppage of transport, of guns, ammunition, food, reinforcements, etc., the strike would indirectly, but none the less surely, sell our lives to the Huns.[53]

This was an appeal to which even the most convinced potential striker might be expected to give full hearing.

Another purpose of the NWAC, less widely advertised, was to orchestrate a black propaganda campaign aimed at the domestic audience. The principal purpose of white propaganda is to inform. It is permissible, of course, to slant news to encourage a target audience to draw certain conclusions. Black propaganda, on the other hand, is often composed of outright lies. Its primary purpose is motivational rather than informational. Its appeal is emotional rather intellectual As we have seen, in wartime, recruiting efforts were one method of government, white propaganda the nation was prepared to accept. Going further, from 1915 the government had been in the business of providing war news, following criticism that no news simply led to the population being left with nothing with which to combat the doom-sayers.[54] Black propaganda, however (atrocity stories, disinformation, etc.), remained a monopoly of the press lords, who, throughout the war, continued to demonstrate an ability to limbo lower than anybody else. The notorious 'corpse conversion factory' sensation of 1918, for instance, was orchestrated by the Northcliffe press after every agency even close to the government, had rejected the story as something the government simply could not use.[55] Even in the last years of the war, in conditions of growing emergency, hysteria and bitterness, government agencies continued to feel uncomfortable handling this sort of material.[56] The NWAC, however – officially unofficial once again – provided an excellent vehicle by which the government could orchestrate a black propaganda campaign while keeping its hands clean.

From the beginning at least some NWAC propaganda crossed the line from information to disinformation, from white to black propaganda – truth being recast for its agitprop value. While this type of material, in theory, was handled by the NWAC alone, the fiction was thin. Although there was an explicit separation of function with government agencies, there was, for instance, unity of personnel. Carson, commissioned to dovetail the work of the NWAC with that of existing organizations – principally the Department, later Ministry, of Information – was himself, for instance, already head of 'home publicity' at the NWAC.[57] Moreover, co-operation between official organizations and the NWAC was routine. In March 1918, for instance, the Ministry of Information took over responsibility for the distribution of film propaganda for the NWAC. The director of the cinema department at the Ministry, Sir William Jury, became the film agent for the NWAC.[58] The RAF, similarly, shared equipment with the NWAC, the NWAC using projectors for propaganda, the RAF using the same equipment for recruiting purposes, back-to-back in the same venue.[59] Sometimes co-operation went even further. In August 1918, for instance, the Chancellor of the Exchequer arranged to borrow NWAC cinema vans for a war-bond drive, combined this with an artillery exhibit from the WO, and agreed to run NWAC propaganda films when the vans were not otherwise in use – and this at the same rallies.[60]

More illustrative still of government collusion was the fact that much of the material being used by the NWAC had been commissioned by the government itself for foreign consumption. No inhibition existed against disinforming foreigners. By 1916, MI7b was producing material of this sort directed at the domestic market, but was unable to distribute it. This did not stop MI7b, however, from commissioning 7,500 pieces of domestic propaganda between September 1916 and November 1918, from 500 different authors. With the formation of the NWAC a suitable conduit was discovered.[61] Admiralty intelligence, similarly, sought assistance in organizing propaganda in industrial centres to contain workers' unrest. Aware that the NWAC was not in that game, it resolved, nonetheless, to co-ordinate its own campaign with that of the NWAC and share appropriate materials.[62] The NWAC, for its part, commissioned propaganda of its own, which it shared with MI7b, Admiralty Intelligence, the Government Information Bureau and other interested agencies.[63] While the amount of material produced by the NWAC is difficult to ascertain, the total must have been substantial. Between October 1917 and February 1918 the NWAC commissioned, published and placed 23 articles and pamphlets by Major-General Sir George Aston alone, between January and June 1918 a total of 28. Most were in the 1,000–2,000 word range. Payments ranged from £3 to £4 for each.[64] Since, in a typical month, the NWAC paid something like £225 for literary and pictorial work,[65] the total number of centrally commissioned works was probably quite substantial. A figure of around 800 pieces seems probable. Champion contributors were Sir George Aston and Wedgwood Benn, the latter contributing at least 68.[66] Note, of course, that other work was undoubtedly being commissioned and placed as part of the publicity campaigns conducted by local committees.

Furthermore, from October 1917 the services were sending representatives to NWAC central meetings to 'co-ordinate' their campaigns with the NWAC.[67] Jan Smuts, in the War Cabinet, had just settled the division of responsibilities between agencies,[68] and other departments had been instructed to co-operate with NWAC and with one another in their home publicity campaigns.[69] By April 1918, co-operation had been formalized. An interdepartmental publicity committee was established, responsible for collecting and organizing materials from all interested agencies; the NWAC to act as the 'clearing house' for all. To facilitate this campaign, the NWAC organized two committees, each divided three ways between coalition parties: a meetings committee (national chairmen: Walter Read MP, Hamar Greenwood MP, and Robert Tootill MP), and a publicity committee (national chairmen: Ronald McNeill MP, Sir W. H. Cowan MP and James Parker MP). On both committees WO, Admiralty, and Treasury representatives would sit as ex-officio members. The Earl of Onslow sat for the army (MI7b), Commander Walcott for the navy (Naval Intelligence), and H. Lloyd M. Bebb for the Treasury. The publicity committee was capitalized, initially, at £10,000 a month. W. H. Smith agreed to assist with distribution.[70] Locally, NWAC committees organized subcommittees in each constituency to arrange for propaganda regarding war aims, war savings, food economy, national service and munitions work.[71] By June 1918 there were something like 250 local committees in existence.[72] Once again, this was certainly an improvement on the rather ramshackle UDC arrangements!

The tangle between official and unofficial became worse when Lord Beaverbrook became Minister of Information and Northcliffe took over at Crewe House (foreign propaganda). Division of responsibilities between the two was arranged essentially as a division of provinces between satraps rather than as a settlement between responsible ministers of the government.[73] In such a situation, when did official information become propaganda directed at a foreign audience become disinformation directed inward become simply Beaverbrook's own editorial line as found in the *Daily Express* or Northcliffe's in the *Daily Mail*? Ultimately, of course, Beaverbrook's attempt to assume control of all information (and thus to produce a real ministry of propaganda) failed due to Secret Service, Admiralty, and especially, FO objections.[74] The question remained, however: where did the government start and stop when Northcliffe (a press proprietor and a government minister with responsibility for propaganda) offered to print 100,000 NWAC 'Holy War' propaganda posters for free (paper, however, being allotted by the government)?[75] It is, and must have been, difficult to see through all of this clearly. Perhaps that was the point.

While, therefore, the NWAC was solely responsible for the domestic distribution of the more disreputable sorts of propaganda, the truth was that the NWAC line and purpose could never be disentangled from that of the government, so fully was it integrated into the existing machinery of state, and tied to the continuing campaigns of Beaverbrook and Northcliffe.

The tone of the propaganda campaign can be gauged from the titles of some of the material produced. In addition to 'Peace at Germany's Price', we find indicated in a list of leaflets current to September 1917: 'A Kalender of Kultur', 'President Wilson on Peace Terms and War Aims', 'Labour and the War', 'What are we Fighting For?', 'There Must Be No Next Time', 'Manpower', 'Close the Ranks', 'The Nation's Vote of Thanks to the Fighting Forces', 'How the Hun Hates', 'What a Red Rag', 'Freedom of the Sea', 'Germany's Plot Against the Peace of the World', 'Is it a Capitalist War?', 'Germany's Two Voices', and 'Murder Most Foul'.[76] 'Red Cross or Iron Cross' (a later production) appears to have been a special favourite, judging by the number of times it was requested. Some of this, quite obviously, was intended to inform. The rest – if the titles are any guide – ranged from white propaganda through to black disinformation, intended, perhaps, to capitalize upon the anti-German hysteria of the latter war years. The films shown by the NWAC were also sometimes of this genre. An example: the prospectus for a movie entitled 'Once a Hun, always a Hun'.

> Two German soldiers are first shown in a ruined French town meeting a women with a babe in arms whom they strike to the ground. The two soldiers gradually merge into two commercial travellers now seen in an English village after the war. One enters a small general store and shows the shopkeeper a pan. The shopkeeper is at first impressed, but his wife enters and reveals the 'Made in Germany' inscription underneath. She calls in a policeman who orders the Germans from the shop. The final words on the screen point up the message, 'there can be no trading with these people after the war'.[77]

This example speaks for itself.

For our purpose, perhaps the most important purpose of the NWAC had nothing to do with propaganda. It was, quite simply, to create the secret machinery by which dissenters could be intimidated and in the extreme physically suppressed. Not only did the NWAC seek to mobilize the populace in a patriotic direction, it also existed to direct the patriots, as required, against the dissenters. For the first time, patriot excess was not only tolerated, but organized, employed, even manufactured by the government.

In November 1917, following a suggestion of Cave,[78] it was arranged for the NWAC through its general secretary, Thomas Cox, to get prior notice of dissenting meetings from the HO in order that it might 'try and arrange out-door or in-door meetings as a counter-blast'.[79] 'We understand', the NWAC had put to the HO,

> that you are kept informed of Pacifist gatherings which are being held throughout the country from time to time, and we should be glad if you would let us have particulars of any such meetings in order that we may set our local Committee machinery going.[80]

According to Cave's thinking, this information would then be most usefully passed to the BWNL WAC – the chosen instrument of suppression.[81] While it seems probable that this type of co-ordination had been going on unofficially for some time, this was the first time that the suggestion was made that connections between the government, the police, the NWAC and the BWNL be put on official footings. The purpose, of course, was obvious: to streamline the process of suppression.

As the author of this arrangement was the Home Secretary himself, co-ordination began forthwith. The NWAC soon began to receive copies of Thomson's CID intelligence reports.[82] It was already receiving copies of military intelligence reports from the Earl of Onslow, which would have included, of course, intelligence gathered through press and postal censorship.[83] At the end of the month, more helpfully still, the HO arranged for local chapters of the NWAC to receive notification of proposed meetings directly from local police sources.[84] As all public meetings had to be registered with the police under DORA, what this arrangement amounted to was a system by which the police passed information to the patriots – organized under the auspices of a committee led by the highest political figures in the land, and organized at a local level by notable patriots (just those sorts of people who had led the patriot onslaught at Cory Hall), often associated with organizations already active in the suppression of dissent. Hitherto, the HO had always operated on a rough laissez-faire principle. If it was nobody's business to tell the dissenters what they might say, patriots were also free to act in response as they saw fit. From this point, however, patriot demonstrations became less spontaneous outbursts which the police could not control than an organized, if covert, suppression of free speech which the police no longer simply ignored but partly inspired.

The result did not always have to be violent. For instance, a NWAC speaker arrived at the town in which he was to speak, in August 1918, and found (how odd!) a socialist meeting in progress. Within ten minutes everybody had been drawn over to the NWAC meeting. He stayed several days, and conducted a series of 'very useful and successful meetings'.[85] Given, however, that the NWAC was linked locally, and organically with other organizations (the BWNL for instance) it would be too much to expect that such foreknowledge did not also forearm patriots more inclined to violence than persuasion.

The NWAC responded to government information in kind. The flow of information was two-way, and the NWAC became, on one level, a gigantic intelligence gathering apparatus, reaching into every community in the country, the members and agents of which reported constantly to the executive in London. Each of its speakers, for instance, filled in a daily report which they forwarded to the central office, concerning the success of any meetings, local feeling, troublemakers, and so on.[86] They were instructed, in particular, to take note of local grievances so that these could be passed by the national committee to the appropriate government agency for action.[87] The NWAC analysed the press as well, and passed on intelligence gathered to its political leadership.[88] When the NWAC felt that something actionable had come to its notice, it informed the authorities who sometimes acted. In September 1918, for instance, the activities of a Mr Barraclough of

Weymouth were brought to the attention of the national committee by a local branch. It was felt that he was acting in a manner likely to prejudice the sale of war bonds. National HQ informed the HO accordingly. Proceedings, shortly thereafter, were initiated against him.[89] Had the war continued, it is probable that the NWAC would have received authority, similar to that granted to the services, to refer cases directly to the DPP. It was certainly amenable to the idea and suggested such an arrangement, but does not appear to have received this power.[90]

As worrying in its implications was the fact that from its inception the NWAC had been targeting the quarter of a million-strong volunteer movement (the VF) as especially amenable to its message, and as a particularly vital target audience. If this was not sedition, it was certainly provocative, particularly when we remember the prominence of uniformed personnel in previous incidents of patriotic violence, and the fact that many volunteers were also police auxiliaries. From the autumn of 1917, the NWAC was sending speakers to volunteer camps,[91] following a decision to conduct outreach missions among the troops.[92] The volunteers' associations were disposed to co-operate. Volunteers who attended NWAC events were excused drills.[93] There was nothing particularly new in the idea of volunteers being exposed to propaganda. From the beginning, the Anglican church hierarchy had been closely associated with both the TA and the VF. Prominent churchmen – Lieutenant-Colonel Bishop Winningham-Ingram, for instance – had been in the habit of attending camps and making powerfully patriotic appeals to the men.[94] What was new, in 1917, was that the government was taking on this job itself. The association of the VF with patriotic organizations, and its continued loyalty to the government, was of some importance. We will see in a later chapter, for instance, something of the part assigned to the volunteers in planning for home defence in 1918.

The government certainly did not disapprove. It is undoubtedly significant, in this regard, that a very strongly worded communication from the National Federation of Discharged and Demobilized Sailors and Soldiers, Coventry Branch, was passed by the HO to the NWAC for action. 'We ... view with anxiety', the letter began,

> the pernicious effect of the pacifist feeling now permeating the ranks of the workers throughout the country.
>
> We have each done our bit ... and we feel that the sacrifice made by us and being made by our comrades in the air, on land, and sea, will be futile if the workers of this country ... continue to foster this pacifist feeling now so prevalent.

We may have a moral obligation to our unions, but we also have a National obligation to our King and Country and a fraternal obligation to those left behind in the Forces.

We have promised that should it be considered necessary we would willingly place our services at the disposal of the Country.

We now feel the time has arrived and we must redeem our promise and we do so willingly feeling certain that only by a 'knock-out' blow can Germany be brought to her knees and an honourable peace concluded and we are of opinion the sooner this is done the better.

We therefore, at an extra-ordinary General meeting have passed by a unanimous vote a resolution placing ourselves at the Service of the Government, Local and National, to maintain order and assist in the carrying out of the 'Manpower Scheme'.[95]

The violence implicit in this communication is not what makes it important. Given the growing social–political polarity of wartime Britain, that was to be expected. What is most important is that the HO passed it to the NWAC for action. What service was it expected that these men would perform? How is it that a government agency was passing to what was (at least officially) a non-government organization an offer to assist, by means unspecified but clear by implication, in the imposition of compulsion and the suppression of dissent? Why was it, similarly, that Cave was most receptive to intelligence sharing with the BWNL WAC? The answer, of course, is obvious. Organizing such patriotic violence was part of what the NWAC was about – part of the reason it had been created by the Lloyd George government.

The result? By the beginning of 1918, the government had organized, and was supporting and financing, a body which claimed to be non-partisan (and was), unofficial (and was not), and concerned solely with popularizing the nation's war aims. This was not even half the truth. The NWAC was also convened to disseminate black propaganda, while organizing and directing the patriots in their role as a popular police force. Meanwhile, by its nature, it consolidated all patriotic organizations into something suggesting a National Party fighting organization: Lloyd George's stormtroopers. Britain had come a long way since 1914. It was to go further still.

NOTES

1. PRO CAB 24/16, 'Report on the Labour Situation', 6 June 1917. The creation of the NWAC has been taken as an indication of government concern that 'war-weariness was beginning to take hold of the British people, and that pacifist propaganda and

calls for a negotiated peace were beginning to attract public support far beyond the narrow circle of pacifists and radicals to which they had previously been confined'. D. Sweet, 'The Domestic Scene: Parliament and People', Liddle, *Home Fires and Foreign Fields*, p. 15.

2. Lord Lansdowne, and his supporters – working for a negotiated peace by 1917 – could absolutely not be touched. Cracking the heads of conservative elder statesmen, after all, was probably further than the BWNL was willing to go. Counter-mobilization against this threat was the only alternative. For the 'Lansdownes', see Lord Newton, *Lansdowne. A Biography*, pp. 468–75.

3. PRO HO 139/9/36 (Item 33), 'Home Propaganda', John Buchan to Lloyd George, 18 May 1917.

4. Thomson, *The Scene Changes*, diary entry for 2 December 1916, p. 355.

5. HLRO, Lloyd George Papers, Derby to Lloyd George, 11 May 1917.

6. See, for instance, A. Bryant, *George V* (London: Peter Davies, 1936), pp. 89–109; Nicolson, *King George the Fifth*, pp. 248–325; Lloyd George, *War Memoirs*, Vol. IV.

7. Thomson, *The Scene Changes*, diary entry for 16 May 1917, p. 368.

8. PRO T 102/3, N. Grattan Doyle (Honorary Secretary, National Patriotic Organisation (NPO); also BWNL, though not writing in this capacity) to Guest (NWAC), 2 August 1917; NWAC to NPO, 25 July 1917.

9. PRO T 102/3, Entente Peoples' Alliance to NWAC, January 1918.

10. PRO T 102/3, Grey Wilson to Doyle, 2 August 1917.

11. PRO T 102/7, NWAC circular letter, 18 September 1918.

12. PRO T 102, J. S. Armitage to Henderson to NWAC, 25 August 1917.

13. See, for example, PRO T 102/5, E. Gibbons (Newcastle Labour Representation Committee) to Peters, August 1917; and Peters to Gibbons, 27 August 1917.

14. PRO T 102/18, 'National War Aims Committee'.

15. PRO INF 4/1B, 'Staff of NWAC'.

16. PRO T 102/16, Statement of Expenditure Compared with Estimate, September 1917. Statement notes exceptional expenditures for August, incurred in 'obtaining special reports of anti-war conferences in August'; probably a reference to the Leeds conference.

17. PRO T 102/16, 'Estimated Expenditure for Six Months Ending March 1918'.

18. PRO T 102/18, 'Special Fees: Speakers', 3 September 1918.

19. PRO T 102/16, 'Estimated Expenditure for Six Months Ending March 1918'.

20. Swartz, *The Union of Democratic Control*, p. 188.

21. PRO T 102/16, Minutes, 10 October 1917.

22. PRO T 102/16, Minutes, 3 October 1917.

23. PRO T 102/7, NWAC to London City and Midland Bank, 29 January 1918; T 102/16, Minutes, 24 October 1917.

24. PRO T 102/7, NWAC to London City and Midland Bank, 29 January 1918.

25. PRO T 102/16, 'Statement of Expenditure Compared with Estimate', September 1917.

26. PRO INF 4/1B, 'Staff of NWAC'.

27. House of Lords Debates, Beaverbrook statement, 8 May 1918.

28. Swartz, *The Union of Democratic Control*, p. 175. See Beaverbrook statement, House of Lords Debates, 12 May 1918. To this purpose Beaverbrook adds two others: keeping the country informed of the war aims of the British Empire and its Allies, and supporting the government in its task of carrying on the war.

29. D. Sweet, 'The Domestic Scene', p. 15.

30. PRO T 102/16, Meeting Department Report, 25 September and 10 October 1917.

31. PRO T 102/16, Meeting Department Report, 25 September and 10 October 1917.

32. See, in particular, PRO T 102/1, T102/3, and T102/5.

33. PRO T 102/4, Admiralty Intelligence to NWAC, 7 December 1917. Remember, for instance, J. Havelock Wilson's reception in Glasgow. McGovern, *Neither Fear Nor Favour*, pp. 46–52.
34. PRO T 102, NWAC to Benn, 6 and 7 November 1918.
35. PRO T 102/4, Admiralty Intelligence to NWAC, 10 November 1917.
36. Wrigley, *Arthur Henderson*, p. 126.
37. PRO T 102/3, Darrow to NWAC, 25 August 1918.
38. A. Bullock, *Ernest Bevin*, p. 54.
39. *Report of the Proceedings at the 49th Annual Trade Union Conference, September 3–8 1917*, p. 69.
40. HLRO, Lloyd George Papers, F/4/2/33, Barnes to PM, 24 September 1918.
41. PRO T 102/18, Instructions to Speakers, in 'Report up to 8th December 1917'.
42. CCC, Churchill Papers (Chartwell Trust), CHAR 9/55, War Aims Speech at Bedford, 10 December 1917.
43. Ibid.
44. Ibid.
45. PRO HO 139/35/147, 'War Aims Committee. Confidential Circular to Editors', October–November 1917.
46. PRO HO 139/35/147, 'War Aims Committee. Confidential Circular to Editors', October–November 1917, 'Military Situation in Italy', File 1, attached.
47. PRO T 102/18, 'Cine Motor Campaign', Report of Attendance 8–13th April 1918.
48. House of Lords Debates, Beaverbrook statement, 8 May 1918.
49. PRO INF 1/4B.
50. House of Lords Debates, Beaverbrook statement, 8 May 1918.
51. See, in particular, PRO T 102/1 and T102/3.
52. PRO T 102/4, E. Green to W. Carter, 7 March 1918.
53. Bagwell, *The Railwaymen*, p. 356.
54. For example, Lords Debates, Series V, 20, Cols. 6–12, 8 November 1915: Lords Selbourne, President of the Board of Agriculture, Milner and Loreburn, all rising to criticize the government for over-strict censorship.
55. Marwick, *The Deluge*, pp. 212–13. The story was that the Germans were sending the corpses of their own dead back to Germany to be rendered for their fat – this used for explosive manufacture and other purposes.
56. For the propaganda work of the NWAC see, in general, Sanders, and Taylor, *British Propaganda*.
57. PRO INF 4/1B, 'Staff of NWAC'.
58. Ibid.
59. PRO T 102/1, RAF Comptroller General of Equipment to NWAC, 8 October 1918.
60. PRO T 102/1, J. C. Davidson to Captain Guest, 28 August 1918.
61. PRO MIN 4/1B, 'Military Press Control, A History of the Work of MI7, 1914–1919'.
62. PRO T 102/4, C. E. Farrar (Directorate of Shipyard Labour, Intelligence Officer) to NWAC, 27 December 1917.
63. PRO T 102/7 various.
64. PRO T 102/19, 'Articles Written and Sent to National War Aims Committee from January 17th to June 21st 1918'.
65. PRO T 102/19, 'Summary of Expenditure for Literary and Pictorial Work'.
66. PRO T 102/19, 'Articles Written for National War Aims Committee, Major-General Sir George Aston'; T 102/21, Books.
67. PRO T 102/16, Minutes, 24 October 1917.
68. PRO 122/1/1.
69. PRO T 102/16, G-18, Department of Information to Carson, September 1917,.
70. PRO T 102/16, Minutes of a Meeting, 4 April 1918.

71. PRO T 102/16, Meeting Department Report, 10 October 1917.
72. PRO T 102/18, 'List of War Aims Committees to Whom Letter of June 27, 1918 was Sent'.
73. If appointed Minister of Information, Beaverbrook would assign to Northcliffe foreign propaganda with access to the PM. Dominions and the services would remain Beaverbrook bailiwicks. Each would have the right of reproducing the other's material. Films would be joint holdings. Paintings would remain the responsibility of Northcliffe's brother, Lord Rothermere, in association with Northcliffe. Routine in the ministry would remain with Beaverbrook. HLRO, Beaverbrook Papers, C/261, Northcliffe minute, 26 January 1918. The agreement eventually broke down over the question of the manner in which Northcliffe would be appointed. Northcliffe to Beaverbrook, 23 April 1918.
74. See HLRO, Lloyd George Papers, F/4/5/21, Beaverbrook to Lloyd George, 13 June 1918; F/4/5/25, Beaverbrook to Lloyd George, 24 June 1918.
75. PRO T 102/3, Mr Simpson (*Daily Mail*) to Thomas Cox (NWAC), 20 September 1917.
76. PRO T 102/3, List of Leaflets, 21 September 1917.
77. Marwick, *The Deluge*, pp. 214–15.
78. Swartz, *The Union of Democratic Control*, p. 189.
79. PRO HO 45 10743/263275, file 265, National War Aims Committee, 16 November 1917. See also De Groot, *Blighty*, pp. 151–2.
80. PRO T 102/5, Thomas Cox to HO, 15 November 1917.
81. Swartz, *The Union of Democratic Control*, p. 189.
82. PRO HO 45/10743/263275/265, Cox to HO, 15 November 1917. See also T 102/5, Metropolitan Police to Cox, 20 November 1917.
83. PRO T 102/16, Minutes of Meeting, 19 September 1917.
84. PRO HO 45 10743/263275, file 265, National War Aims Committee, 16 November 1917.
85. PRO T 102/16, Speakers Daily Reports, Weston (?), 26 August 1918.
86. PRO T 102/16, Speakers Daily Reports.
87. PRO T 102/18, 'Report up to 8th December 1918'.
88. For example, NWAC analysis of impact of Lansdowne letter, PRO T 102/16, 'Public Opinion of Lord Lansdowne's Letter', September 1917.
89. PRO T 102/5, HO to T. Cox, 1 November 1918.
90. PRO T 102/18, Minutes of Meeting, 13 December 1917.
91. For example, PRO T 102/5, NWAC to Wilfrid Hill, 3 October 1917; *Daily Mail*, 22 July 1918 (NWAC speaker talking to 8th City of London Volunteers).
92. PRO T 102/16, Report of Meetings Department, 25 September 1917.
93. PRO 30/69, Ramsay MacDonald Papers, 30/69/1042, Free Man, May 1918.
94. For example, Wilkinson, *The Church of England*, p. 33; Marrin, *The Last Crusade*, p. 139.
95. PRO T 102/5, National Federation of Discharged and Demobilized Sailors and Soldiers, Coventry Branch, to HO, 31 January 1918; HO to NWAC, 11 February 1918.

10

1918

B Y 1918 the system by which dissent was suppressed had developed to the point where Britain possessed something like a Ministry of the Interior armed with emergency powers. It is true that military involvement was covert, and that the police operated with discretion, and true, moreover, that the opposition was not entirely silenced. It is also true that where neither the arrest of an individual nor censorship was an appropriate response, the patriots were more than willing to silence opposition, and true, as well, that they had been linked into the system of suppression through the NWAC, the militant expression itself of Lloyd George's new national coalition. It was true, finally, that wherever dissent was thought dangerous enough, censorship, in one form or another, could be quite ruthless, and that even where it was tolerated, dissent was marginalized and manipulated for its propaganda value.

The government, in short, had gone about as far as it could without doing considerable, perhaps irreparable, harm to the constitution. By 1918, two major steps remained by which the government could increase pressure on the dissenters. The first step would be simply to recognize, officially, what had happened. Legal status could be given to the de facto constitution which had developed by 1917. What was unofficial, covert and applied on a case by case basis, could be made official and obvious and universal. Lloyd George's coalition would be formalized. The old parties would be effectively dissolved, and the National Party created as the antidote to apprehended revolution. The NWAC amalgam would become official twice over – both as an instrument of the party and as an agency of the state. It would come to occupy the same symbiotic position in the political nation, as for instance, did elements of the National Fascist Party in Italy after 1922. Finally, censorship and police repression would come to be directed pre-emptively at categories, rather than in reaction to punish individual breaches of regulations. Arrest of opponents of the government without warrant, and perhaps without a crime having been committed, as had already occurred once in the case of the ASE strike leaders, would become common. MacDonald, Trevelyan, Snowden and the other active parliamentary dissenters might well find themselves going the way of Lupton. More thoroughgoing still – the second threshold – civilian control could disappear, and as in Germany, war government could be overtly militarized. Military requirements expressed through civilian agencies could become outright martial law imposed by armed force. In both eventualities, national life would move to a beat established by a universal and uniform propaganda system in which functional distinctions between the government, the NWAC and the private press would cease to have any meaning at all. These systems were not contradictory, and could be implemented in tandem or succession as the situation warranted. What would emerge, of course, would be something like an authoritarian, corporatist, militarist government of national consolidation – a clerical fascist state.

Throughout 1918, to its credit, the Lloyd George government steadily refused to implement either alternative because of its acute political perception that neither was yet required, while both would involve greater costs than benefits. Both, certainly, were prepared and suggested, and would probably have been implemented if conditions of greater emergency had developed. A dissent which eliminated what few inhibitions remained would have had to develop first. The trigger for the legitimization of the informal constitution very probably would have been widespread industrial action – perhaps a general strike. In the last years of the war, a general strike was always possible. If such a strike took a syndicalist direction, it would, in fact, have a revolutionary agenda. The prompt for militarization, or for the implementation of both systems in tandem, would have been apprehended revolution, becoming civil war. These eventualities, it is clear, were foreseen at the time. The logical response to both was prepared. Remember, finally, that the end of the war, by 1917, was projected several years in the future. Had the war continued longer than it did, and had social cleavages widened still further, HMG might well have had to face what it most feared.

We will deal with preparation for this new departure, for the most part, in chapter 11. In what follows, we will consider the attempt to manage, in 1918, the crumbling home front with the powers which the government had already assembled and how the failure of these powers contributed to a growing sense of emergency all too apparent in the war's last year.

By this point in the war, the only alternative to universal patriot suppression was probably simply to ban dissenting meetings which were likely to be inflammatory – which is to say all of them. While a total prohibition was never imposed – it would probably produce a powerful backlash requiring harsher measures still – during 1918, increasing use was made of DRR 9A to forbid dissenting meetings on a case by case basis. A labour meeting proposed for Finsbury Park for 2 May 1918, for instance, was flatly forbidden.[1] A WPC meeting, about the same time, was also banned without explanation.[2] Another meeting scheduled to commemorate May Day, in north London, was prohibited despite a protest from the NCCL which was seconded by the Society of House and Ship Painters, and more ominously, by the bumptious National Union of Railwaymen (NUR).[3] In the House of Commons, Cave was forced to defend this last prohibition. This particular meeting had been sponsored by eight local TUCs with 100 union branches scheduled to attend. Cave responded to calls for a justification by simply asserting that not only would the meeting not be permitted, but that there would be no point in rescheduling a May Day parade for a later, less provocative date. The reasons for the prohibition would still apply. Permission had been withheld, he said, because the HO apprehended 'grave disorder' if the meeting went ahead.[4]

May Day 1918 was such an issue because total manpower compulsion appeared, once again, to be on the near horizon, and the unions were determined to oppose it by whatever means were necessary. Once again, the problem was total war. In the aftermath of Passchendaele, it was difficult to see how the strength of the army could be maintained without a thorough combing of the home front. Taking its courage in its hands, in January 1918 HMG passed a new Military Services (No. 3) Act which gave the National Services Department (NSD) the right unilaterally to reschedule occupations and cancel exemptions without consultation with the unions. The act was only passed against strenuous objection – by the ASE and miners particularly, which had defended their privileges successfully in 1916 and again in 1917.[5] Sir Auckland Geddes, the new Minister of National Service, simply could see no other way to get more men for the army. This meant that, whatever the political cost, the unions must somehow be deprived of the right to make exemptions. By May Day, in the face of fantastic pressure from the unions, the Act was less shelved than stalled in implementation. The government lacked sufficient resolution to force it down the throat of the triple alliance.[6] There was never much doubt that reprisal would take the form of a general strike; nor that this was a show-down desired by at least a portion of the labour leadership.[7] Ultimately, whatever extra men the measure provided came through increases in efficiency rather than the implementation of the new legislation.[8] Meanwhile, HMG began seriously, if briefly, to consider the next logical step – conscription for Ireland.[9] All the government managed to do, even by discussing the issue, was to drive organized labour, the nationalists and Sinn Féin together.[10]

The social–political situation was ugly. If the patriots were pushing the government to greater action, the dissenters, having worked to politicize wartime grievances, were, increasingly, compelled to speak to the constituency which they had, in part, created. The combative Charles Trevelyan, for example – like Snowden – during 1917–18 was steadily moving towards a position of outright opposition to the government. In a speech in Halifax, a report of which was passed to the HO by 'a loyal Englishman', Trevelyan attacked the army for its deplorable waste of manpower and for the associated disappearance of British freedom as it struggled to make this wastage good. Conscription for Ireland would, he said, be the most 'deliberate and wanton crime in the history of any Government'. Britain was being ruled, he claimed,

> by a braggart and gambler [Lloyd George] who has failed, and who wants to hide the ruin he is bringing on his country by this frantic, useless, and ill timed measure [Irish conscription, and compulsion at home]. It is the way of all braggarts. They are most liable of all men to panic. They are wild and unsound in their hopes, and wild and unsound in their fears.[11]

'This boaster of the "knock out" blow', Trevelyan continued, 'who would not try for peace when the Germans were squealing for peace', now might be forced towards peace in less favourable circumstances.[12] The requirement that there must be peace he no longer troubled to conceal. But still, there was no legal action against Trevelyan. His notoriety – if not his parliamentary immunity – protected him, if only just. The HO might judge his excesses 'deplorable', but it was not prepared to move against him – on grounds of utility, perhaps, as much as on grounds of principle.

The agitation to hold some sort of May Day meeting continued, and accordingly – aware that it was producing, rather than suppressing, dissent by its policies – HMG began to modify the degree of its opposition. As always, the Lloyd George government was adept at identifying elements of its policy which, while perhaps sensible, were politically unwise. While it was not inclined *at all* to let the meeting go ahead, particularly when the German offensive in Flanders began to unfold at the end of the month, the HO was eventually brought to sanction the meeting in June, though not in Hyde Park, as had been planned, but in the much smaller venue of Finsbury Park. The less restrictive attitude adopted by the HO undoubtedly owed much to the virtual cessation of strike activity while the emergency in France continued.

Initially, the government had not been so confident that bad news at the front would quiet, rather than encourage, dissent. In February, the government had already been in a touchy mood and there had been an 'epidemic of prosecutions', the most famous of which was that of Bertrand Russell.[13] Russell later wrote about his trial that he had 'never felt anything equal to the concentrated venom of the magistrates in sentencing me: it was a blast of hatred quite astonishing'.[14] Russell was prosecuted for the anti-American article which had landed him in trouble in 1917, and which had reappeared in the 8 January edition of *The Tribunal*, and was imprisoned.[15] On appeal, the conditions under which he was held were mitigated following representations from many prominent persons. In June, Russell was released into his brother's keeping for recuperation, and the prohibition on his movements was withdrawn.[16] At this time also, not only was *The Tribunal* seized, but the National Labour Press, where it was printed, was invaded and the press removed under DRR 51. In March, with news of disaster at the front, Christopher Addison, Minister of Reconstruction, was commissioned to consider what special steps should be taken, and what powers would be needed to enable the government 'to deal at short notice either before or immediately upon the conclusion of the War with emergency measures, which, in ordinary course, would lapse either on or with the termination of hostilities'.[17] He received this charge the day after the *Kaiserschlact* started and news of disaster began to arrive. The question, of course, was whether the government expected defeat and the disruption which might precede, accompany and follow it; or whether it considered, even, that the home front was so fragile that bad news accompanied by a call for still greater effort might not finally produce a compelling demand to end the war. Given the correlation of dates, either inference would be entirely justified. Even the Society of Friends, which the government had been seeking to detach from dissent a year previously, became a focus of official paranoia. In May 1918 the members of the Friends service committee – Mr Harrison Barrow, Mr Arthur Watts and Mrs Edith Ellis – were all arrested for breach of censorship for authorizing the printing of a leaflet without first passing it through the press bureau. Burrows and Watts were sentenced to six months' imprisonment each, and Mrs Ellis was fined £100. The chairman of the quarter sessions, Sir Alfred J. Newton, in sentencing them, gave as his opinion that

One can scarcely contain oneself, and restrain one's indignation. The law had been deliberately and wilfully and ruthlessly broken. For the protection of the Empire and of the civilized world it has been decided that a check should be put on the publication of certain literature. Here is a body which deliberately flaunts everybody and everything. This Bench will not sanction any such proceedings.[18]

Even many patriots must surely have thought that Newton was laying it on a little thick.

If the government feared that domestic enemies would seek to exploit foreign defeats, they profoundly underrated the residual loyalty of even the most intransigent dissenters. When bad news began to arrive from France, even the strike arrangements committee of the shop stewards' movement banned strike action at this time of national emergency.[19] In November 1917, at the nadir of allied fortunes in the war, nearly a million days had been lost to strikes in the munitions industry alone. December 1917 and January 1918 had also been bad months. In April 1918, however, so powerful was the response of the population that only 15,000 days were lost. Smillie's miners voluntarily filled their comb-out quota, and '[t]he response to the Government's appeal to ... work over the Easter holidays proved almost embar-rassing'.[20] The Yorkshire miners were typical. While voting in March by a very narrow margin (39,847 to 35,558) to oppose withdrawal of exemptions, they also voted more than two to one to find the men the government required to fill out the army, and again in April, to find still more men for the front.[21] Even Ramsay MacDonald, at this time of national emergency, thundered to his supporters that they must be prepared to do whatever was necessary to win the war; neither defeat nor surrender, he claimed, were in his vocabulary.[22] The new Military Service Act was now less stalled than, for the moment, unnecessary. In April 1918, so quiet was the home front that Cave could claim that dissent had been defeated – the long fight had finally been won.[23]

The workers were allowed their day of international solidarity in June. Despite the still existing industrial truce it ended with the resolution – forwarded to the HO – of the 'Mass Meeting of Trade Unions, Labour & Socialist Organisations',

that they may anytime exercise the right to protest against reactionary legislation and *especially that organized Labour affirms its abiding faith in the unity of the Working Peoples of all countries as the only means of maintaining the Peace of the world.*[24]

While predictable, given the shift in the labour balance of power evident a year earlier, both the language and the stridency of the resolution were new in wartime England and were a sign that the truce of the spring could hardly be expected to last for long. Shortly thereafter, at a Labour Party conference (in London, on 26–28 June 1918), a resolution sponsored by Robert Smillie and Sylvia Pankhurst, calling upon the Labour Party to withdraw from the government, was almost passed. In the end, it was defeated only following explicit warnings from George Barnes that such a vote would split the party, and make the position of Labour MPs impossible. Better to wait, he pleaded, until the end of the war.[25] Ben Tillett was frightened at the direction dissent was taking, and convinced that the continued association of trade unions with political grievances could only have revolutionary con-sequences. Did the dissenters, he wondered, want to produce another Russia?[26] J. Havelock Wilson went one better and threatened to take the TUC in its entirety out of the Labour Party if such a motion were even seriously considered. If the TUC wouldn't come entire, then it could come in part.[27]

The position of Tillett and Wilson was undoubtedly affected by the offensive recently launched by the dissenters against Lloyd George's Labour supporters. In December 1917, the MFGB had informed the Labour Party that it had grounds for believing that the BWNL was going to run its own candidates in the next election. Determined to preserve discipline, the party informed its BWNL members that if this were the case they risked expulsion. Some, Hodge and Tillett, for instance, began to distance themselves from the BWNL – but would this be enough?[28] With the growth in dissent it appeared that the position of the patriots within the Labour Party might not be tenable for much longer. They could leave or be kicked down the stairs. Neither side desired, nor was yet ready for an overt breach. The first casualty of further, radical agitation, it appeared, would be the Labour Party, experiencing on a national level the same schism which had already occurred locally in Liverpool and Birmingham. For the moment, the dissenters advanced with greater caution.

Things were to get worse still. When it was obvious that the emergency had truly passed, by July 1918, 'a wave of unrest swept across the factories'; while,

> beneath the surface, always ready to exploit any psychological reaction, lurked the pacifist and subversive elements of the labour world.

Such is the testimony of Winston Churchill, then Minister of Muni-tions.[29] The leading edge of dissent had finally arrived at something like the Bolshevik position: peace certainly, but not for itself alone, and necessarily accomplished by total social realignment. At a meeting of the Socialist Labour Party, held in Glasgow in August 1918, the party chairman, Tom Bell, spoke in a straightforward revolutionary manner. The party was growing rapidly, he said. Branches were appearing everywhere. *The Socialist* had tripled in circulation. The party had adopted a revolutionary programme.

> ... [T]he SLP had conducted an active anti-militarist agitation during the past year. Since last November, the party had carried on a virile propaganda against the war, hand in hand with the Russian wing of the SLP, the Bolsheviks. While labour leaders of the sentimental type, Mr. Ramsay MacDonald, MP, were repudiating the Bolsheviks, this conference would be asked to pass a resolution congratulating the revolutionary Socialists of Russia for their heroic stand.[30]

The feelings of those reading the police report of this conference can be imagined, particularly as Bell was, as we have seen, no stranger to the police. The October Revolution, moreover, was already a year old, so that Bell could not claim ignorance of what was happening in Russia. But what to do? Bell had already been jailed, and far from being silenced, he had emerged with greater conviction and vigour to lead a movement which had tripled in size.

The government's attitude, once again, began to alter in keeping with the threat perceived. Authorities began to press for the power simply to prohibit expression of dissent. At this time, for instance, the Chief Constable of Weymouth requested blanket power to prohibit all meetings of socialist and Labour organizations.[31] Such official stridency was new. The HO still refused to grant him this power: though now, not because it did not want to, but because it did not feel that it had the available forces. The question, it was felt, was not of principle (all such meetings should be stopped), but whether there were sufficient police to enforce such a ruling. As there were not sufficient police, policies of either total tolerance or total prevention were impossible, unless, of course, the decision were made to bring in the army. The government was not yet ready for that. Besides, '[i]t [was] notorious', an HO official minuted the request from Weymouth, 'that opposition to Pacifist meetings [was] being organized: representatives of the minority [were] not to be allowed to hold public meetings for the purpose of passing unanimous resolutions wh[ich] in the opinion of the majority [were] not only detestable, but [might] also be highly injurious to the public interest'.[32] The patriots might yet work their old magic. In 1918, given ongoing police–patriot liaison, suppression of dissent by patriot gangs became systematic and this method continued to be adequate to contain most simple anti-war dissent. The patriots, only too aware that HMG was unlikely to do anything to stop them – and why should it, when it was inspiring, co-ordinating, even organizing their activities? – began to operate with almost astonishing impudence and violence. More examples of this type of activity would be redundant. Let one speak for all. Before the suppression of an Abbey Woods meeting in September 1918, for instance, not only were 'open and elaborate plans made', but a reward was offered 'to the first man who caused Mr. Ramsay MacDonald to be taken away on a stretcher'.[33] This was a long way from the threat, in 1914, to boo MacDonald down. Where this solution was insufficient, the threat of violence could still be used to justify individual, case by case, prohibitions. A combined WIL–WPC meeting, for example, scheduled for Hyde Park in July, was refused police permission to proceed under DRR 9A, certain violence being apprehended.[34]

Official policy was no different from that in 1917. Where individual meetings could not be prevented, the best policy, it was thought, was to permit the pacifist–patriot dialogue of fists to take place unimpeded. The authorities would assist in this process only by ensuring that those dissenting meetings permitted were restricted to such venues as denied the dissenters access to a wide audience, while ensuring that such 'scuffles' as developed ended 'without any serious public disorder ensuing'; that is, such that 'no-one will be seriously incommoded except those attending them'.[35] So stood HO opinion at the end of the war. Dissenters could not publish, but they could say what they wished. That was their right. They could only express their opinions, however, in forums unfavourable to the propagation of their message. It was understood, meanwhile, that it was not a police responsibility to protect them from their more vocal, more numerous and more violent adversaries. This dynamic was intensified, of course, by the fact that the HO covertly assisted in the organization of the anti-pacifist backlash. A rather effective censorship by riot and counter-riot remained government policy until the end of the war.

And yet dissent continued to grow, while becoming steadily more radical. Worse, through its association with militant labour, the dissenters gained access to venues in which suppression by patriots could only be counter-productive. MacDonald was vulnerable if addressing an NCCL meeting in Cardiff; what if Snowden addressed striking workers in an armaments plant? Patriot violence was certainly sometimes attempted against disgruntled workers. For instance, a meeting of Royal Arsenal workers in July 1918, which Ramsay MacDonald was to have addressed, was broken up with considerable violence by a band of patriots. The police declined to intervene, even though the patriot counter-demonstration had been 'previously organized [by men] and methods known ... to the police authorities'.[36] This sort of intervention, however, could never have become a general solution. The perception that free play of fists would not work on strikers was confirmed by patriotic labour. An attempt to deal with disgruntled workers by force would backfire, they warned, and only increase unrest.[37] In the meantime, of course, war production would be jeopardized. An intimidated worker is not a productive worker, is, more than likely, an angry worker, more disposed to listen to incendiary appeals than otherwise.

Patriotic counter-mobilization was tried, and sometimes did the trick. A wave of munitions strikes, in July 1918, which encompassed workers in Sheffield, Avonmouth, Oldham, Coventry, Gateshead, Farnham, Birmingham, Manchester, Hardon, Gainsborough and Newport, was brought to an end by the NWAC. Following appeals to their patriotism (and threats from Churchill that they were about to be called up), all the workers except those in Coventry returned to work. That Friday, members of the NASFU, led by J. Havelock Wilson himself, entered Coventry behind their branch bands. The WSPU was on hand in strength, led by no less notable a patriot than Christabel Pankhurst. The town was treated, throughout the weekend, to non-stop speakers, propagandists and canvassing. The following Monday, the strike collapsed.[38]

Such methods, however, did not always work, though some solution always had to be found to contain industrial unrest. The railway workers, for instance, could not be permitted to say what they liked or do as they wished. They were, however, in a condition of imminent strike from August 1917. Moreover, as part of the triple alliance, a general rail strike, like the engineers' strike of 1917 – which, remember, had produced the war's only pre-emptive arrests under DRR 14 – was potentially a general strike. How were the railway men to be handled?[39] There were too many to intimidate; they were too dispersed and angry to be easily convinced.

Attempting to restrain industrial unrest by prohibiting certain types of effective action was one solution. In August 1917, for instance, in the face of picketing by railway workers, it had been decided to arrest the picketers under DRR 56. In addition, the Staffordshire chief constable gave as his judgement that, under DRR 42 and in accordance with the Munitions Act of 1915, any striking railway workers were liable to be fined £5 a day for each day they were on strike. A poster, prepared to deal with a strike that did not last long enough for it to be posted, informed railway workers that anybody actually attempting to prevent the working of the railways would be imprisoned for six months.[40] It is possible that the government would have had a chance to try out these powers had the leader of the NUR, J. H. Thomas, not threatened to resign unless his men went back to work. If the railworkers emulated the ASE membership, then they would strike without him. A strike at this point in the war, Thomas fumed, 'was [as] wicked as dangerous', to be fought, not tolerated.[41] In 1917 the leadership was strong enough and such intimidation was effective enough to stop this potential strike in its tracks.

A year later, however, the railworkers did go on strike, regardless of warning, as part of an orgy of industrial action which saw policemen, cab drivers, omnibus conductresses, Lancashire cotton operatives, spinners, jute workers and miners take to the streets[42] – 'every day the signs of unrest at home increas[ing]'.[43] In some workplaces the impetus appears to have been attempts to restore prewar practice, the emergency being over and the end of the war apparently approaching. In Dundee, for instance, membership of the jute workers' union had quadrupled during the war. Conditions of work had much improved. Wages had increased greatly. A 40-hour working week became the norm. The political power of the union had grown. By 1918, there were 20,000 members of the jute workers' union in a total population in Dundee of 170,000, jute being the principal component in canvas and sandbags. None of this was surprising or exceptional, since the industry was essential to the war effort. In September 1918, however, production was deregulated, and producers were informed that they should move to prewar levels of production. The employers, in short order, were seeking to lay off excess staff, slash wages, and return to a 55-hour week. They did not bother to consult the union over any of this. When the workers refused to work under these conditions, employers simply withheld three-elevenths of their pay. Dundee exploded, and remained restive throughout 1921.[44]

Of all the 1918 strikes, the rail strike was probably the most dangerous, both in scale and, potentially, to the war effort. If some disruption could be tolerated in Dundee among workers whose product was no longer essential, work stoppages on the Great Western could never be permitted. While contained by exceptional efforts, the rail strike of 1918 was widespread enough to cause considerable short-term disruption.

What happened? On 22 September men at the Alexandra Dock and Railway Company in Monmouthshire and south Wales voted to stop work at midnight. Over the next three days the strike spread over many of the major lines in the west and south-west. Paddington station went out on 24 September. That same day, at a meeting at the Board of Trade, military, HO, and other officials co-ordinated procedures for fighting the strike. By this time such co-ordination was routine; the HO, once again, was the leading agency. A poster, prepared a year earlier, was dispatched for circulation. A telegram containing instructions on how to deal with picketers was sent to chief constables in affected areas. A request for military assistance was forwarded to the DMI, General Macdonogh, and a similar request to his counterpart at the Admiralty. It was of 'paramount importance', the request read, that order be maintained and that the strike be prevented from affecting the conduct of the war. Assistance was requested in the protection of property and in the conveyance of workers willing to work to their place of employment. Local police officials were advised that they had the right to call for military assistance without reference to the HO.[45] The next day six battalions in Aldershot were placed in readiness to move, and two brigades of the City of London Garrison were mobilized. One brigade was in fact dispatched to Newport, while a company of the Scots Guards was sent to Stratford in east London to contain picketing along the Great Eastern line there. The day after that, 26 September, while men of the Labour Corps were being called upon to run the railway, the railwaymen began to return to work, and J. H. Thomas, their leader, advised the army that the remainder of his men would go to work the following day. Most did. By the following morning, the railways were back in operation. The press was immensely supportive of the government's stance, and *The Times* went so far as to advocate the militarization of the railways for the duration.[46] In many ways, however, the rail strike of 1918 was a rehearsal for the General Strike of 1926, though, for the moment, a policy of incremental coercion had worked.

Less dangerous but as worrying was the police strike of August 1918. Who would watch the home front if the watchers themselves were no longer dependable? The police had been shaping for a strike for some time. In the years before the war, discontent had risen. During the war, the workload had risen while the number of police had declined markedly. Police pay, meanwhile, had not kept pace with a rapidly rising cost of living. Already by 1913, a secret police union – the National Union of Police and Prison Officers (NUPPO) – was in the process of formation. By 1918, the NUPPO was seeking trade union affiliations. In August, a provincial organizer, Thomas Theil, was dismissed for his union activities. The NUPPO called for his reinstatement and submitted additional demands. The government refused to bargain. On 30 August 1918, most MEPO and City of London constables failed to report for work, while NUPPO officials sounded out other unions regarding the possibility of sympathy strikes. The government plainly panicked, faced with what appeared to be a police mutiny, with the potential that it might encourage, even provoke, further industrial unrest. That day soldiers took position around vital points, marines surrounded the Admiralty, and garrisons in the city were placed in readiness for action. The attitude of the strikers, however, made it obvious very quickly that they had no political agenda. This was a good thing, because it was also quickly obvious that the soldiers in the city might not be willing to act against them. The government moved quickly to meet most of the strikers' demands. A day later, the police were back at work. Britain, Lloyd George said, had been closer to Bolshevism during the police strike than at any time before.[47]

Most of the strikes of 1918, once again, were not politically motivated. Industrial action still tended to develop from discontent produced by violations of what workers considered fair practice. The English working class, for the duration of the war, remained fundamentally uninterested in 'far-reaching industrial and political programmes and … [un]willing to act unless for quite definite and immediate aims'.[48] Politically, throughout 1918 the patriots were firmly back in the ascendant. In the early months, national solidarity re-emerged in the face of bad news from the front. In the final months of the war labour political militancy generally took the form of calls for vengeance against Germany.[49] None of this meant, however, that a return to the confident, widespread dissent of 1917 was impossible. Nor did it mean that politicization of workers' grievances was not in the offing. Nor did anything prevent radical dissenters in the labour movement from attempting to turn any strike into a political act. It is probable, finally, that had the war continued through succeeding years, simple frustration and war weariness would have produced greater interest in far-reaching schemes. And all of this notwithstanding, working-class unrest was dangerous. When provided with a socialist gloss by the dissenting leadership, it seemed less a series of unrelated protests at conditions of work than a well-ordered conspiracy to change society. Unheeded, industrial unrest could produce the type of mass dis-affection from the war effort which would lead to certain defeat, or at least, a certain withdrawal from the war, with significant implications for the home front in the postwar world. Moreover, if the workers were themselves not revolutionary, the perception that they were – common to much of the administration – could lead to pre-emptive, premature counter-revolutionary actions which might well produce exactly the type of political dissent which they were designed to combat.

In the aftermath of the rail strikes, the HO began preparing exactly such pre-emptive activity, both on its own, and in co-ordination with other ministries. Systematic police surveillance, as we have seen, had already been instituted. Seeking to turn this to good effect, by 1918 the HO was considering the posting of a circular to chief constables requiring them to furnish London with the names of fomenters of strikes and agitators so that pre-emptive proceedings might be taken against them when the occasion warranted – as against the engineering shop stewards in 1917. Fortunately, the HO did not need to go this far, because peace came before such a step proved necessary. It is enlightening, however, that it was even considered. Even without this step, the ordinary rights of labour were not fully restored until the end of 1919,[50] and in the interim much of the machinery of police surveillance remained in place. Until well into 1919, for instance, a special intelligence office in the CID was operating under Director of Intelligence, Basil Thomson. It co-ordinated information about 'seditious meetings and conspiracies, threatened disturbances and revolutionary movements'. In addition, Thomson was charged with the preparation of confidential reports for the government on labour unrest, based upon the reports of detectives dispatched a year earlier when system-atic surveillance of the working class began.[51] Thomson's office was a legacy of the rail strike of 1918, insofar as it had been a common complaint then that no pre-emptive action was possible due to the difficulty of getting names of persons against whom proceedings might be instituted. It followed, as well, from a suggestion of Carson's that the time had come to treat all forms of discontent as a single phenomenon – very possibly funded by Germany, certainly acting in Germany's interests.[52] Certainly, if this was the perception of the government, then Thomson was a good man for the job – he was, it has been claimed, unable to distinguish between radicalism and revolution, dissent and unrest, dislike of the war and dislike of the system.[53] Thus if pre-emptive arrest of the dissenting leadership did not become government policy, this must not be taken to mean that it was not fully prepared and the government inclined to implement it, should a sufficient threat develop.

Other methods continued to function, providing an automatic brake on dissent. The employment of conscription, as a tool to combat dissent, we have already seen. Part of the Lloyd George solution to problems of all sorts was simple government control. Government control implied government power. Any sort of power, during a Great War, could become power to coerce. During the Lloyd George period, whole industries were effectively nationalized for the duration. In order to ensure adequate food supplies, while preventing profiteering, purchasing and distribution of food became a government monopoly – the price of food was regulated and food itself ultimately rationed. Meanwhile, the shipping industry was controlled to ensure an adequate supply of ships, and to make certain that sufficient tonnage was allocated to secure enough food to keep the home front quiet. Industries like coal mining and shipbuilding followed munitions production into government control. Specific ministries were created to deal with the most important of these – food and shipping most particularly. The rationale behind all of this was to ensure fair play in the workplace, and therefore to prevent strikes; to silence criticisms of profiteering, by removing essential industries from private control for the duration. It was also, of course, to control and assure production. Some success, at least, was achieved. By the summer of 1918, increased building, rationing, and controls had ensured that enough food was reaching the United Kingdom to make certain that acute shortages in themselves did not become the source of disruption on the home front.[54] This was simple palliation of dissent, as always the favoured strategy.

As with conscription, however, it was possible that the government attempted to do far more than remove cause for grievance and ensure efficiency by taking control of different aspects of national life. It is very likely that Lloyd George's nationalization programme contributed to the realization of another agenda altogether. It is certain, for one thing, that he looked to government control to modernize and rationalize obsolescent industries. This purpose was relatively benign, and in keeping with the long-range programme of his government.

There were, however, other tools applicable to the fight against dissent which Lloyd George gained by instituting industrial control. One of these was certainly the ability to threaten other industries with regulation if either management or the unions failed to play their part in the war effort – which meant, essentially, if they did anything to jeopardize production or continued domestic peace. We have already seen how this threat was used on one occasion – against the railwaymen in 1917 – to end a strike. Control was all the more daunting because it placed in government hands another weapon which those workers in privileged, war-essential industries, could not be expected to ignore: the threat to cancel exemptions. If industrial action ever reached the stage where it imperilled Britain's performance in the war, not only could industries become subject to government control, but in so becoming would make obsolete special deals made in the past. Exemptions would be unilaterally cancelled and the workplace subjected to thorough-going reorganization – perhaps, as with the railwaymen, militarization.

Those rendered redundant and therefore expendable would shortly thereafter be on their way to the front. This was not a threat which the Lloyd George government ever much scrupled to employ. Faced with the munition workers' strike in July 1918, for example, Churchill, then the Minister of Munitions, declared that '[i]f the men won't work, they ought to fight'.[55] The strike, he told the assembled press proprietors, 'can only be regarded as an attempt to subvert and deflect the avowed policy of the state in time of national danger'.[56] Such was the message and the warning that their newspapers carried, with very supportive editorial content. Shortly thereafter, Lloyd George threatened that if the strike were not over within three days, all the strikers would find themselves in khaki.[57] The strike collapsed almost immediately. Constant intimidation of this sort was probably the greatest reason why labour strife was contained at manageable levels until 1919.

There was another method held in reserve by the Lloyd George government, useful for bringing dissent of any kind to heel, but only to be employed when all other options had been tried and failed. By 1918, having assumed monopoly responsibility for importing, growing and distributing food, the government was placed in a position where it could respond to dissent of any kind, if necessary, with the imperative 'no co-operation, no food'. There is some suggestion that Lloyd George himself considered using this method during 1918, and that the method was threatened if not employed. Understandably, it was rather effective. What price making a political point if the result were starvation? There is the suggestion, moreover, that the ability to use this method was deliberately retained after the war against the eventuality that industrial relations deteriorated to a dangerous degree.[58] All of this was a sign, of course, of how serious the government considered dissent on the home front to have become by 1918. Once again, it is fortunate that the government did not feel compelled to go so far.

The fact that the iron fist was not yet required in 1918 and, therefore, that the working class had not yet entirely aligned itself with dissent, that the patriots continued to keep a lid on things, and that a revolutionary situation had not yet developed, was cold comfort through the late summer and early autumn of 1918. With victory uncertain, and near victory unlikely, it was impossible to know whether the process of consolidation, radicalization and politicization of dissent would continue or where it would lead. And, if it cannot be said that the majority of the working class ever achieved a revolutionary consciousness, neither can it be said with confidence that the government had failed to adopt a counter-revolutionary consciousness. Civil war, like war between states, does *not* require two players. By 1918, the Lloyd George combine was a white reaction in the process of formation. It may well be the fact that Britain got off the steam-train of history only one or two stops short of civil war. HMG was preparing to turn a corner. Just how sharp this corner could be we will see in the chapter which follows.

NOTES

1. PRO HO 45 10810/311932, file 59, 2 May 1918.
2. Wiltsher, *Most Dangerous Women*, p. 197.
3. PRO HO 45 10810/311932, file 61, North London Labour Demonstration, 5 May 1918.
4. Ibid., file 62, May 1918.
5. Adams and Poirier, *The Conscription Controversy*, p. 227. By 1917, the Welsh miners in particular were returning to radicalism. The Russian revolution was welcomed and the valleys 'seethed with bitterness'. Morgan, *Rebirth of a Nation*, pp. 175–6.
6. Adams and Poirier, *The Conscription Controversy*, p. 227.
7. G. D. H. Cole, for instance, at this point a confidential advisor to the ASE, and no radical, told C. P. Scott that he was anxious for the shop stewards to stop the war by organizing a general strike. Wilson, *The Political Diaries of C. P. Scott*, diary entry for 3–5 February 1918, p. 333.
8. See Grieves, *The Politics of Manpower*, pp. 149–99. Grieves argues, however, that the improvement in method represented the war's first real attempt actually to exercise manpower control.
9. Adams and Poirier, *The Conscription Controversy*, pp. 236–8; Wilson, *The Political Diaries of C. P. Scott*, diary entry for 19–21 April 1918, p. 342.
10. E. O'Connor, *A Labour History of Waterford* (Waterford: Waterford TUC, 1989), p. 142.
11. PRO HO 144 1459/316786, file 6, 22 April 1918.
12. Ibid.
13. MUH, Russell Papers, Volume 410, Clifford Allen to Bertrand Russell, 11 February 1918. This was enough for Russell, who could no longer see how the dissenters could possibly win the support of the country, the government being what it was. By the end of 1917 Russell had already resolved to withdraw from propaganda work (MUH, Russell Papers, Volume 410, Statement of BR [G. Murray], 8 April 1918. In December 1917 he informed the WO of this fact (Volume 410, Lord Russell to Cockerill, 15 December 1917, and Cockerill to Lord Russell, 17 March 1918). Russell was prosecuted for the anti-American article which had landed him in trouble in 1917, and which had reappeared in the 8 January edition of *The Tribunal* (Volume 806, 'Rex vs Russell' 1918), and imprisoned. In June, he was released into his brother's keeping for recuperation and the prohibition on his movements withdrawn (Volume 410, Lord Russell to Cockerill, 5 July 1918, and Cockerill to Lord Russell, 17 July 1918).
14. *Collected Works of Bertrand Russell*, Vol. XIV, p. 390. It is quite possible that there was something personal in the persecution of Russell at this time, after he had promised to stop propaganda work. The magistrate presiding at his trial spoke of his attainments and position in passing sentence – an indication, perhaps, of violated class feeling, as dissent was ever more closely aligned with social unrest. The attorney who drove the campaign against Russell, *The Tribunal* and the National Labour Press (Sir Archibald Bodkin) had been prosecutor in the earlier Everett case. In 1918, he was working for the DPP in the Russell case, and for the HO and MI5, providing legal advice regarding censorship. Ibid., p. 390.

15. MUH, Volume 410, 'Rex vs Russell', 1918; and Volume 410, Lord Russell to Cockerill, 5 July 1918, and Cockerill to Lord Russell, 17 July 1918.

16. *Collected Works of Bertrand Russell*, Vol. XIV, item 410, Lord Russell to Cockerill, 5 July 1918, and Cockerill to Lord Russell, 17 July 1918.

17. BLO, Cave Papers, Cave 62476, Addison to Cave 22 March 1918.

18. Snowden, *Autobiography*, p. 428.

19. Waites, *A Class Society at War*, p. 232.

20. Ibid., pp. 232–3.

21. C. Baylis, *A History of the Yorkshire Miners 1881–1918* (London: Routledge, 1993), p. 404.

22. Commons Debates, Series V, Volume CVII, column 591, 20 June 1918.

23. Playne, *Britain Holds On*, p. 314.

24. PRO HO 45 10810/311932, files 64 and 65, North London Labour Committee, May 1918.

25. Brand, *British Labour's Rise to Power*, p. 51.

26. Schneer, *Ben Tillett*, p. 196.

27. Brand, *British Labour's Rise to Power*, p. 51.

28. Clegg, *A History of British Trade Unionism*, Vol. II, p. 231.

29. W. Churchill, *The World Crisis* (New York: Charles Scribner, 1927), Vol. II, p. 205.

30. PRO HO 139/23/96, Part 2, File 34, 'Socialist Labour Party Conference at Glasgow, 4 August 1918', police transcript of Chairman's address appended.

31. PRO HO 45 10810/311932, file 67, 31 August 1918.

32. Ibid.

33. PRO 30/69/1162, Herbert Morrison to Ramsay MacDonald, 25 September 1918.

34. Wiltsher, *Most Dangerous Women*, p. 197.

35. PRO HO 45 10810/311932, file 67, 31 August 1918.

36. PRO 30/69/1162, Herbert Morrison to Lloyd George, 25 September 1918.

37. See, for example, PRO CAB 24/26, GT 2073, 'Labour in Revolt', 20 September 1917.

38. Churchill, *The World Crisis*, Vol. II, pp. 206–7.

39. PRO HO 45 10884/346578, Railway Strike 1917–1918.

40. Ibid., file 6, Railway strike, August 1917. HO opinion, however did not support him on this. The right to strike, it was thought, remained, though an attempt at arbitration was necessary first. Picketing, however, remained an offence under DRR 42. See also file 7, Threatened Railway Strike: The Government's Prompt Action, Press Cuttings, September 1917, for the favourable public reaction to the actions of the government which headed off the threatened strike.

41. Bagwell, *The Railwaymen*, p. 356.

42. See Williams, *Home Fronts*, pp. 256–7.

43. Mallet, *Lord Cave*, p. 216.

44. Walker, *Juteopolis*, pp. 394–408.

45. PRO HO 45 10884/346578, file 9, Railway Strike September 1918, 24 September 1918.

46. PRO HO 45 10884/346578, file 11, Railway Strike, September 1918.

47. K. Jeffery, *States of Emergency. British Governments and Strikebreaking since 1919* (London: Routledge & Kegan Paul, 1983), p. 5; Morgan, *Conflict and Order*, pp. 66–71.

48. Waites, *A Class Society at War*, p. 207.

49. Ibid., p. 193.

50. PRO HO 45 10785/290314, file 17, *Restoration of Pre-war Practices Act 1919*, 29 September 1919.

51. PRO HO 144 1484/349684, HO to Chief Constables (Circular), 22 April 1919.

52. PRO CAB 24/4, G157, 'Memorandum on Pacifist Propaganda', 3 October 1917.

53. Swartz, *The Union of Democratic Control*, p. 183.

54. S. Armitage, *The Politics of Decontrol of Industry* (London: London School of

Economics, 1969), pp. 22–3, 28–31. See also Webb, *The History of Trade Unionism*; Salter, *Allied Shipping Control*, idem, *Memoirs of a Public Servant*, pp. 73–122, and idem, *Slave of the Lamp*, pp. 59–69; Winter, *The Great War*.

55. Adams and Poirier, *The Conscription Controversy*, p. 243.
56. Churchill, *The World Crisis*, Vol. II, p. 206.
57. Adams and Poirier, *The Conscription Controversy*, p. 243.
58. R. Desmarais, 'Lloyd George and the Development of the British Government's Strike Breaking Organisation', p. 1.

11

Towards the Abyss[1]

BY 1918, many feared that a situation was developing in Britain similar to that which had come about in Russia a year previously, and which unfolded in Germany in the autumn. Against this eventuality HMG was plainly preparing to cross the militarization threshold previously identified. By 1918, not only was the domestic threat considered sufficient to necessitate the retention in the United Kingdom of a considerable number of soldiers, but it became the implicit rationale behind home defence planning. With revolution possible, counter-revolution – the military counter-strike by which it would be contained – was prepared. Planning for this eventuality was the logical conclusion of the evolving process by which dissent was contained. It should be stated at the outset that what follows will depend almost entirely upon circumstantial evidence. No agency was ever ready to admit that HMG was prepared to go so far. Given the powerful inhibitions within British political life – the fact that much of the machinery we have already described remained throughout the war unofficial, covert, and circumscribed – it would be strange indeed if we were to find open admissions of something which was for many not only inadmissible but unthinkable. Nevertheless, enough can be established about military dispositions, planning and co-ordination to suggest powerfully that a military counter-stroke was being prepared.

First it is necessary to revisit the old question of just what force was retained in the United Kingdom during 1918. If few troops were retained, then home defence planning cannot be held to reflect, necessarily, government policy. If all available troops were sent to France in 1918 in response to the emergency there, we might be excused for concluding that their presence in Britain earlier in the year was simply military inertia. If, however, troops were present in Britain in substantial numbers throughout the year there is reason to address the question of why they were being kept there.

The number of troops in Britain at the beginning of 1918 is not open to much question. In January 1918, according to the AG's department, there were something like 1.5 million soldiers in the United Kingdom. In November 1918, there were still about 1.4 million: hardly a substantial reduction. Not all of these men, of course, were dedicated to home defence. When wounded men, the garrison of Ireland, trained men under-age for overseas service, troops in training, those serving in various support roles or static guards, and those committed to air defence are deducted, however, a residual number of something like 175,000 men remained at the beginning of the year.[2] This figure represented trained men otherwise available for active service but kept in the UK for home defence. It is about the figure that we would expect, given that there were, in January 1918, eight manoeuvre divisions in the United Kingdom – two short of the ten which had been there in 1917 and which the army had previously judged necessary for home defence.

Whatever cosmetic changes might have been made to UK manning levels in 1918, the actual number of manoeuvre troops dedicated to home defence appears to have changed little, even following the reduction in the number of actual divisions retained at home.[3] In his memoirs, Sir William Robertson wrote that upon leaving his post as CIGS and taking up position as Commander Eastern Command (the most important home command), in February 1918, he set himself to reduce the number of troops in Britain. He continued this campaign as Commander Home Forces after June 1918.[4] Robertson clearly designated trained eighteen-year-olds, in particular, to commence their active service early; considerable numbers of these found their way to France in 1918.[5] An additional loss to home defence manpower totals occurred early in the year when eight brigades of Yeomanry cyclists were despatched to Ireland. There they joined seven territorial cyclist battalions who had apparently been deployed a little earlier.[6] Most of the troops kept at home, Robertson suggests, were in the eighteen-year-old category, and thinning them out by sending them to France solved the problem of combat-ready soldiers kept at home. When we look at WO figures, however, while the under-age men may have formed a substantial proportion of the troops in Home Commands, they do not seem to have provided much of a contingent in those units actually dedicated to home defence. Even the dispatch of the cyclists did not have much of an effect on the total number of able men retained in Britain proper. In fact, by November 1918, judging by the number of active formations still in the United Kingdom and the type of unit from which these were formed, the number of trained troops dedicated to home defence is unlikely to have changed much at all. When the fighting ended in France, there were still four formed Territorial Force

(TF) infantry divisions, one cyclist division,[7] six independent mixed brigades, and various other support and unallocated units distributed throughout the country. The global total, as we will see, was roughly equivalent to the eight divisions in Britain at the beginning of the year.

The bulk of the manoeuvre troops were with XXIII Corps in East Anglia, under the command of General Pultney: 64th (Highland) Division Territorial Force (TF), HQ Norwich; 67th (Home Counties) Division TF, HQ Colchester; and 68th (Welsh) Division TF, HQ Bungay;

FIGURE 6: HOME DEFENCE DEPLOYMENT, 1918
(MANOEUVRE TROOPS)

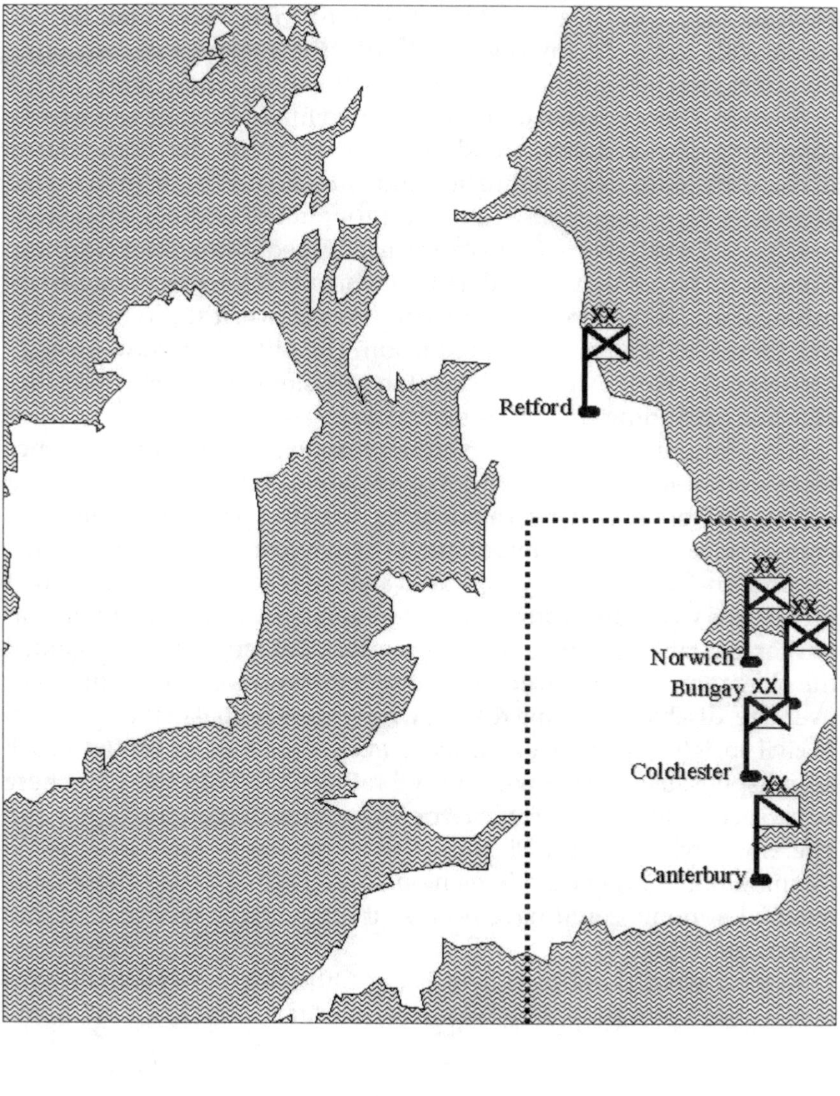

with 1st Cyclist Brigade (Yeomanry) at Beccles (attached 68th Division), 223rd Mixed Brigade (TF) at Sheringham (attached 64th Division), 224th Mixed Brigade (TF) at North Walsham (attached 64th Division), 225th Mixed Brigade (TF) at St Olaves (attached 68th Division), 226th Mixed Brigade (TF) at Clacton (attached 67th Division), and 227th Mixed Brigade (TF) at Saxmundham (attached 67th Division). In Kent, there was a cyclist Division (aka 'The Kent Independent Force'), with three cyclist brigades in and about Canterbury (5th, 11th and 12th Yeomanry); while two attached mixed brigades were centred on Sandwich (221st Mixed Brigade, TF) and Margate (222nd Mixed Brigade, TF). In Northern Command could be found, finally, the 69th (East Anglian) Division (TF) with headquarters at Retford.[8] The tally? One formed corps with three TF divisions and with the makings of two other divisions attached in the independent brigades; rather more than a division in Kent (a cyclist division with two mixed brigades attached – something like a division and two-thirds); a full Territorial Army division in Northern Command; and this, finally, with unallocated Territorial Army battalions scattered throughout the other commands – eight cyclist battalions, for instance, garrisoned throughout Northern Command. Given that Ireland had been hived off into a separate establishment under the direct control of the War Office, it seems impossible that there had been much of a reduction. The difference between eight divisions (including Ireland), and five divisions with eight brigades attached (excluding Ireland) is negligible.

Furthermore, since the formations responsible for home defence were second-line TF, the men retained should have been suitable for service in France. Other formations of this kind had been fighting in France since 1915.[9] It is important to remember, in this regard, that 'second-line' did not imply a reduced state of readiness, but rather that these units were raised after the declaration of war in excess of prewar territorial establishments and under new terms of service which included the obligation to serve overseas. Those men who were truly under- or over-age, disabled for some reason, who were essential to the operation of civil society, or who were army reservists retained or brought back as indispensable, served with the VF rather than with the TF.[10] These were 'second-line' units as the term was understood on the Continent. Therefore, while within TF units there appears to have been some thinning out of higher grade men on an individual basis,[11] those units retained at home could have been sent on overseas service, had that been required.

So why were these men held back? Officially, the eventuality for which they were preparing was a German invasion. Even the home

FIGURE 7:
MANOEUVRE TROOPS, HOME COUNTIES, 1918

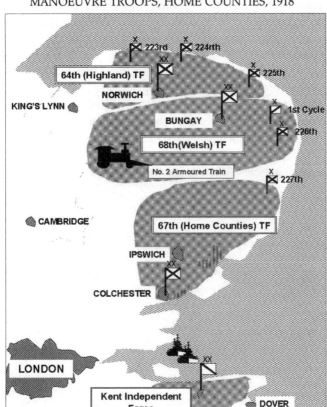

defence plans as revised in April 1918 continued, in theory, to be predicated upon a potential German 'bolt from the blue', while the actual deployment of the home defence forces, it seems obvious, continued to be directed at this threat. Why look deeper when so much seems obvious? Consider, for a start, the degree of the identified threat which seemed to require the retention of so many men.

The whole coast north of Cromarty, the west coast (including Ireland) and the south coast from Land's End to Selsey Bill, it was thought, might be the target of a German raid by a force of 500–600 men landed suddenly from fast merchantmen supported by two cruisers. The east coast north from the Wash to Cromarty, on the other hand, was more exposed. Here, it was considered, the Germans might attempt a raid in divisional strength, with light artillery and howitzer support. Finally, the east coast south from the Wash to Dover might be the site of a possible landing of a German force of, perhaps, 30,000 men with some light transport and artillery. Only the south coast from Dover to Selsey Bill was considered absolutely secure. Here, any attempt to get ashore would be 'extremely hazardous'. So much for potential threats. The most probable direct threat, it was considered – in the unlikely event that the Germans were to attempt a landing – would be a sudden strike at London following a landing somewhere east of Selsey Bill.[12] In practice, therefore, if the Germans *did* choose to attack, they would probably seek to land something like a light corps, somewhere between the Wash and Dover in an attempt to capture London quickly. Even the maximum figure of 30,000 potential German raiders was a considerable

FIGURE 8: THE THREAT, APRIL 1918

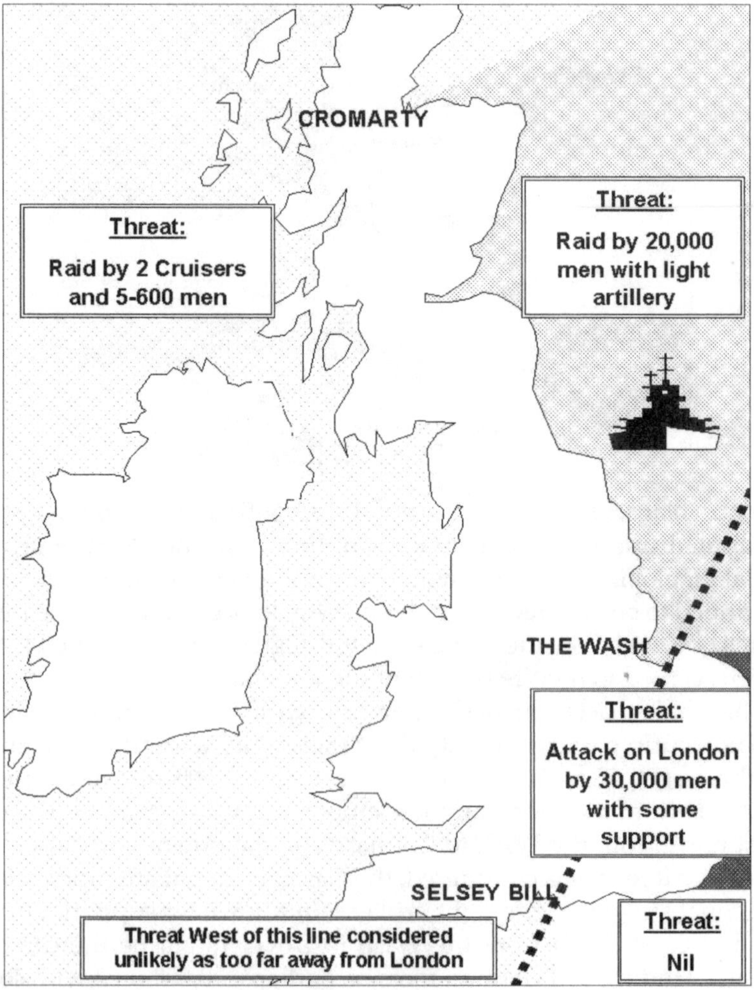

CROMARTY

Threat:
Raid by 2 Cruisers and 5-600 men

Threat:
Raid by 20,000 men with light artillery

THE WASH

Threat:
Attack on London by 30,000 men with some support

SELSEY BILL

Threat West of this line considered unlikely as too far away from London

Threat:
Nil

increase from prewar thinking. In 1908, at the time of the original 'bolt from the blue' agitation, 12,000 men was considered to be the largest invasion force the Germans could put ashore.[13] In what follows, the larger figure will be taken to be the maximum threat, even though it was probably the product of wartime inflation.

How likely was it that the expectation of such a threat necessitated the retention of the fighting elements of nearly eight divisions? Not very likely at all. Consider first the disparity of the forces involved. Consider, as well, that the approaches to London from the south and east had been fortified in 1914.[14] These defences, moreover, were being constantly improved, after October 1915, by work parties from the VF.[15] A small, poorly supported German corps landed to seize London, and cut off from all supply when the Royal Navy interrupted landing operations 32–36 hours after hostile troop transports or troops were sighted was not only unlikely to accomplish its objective; it was highly doubtful that it could even maintain itself in being for any significant period. Even the maximum German invasion attempt, therefore, would be a forlorn hope rather than a useful combination of war.

It could be asserted that the British had not been rational about the defence of the British Isles for some time past. Sensible dispositions, therefore, should not be expected. Such a position would be rather hard to maintain. While there had always been popular fears of invasion from the continent – best exemplified by the success of thrillers such as *The Riddle of the Sands* (1903) and *The Battle of Dorking* (1871) and plays like 'An Englishman's Home' – it must be stressed that these were *popular* rather than *official* fears. In the prewar period the most probable direct threat from Germany was always considered to be that of commerce raiding. The answer to that, as Churchill insisted on more than one occasion while first Lord of the Admiralty, was more ships rather than more men or heightened 'bricks and mortar' preparation within the United Kingdom. On the other hand, it was also recognized, that significant interruption of British trade, since Britain was import-dependent, might produce popular unrest. This was the real German threat as seen by British policy-makers (as distinct from British scaremongers) even before a shot was fired. Julian Corbett described the findings of a 'War Council' called before the war in this way:

> The Staff studies of recent years had all pointed to the probability that our most formidable danger in going to war was an internal danger. Since the Navy could not guarantee the flow of food and raw materials to this country during the first weeks of the war, it was apprehended that our preparations might be paralysed by popular disturbances

aroused by the menace of starvation and widespread cessation of employment. Labour, in fact, might be forced by hunger into an attitude of dangerous antagonism and it was from representatives of labour that the opposition came.[16]

Before the war Britain was planning, if necessary, on producing exactly this type of situation in Germany by blockade. Their plans against Germany, as Avery Offer correctly notes, were the mirror-image of their knowledge of British vulnerability, while their domestic fears were a product of their planning against Germany. In the early months of the war, fears that trade dislocation produced by war would lead to civil unrest underlay HO planning to arm the police against rioters. The army, meanwhile, composed a plan for the 'Suppression of Civil Disturbance in London'.[17] The policy-makers, it needs hardly be added, were pleasantly surprised to discover that the war against Germany was genuinely popular. Contrary to prewar expectations, actual military planning against a domestic enemy was not necessary in the war's early years.

This was not the only threat which, it was thought, could safely be relegated to the back burner. The possibility of a direct German attack was also effectively excluded. Shortly before the war, it was considered that the maintenance of two divisions in the UK would protect it against all possible foreign invasion.[18] Going further, in 1914, a German 'bolt from the blue' was considered so unlikely that the United Kingdom was denuded of regular troops, while every influence was brought to bear on members of the TF to inspire them to enlist for overseas service.[19] The VF was actively discouraged as apt to keep useful men from France.[20] By December 1915, so unlikely did any German strike at Scotland appear that lord lieutenants were instructed by the WO to suspend their planning for the destruction of property in the event of a German invasion.[21] By 1916, in the aftermath of Jutland, any sort of German invasion at all was viewed as a very remote contingency indeed.[22] In the latter part of the war, as CIGS, Commander Eastern Command and Commander Home Forces, Robertson made it clear that he was virtually certain that the Germans would not invade.[23] In 1918, one of the primary premises upon which Wilson, by this time military advisor to the Supreme War Council and about to become CIGS in succession to Robertson, was basing his planning for the coming year was that

> the United Kingdom was safe from all serious invasion and that the necessary measures, both naval, military and air for its defence against the contingency of an attack involve no interference with the operations of the British forces overseas.[24]

FIGURE 9: EMERGENCY SCHEME K, AUGUST 1916

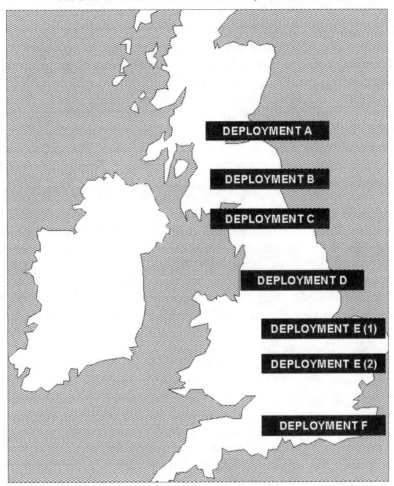

No dispositions against Germany were required, because no German attack was possible. This was British policy for most of the war.

Home defence troops were retained in Britain, therefore, without a realistic foreign threat – and this while the BEF was dying of anaemia. What is to be understood from the foregoing, of course, is that the perceptions which had produced prewar home defence planning aimed at the suppression of possible domestic unrest returned with a vengeance in the last years of the war. Home defence planning against Germany meant, in 1918 as in 1914, preparation to suppress the civil dissent which would be produced or accentuated by the most effective kind of blow (commerce interruption) Germany could land. Let us consider the content of home defence contingency planning to see if there is any evidence that it was being driven, at this juncture, by considerations of internal security.

Until 1918 it is likely that home defence planning was directed against a German invasion threat, however unlikely that contingency was judged to be. Emergency Scheme K, which dates from August 1916 and which survived amid a host of later plans, is quite plainly directed against a threat from Germany. It was a plan to repel a hostile force landing anywhere on the east coast of Britain as close to the site of the initial landing as possible. The east coast, therefore, was divided into potential theatres of operations: A, the Firth of Forth; B, Tyneside–Teeside; C, north of the river Humber; D, south of the river Humber; E(1), East Anglia north; E(2) East Anglia south; and F, south of the river Thames. If a German landing took place in the region of Scottish or Northern Commands, these would be reinforced from other areas. Troops available for redeployment elsewhere were identified as one or more of the divisions of XXIII Corps, the cyclist division from Canterbury, or one or more of its attached mixed brigades.[25] While the army moved to the coast, the civilian population would retire into the interior, destroying all stock, mills and food as they went.[26] Volunteers, meanwhile, would begin operations in the abandoned regions with the aim of denying sustenance to the enemy.[27]

Until April 1918, Emergency Scheme K appears to have been the only home defence plan in existence. Considering the nature and scale of the threat identified, it was more than adequate, and if a possible German landing continued to be the only case driving planning, it probably would have continued to stand alone. Now, setting aside for a moment the possibility that later plans may have derived from the arrival as Commander Home Forces of Robertson – a highly energetic, talented, and underemployed staff officer – it seems probable, from internal evidence, that a different threat was driving some of the plans which began to appear from the spring of 1918.

Some of this later planning we can exclude from consideration as obviously intended to dovetail with Emergency Scheme K, or for that matter, with any other defence scheme. Emergency Scheme E, for instance, dealt with the potential reinforcement of XXIII Corps by 69th Division, drawn south from Northern Command.[28] Emergency Scheme H called for the potential reinforcement of XXIII Corps by, in addition, two special service cavalry brigades and two special batteries Royal Horse Artillery from Aldershot Command and Salisbury plain.[29] Emergency Scheme M considered the possible despatch of all mobile forces to reinforce troops fighting on the beaches. This was not an unreasonable provision, considering that it was the British intention to stop the Germans as close to their landing places as possible.[30] Emergency Scheme O dealt with alternative deployments for 67th Division from XXIII Corps area.[31] Emergency Scheme Q allowed for the provision of mechanized transport and for the supply of troops operating in XXIII Corps area.[32] Finally, Emergency Scheme T provided for the use of tanks in XXIII Corps area.[33] At least two of the plans produced in this period, however, catch the eye as not quite in keeping with the declared intention of providing for the contingencies of either a minor German landing aimed at London or at raiding elsewhere in the United Kingdom.

One of these, Emergency Scheme Z, had nothing to do with any German threat. It called for the despatch of forces to Ireland: the whole of 69th Division, with a portion of the forces called for under Schemes O and H – a maximum deployment to Ireland, therefore, of something like two infantry divisions (69th and elements of the 67th) with two special service cavalry brigades and two RHA batteries.[34] Since the only German threat to Ireland identified in the master document describing home defence planning was a possible raid by 500 or 600 men, supported by two cruisers, this could not possibly be the contingency predicating such a large deployment – especially given that a German force of rather less than battalion strength would be outnumbered at least 32 times by the forces already garrisoned in Ireland! It seems obvious, therefore, that Emergency Scheme Z was aimed at providing the force required should there be a recurrence of troubles in Ireland – once again, by this time, a separate command – perhaps supported by a German raiding party, as in 1798.

Now, lest it be thought that the Irish situation was itself the rationale behind the retention of troops in the British Isles, consider that Ireland had been separated from the rest of the United Kingdom for command purposes; hence the requirement for this kind of contingency planning – planning for the transfer of troops between commands. If Ireland was the reason the troops were not in France, then we would expect to find them in Ireland, not in Britain. Nor, if this were the case, would Ireland have required separate planning and handling and, therefore, a discrete command establishment. Consider, as well, that all through 1918 Lord French constantly badgered the WO for more troops without much success. He was, therefore, reduced to warning that the troops he had at his disposal would only be sufficient to maintain order, should troubles re-emerge, 'if they are used without any kind of doubt, hesitation, or interference'. He followed this by advising his subordinate commanders that they must 'act [in the event of trouble] with the utmost promptitude when the occasion arises and show firm determination to put down all opposition at all costs'.[35] If French was reduced to ordering a policy of instant repression due simply to the lack of force immediately available to him, and if the only promise of reinforcement he ever received was the potential deployment of troops held to meet, first, another (and therefore more important) contingency, the situation in Ireland could not have been the reason for the maintenance of such a powerful garrison in the British Isles. It is revealing, however, that a contingency plan so nakedly directed towards a threat to the civil peace in Ireland was included among planning *all* of which was officially predicated upon a German threat.[36]

Let us turn, finally, to Emergency Scheme L, which can only be described as a plan to meet something like a doomsday scenario. Scheme L, basically, was a plan for the formation of composite infantry and artillery brigades, and other units, from forces held in the United Kingdom but not dedicated to home defence. This would be followed by a *levée en masse* of volunteers,[37] and the effective cessation of civilian authority in the British Isles.

Under Scheme L, four infantry brigades were to be formed from troops in Aldershot Command. Southern Command would produce three infantry brigades, four companies of Royal Engineers (RE) with other support troops; Western Command, four infantry brigades, one pioneer company with additional support units and sub-units; Southern Command, two infantry brigades, one company RE, five machine-gun groups, with other echelon troops; and Eastern Command would field two infantry brigades, two companies RE, four machine-gun companies, and half a cyclist company. Meanwhile, Canadian troops based in the United Kingdom would kick in with a brigade for the garrison of Dover, and the entirety of 5th Division CEF held in the United Kingdom for the reinforcement of the Canada Corps, and quartered in Bramshott Camp on Salisbury plain.[38] Other forces – two cyclist brigades, eight non-allocated cyclist battalions, two field batteries Royal Artillery (RA), and six field companies RE would be consolidated from detached sub-units – while the siege artillery schools would form one Battery of 6-inch, and one of 9.2-inch howitzers for the defence of London. All of these were in addition to mobile units formed under Schemes H, M, Q and T. Assistance, moreover, would come from No. 6 Brigade, Royal Air Force.[39] The total? Nineteen infantry brigades (15 British, four Canadian) with a host of support and service formations, units and sub-units.

These would, upon formation, be deployed into three concentration areas identified in the plan, in six brigade packets – the left-over brigade

FIGURE 10: SCHEME L

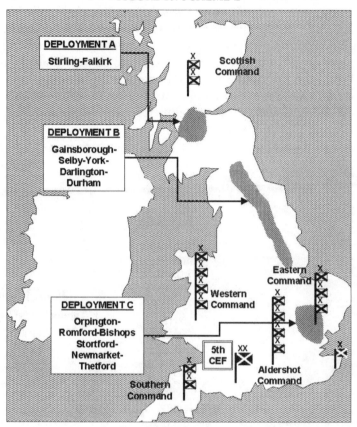

being the Canadian garrison of Dover. One such force would concentrate under Scottish Command, in the area Stirling/Falkirk. Another would go to Northern Command, in the region Gainsborough/Selby/York/Darlington/Durham. The third would find itself under Eastern Command, in the areas Orpington/Romford/Bishop's Stortford/Newmarket/Thetford, troops deployed to Orpington and Romford being administered by London, rather than Eastern Command itself. In short, the fighting elements of yet *another* six divisions (with attachments) were to be mobilized, in addition to the forces already deployed for home defence. Once again, officially, all of this sound and noise was intended to counter the threat from a maximum German landing force of two anaemic divisions, with little support, and (best case) cut off from supplies within a day-and-a-half of having landed.

These were, however, not the only provisions of Scheme L and what appears to be associated planning. Under Scheme L, upon mobilization, all leave would be halted. All troops would be recalled from detached service. Home forces, and district headquarters would be mobilized. Motor-bus columns would be organized in the City of London. Volunteers would be called up, and were expected to produce 42 mobile and 11 semi-mobile battalions in London alone. Meanwhile, Robertson and his staff would move to a mobile headquarters – a train held by the Great Eastern Railway specifically for this purpose. The civil

FIGURE 11: AREAS OF CHRONIC UNREST, 1916–18

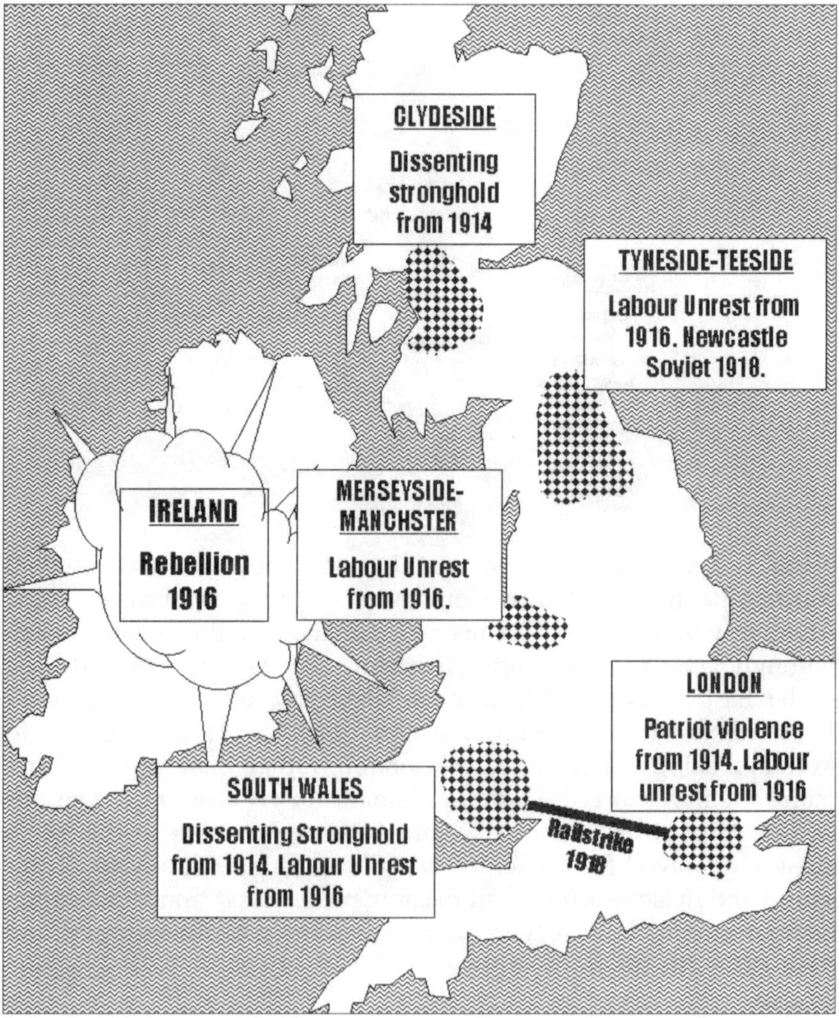

CLYDESIDE
Dissenting stronghold from 1914

TYNESIDE-TEESIDE
Labour Unrest from 1916. Newcastle Soviet 1918.

IRELAND
Rebellion 1916

MERSEYSIDE-MANCHSTER
Labour Unrest from 1916.

LONDON
Patriot violence from 1914. Labour unrest from 1916

SOUTH WALES
Dissenting Stronghold from 1914. Labour Unrest from 1916

Railstrike 1918

population, finally, was to be strictly controlled. Increased military vigilance was to be instituted. Under associated planning, the communications net would come under military control.[40] The right of trial by jury was to be suspended by annulling Section 1 of DORA. Dangerous people were to be arrested by the civilian police and interned by the army with neither warrant nor trial. Lists, we read, were to be prepared in advance by the HO, advised by military authorities.[41]

Let us anticipate what might be the focus of the argument in what remains. Scheme L, it appears probable, like Scheme Z, was not directed against any possible German threat. What seems most likely is that Scheme L was intended to anticipate the emergence of revolutionary dissent within the United Kingdom, perhaps, as in the case of Ireland, accompanied by German intervention. Before we turn to the consideration of why this seems probable, it would be best, first, to attempt to determine briefly if the army perceived this possibility and if it considered such a scenario likely.

In wartime propaganda and in postwar memories (at least in countries in which revolution does not actually develop) all home fronts are solid, and all sections of the population are equally resolute. Indeed, even in consideration of countries brought down, finally, by internal dissent, historians often ascribe a false solidity to the home front up to the moment when revolution, seemingly without any sign of approaching trouble, appears. The truth is that total war accentuates all national cleavages and no home front is entirely solid. The truth is, as well, that the attempt to assess the strength and effectiveness of wartime dissent, prior to revolution, is always difficult, since wartime censorship ensures that the surviving paper trail will always understate dissent's scale and scope. In Britain, by 1918 there were numerous signs that the complex dissent we have noted was reaching the stage where it was already inhibiting Britain's performance in the war, and might well have taken a violent turn had the war continued longer than, in fact, it did. Remember again that the probable end of the war was typically projected, in wartime Britain, into 1919 or 1920, if not 1921. Signs of this dissent, the way in which it was interpreted, and the growing insufficiency of the restricted means employed to deal with it, we have seen. It is not surprising that something more thoroughgoing was prepared.

Did the army have grounds for believing that things would get worse? It is undoubtedly significant that the April Home Defence revision was taking place just as Lloyd George was taking the final steps toward assuming total control of labour.[42] This planning was happening, as well, just as the German submarine offensive was making the greatest headway – sinkings during 1917 continuing at frightening,

perhaps war-losing levels. In response, rationing was being implemented, and proving provocative rather than an adequate solution.
Meanwhile, dissent of all kinds burgeoned in scale and scope. The
link with prewar perceptions is obvious. Successful blockade would
produce famine, would give rise to dissent, and perhaps revolution. By
1918, if more concrete evidence were required, there was more than
enough evidence of war weariness, defeatism and social cleavage. By
1918 Britain appeared to be faced with a type of amalgamated dissent
it could no longer restrain with the tools it had employed until this time.
Britain was sliding down a slope which might begin with social unrest
but which passed through defeat to national collapse and revolution.
The home front came to be regarded in a new, much more sceptical
light. It is surely significant that the answer of the government to one
of the most worrying strikes of 1918 – the rail strike in September – was
to threaten to use troops to militarize the railways while calling up the
workers, hitherto exempt, for military service.[43] Intimidation, even
coercion, of a recalcitrant working class might be necessary.

By 1918 the HO and police feared the way things at home were
tending. The Cabinet was at a loss.[44] Britain's ally, the French Prime
Minister Georges Clemenceau (in a prior political incarnation a very
heavy-handed prewar Minister of the Interior), never disguised the fact
that he was very worried about his own home front. In March 1918, four
cavalry divisions were deployed to the French interior and held there
for the remainder of the war to break strikes and suppress anti-war
agitation.[45] It would be odd if Britain's generals were not coming to the
same pessimistic conclusions as their political masters, or beginning to
think that the French example might not have to be followed. This much
is certain: the soldiers were enthusiastic partisans of intervention in
Russia from the beginning, largely because they feared the Bolshevik
example.[46] The evidence suggests that in their appreciation of what was
likely to happen at home, Britain's generals were no more optimistic
than Britain's politicians, and that they were indeed anticipating the
requirement for a Clemenceau solution to British dissent.

Consider, for instance, Robertson's summary of the domestic situation to Haig in September 1917. Remember that Robertson was CIGS
until February 1918, Commander Eastern Command until June, and
Commander Home Forces thereafter. He was, therefore, principally
responsible for the home defence planning of the spring–summer 1918.
'[T]here is no getting away from the fact', he told Haig,

> that there is a state of great unrest in the country now as a result partly
> of the Russian revolution. There have been some bad strikes recently

and there is still much discontent. An announcement even appeared in some newspapers yesterday with regard to the calling together of a committee of workmen and soldier delegates to consider the political solution. This shows the way the wind is apt to blow.[47]

According to Sir Henry Wilson (CIGS following Robertson) Robertson was 'constantly' writing and speaking in 'that strain'.[48] Wilson, if his correspondence and diaries, published and unpublished, are anything to go by, was inclined to agree. Rawlinson (British Representative to the Supreme War Council until April 1918, and a postwar CIGS designate) of all British generals was perhaps most unrestrained. 'A grave and critical situation has arisen in England', he wrote to Lord Derby in October 1918.

[T]he Masses, strained and war-weary, are becoming articulate. The people wish to take charge of the country and of the War. The Government and Parliament have lost control … Now the Bolsheviks may be visionaries and idealists, but they simply aim at social revolution and upheaval in the world. … There is a real danger of Bolshevist propaganda being spread throughout this country … The so-called popular movement in Germany and Austria will certainly aggravate the situation here and in France and act as a decoy to our working classes. Unfortunately the German and Austria Governments have better means and more power of controlling these strikes and plots. Here, any repressive measures would probably set a spark to all this inflammable material.[49]

Whom did Rawlinson identify as probable British 'Bolsheviks', as the substance of this 'inflammable material'? The ILP certainly, the UDC, the shop stewards' movement ('a purely revolutionary organization'), Sinn Féin and Sylvia Pankhurst's suffragettes all had him worried. Even the common soldiers at the front were sensing something in the air. Captain J. C. Dunn – the medical officer of an infantry battalion in France – for instance, on at least three occasions between August 1917 and the end of the war, noted that cracks in the British home front were apt to lose the war for the allies.[50]

It is certain, therefore, that Britain's leadership, both military and civil, was worried about the domestic situation. The equation 'dissenter = pro-German' had developed by 1915, and 'dissenter = revolutionary' in the aftermath of the Russian revolution. By 1918, many British leaders had come to view revolution as a distinct possibility, rather along the lines of the Bolshevik example. As in Russia, the war would be lost incidentally. This could not, of course, be allowed to happen. The retention of sufficient force at home was surely the first step. Planning for the employment of military forces domestically and for the partial militarization of civil procedure followed. Once revolution was apprehended, planning would become operations. The HO would cease to be the leading agency in the fight against dissent: the WO would take over. Is seems likely that this scenario, rather than a potential German invasion, lay behind Emergency Scheme L.

Then why the German blind? Perhaps it was not entirely a blind. Remember that the examples which must have sprung most readily to official minds, in 1918, were Ireland in 1916 and Russia in 1917. In Ireland, Sir Roger Casement had been landed by German submarine, and the Irish Volunteers were assisted by the Germans at the time of the Easter Rebellion. By 1918 it was firmly established in official minds that Germany had supported and continued to support Irish national-ism.[51] Echoes of fears about Ireland can be readily found in documents relative to the state of affairs on the British home front. For instance, having been apprised that the Clyde detainees were to be released, Basil Thomson recorded his worries that 'this is just the sort of atmosphere that brought about the rebellion in Ireland'.[52] In Russia, similarly, Lenin had been returned, and the Bolshevik movement succoured by Ludendorff. Official documents of the period demonstrate the con-viction that Lenin was not only a dangerous man in himself, but also a German agent. The Cabinet, Thomson considered, in the aftermath of the October revolution, was simply 'aflutter' with worries about the dissenters. They believed, given the example of what had happened in Russia, that these must be supported by Germany and have a revo-lutionary agenda. They looked to Thomson to find the evidence.[53] A far more likely threat from Germany than outright invasion, therefore, seemed to be that it might attempt to capitalize upon unrest – itself, in part, a product of submarine warfare – in an attempt to push Britain over the brink into domestic conflict.

Even so, we can hardly expect that Britain's military leaders would admit, in 1918, that troops were being retained in the United Kingdom to meet the eventuality of civil conflict, nor that they would much boast about it after the war. For one thing, there was the correct per-ception that repressive measures, even open preparation for repressive measures, might 'set a spark to all of this inflammable material'. Preparation would, in any case, certainly give a fillip to discontent. It would also both encourage the enemy and undo *much* propaganda, both domestic and foreign, about the solidity of the home front and the degree of British resolution to see the war through to a successful conclusion. Finally, open and admitted preparations against internal dissent might well prove politically impossible. The National Government, after all, was a coalition including representation from the Labour Party. The position of Coalition Labour, already difficult, would quickly become untenable. We cannot expect that if home defence planning by 1918 was driven by domestic fears that this would leave much of a formal trace. For evidence, therefore, we must look to the content of home defence planning, and to the context in which it occurs.

Consider Emergency Scheme L. The disparity of the force which it would seek to bring against any possible German invasion is obvious from the start. The German threat had not grown greater since 1914, but smaller. Scheme L was Scheme K plus. What is less obvious from a casual reading of the surviving documentation is that the three concentration areas indicated in the plan, while they certainly lay behind possible invasion sites, ran against the general thrust of British planning to meet a German invasion in that they would be useless unless it were the British intention to meet the Germans inland. It was the British plan, however, to meet the Germans on the beaches and to commit whatever forces were available *immediately* to prevent them from gaining even a foothold. This did not change. There was never any other plan. Basil Thomson was informed by the AG, following what appears to have been a 1917 invasion scare, that as soon as it had been ascertained that a German invasion was in progress every available soldier would be sent to the east coast immediately. Only 100 men would be left behind to guard the London sewage works which, it was considered, was a more vulnerable target for sabotage than the War Office.[54] The AG's description was, quite plainly, a vulgarized explanation of Scheme K – not the far more comprehensive Scheme L.

Another thing which appears odd about the Scheme L concentration areas is that they were located near – and in one case, overlapped – regions of chronic unrest. This fact is the more significant in that, under the provisions of Emergency Scheme L, all three sites would be occupied *simultaneously*, which is odd considering that the Germans were believed to be incapable of attempting more than a single 'bolt from the blue'. The site of the German landing would be a known quantity by the time the plan could be implemented. What was the point in deploying six ad hoc brigades, for instance, to the concentration area Stirling–Falkirk in the event of a German landing in East Anglia? If, however, revolutionary conditions emerged in London or Newcastle, having six brigades outside Glasgow might prove rather handy. Moreover, the fact that the areas of concentration lay outside possible areas of domestic disturbance is itself interesting. It is of the first importance in the suppression of dissent that troops dedicated to this task *not* be given the chance to fraternize with the rebels before they can be used. They cannot, therefore, be left hanging about a disaffected region while being assembled. Also, the most effective suppression of domestic unrest occurs when reliable troops are committed in overwhelming force. Six brigades, perhaps 30,000 men, with the 53 battalions of 'volunteers' called for in Scheme L, might well have over-awed even industrial London. This would be especially so if these forces were assembled into a coherent mass north of the city. In the event, when a Bolshevik rising was actually apprehended in Glasgow in January 1919, 19 battalions with tanks were deployed to the city.[55] Nineteen battalions looks suggestively like the six brigades called for under Scheme L. It would be interesting to find out if they were deployed following contingency planning carried out under this defence scheme. Hardly surprisingly, a force this massive was sufficient to stop manifestations of unrest in the city.

An aside. Just who the volunteers called for in Scheme L were is itself an interesting question to which there can be no easy answer. In home defence planning, the only role allocated to the VF was action as guerrillas in areas of the country abandoned following an invasion.[56] Defence of vital points and deployment as special constables can be assumed. A plan which called for their formation into battalions and their concentration, very probably, into even larger forces is from the beginning more than a little odd. Also, as we have seen, Scheme L called for the mobilization of 53 battalions of volunteers from the London area alone. Returns of strength for the VF, for this period, indicate that there were only 30 battalions parading in London, with one battalion of engineers and two motor volunteer corps.[57] And, against the possibility that the extra 23 battalions represented projected growth, it should be recalled that the VF was, by this time, a declining rather than a growing force. There had been, for instance, 32 battalions in the London area a year previously.[58] More puzzling still, even in the event of invasion it was not envisioned that all volunteers would be called to the colours. Only Sections A (over-age but fit) and B (of age and fit, but badged) men would be called up. Others – the young, the infirm, and those occupied in essential services and industries – would remain at home. Some of those left behind were simply too valuable to be taken whatever the emergency; the others were the sort of very old, very young or very unfit men who, despite their patriotism, had filled *Country Life* and *Punch* with jokes of the species 'if England has to fall back on they chaps, we's done'.[59] The total pool of official volunteers available to meet an invasion was, therefore, roughly half what total VF strength figures implied.[60] Scheme L, then, called for the deployment of three to four times as many volunteers as actually existed in authorized units. One explanation is that the total included at least some men who were already enrolled in the army but retained at home in agricultural companies and dock and labour battalions.[61] There were, however, simply not enough men so employed to make up even the discrepancy for London alone. Nor was the army likely to assign any very vigorous role to the labour battalions. They were by definition composed of men who were C-3 (of scarcely any military use at all).[62] Who were these other volunteers? This is a question for which a very tentative answer will be provided shortly.

Consider, as well, the import of certain of the provisions for the militarization of civil society detailed both in Scheme L and in associated planning. If it would be a rather good idea to militarize the communications network in the event of a German landing, this would also, equally obviously, be essential in the event of a revolutionary situation. Just who would be leaking information to the Germans is problematic, given that suspected spies had been apprehended and enemy nationals interned in 1914. Preventing communication between a region in which dissent had taken a dangerous turn and other regions in which imitation was possible would be *essential*; especially when we remember that the most probable form that an attempted revolution would take in Britain, at least initially, would be a national, general strike.[63]

Perhaps most revealing, however, are the provisions for the militarization of the system of justice: for the suspension of civil legal procedures, and for the pre-emptive military detention of suspected troublemakers. Scheme L called for lists of potential subversives to be drawn up by civil authorities in correspondence with their military counterparts. The content of such lists – if surviving HO documentation is to be trusted – consisted entirely of the leadership of the anti-war movement and known industrial agitators.[64] These were hardly the people one might expect to be co-operating with the Germans, unless, of course, Germany intervened while a social revolution or general strike was already incipient or in progress. In any case, we have seen how the HO and police were in the game of drawing up blacklists from December 1916. We have seen, as well, how such a list very probably lay behind the pre-emptive arrest of engineering strike leaders in the spring of 1917.[65] It is unlikely that there were any other lists. What the Scheme L lists represented, probably, was the revision of police lists in such a way as to reflect military requirements more fully.

Let us note, finally, that throughout 1918 the WO was obviously 'up to something' and 'something', moreover, in co-operation with the HO.

In July 1918 – and the importance of this will be immediately obvious to anybody with experience in 'aid to the civil authority' or 'aid to the civil power' operations – the boundaries of military districts were redrawn to correspond to those of police districts. These were the same district headquarters which were to assume their command functions in the event of the 'emergency' foreseen in Scheme L. Each of the major industrial areas, more importantly, became a single military district, coterminous with a single local police authority. In each military district so created, a military commander corresponded routinely with the police chief. In each, as well, an assistant CMA was appointed whose sole purpose was co-operation with the police and associated agencies.[66] Shortly thereafter, local police authorities were instructed that they need not appeal to London for military support. They were to deal directly with local military officials.[67] Together local police chiefs and assistant CMAs were to co-ordinate plans for the provision of assistance under the DRRs, provide for the control of 'dangerous persons' in the event of an emergency, 'liaise with local "emergency committees" and other relevant agencies, establish an effective command structure in the event that an emergency occurred, and investigate 'suspicious persons or occurrences'.[68]

There was significant and revealing precedent for this type of civil–military collaboration. The emergency arrangements of 1918 were, in large measure, the formalization and general application of ad hoc local arrangements made during periods of prewar unrest. During the unrest in south Wales, in 1911, 'strike areas' were identified. In each, a joint WO-HO committee was formed for the duration and a 'strike area commander' identified.[69] The local police intelligence-gathering network began to provide information to this committee, while informal liaison commenced with local magistrates, who remained, throughout, the leading agents.[70] Had the situation not been contained, the magistrates would have stepped back, and the strike area commanders would have restored order by exceptional measures. The army, in short, would have become the lead agency and applied greater force. Meanwhile, two Welsh-speaking CID constables were posted to each area for special operations, with one HO representative at the headquarters of General Macready (GOC) to facilitate direct communications with the Home Secretary.[71] The similarity of arrangement would suggest similarity of contingency – fears that industrial unrest would grow to threaten the national interest and perhaps take a political direction. The universality of the 1918 arrangements, however, suggests that more than simply local disruption was apprehended.

Neither 'local emergency committees', nor 'dangerous' and

'suspicious persons' are defined in the existing, open documentation. Local emergency committees had been formed in 1914 by the lord lieutenants to deal with the German threat of the day.[72] Such committees would be of some consequence in the event of civil unrest, since lord lieutenants and local magistrates retained, even after local government reform in 1889, considerable residual powers.[73] The local county establishment, moreover, normally provided the leadership of the TF and VF: useful collaborators to say the least. By 1918 there was probably considerable identity of membership not only between the 1914 emergency committees and volunteer leadership, but the local chapter of the NWAC as well.

Why is this inference justified? Consider, for instance, the extent to which local government continued to be dominated by local notables. In the county council for Bedfordshire, for instance, the elected chairman was the Duke of Bedford. He was also the Lord Lieutenant, seconded as aldermen by his kinsman Lord Ampthill and his agent Robert Prothero.[74] All were volunteers. All had been members of the NSL. All were prewar die-hards – precisely that element in the British society most likely to support, by the use of violence if necessary, the national war effort and the maintenance of the existing constitution. Bedfordshire was not unique. In 1911, one-fifth of all members of English county councils were listed in *Walford's County Families*. They were drawn from families which tended, disproportionately, to die-hard Unionism and social conservatism, and which served disproportionately in the army, reserve, local militia, territorial, Yeomanry and volunteer movements.[75]

The gentry was not the only level of society at which we witness a gradual coalescence of function and politics, anticipating white reaction.[76] Birmingham's John Beard, whom we have already seen at work splitting the local TUC – a Workers' Union leader, volunteer and BWNL activist – was not unique in wartime Britain. He was a member of a group never properly delineated: working-class leaders become prominent local patriots and volunteers. Another such was the Londoner Will Thorne, whose passage was, in may ways, still more remarkable. In 1914 a Worker's Union organizer and champion of militant action, Thorne had become, by 1916, MP for West Ham, a lieutenant-colonel in the VF and, like Beard, a collaborator with both the NWAC and the BWNL. Attacked by Snowden for his 'unlettered ignorance and unfitness of parliament', Thorne was a highly popular figure in his multifarious patriotic capacities.[77]

Consider, as well, some of the facts we have already examined. It was asserted at the time that NWAC demonstrations were strongly attended by conscripts and volunteers, with drills-excused men participating.[78] It is certain, moreover, that the HO had already allowed, in November 1917, for local liaison between police authorities and local chapters of the NWAC.[79] It is certain, as well, that through the NWAC the government was organizationally linked with the very combative BWNL, veterans' organizations, and so on. Co-ordination between the local NWAC committees and both police *and* military authorities for co-operation in the event of rebellion was only the logical next step; the next after that was operation as a civilian emergency committee. It is highly suggestive, finally, that those who were probably the members of one 1914 emergency committee – that for Cardiff and Monmouth-shire – led by the Lord Lieutenant, seconded by the local MPs, Justices of the Peace, deputy Lord Lieutenants, and prominent VF leaders, could be seen openly supporting, indeed convening, patriot mobs to suppress pacifist demonstrations, as early as autumn 1916, during the Battle of Cory Hall. In September 1917, when local notables likely to be interested were contacted by the NWAC and began to form local com-mittees, what this amounted to, in effect, was the consolidation of all of these tendencies within an umbrella organization. The NWAC was certainly not alone in blurring the lines between what was official and what was not. The lines were already blurred. The questions then arise: when did the volunteer cease to be BWNL, or NWAC; when did the magistrates and volunteer officers serving on local emergency commit-tees and acting locally for the NWAC serve in an official and when in an unofficial capacity – when were they magistrates, when soldiers, when propagandists, and when representatives of the sovereign? The answer, of course, was that the leadership and its followers were always patriots.

If an essential identity between emergency committees, VF associ-ations, and NWAC local committees existed, and given that local liaison between all of them and with military and police authorities was not only permitted but positively enjoined, then perhaps, the question of the missing volunteers becomes easier to answer. In addition to VF personnel *per se*, 'volunteers' as defined in Scheme L might have included persons organized, not by the army directly, but by organi-zations associated with the NWAC. They would include, at a minimum, members of the BWNL[80] and the National Federation of Discharged and Demobilized Sailors and Soldiers.[81] Surely this suggests some level of organization; and certainly it suggests, as well, that the government knew of and facilitated this organization, while recognizing and approving of its purposes.

'Dangerous, suspicious persons', on the other hand, is less of a poser. Almost certainly these would be the type of anti-war, industrial agitators the CID had been monitoring since 1916. It is hardly surprising, therefore, that it was at precisely this time that Thomson's special CID office was formed and charged with gathering information about 'seditious meetings and conspiracies, threatened disturbances and revolutionary movements'.[82] Locally, chief constables were instructed to share intelligence about industrial unrest with their army opposite numbers at district headquarters. What all of this meant, of course, was generalization, centralization and partial militarization, of surveillance measures already implemented by local police authorities.

While police authorities were not always happy with these arrangements, their protests were ineffective. This was largely because the incoming MEPO Commissioner was – no surprise – the outgoing AG, Sir Nevil Macready. Macready had been brought in, at least apparently, to deal with the ongoing police strike following the resignation of his predecessor, Sir Edward Henry.[83] Rather to the point, as well, Macready was the only serving British general with experience of commanding a mixed force of police and soldiers in suppression of a civil disturbance. He had been appointed local District Commander in south Wales at the time of the prewar Tonypandy disturbances.[84] He was also the man despatched in 1914 by the Asquith government seemingly to suppress the Ulster Unionists had that become necessary.[85] He was later to become, as is well known, GOC Ireland during the height of the troubles. His appointment as Commissioner of Police, in 1918, should therefore constitute something of a red flag. Macready was himself aware of the significance of his appointment. He had been made commissioner at this juncture, he knew, for political and national reasons, because he had 'caught the public eye in the past' for civil–military operations. His appointment *was* a red flag; it was intended to be a red flag. He suspected that he had been appointed, as well, for the purpose of 'dragooning' the striking policemen into obedience. He considered that this was impossible and feared that it would look as if he was being forced out of the army for political disagreements with past home secretaries. He believed also that if a steady hand might be required at Scotland Yard, then it was equally essential at the WO at this juncture of the war.[86] Whatever his misgivings, Macready remained in office, a standing threat, almost the equivalent in himself of a reading of the riot act.

What the HO was co-ordinating with the WO, therefore, was rather obviously, in the first instance, an attempt to head off any chance that industrial unrest and anti-war dissent might become political insurrection, and if it proved necessary, their joint reaction to revolutionary conditions. It was doing so, note, at the same time that Emergency

Scheme L was being written, and at the same time, moreover, that the elements of eight divisions were being retained in Britain to meet the threat, all agreed to be unlikely, of a lightly supported and unsupplied invasion attempt, launched by a maximum of 30,000 men.

Was it surprising that troops were retained in Britain, blacklists of potential domestic opponents of the war composed, and suppression of violent social unrest both planned and co-ordinated by the police and the army? Hardly.

So where have we arrived? It is to be hoped that it will be obvious. During 1918 not only were the HO and WO co-operating in the suppression of dissent, they were also co-ordinating their response to the development of a more dangerous dissent still. At the same time, the WO was also feverishly revising its plans for home defence. While all of these were, officially, predicated upon a possible German landing, at least one of them (Emergency Scheme L) was probably intended as the army's reaction to the emergence of revolutionary conditions. It is certain that revolution was believed possible, even probable, by much of Britain's leadership – including those generals (Wilson, CIGS, Robertson, Commander Eastern Command and later Commander Home Forces, and Rawlinson, British Representative to the Supreme War Council) with principal responsibility for planning. It is certain, as well, that at least one other home defence scheme (Emergency Scheme Z) was not directed at a German threat at all, but rather intended to cater for potential trouble in Ireland. The generals, therefore, were not above officially predicating planning on one contingency while considering, in fact, rather a different case altogether. It is certain, furthermore, that there were excellent reasons for following a similar policy in regard to Emergency Scheme L. All of this might be circumstantial evidence. We can expect to find no other kind. Taken together, however, the evidence suggests rather forcibly that the reason why so many troops were being retained in the United Kingdom during 1918 had little to do with anything the Germans might do, nor was it likely to be the result of simple inertia, nor was Lloyd George responsible. The real reason had rather a lot to do with fears that cracks in the home front might well take Britain out of the war by producing a revolutionary situation – particularly if the war, as projected, lasted into succeeding years.

The last stage of the war on the home front? Planning for the militarization of the war against dissent, the abandonment of remaining inhibitions and most of civilian procedure, and, *in extremis*, for civil war. Fortunately for Britain, conditions never developed which were sufficient to justify the implementation of such planning.

NOTES

1. Much of what follows has appeared as B. Millman, 'A Note on British Home Defence Planning and Civil Dissent, 1917–1918', *War in History*, 5, 2 (1998), pp. 204–32 and appears here with permission of the publisher.
2. PRO CAB 3, 'Troops Required for Home Defence', Robertson, 15 January 1918. See also WO, *Statistics of the Military Effort of the British Empire During the Great War 1914–1920* (London: HMSO, 1922). The figures here are similar, but not identical, to those presented by D. Woodward in 'Did Lloyd George Starve the British Army of Manpower Prior to the German Offensive of 21 March 1918?', *History Journal*, Vol. XVII, no. 1 (1984), pp. 199–224. Unlike in Woodward, however, the task here is not to establish how many troops were in the UK, or even if it were Lloyd George or the generals who kept them there. It will be understood, as Woodward demonstrated, that everyone knew roughly how many soldiers were in the UK and approved of their retention.
3. The Maurice debate – the suggestion, in April 1918, that Lloyd George was keeping troops in the UK in order to keep them away from Haig – is entirely peripheral. Troops were kept in the UK before the German offensive. They were there in nearly equivalent numbers after the German offensive. They were still there at the end of the war. If there were men in the UK, the army knew it and concurred with their retention. Not even Haig appears to have had a problem with the retention of men at home. Maurice was trying to bring Lloyd George down by implicating him in a scandal from which the truth might extricate him, but only by creating a bigger scandal still. Lloyd George sidestepped the issue by revealing that Maurice had known the truth (whatever it was) all along. While this is not his argument, the best general description of the Maurice debate is by Woodward in 'Did Lloyd George Starve the British Army?'. The tragedy of the Maurice debate is that it has stolen the focus from a more important question: 'why were troops retained in the UK during 1918?'.
4. W. Robertson, *From Private to Field Marshal* (London: Constable, 1925), pp. 343–4. Robertson's predecessor, Sir John French, became commander-in-chief in Ireland.
5. Previously, trained eighteen-year-olds were kept in Britain until they had reached their nineteenth birthday and thus became eligible for overseas service.
6. *Stand to! The Journal of the Western Front Association*, no. 20 (Summer 1987), p. 20.
7. If 35 Yeomanry cyclist battalions (eight brigades) went to Ireland in 1918, along with seven first-line cyclist battalions, 30 were still retained for home defence proper.
8. PRO WO 33/904, 'Distribution of the Forces in Great Britain including Reserve and Cadet Units', 1 November 1918.
9. The TA divisions indicated were second-line territorial divisions. The cyclists were either prewar TA cyclist units, or converted second-line Yeomanry. Several second-line TA Divisions served overseas, as did Yeomanry units. The elements of the 45th Division, a second-line territorial division, saw service in India from December 1914. Later, the 57th, 58th, 59th, 60th and 61st arrived in France – all between May 1916 and February 1917. At about the same time, the 74th Territorial Yeomanry Division was formed overseas of units identical to those retained in Kent. See, in addition to *Statistics of the Military Effort of the British Empire*, A. Becke, *Order of Battle of Divisions*; D. Filsell, 'On Cycles to War', *Stand to! The Journal of the Western Front Association*, no. 16 (Spring 1986); 'Army Cyclists', *Stand to!*, no. 20 (Spring 1987); T. Cave, 'The Territorial Infantry Division', *Stand to!*, no. 8 (Summer 1983).
10. While it was generally accepted that all men who could serve should serve (PRO WO 161/105, Supplementary Instruction E to Lord Lieutenants from the HO, 30 November 1914), it was recognized that the service of some would be more valuable

at home than abroad. These, it was thought, would join the volunteers, who had no obligation to go on overseas service. Section W volunteers were all those deemed more valuable at home by reason of occupation (Army Order 203, 1916); Sections T, P and P(T) were skilled tradesmen who had contracted disabilities in the services; Section R were those required in urgent war work (WO 161/107, 'VF: Organisation and Administration' Central Association VF Memorandum); Section B men had been exempted by tribunal (WO 114/56, 'Volunteer Force. Return of Strength, 31 May 1917–31 October 1918'). Section A were over-age. Section C men were the truly under-age – one could join the TF at age 17 (WO 161/108, 'Army Council Instruction Ref: VF, 1916–1918').

11. I. Beckett, 'The Territorial Force in the Great War', in Liddle, *Home Fires and Foreign Fields*, p. 23.
12. PRO WO 33/872, 'General Summary of Home Defence Schemes'.
13. Adams and Poirier, *The Conscription Controversy*, pp. 36–7.
14. PRO HO 45 10690/228849, 'Defence of the Realm Act and Amendments, 1912–1914', files 2, 33 and 37, dated 2 August, 19 November, and 11 December 1914.
15. PRO WO 161/107, 'VF Organization and Administration', Mr Mordan (Central Association) Memorandum. From October 1915, 4,500–5,000 men a week were working on trenches outside London.
16. Quoted from A. Offer, *The First World War: An Agrarian Interpretation* (Oxford: Clarendon, 1989), p. 309.
17. Ibid., p. 311.
18. Adams and Poirier, *The Conscription Controversy*, p. 47.
19. Remember, of course, that the Territorial Army was designed not only to provide follow-up forces for the BEF, but as a successor to the militia and volunteers, to provide for home defence against direct threats.
20. This last is clearly demonstrated by J. Osborne, in 'Defining Their Own Patriotism: British Volunteer Training Corps in the First World War', *Journal of Contemporary History*, 23, no. 1 (January 1988).
21. Dalmeny Estate, Rosebery Papers, A. G. Asher (clerk, Lieutenancy of Midlothian) to Rosebery, 31 December 1915. Many thanks to Graham Thompson for this reference.
22. PRO CAB 3, 'Troops Required for Home Defence', Robertson, 15 January 1918.
23. 'The arrangements for home defence, on land, had been greatly improved under the direction of Lord French. There was, for reasons that need not be described, little probability that they would ever be put into execution …'. Robertson, *From Private to Field Marshal*, p. 347.
24. HLRO, Lloyd George Papers, F 47/7/9, Wilson to Lloyd George enclosing 'Joint Note No. 12 to the Supreme War Council', 20 January 1918. Note that at this time Wilson was not yet CIGS; his thinking had not changed, however, by March.
25. PRO WO 33/867, 'Emergency Scheme K'; WO 33/872, 'General Summary of Home Defence Emergency Schemes', Annex II.
26. HLRO, Beaverbrook Papers, BBK B/9, Secret 83-A 'Instructions to Local Authorities in the Event of Belligerent Operations in the United Kingdom' [CID], November 1914.
27. Dalmeny Estate, Rosebery Papers, Hankey to Rosebery, 15 December 1914. Many thanks to Graham Thompson for this reference.
28. WO 33/872, 'General Summary of Home Defence Emergency Schemes'; WO 33/888, 'Emergency Scheme E (Provisional)', June 1918.
29. WO 33/872, 'General Summary of Home Defence Emergency Schemes'.
30. PRO WO 33/872, 'General Summary of Home Defence Emergency Schemes'. Troops available within six hours of mobilization: six machine-gun companies, and two motor machine-gun batteries, drawn from the machine-gun training school at

Grantham; ten companies at Belton Park, with a further six at Clipstone with some transport. PRO WO 33/875, 'Emergency Scheme M', April 1918.

31. PRO WO 33/872, 'General Summary of Home Defence Emergency Schemes'.
32. Ibid.
33. Ibid.
34. Ibid.
35. PRO CAB 1/26, 'Measures to be Taken in Ireland Should Military Assistance Become Necessary', French, 19 April 1918.
36. Interestingly, the army was apparently not the only service in which deployments were inconsistent with stated rationale. There survives, for instance, a letter from the incoming First Lord of the Admiralty (Lee) to his predecessor (Balfour) in which he queries the reason for the deployment of four 'King Edward' class pre-Dreadnoughts in the Thames estuary. Since these battleships served no apparent naval function, were they, Lee asked, deployed there to serve a political purpose? What that purpose might have been is not addressed. PRO FO 800, Admiralty to Balfour, 8 April 1918.
37. The Volunteers were the First World War equivalent of the Home Guard. Initially simply collections of patriotic enthusiasts, too old to enlist in the army, by 1916 the Volunteers were being organized by the army, by 1917 receiving weapons and some support staff, and by 1918 they were being mobilized in company strength for coastal and static defence. 'The Home Front: 13, The Volunteers – WWI Home Guard', *Stand to! The Journal of the Western Front Association*, no. 21 (Winter 1987). By November 1918, 248,444 volunteers had been enrolled. WO, *Statistics of the Military Effort of the British Empire During the Great War 1914–1920*. See also Osborne, 'Defining Their Own Patriotism'. See, finally, PRO WO 114 and 161 for information regarding the volunteers. Another useful source for general information is the House of Lords debates, where Lords Desborough, Derby and French, in particular, are often recorded speaking on the subject of the volunteers.
38. If, as will be argued, the contingency upon which Scheme L was based was the suppression of internal dissent rather than a German landing, then the Canadians would surely have proved useful troops. For one thing, they were, of course, not British. Perhaps another thing which did not escape the notice of the AG's Department was that they had been sworn in, in Canada, for active service starting in the United Kingdom. This would have made it much easier for them to be used in a suppressive role, escaping possible prosecution by civilian magistrates, than British troops.
39. PRO WO 33/877, 'Emergency Scheme L', May 1918; WO 33/872, 'General Summary of Home Defence Emergency Schemes'.
40. PRO WO 33/880, 'Home Defence Emergency Arrangements', May 1918. Under this, a scheme for 'the suspension of telegraphic and telephonic communications in certain districts of Great Britain and for the taking over of communications in certain zones by the Army Signal Service in the event of invasion', the army was to inform civilian authorities of just where an emergency existed, and it would then take control of all local communications. As a general rule, in such an area, no communications within a town or a 'suspended district' were authorized. No local calls would be permitted except to the fire department or ambulance. The declared intention of all of this, of course, was to prevent leakage of information to the enemy and to clear lines for military use. This plan also exists in SRO HH 31/20 (thanks to Graham Thompson for this reference).
41. PRO WO 33/872, 'General Summary of Home Defence Emergency Schemes'.
42. See French, *The Strategy of the Lloyd George Coalition*, Chs 3 and 8 for instance.
43. See, for the relevant HO documentation, PRO HO 45 10884/346578, Railway Strike

1917–1918, especially files 6, 9, 11, 17. The troops involved were drawn from Aldershot Command and the garrison of London. It would be interesting to know if they were mobilized under the provisions of Emergency Scheme L.

44. See, for example, PRO CAB 23/5, WC 364, 12 March 1918, for the minutes of a War Cabinet meeting at which 'the revolutionary attitude on the Clyde' is discussed. See also Cabinet reaction to the rail-shipwright strike of September 1918 in PRO CAB 23/7, WC 477, 25 September, and WC 478, 26 September 1918.

45. Williams, *The Home Fronts*, p. 269. When workers in Saint-Etienne attempted to strike in March 1918 the strike was broken by cavalry and *gendarmes* – the older workers were retained with raised pay, and the younger workers sent to the front.

46. B. Millman, 'The Problem with Generals: Military Observers and the Origins of the Intervention in Russia and Persia', *Journal of Contemporary History*, 33, 2 (1998), p. 291.

47. KCL, Robertson Papers, 1/23, Robertson to Haig, 15 September 1917. The announcement was probably Bertrand Russell's attempt to start a soviet in London. As we have seen, it failed, following one of the most violent patriot attacks for which evidence remains.

48. IWM, Wilson Papers, 1/26, Wilson Diary, entry for 27 May 1917.

49. NAM, Rawlinson Papers, 5201/33/74, Rawlinson to Derby, 24 October 1918, 'Memorandum on Situation in England' (attached). See also, for army thinking on the domestic social/political question, K. Jeffery, *The British Army and the Crisis of Empire 1918–1922* (Manchester: Manchester University Press, 1984), as well as works dealing with Robertson, Wilson and Rawlinson.

50. J. C. Dunn, *The War the Infantry Knew* (London: Cardinal, 1989 [1938]).

    Entry for 6 August 1917: '… There is great unrest, and an intense feeling and determination that make certain the coming of great political and social disturbances after the War, the early phase may precede the end of the war'.

    Entry for 25 January 1918: '… Officers and men rejoining off leave say that "fighting is over", according to common talk on the home front. It looks like a toss-up if the Anglo-French home front doesn't crack before the Germans'.

    Entry for 19 May 1918: 'There are those like me who think the immediate outlook very bad, but I fancy that the men as a body look on with the incomprehension that has saved so many situations. Anyhow, we'll know soon; but we'll win in the long run if the home front holds. The poisonous atmosphere there is disheartening. Intrigue and chicanery and inspired half-truths are the media through which the most important decisions affecting us are come to … '.

51. HLRO, Lloyd George Papers, F 46/9/1, Basil Thomson to Sutherland, 22 May 1918: Correspondence with supporting documentation from intercepts, establishing German support for Irish nationalist movement.

52. Thomson, *The Scene Changes*, diary entry for 2 December 1916, p. 355.

53. Ibid., p. 392.

54. Ibid., p. 360.

55. J. Morgan, *Conflict and Order: The Police and Labour Disputes in England and Wales 1900–1939*, p. 76.

56. Dalmeny Estate, Rosebery Papers, Hankey to Rosebery, 15 December 1914. Many thanks to Graham Thompson for this reference.

57. PRO WO 114/56, 'Volunteer Force. Return of Strength, 30 April 1918'. There were, in these, a total of 24,793 men and 733 officers, with unit strength being anywhere from 537 and 1,467 all ranks.

58. Ibid. Total strength, May 1917: 32,873 all ranks. This followed from the WO's failed attempt to make the VF more effective. Part of the attempt to increase efficiency

included reducing the total strength of the VF and organizing these on approved military lines. Many volunteers thereafter quit. S. Mackenzie, *The Home Guard* (Oxford: Oxford University Press, 1995), p. 15.

59. Dakers, *The Countryside at War*, pp. 122–3. The 'GR' on volunteer armbands was said to stand for 'George's Wrecks' or 'Genuine Relics'. Mackenzie, *The Home Guard*, p. 16.

60. PRO WO 114/56, and WO 161/107 'VF: Organisation and Administration', 'Memorandum on Volunteer Force', 12 October 1916. Of a total strength of 280,106 men in the UK, 53,763 were in Section A, and 80,012 in Section B.

61. See, for example, Grieves, *The Politics of Manpower*, p. 208. Grieves believes that these men were retained at home through 1918 to counter a potential threat from Germany.

62. Inspecting a labour battalion, in June 1917 the Surgeon General, General Bedford, was so horrified at the men's physical state that he immediately sent out orders to 'stop passing the lame, the halt, and the blind, examples of whom he had just seen in uniform'. Winter, *The Great War and the British People*, p. 52.

63. The scheme for the militarization of the telephone and telegraph system survived in later British home defence planning as the Telephone Preference System (TPS). A sign that, at a later date, it was not unthinkable that such planning would be employed to cover a different, unforeseen contingency, came in 1996, when implementation of the TPS was considered following the shootings at the Dunblane primary school. Many thanks to Graham Thompson for this reference.

64. PRO HO 144/1484/349684, especially file 3, 'Industrial Unrest'.

65. Geary, *Policing Industrial Disputes*, p. 59.

66. PRO HO 144/1484/349684, file 3, 'Industrial Unrest', Police Reports to CMA or Military Intelligence Officers, 28 March 1918.

67. PRO HO 10884/346578, file 9, 'Railway Strike, September 1918', 24 September 1918.

68. PRO HO 144/1484/349684, file 3, 'Industrial Unrest', Police Reports to CMA or Military Intelligence Officers, 28 March 1918.

69. Peak, *Troops in Strikes*, p. 30.

70. Geary, *Policing Industrial Disputes*, p. 35.

71. Ibid., pp. 38–9.

72. HLRO, Beaverbrook Papers, BBK B/9, Secret 83-A 'Instructions to Local Authorities in the Event of Belligerent Operations in the United Kingdom' [CID], November 1914. Also, SRO HH 31/20. Thanks to Graham Thompson for this reference.

73. See, for instance, Geary, *Policing Industrial Unrest*, p. 23; Peak, *Troops in Strikes*, p. 41. It was always the army's preference to work hand in glove with local, legal authorities. In 1918, recent precedent suggested that a soldier was apt to find himself in the dock very quickly if he employed force at home without the authorization of a magistrate.

74. Phillips, *The Diehards*, p. 69.

75. Ibid., p. 87. Of die-hard peers, 72.3% had prior military experience, against 43.4% of all peers. Die-hards and non-die-hards were powers in the local volunteer establishments (p. 87). Even non-die-hard peers and their attachments could be counted upon as safe in the domestic context of the latter war years.

76. 'White', of course, in two senses: legitimist (nineteenth-century sense), and anti-socialist (twentieth-century sense).

77. Laybourne, *Philip Snowden*, p. 68.

78. PRO 30/69, Ramsay MacDonald Papers, 30/69/1042, *Free Man*, May 1918.

79. PRO HO 10743/263275, 'Pacifist Agitation', file 265, 'National War Aims Committee', 16 November 1917.

80. BWNL: as we have seen, principal inheritor of the NSL (BLO, Milner 44 and 45;

especially, Milner 44, 'Report on Meeting of Joint Conference of a Sub-Committee of the National Service League and the British Workers' National League, Which Took Place on August 23rd 1916, at 3:00 p.m.'), and by 1918 organized into more than 150 branches, dedicated to a policy of mandatory national service and combating by violence if necessary the 'anti-nationalism' of the dissenters (LSE, MacDonald Papers, J8 Vol. VI, 'Memorandum L.U. No. 4 'The Rank and File Movement', 14 September 1918; also, BLO Milner Papers, Milner 44, National Service League to Milner, 16 April 1916).

81. NFDDSS, whose offer to do whatever it could for the government to combat pacifism and maintain order had been passed by the HO to the NWAC, and by the NWAC to the WAC of the BWNL.

82. This office continued to collect and collate information on potential industrial 'subversives' well into 1919. PRO HO 144/1484/349684, HO to Chief Constables, April 1919.

83. Mallet, *Lord Cave*, p. 20.

84. See J. Sweetman (ed.), *The Sword and the Mace: Twentieth-Century Civil–Military Relations in Britain* (London: Brassey, 1986), p. 7; M. Midlane, 'Military Aid to the Civil Authorities', in Sweetman, *The Sword and the Mace*, p. 112; Geary, *Policing Industrial Disputes*, pp. 27–31. Geary's is the best account.

85. E. Marjoribanks, *The Life of Lord Carson* (London: Gollancz, 1932), Vol. II.

86. HLRO, Lloyd George Papers, F/38/4/10, Macready to Lloyd George, 1 September 1918.

Conclusion

THE WAR ended as suddenly as it had begun. By 1918 the Lloyd George government had produced a strategy for containing such dissent as existed while anticipating those measures which would be required if either anti-war dissent or industrial unrest came to imperil Britain's war effort. For the moment thoroughgoing censorship, decapitation of the dissenting machine and patriot violence were sufficient – none of these tactics either was admitted or was the product of special legislation, but all were organized and co-ordinated by the government. Against the possibility that a more dangerous dissent developed, a more thoroughgoing suppression was prepared. This would involve methods which would never have been envisioned, much less permitted, in 1914. By 1918, however, social–political polarization had increased to the point where a working consensus in British society would not only follow the government, but was seeking to drive it to contain dissent and win the war by whatever means were necessary.

By 1918, the choice was no longer victory with Lloyd George or negotiated peace with Ramsay MacDonald. Things had moved beyond that. Both dissent and the Lloyd George government were beginning to realize the form implicit in the logic upon which each was founded. Neither was a finished product but an interim stage in an ongoing process. By 1918, the final form of each was anticipated but not yet realized. The more convinced dissenters had moved far beyond Ramsay MacDonald. The dissenters, in linking anti-war dissent to residual class and union grievances accentuated by the war had harnessed a horse which they could not control and which evidenced some determination to pull in a direction which they would never had approved. Lloyd George's perception that MacDonald in power might be, at best, a sort of tumbledown Kerensky, was probably correct.[1] Lloyd George, meanwhile, seemed to many patriots to be too soft to deal with a real emergency. If MacDonald had the makings of a Kerensky, was not Lloyd George, far from being a Cromwell, only a slighter, harder Bethmann Hollweg – perhaps a parliamentary Kornilov?

If the war had continued, real, total compulsion – of exempted industries, in Ireland, and so on – would have been a prerequisite if Britain were to continue in the struggle. Manpower projections for a war continuing through 1919 made this clear. Had this been imposed, real disturbance on the home front would have been inevitable. Given the linkage of industrial and class disaffection to anti-war dissent this would probably have taken the shape of a general strike. In the minds of both syndicalist dissenters and the government a general strike was revolution. An attempted general strike in wartime, even the consolidation of organized labour behind the dissenting programme, would probably have been pre-empted by Lloyd George's most convinced colleagues, if Lloyd George had not been willing to go the distance himself. In the main, Carson, Milner, Beaverbrook and the generals had been preparing a patriotic alternative from the autumn of 1916. In an open struggle between the patriots and the dissenters, the patriots would have prevailed. They were more numerous, more militant, better organized, in control of the state, and in sympathy with its most powerful agencies. The most probable result, therefore, of social contradiction accentuated by the war, being brought to a head by compulsion would have been the emergence not simply of a total war government, or of an HO become Ministry of the Interior, but of something like the Fatherland Front amalgam which ruled in Germany after the summer of 1917: government by the Unionists (with or without Lloyd George and Bonar Law), the armed services, the press lords and the patriots, aligned behind a total war programme and internal policies of social reintegration and, where that was not possible, pre-emptive repression. The dissenters, for their part, nearly did mobilize at least a critical mass of the labour movement, and by the end of the war had organized this behind a socialist programme, had unwittingly produced something like a general strike in September, and shortly thereafter, in October, had engineered a vote in the Labour Party calling for a movement out of coalition and into opposition, despite the best efforts of the patriots.[2] Had any of this come even a few months earlier, when the issue of the war was still in doubt, it is unlikely that the government would have withheld its hand. How close it was to acting, in September, we have already glimpsed. Reaction, if not revolution, was always incipient during 1918, and may well have been months, even weeks away, when the war ended – suddenly and unexpectedly – in November.

While perhaps all of this seems a strange passage in retrospect, the record of the other major combatants in the war deprives us of the luxury of either scepticism or criticism. The worst was never realized, though it was anticipated. Moreover, the policing of the home front is an essential part of modern, especially total, war. Nations which are too restrictive, as were perhaps Russia and Germany during the First World War, run the risk that there may be an explosion where there might have been a protest. Nations which are too permissive gamble that civil dissent will not end in the collapse of the war effort. Both France in the Algerian conflict (1946–59) and the United States in Vietnam were countries which, it might be maintained, saw the prospect of victory evaporate not due to defeats in the field but to the collapse of the home front – and in both these cases, the pressures, cost and perils of conflict were considerably less than those faced by Britain in the Great War. It is pointless to deplore that which cannot be avoided – that without which victory is impossible. The truth is, as well, that even this notwithstanding, Britain preserved the greatest level of civic freedom of any country on either side of the conflict, and throughout the war maintained a comparatively, even surprisingly, high degree of civil liberty – and this despite the gradual hardening of the means by which dissent was contained as McKenna and Simon gave way to Samuel and then Cave at the HO. This was so because the response of the government to the domestic challenge of war was extremely flexible and continually modulated to reflect the degree of dissent, which – given some opportunity to express itself – though it did become dangerous, never developed to fatal or revolutionary levels. Under no administration did the government prohibit, where it could discourage, or discourage where it was safe or politic to ignore. However, it *always* noticed, continually recorded, and remained half a step ahead of the dissenters. The very tolerance of the system which emerged was something which even the dissenters themselves were prepared to recognize, once wartime passions had abated. 'It will always be to me', Snowden later wrote,

> a matter of surprise and gratitude that we were permitted to carry on an active propaganda for peace, by public meetings and in our own press, and by the distribution of leaflets and pamphlets during the four years of the war.[3]

It is doubtful if Liebknecht ever wrote such a tribute to the tolerance of the Kaiser, or Lenin about the forbearance of the Czar. But then, neither Wilhelm II nor Nicholas II would have been in a position to appreciate such praise, had it been offered, for ineffective systems for dealing with dissent, had, in large measure, led to the destruction of both.

Finally, the machinery constructed to contain dissent *was* unofficial, and the product of agreed practice, rather than of special wartime legislation. The worst never happened. Once peace returned, much of the practice quickly dropped away. Even before the end of the war, in October 1918, with victory in sight, the Ministry of Reconstruction was envisioning a rather rapid transition to peacetime practice, retaining only those elements of wartime practice which seemed to be essential for a smooth passage – for instance, the ability to forbid processions and meetings, to retain men with the colours or call them back if required,[4] to control the food supply, and to monitor industrial dissent.[5] Emergency committees were stood down in December 1918.[6] The patriots, after a time, disappeared and were, by and large, forgotten. The BWNL looked a success during the coupon election: in the election that followed, it ceased to exist. While the political style of the government, for some years after the war, remained combative and divisive, Lloyd George's projected National Party became, by 1923, merely Baldwin's Tory Party.[7] In 1919, it is true, there was an explosion of unrest. A general strike was constantly apprehended, and sometimes tried.[8] Ultimately, however, the dissenting machine was transformed into the lack-lustre Labour Party of the interwar years. Despite some anxious moments in the early postwar years[9] the closest Britain ever came to revolution or counter-revolution was the General Strike of 1926 – a far cry from the Bolshevik revolution or Fascism, and the rather tame after-shock of wartime cleavages. Ultimately, indeed, rather quickly, peacetime tolerance and relative social stability re-emerged. There were, of course, profound party political consequences following from the patriot–dissenter divide. These, however, are not our concern.

Some tricks the government did not forget; some inhibitions it never regained. There was, for instance, continued surveillance of the working class and suspected organizations after 1918 – something unthinkable in 1914. Thomson's special office was renamed, but remained and retained its function.[10] DORA became the Emergency Powers Act (1920). Contingency planning against the possibility of social violence began during the war and subsequently remained a recognized function of government. In 1919, for example, Churchill ordered the army 'to prepare a complete scheme and organization of Military Forces throughout the United Kingdom to act in aid of the Civil Power in the event of a national strike of revolutionary character' – shades of Scheme L![11] Peace having returned, however, the army returned to its more customary policy of attempting to limit its involvement at home.[12] In Ireland, however, the system adopted during the postwar troubles, particularly the depredations of the 'Black and Tans', indicate how many inhibitions had been lost in the course of the war, and how far the Lloyd George government would have been willing to go at home if pressed. When war returned, in 1939, the government began by formally assembling many of the tools it had silently taken up during the First World War.[13] Censorship was ruthless from the beginning. The Ministry of Information started with the powers which had eluded Beaverbrook. Clement Attlee (Deputy Prime Minister), Bevin (Minister of Labour) and Morrison (Home Secretary) – all Labour members of the government – dealt with dissent with far greater rigour, and fewer inhibitions, than their predecessors of the First World War.[14] They sat comfortably beside their colleagues in government: Winston Churchill and Lord Beaverbrook.

In the end, the government managed to survive the war without either impairing civil liberties to the point where they could not have been restored, or to an extent inconsistent with the situation in which Britain found itself; and, of course, Britain outlasted its enemies and won the war. All in all, it was an effective and a creditable performance … whatever Charles Trevelyan might have said at the time.

NOTES

1. Marquand, *Ramsay MacDonald*, p. 208.
2. Brand, *British Labour's Rise to Power*, p. 53.
3. Snowden, *Autobiography*, p. 411.
4. BL, Cave Papers, Cave 62476, 'Memorandum on the Continuance of Emergency Legislation After the Termination of the War', [Addison], 19 October 1918.
5. Desmarais, 'Lloyd George and the Development of the British Government's Strike Breaking Organisation', p. 1. Food controls, necessary in themselves, were possibly retained as a possible and powerful weapon against the possibility of labour disruption. Similarly, the Industrial Unrest Commissions – the 'general staff' of suppression – were formalizations of the interbureau working groups established during the war.
6. SRO HH 31/20, 'Scottish Emergency Committees', Scottish Office to Lords Lieutenants, December 1918. Thanks to Graham Thompson for this reference.
7. For example, when Churchill stood for election in Dundee in 1918, against him were united 'all the Bolsheviks and pacifists of the city and as many of the Irish Nationalists who care to follow the caucus orders'. His supporters needed, he said, to 'go forward against the foes … of Britain, whether they be the Huns abroad or the pacifists, Bolsheviks, and Sinn Feiners at home'. Walker *Juteopolis*, p. 453.
8. In 1919, for example, there was a general strike in Glasgow put down by troops. In Liverpool, meanwhile, there was looting and rioting put down by tanks and sailors from a battleship deployed for this purpose. In 1921, and on several occasions through 1926, there were attempts to organize national general strikes. See, for example, Geary, *Policing Industrial Disputes*, pp. 48–55.
9. HLRO, Lloyd George Papers, F/46/9/11, Thomson Memorandum, Summer 1920. Summary: situation at home not good. Might be something afoot. First blow would probably be a rail strike. Some dreaming of a general strike, constituting something like a *coup d'état*. England denuded of troops. Nothing left for aid to the civil power. London sound, but reaction of authorities on the Clyde and in Lancashire, where there were a lot of armed Irishmen, would be problematic.

10. Geary, p. 59. See also Thurlow, *The Secret State*, p. 50.
11. Morgan, *Conflict and Order*, p. 77.
12. Peak, *Troops in Strikes*, p. 41; Thurlow, *The Secret State*, p. 53. See also the works of Brian Bond and Keith Jeffery.
13. See, for example, Geary, *Policing Industrial Disputes*, pp. 53–5. Geary: 'It was only in the years immediately following the First World War that contingency planning in relation to industrial disputes became a prominent function of central government' (p. 53). Leopold Amery, commenting on plans to suppress an apprehended general strike in 1921 noted that the plans had 'gone off like clockwork' (p. 55). These plans seem to have had considerable continuity with those made during the war.
14. See, for example, Donoughue and Jones, *Herbert Morrison*, pp. 279–321.

Chronology of Events

Date	Western Front	Elsewhere	Government actions	Patriots	Dissenters
1914 August	Declaration of war.		Liberal Government. Asquith PM. McKenna Home Secretary. DORA implemented. Postal and press censorship instituted.	Splits in Labour Party apparent. MacDonald resigns leadership. Anti-foreign outrages.	Foundation of UDC.
September	Battle of the Marne.				UDC begins to contact interested organizations.
October	I Ypres.				
November		Turkey enters the war.			
December				BSP splits. Leadership resigns.	Foundation of NCF. Foundation of FOR.
1915 January			*Forward* and *Worker* suppressed, Glasgow leaders imprisoned.		
February	II Ypres.				Strikes on the Clyde and in south Wales.
March	Neuve Chapelle.				
April		Landing at Gallipoli.		Tillett commences propaganda campaign in support of the war. SNDC formed. WSPU commences patriotic activity.	
May		*Lusitania* sunk. Italy enters the war.			

Date	Western Front	Elsewhere	Government actions	Patriots	Dissenters
June			First Asquith coalition. Simon Home Secretary. Munitions of War Act.		
July			National Register Act. Police postulate unity of dissent with German backing.	*Daily Express* commences campaign against dissent. First patriot riots. BWNL formed. Monster pro-war WSPU rally in London.	UDC anti-conscription campaign stillborn.
August			Press bureau seeks, and is denied, coercive powers. Carson orders raids against dissenting publications. Government backs down.		
September	Battle of Loos.				Death of Keir Hardie.
October			Derby Scheme.	Milner begins to attempt to unify patriotic forces.	
November				Stanton victory in Merthyr Tydfil by-election.	Morel plan to unify dissent in the UDC and to use unity to dominate the peace.
December		Withdrawal from Gallipoli.		*Britannia* suppressed.	

Date	Western Front	Elsewhere	Government actions	Patriots	Dissenters
1916					
January			Second Asquith Coalition. Samuel Home Secretary. Press bureau becomes MI7a. Conscription for single men introduced (Military Service Act). Chief constables instructed on how to handle dissenting literature.	*Herald* meetings come under attack.	Society of Friends declares war on the government. First billboard and Leaflet campaign.
February	Battle of Verdun begins.		Processes for prosecution for breach of censorship streamlined. Picketing in controlled establishments ruled illegal.		ASE strike at Abbey Woods.
March			Conscription for married men (Military Service (No. 2) Act).		
April		Easter Rebellion in Ireland. Surrender at Kut al Amara.		Easter 'monster rally' of dissenters in Trafalgar Square broken up.	BSP purges patriots.
May			Snowden informed that HMG could no longer guarantee his safety.		NAC announces plans for a series of outdoor dissenting rallies.
June	Battle of the Somme begins.		Offices of NCF raided under military warrant. NAC destroyed. Russell fined for breach of censorship. Russell's movements restricted. Dissenting leadership attacked (Brockway, Allen, Norman arrested).		Russell, Snowden and Trevelyan canvass south Wales. Morel plans to link triple alliance to dissent, to produce a general strike.

Date	Western Front	Elsewhere	Government actions	Patriots	Dissenters
July					
August				BWNL/NSL union.	
September					NCF begins to find working class audience.
October			UDC offices raided.		
November			Decision to implement compulsion, if necessary.	Carson attempts to oust Asquith. Battle of Cory Hall.	Sheffield engineering strike.
December		Unrestricted U-boat warfare begins.	Lloyd George Prime Minister, Cave Home Secretary. Police surveillance of organized labour groupings. Parliamentary dissenters come under close police scrutiny. King George V visits the north.		
1917 *January*					
February					
March		First Russian revolution.		Liverpool TUC splits.	Second General Conference, Rank and File Movement. Albert Hall meeting.
April	Battle of Arras.	United States enters the war. Height of the U-boat offensive (850,000 tons sunk).	Decision to institute systematic surveillance of the working class. Thomson bureau formed. Creation of Commission on		

Date	Western Front	Elsewhere	Government actions	Patriots	Dissenters
May			Industrial Unrest. 34 COs sentenced to death. Civil custody instituted.		Engineers' strike.
June				Foundation of NWAC. Xenophobic demonstrations become endemic.	Leeds Labour conference. ILP and BSP form short-lived united Socialist council. Stockholm agitation begins.
July	III Ypres (Passchendaele).	Ludendorff coup in Germany.		Attempt to form new 'National Party'. Bottomley agitation in high gear. London Soviet suppressed by rioting.	Attempts to convene soviets. Nottingham TUC conference.
August					Henderson leaves government.
September			Imprisonment of E. D. Morel.	Return of Mrs Pankhurst from Russia. WSPU enters a period of frantically patriotic activity. TUC brought to oppose Stockholm idea. NWAC begins contacting local notables.	
October		Orlando becomes Premier in Italy.	NWAC financed by the government. Government representatives begin attending committee meetings. NWAC begins targeting volunteer movement. London Conference of Trade Unions of the Entente Powers.		

Date	Western Front	Elsewhere	Government actions	Patriots	Dissenters
November		Clemenceau Premier in France. Bolshevik revolution.	Unionist association with BWNL approved. Foundation of Women's Party. HO and police begin sharing intelligence with NWAC.		
December	Cambrai.	Capture of Jerusalem.	BWNL begins planning to run its own candidates.		Dissenters begin offensive against Labour patriots.
1918 January		Allied war planning predicts war lasting to 1919 at least.	Lloyd George War Aims formally unveiled before TUC audience. President Wilson's 14 points. Birmingham TUC splits. Nottingham Labour conference reveals that patriots are still ascendant. Beaverbrook at MIN. Northcliffe at Crewe House. Rationing introduced. Government assumes power to reschedule occupations and cancel exemptions to introduce total manpower compulsion (Military Service (No. 3) Act).		Triple Alliance promise that it will resist compulsion with a general strike.
February	Wilson becomes CIGS. Robertson assumes Home Command.		Arraignment of Arnold Lupton MP (violation of parliamentary immunity). *Tribunal* seized. National Labour Press invaded; press removed. Russell imprisoned.		Labour Party adopts socialist platform.
March	German spring offensive.	Clemenceau redeploys four divisions to the interior to deal with French dissenters.	Addison commissioned to consider elements of wartime practice which should be retained in peace.		Strike Arrangements Committee of Shop Stewards' Movement bans strike action during emergency.

Date	Western Front	Elsewhere	Government actions	Patriots	Dissenters
April	German offensive in Flanders		Home defence plans revised.		
May	German offensive against French: 2nd Battle of the Marne.	Treaty of Brest Litovsk.	Labour Day demonstrations prohibited. Friends' Services Committee arrested.		
June			J. Havelock Wilson threatens to take TUC out of Labour Party.		Belated May Day celebrations. London Labour Party conference almost passes resolution to end coalition.
July		Ongoing intervention in Russian civil war authorized.	ASE strikes ended by NWAC counter-mobilization. Government threatens unilateral restructuring and conscription of strikers. Army and police boundaries redrawn. Intelligence sharing and local co-operation institutionalized. Process for civil–military co-operation streamlined.		Intense industrial unrest begins. National engineering strike.
August	Allied counter-attack – 'The Hundred Days'.				Police strike.
September			Threat to militarize railways. Macready appointed MEPO Commissioner.		Rail strike.
October		Collapse of Germany's allies.			Labour Party leaves coalition.
November	Armistice.				

Bibliography

UNPUBLISHED DOCUMENTS

Unpublished Documentary Collections (Indicated by Class Number)

British Library (India Office)
BLIO L/MIL/3
BLIO L/MIL/17/14
BLIO L/P&S 11

National Army Museum
NAM – 5201/33, 6111/93, 6302/61, 6403/2, 7207/19, 8202/3

Public Record Office (PRO)
PRO ADM – 1, 116, 137
PRO AIR – 1
PRO FO – 371
PRO HO – 45, 65, 139, 144, 173
PRO INF – 4
PRO CAB – 1, 2, 3, 6, 7, 8, 16, 21, 22, 23, 24, 25, 26, 27, 28, 29, 41, 42
PRO MEPO – 1, 2, 5, 6
PRO MH – 47
PRO MUN – 2, 3, 4
PRO PRO – 57
PRO T – 102
PRO WO – 33, 71, 79, 81, 83, 84, 86, 95, 106, 114, 154, 160, 161, 213, 256

Scottish Records Office (Courtesy of Graham Thompson)
SRO HH 31

Private Papers

Bodleian Library Oxford
Milner

Ponsonby
Simon

British Library
Burns
Cave
McKenna
Simon

British Library (India Office)
Chelmsford
Curzon

Churchill College Cambridge
Brockway
Churchill
Esher
Hankey
McKenna
Rawlinson

Dalmeny Estate (Courtesy of Graham Thompson)
Rosebery

House of Lords Records Office
Beaverbrook
Blumenfeld
Bonar Law
Lloyd George
Samuel

Imperial War Museum
Wilson

Liddel Hart Archives for Military Study, King's College London
Robertson

London School of Economics
Lansbury
MacDonald
Morel
Passfield

McMaster University Hamilton
Russell
Ogden

National Army Museum
Rawlinson

Public Record Office (Kew, London)
Balfour	(PRO 800 199/207)
Cavan	(PRO WO 79)
Cecil	(PRO 800 197/198)
Curzon	(PRO 800 147-158)
Derby	(PRO WO 137)
Drummond	(PRO FO 800/197)
Geddes	(PRO SUPP 12/1)
Haig	(PRO WO 256)
Hankey	(PRO CAB 63)
Lloyd George	(PRO MUN 9)
MacDonald	(PRO 30/69)
Macdonough	(PRO WO 196/1510)
Thomas	(PRO WO 79)
Von Donop	(PRO WO 79)

University of Birmingham
Chamberlain

PUBLISHED WORKS

Balfour, A. *Opinions and Arguments From Speeches and Addresses of the Earl of Balfour* (New York: Doubleday, 1928)

Bertie, Lord. *The Diary of Lord Bertie of Thame 1914–1918* (London: Hodder & Stoughton, 1924)

Brett, M. (ed.). *Journals and Letters of Reginald Viscount Esher* (London: Ivor Nicholson & Watson, 1934)

Boreston, J. (ed.). *Sir Douglas Haig's Despatches* (London: J. M. Dent, 1919)

Boyce G. (ed.). *The Crisis of British Unionism: Lord Selbourne's Domestic Political Papers* (London: THP, 1987)

Callwell, C. (ed.). *Field Marshal Sir Henry Wilson: His Life and Diaries* (London: Cassell, 1927)

Clark, A. (ed.). *A Good Innings: The Private Papers of Viscount Lee of Farnham* (London: John Murray, 1974)

David, E. (ed.). *Inside Asquith's Cabinet* (London: John Murray, 1977)

Degras, J. (ed.). *Documents on Soviet Foreign Policy* (London: Oxford University Press, 1951)

Gathorne-Hardy, R. (ed.). *Ottoline at Garsington* (London: Faber & Faber, 1974)

Gilbert, M. (ed.). *Lloyd George: Great Lives Observed* (New Jersey: Prentice Hall, 1968)

Gilbert, M. and R. Churchill (eds). *Winston S. Churchill* (London: Heinemann, 1971–88)

HMSO. *Debates, Commons*

HMSO. *Debates, Lords*

HMSO. *The War Cabinet Report of the Year 1917* (London: HMSO, 1918)

Jeffery, K. *The Military Correspondence of Field Marshal Sir Henry Wilson 1918–1922* (London: Army Records Society, 1985)

Middlemas, K. (ed.). *Whitehall Diary* (London: Oxford University Press, 1967)

Morgan, K. (ed.). *Lloyd George's Family Letters 1885–1936* (Cardiff: University of Wales Press, 1973)

Petrie, C. (ed.). *The Life and Letters of the Right Honourable Sir Austen Chamberlain* (London: Cassell, 1940)

Riddell, Lord. *War Diary* (London: Nicholson & Watson, 1933)

Robertson, N. (ed.). *British Trade Unionism: Selected Documents* (Oxford: Basil Blackwell, 1972)

Self, R. (ed.). *The Austen Chamberlain Diary Letters* (Cambridge: Cambridge University Press, 1995)

Smuts, J. *Towards a Better World* (New York: World Book Co., 1944)

Taylor, A. (ed.). *My Darling Pussy: The Letters of Lloyd George and Frances Stevenson 1913–1941* (London: Weidenfeld & Nicolson, 1975)

TUC. *Report of the Proceedings at the 49th Annual Trade Union Conference, September 3–8, 1917* (Manchester: Cooperative Print Society, 1917)

Various. *Collected Works of Bertrand Russell*, 14 Vols (New York: Routledge, 1995)

War Office. *Statistics of the Military Effort of the British Empire During the Great War* (London: HMSO, 1922)

Wilson, T. (ed.). *The Political Diaries of C. P. Scott* (London: Collins, 1970)

OFFICIAL HISTORIES

Ministry of Labour

Ministry of Munitions

Ministry of Reconstruction
Press Bureau (unpublished)

SECONDARY SOURCES

Adams, R. and P. Poirier. *The Conscription Controversy in Great Britain* (London: Macmillan, 1987)
Addison, C. *Four and A Half Years* (London: Hutchinson, 1934)
——. *Politics from Within* (London: Herbert Jenkins, 1924)
Albrecht-Carrie, R. *The Meaning of the First World War* (Hoboken, NJ: Prentice Hall, 1965)
Allen, C. *Britain's Political Future* (London: Longman Green, 1934)
Amery, L. *My Political Life*, 2 vols (London: Hutchinson, 1953)
Angell, N. *The Great Illusion* (London: Heinemann, 1910)
Armitage, S. *The Politics of Decontrol of Industry* (London: London School of Economics, 1969)
Arnot, R. *The Miners: Years of Struggle* (London: George Allen & Unwin, 1953)
——. *The Miners: One Union, One Industry* (London: George Allen & Unwin, 1979)
Arthur, G. *George V* (New York: Jonathan Cape & Harrison Smith, 1930)
Asprey, R. *The German High Command at War* (New York: William Morrow, 1991)
Asquith, H. *Moments of Memory* (New York: Scribner, 1937)
——. *Memories and Reflections* (London: Cassell, 1928)
Bainton, R. *Christian Attitudes Toward War and Peace* (New York: Abingdon Press, 1960)
Bagwell, P. *The Railwaymen* (London: George Allen & Unwin, 1963)
Barker, P. *The Eye in the Door* (London: Plume, 1993)
Barnes, G. *From Workshop to War Cabinet* (London: Herbert Jenkins, 1924)
Barnett, C. *The Swordbearers* (London: Eyre & Spottiswoode, 1963)
Basker, R. 'Political Myth. Ramsay MacDonald and the Labour Party', *History*, 61 (1976)
Baylis, C. *A History of the Yorkshire Miners* (London: Routledge, 1993)
Beaverbrook, Lord. *The Decline and Fall of Lloyd George* (London: Collins, 1963)
——. *Men and Power 1917–1918* (London: Hutchinson, 1956)
——. *Politicians and the War* (London: Thorton Butterworth, 1928)
Beloff, M. *Britain's Liberal Empire 1897–1921* (London: Methuen, 1969)
——. *Wars and Welfare* (London: Edward Arnold, 1984)
Bentinck, H. *Tory Democracy* (London: Methuen, 1918)

Birkenhead, Lord. *Frederick Eden Earl of Birkenhead* (London: Thorton Butterworth, 1935)

Birnbaum, K. *Peace Moves and U Boat Warfare* (Stockholm: Almqvist & Wikell, 1958)

Blake, R. *The Unknown Prime Minister: The Life and Times of Andrew Bonar Law, 1858–1923* (London: Eyre & Spottiswoode, 1955)

Bond, B. *British Military Policy Between the World Wars* (Oxford: Clarendon, 1980)

Bourne, J. *Britain and the Great War* (London: Edward Arnold, 1989)

Brand, C. *British Labour's Rise to Power* (Stanford: Hoover War Library, 1941)

Braybon, G. *Women Workers in the First World War* (London: Croom Hall, 1981)

Brockway, F. *Thirty Years Inside the Left* (London: George Allen & Unwin, 1947)

Brome, V. *Aneurin Bevan* (London: Longman, 1953)

Bruntz, G. *Allied Propaganda and the Collapse of the German Empire in 1918* (Stanford: Stanford University Press, 1972)

Bryant, A. *George V* (London: Peter Davies, 1936)

Buitenhuis, P. *The Great War of Words* (Vancouver: University of British Columbia, 1987)

Bullock, A. *The Life and Times of Ernest Bevin* (London: Heinemann, 1960)

Bullock, A. (ed.). *Sylvia Pankhurst* (London: Macmillan, 1992)

Burke, K. (ed.). *The War and the State: The Transformation of British Government 1914–1919* (London: George Allen & Unwin, 1982)

Carsten, F. *War Against War* (Berkeley: University of California Press, 1982)

Catchpool, T. *Letters of a Prisoner for Conscience' Sake* (London: Friends Book Centre, 1972 [1941])

——. *On Two Fronts* (London: Friends Book Centre, 1971 [1918])

Ceadel, M. *Pacifism in Britain 1914–1945: The Defining of a Faith* (Oxford: Clarendon, 1980)

——. *Thinking About Peace and War* (London: Oxford University Press, 1987)

Cecil, R. *All the Way* (London: Hodder & Stoughton, 1944)

Chamberlain, A. *Down the Years* (London: Cassell, 1935)

——. *Politics from Inside* (New Haven, CT: Yale University Press, 1937)

Chambers, F. *The War Behind the War* (London: Faber, 1939)

Charles, R. *The Development of Industrial Relations in Britain* (London: Hutchinson, 1973)

Chisholm, A. and M. Davie. *Beaverbrook: A Life* (London: Hutchinson, 1992)

Churchill, R. *Lord Derby: King of Lancashire* (London: Heinemann, 1959)

Churchill, W. *The World Crisis* (London: Thorton Butterworth, 1923; New York: Charles Scribner, 1927)

Clark, T. *Northcliffe in History* (London: Hutchinson, 1950)

Clarke, P. *Liberals and Social Democrats* (Cambridge: Cambridge University Press, 1978)

Clayton, A. *The British Empire as a Super-Power 1919–1939* (London: Macmillan, 1986)

Clegg, H. *A History of British Trade Unions since 1889*, 2 vols (Oxford: Clarendon, 1985)

——. *Trade Union Officers* (Oxford: Basil Blackwell, 1961)

Cline, C. E. D. *Morel 1873–1924: The Strategies of Protest* (Belfast: Blackstaff, 1980)

Cole, G. *History of the Labour Party from 1914* (New York: Kelley, 1969)

——. *Labour in the Coal Mining Industry* (Oxford: Oxford University Press, 1923)

——. *Labour in Wartime* (London, 1915)

——. *Self Government in Industry* (Freeport, CT: Books for Libraries, 1971)

——. *Trade Unionism and Munitions* (Oxford: Oxford University Press, 1923)

——. *Trade Unionism in Wartime* (London: George Allen & Unwin, 1917)

——. *The World of Labour* (London: G. Bell, 1913)

Cook, C. *Sources in British Political History, 1900–1915* (London: Macmillan, 1975)

Corbett, J. *The Birmingham Trade Council, 1866–1966* (London: Lawrence & Wishart, 1966)

Craig, F. *Minority Parties at British Parliamentary Elections* (London: Macmillan, 1975)

Crangle, J. and J. Baylen. 'Emily Hobhouse's Peace Mission 1916', *Journal of Contemporary History*, 14 (1979)

Dakers, C. *The Countryside at War* (London: Constable, 1987)

Davies, J. *The Prime Minister's Secretariat, 1916–1920* (Newport: R. H. Jones)

De Groot, G. *Blighty: British Society in the Era of the Great War* (London: Longman, 1996)

Desmarais, R. 'Lloyd George and the Development of the British Government's Strike Breaking Organization', *International Review of Social History*, 20 (1975)

Dewey, P. 'Military Recruiting and the British Labour Force During the First World War', *History Journal*, 27, 1 (1984)

——. *Britain 1914–1945* (London: Longman, 1997)

Donoughue, B. and G. Jones. *Herbert Morrison: Portrait of a Politician* (London: Weidenfeld & Nicolson, 1972)

Douglas, R. 'The National Democratic Party and the British Worker's League', *Historical Journal*, 15 (1972)

Dowse, R. *Left in the Centre: The Independent Labour Party* (London: Longman, 1966)

Dudd, D. *Balfour and the British Empire* (London: Macmillan, 1968)

Duff-Cooper, A. *Haig* (London: Macmillan, 1935)

Dunn, J. C. *The War the Infantry Knew* (London: Cardinal, 1989 [1938])

Dutton, D. *His Majesty's Loyal Opposition: The Unionist Party in Opposition, 1905–1915* (Liverpool: Liverpool University Press, 1992)

Elton, Lord. *The Life of James Ramsay MacDonald* (London: Collins, 1939)

Eoff, S. *Viscountess Rhondda: Egalitarian Feminist* (Cleveland, OH: Ohio State University Press, 1991)

Erzensburger, H. *Civil Wars* (New York: New Press, 1995)

Ferris, J. *Men, Money and Diplomacy: The Evolution of British Strategy* (Ithaca, NY: Cornell University Press, 1989)

Foot, M. *Aneurin Bevan* (London: MacGibbon, 1962)

Francis, H. and D. Smith. *The Fed: A History of the South Wales Miners in the Twentieth Century* (London: Lawrence & Wishart, 1980)

French, D. *The Strategy of the Lloyd George Coalition* (Oxford: Clarendon, 1995)

Fuller, K. *Radical Aristocrats: London Busworkers From the 1880s to the 1980s* (London: Lawrence & Wishart, 1985)

Gallacher, W. *Revolt on the Clyde* (London: Lawrence & Wishart, 1949)

Geary, R. *Policing Industrial Disputes: 1893 to 1985* (Cambridge: Cambridge University Press, 1985)

Gibbs, P. *George the Faithful* (London: Hutchinson, 1936)

Gilbert, D. *Class, Community and Collective Action* (Oxford: Clarendon, 1992)

Gilbert, M. (ed.). *Lloyd George* (London: Prentice Hall, 1968)

Gilbert, M. *Plough My Own Furrow* (London: Longman, 1965)

Gollin, A. *Proconsul in Politics* (London: Anthony Blond, 1964)

Grainger, J. *Patriotisms* (London: Routledge & Kegan Paul, 1986)

Grayzel, S. 'The Outward and Visible Signs of Her Patriotism: Women, Uniforms and National Service during the First World War', *Twentieth Century British History*, 18, 2 (1997)

Grey, E. *Twenty-Five Years: 1892–1916*, 2 vols (London: Hodder & Stoughton, 1925)

Grieves, K. *The Politics of Manpower 1914–1918* (Manchester: Manchester University Press, 1988)

Guinn, P. *British Strategy and Politics 1914–1918* (Oxford: Clarendon, 1965)

Hain, P. *Political Strike: The State and Trade Unionism in Britain* (London: Viking, 1986)

Halperin, V. *Lord Milner and the Empire* (London: Odhams, 1952)

Hamilton, M. *Arthur Henderson* (London: Heinemann, 1938)

Hanak, H. 'The Union of Democratic Control During the First World War', *Bulletin of the Institute of Historical Research*, 36 (1963)

Hankey, Lord. *The Supreme Command 1914–1918* (London: Allen & Unwin, 1961)

Hazelhurst, C. *Politicians at War 1914–1915* (New York: Alfred Knopf, 1971)

Hind, P. *Beaverbrook: A Study of Max the Unknown* (London: Hutchinson, 1964)

Hoover, A. *God, Germany and Britain in the Great War: A Study in Clerical Nationalism* (New York: Praeger, 1989)

Hyman, R. *The Worker's Union* (Oxford: Clarendon, 1971)

Jeffery, K. *The British Army and the Crisis of Empire 1918–1922* (Manchester: Manchester University Press, 1984)

——. *States of Emergency: British Governments and Strike Breaking Since 1919* (London: Routledge & Kegan Paul, 1983)

Jeffereys, J. *The Story of the Engineers, 1800–1945* (London: Johnson Reprint, 1970)

Jenkins, E. *From Foundry to Foreign Office* (London: Grayson & Grayson, 1933)

Jenkins, R. *Asquith* (London: Collins, 1964)

Jones, G. *Modern Wales* (Cambridge: Cambridge University Press, 1984)

Judd, D. *George V* (London: Weidenfeld & Nicolson, 1973)

Keddal, W. *The Revolutionary Movement in Britain 1900–1921* (London: Weidenfeld & Nicolson, 1969)

Kendle, J. *Walter Long, Ireland and the Union 1905–1920* (Montreal: McGill Queens, 1992)

Kennedy, P. *The Realities Behind Diplomacy* (London: Fontana, 1981)

Kennedy, P. and A. Nicholls (eds). *Nationalist and Racialist Movements in Britain and Germany Before 1914* (London: Macmillan, 1981)

Kirkwood, D. *My Life of Revolt* (London: Harrap, 1935)

Koss, S. *Asquith* (London: Penguin, 1976)

Lansbury, G. *My Life* (London: Constable, 1927)

Laybourne, K. *Philip Snowden: A Biography* (London: Temple Smith, 1988)

Lees-Milne, J. *The Enigmatic Edwardian: The Life of Reginald 2nd Viscount Esher* (London: Sidgwick & Jackson, 1986)

Leventhal, F. *Arthur Henderson* (Manchester: Manchester University Press, 1989)

Liddle, P. *Home Fires and Foreign Fields: British Social and Military Experience in the First World War* (London: Brassey's, 1985)

Lloyd George, D. *War Memoirs* (London: Odhams, 1938)
——. 'When the War Will End', pamphlet (London, 1917)
——. 'The Allied War Aims', pamphlet (London, 1918)
Lloyd, T. *Empire to Welfare State* (Oxford: Oxford University Press, 1986)
Ludendorff, E. *Concise Ludendorff Memoirs 1915–1918* (London: Hutchinson, 1945)
Lutz, R. *The Causes of the German Collapse in 1918* (London: Archon, 1968)
Lyman, R. 'James Ramsay MacDonald and the Leadership of the Labour Party, 1918–1922', *Journal of British Studies*, 2, 1 (1962)
McEwan, J. 'The Coupon Election of 1918 and the Unionist Members of Parliament', *Journal of Modern History*, 34, 3 (1962)
McCormick, D. *The Mask of Merlin* (London: MacDonald, 1963)
McGovern, J. *Neither Fear Nor Favour* (London: Bloomfield Press, 1960)
McKenna, S. *While I Remember* (London: Butterworth, 1921)
Mackenzie, F. *British Railways and the War* (London, 1917)
Mackenzie, J. M. *Popular Imperialism and the Military* (Manchester: Manchester University Press, 1992)
Mackenzie, S. *The Home Guard* (Oxford: Oxford University Press, 1995)
Macmillan, H. *The Past Masters* (London: Macmillan, 1975
Macready, N. *Annals of an Active Life* (London, 1925)
Mallet, C. *Lord Cave: A Memoir* (London: John Murray, 1931)
Marjoribanks, E. *The Life of Lord Carson* (London: Gollancz, 1932)
Marlowe, J. *Milner: Apostle of Empire* (London: Hamish Hamilton, 1976)
Marquand, D. *Ramsay MacDonald* (London: Jonathan Cape, 1977)
Marrin, A. *The Last Crusade: The Church of England in the First World War* (Durham, NC: Duke University Press, 1974)
Marwick, A. *Clifford Allen: the Open Conspirator* (Edinburgh: Oliver & Boyd, 1964)
——. *The Deluge: British Society and the First World War* (New York: Norton, 1965)
——. *Total War and Social Change* (New York: St Martin's Press, 1988)
Maurice, F. *The Life of General Lord Rawlinson of Trent* (London: Cassell, 1928)
Mayer, A. *The Political Origins of the New Diplomacy* (New Haven, CT: Yale University Press, 1959)
Meynell, A. 'The Stockholm Conference of 1917', *International Journal of Social History*, 5, 1–2 (1960)
Middlemas, K. *The Clydesiders* (London: Hutchinson, 1965)
——. *Politics in Industrial Society: The Experience of the British Since 1911* (London: A. Deutsch, 1979)
Millin, S. G. *General Smuts* (London: Faber & Faber, 1936)

Millman, B. 'Henry Wilson's Mischief: Field Marshal Sir Henry Wilson's Rise to Power, 1916–1918', *Journal of Canadian History* (January 1996)

——. 'A Note on British Home Defence Planning and Civil Dissent', *War in History*, 5, 2 (1998)

——. 'The Problem with Generals: Military Observers, and the Origins of the Intervention in Russia and Persia', *Journal of Contemporary History*, 33, 2 (1998)

Mitchell, D. *Women on the Warpath* (London: Jonathan Cape, 1966)

Morgan, J. *Conflict and Order: The Police and Labour Disputes in England and Wales 1900–1939* (Oxford: Clarendon, 1989)

Morgan, K. *The Age of Lloyd George* (London: George Allen & Unwin, 1971)

——. *Conscience and Disunity: The Lloyd George Coalition Government, 1918–1922* (Oxford: Clarendon, 1979)

——. 'Lloyd George and Germany', *Historical Journal*, 39, 3 (September 1996)

——. *Rebirth of a Nation: Wales 1880–1980* (Oxford: Clarendon, 1981)

——. 'Peace Movements in Wales', *Welsh History Review*, 10, 1 (1988)

Morgan, P. and D. Thomas. *Wales: The Shaping of the Nation* (Newton Abbot: David & Charles, 1984)

Morris, A. C. P. *Trevelyan: Portrait of a Radical* (Belfast: Blackstaff, 1977)

——. *Radicalism Against War* (London: Longman, 1972)

Moynihan, Lord. *God on Our Side* (London: Leo Cooper, 1983)

Newton, Lord. *Lansdowne: A Biography* (London: Macmillan, 1929)

Nicolson, H. *Curzon: The Last Phase 1919–1925* (London: Constable, 1934)

——. *King George the Fifth* (London: Constable, 1952)

O'Brien, A. 'Patriotism on Trial: The Strike of the South Wales Miners, July 1915', *Welsh Historical Review*, 30 (1984)

O'Connor, E. *A Labour History of Waterford* (Waterford: Waterford TUC, 1989)

Offer, Avner. *The First World War: An Agrarian Interpretation* (Oxford: Clarendon, 1989)

Orwell, G. *The Road to Wigan Pier* (London: Gollancz, 1937)

Owen, F. *Tempestuous Journey: Lloyd George: His Life and Times* (London: Hutchinson, 1954)

Pankhurst, Sylvia. *The Home Front* (London: Cresset, 1987)

Peak, S. *Troops in Strikes: Military Intervention in Industrial Disputes* (London: Cobden Trust, 1984)

Pelling, H. *A History of British Trade Unionism* (London: Macmillan, 1963)

Perry, F. *The Commonwealth Armies* (Manchester: Manchester University Press, 1988)

Petrie, C. *The Life and Letters of the Right Honourable Sir Austen Chamberlain* (London: Cassell, 1940)

Phillips, G. *The Diehards: Aristocratic Society and Politics in Edwardian England* (Cambridge, MA: Harvard University Press, 1979)

Pimlott, B. (ed.). *Trade Unions in British Politics* (London: Longman, 1982)

Playne, C. *Britain Holds On: 1917, 1918* (London: George Allen & Unwin, 1933)

Ponsonby, A. *Democracy and the Control of Foreign Affairs* (London, 1912)

——. *Falsehood in War: This Containing an Assortment of Lies Circulated throughout the Nations during the Great War* (New York: E. D. Dutton, 1929)

——. *Social Reform Versus War* (London, 1912)

Postgate, R. *The Life of George Lansbury* (London: Longman, 1951)

Pribicevic, B. *The Shop Stewards' Movement and Workers Control* (London: Oxford University Press, 1959)

Pugh, M. *The Making of Modern British Politics 1867–1939* (Oxford: Basil Blackwell, 1982)

Read, J. *Atrocity Propaganda 1914–1918* (Oxford: Oxford University Press, 1941)

Reeves, N. *Official British Film Propaganda during the First World War* (London: Dover, 1986)

Repington, C. *The First World War 1914–1918* (Boston, MA: Houghton-Mifflin, 1920)

Rhondda, Lord. *This Was My World* (London: Macmillan, 1933)

Robbins, K. *The Abolition of War – the Peace Movement in Britain, 1914–1919* (Cardiff: University of Wales Press, 1976)

Robertson, W. *From Private to Field Marshal* (London: Constable, 1925)

——. *Soldiers and Statesmen 1914–1918* (London: Cassell, 1926)

Roetter, C. *Psychological Warfare* (London: Batsford, 1974)

Roskill, S. *Hankey: Man of Secrets* (London: Collins, 1970)

Rowbotham, S. *Friends of Alice Wheeldon* (London: Pluto, 1986)

Rowland, P. *Lloyd George* (London: Barrie & Jenkins, 1975)

Russell, B. *The Autobiography of Bertrand Russell*, Vol. II (Toronto: McClelland & Steward, 1968; London: George Allen & Unwin, 1968)

Sacks, B. J. *Ramsay MacDonald in Thought and Action* (Albuquerque, NM: University of New Mexico, 1952)

Salter, A. *Allied Shipping Control* (Oxford: Oxford University Press, 1922)

——. *Memoirs of a Public Servant* (London: Faber & Faber, 1961)

——. *Slave of the Lamp* (London: Weidenfeld & Nicolson, 1967)

Samuel, Lord. *Memoirs* (London: Faber & Faber, 1945)

Saunders, M. and P. Taylor. *British Propaganda During the First World War* (London: Macmillan, 1982)

Schneer, J. *Ben Tillett* (London: Croom Helm, 1982)

——. *George Lansbury* (Manchester: Manchester University Press, 1990)

Scully, R. *The Origins of the Lloyd George Coalition* (Princeton, NJ: Princeton University Press, 1975)

Searle, G. *Country Before Party: Coalition and the Idea of National Government in Modern Britain, 1885–1987* (London: Longman, 1995)

——. *The Quest for National Efficiency* (London: Ashfield Press, 1971)

Semmel, B. *Imperialism and Social Reform* (London: George Allen & Unwin, 1960)

Sewell, B. *Cecil Chesterton* (Faversham, Kent: St Albert's Press, 1975)

Shinwell, E. *Conflict Without Malice* (London: Odhams Press, 1955)

Simon, Lord. *Retrospect* (London: Hutchinson, 1952)

Simpson, B. *Labour: The Unions and the Party* (London: George Allen & Unwin, 1973)

Slowe, P. *Manny Shinwell: An Authorised Biography* (London: Pluto, 1993)

Smillie, R. *My Life For Labour* (London: Mills & Boon, 1924)

Smith, P. *Government and the Armed Forces in Britain* (London: Hambledon Press, 1996)

Snowden, P. *An Autobiography* (London: Ivor Nicolson & Watson, 1934)

Squires, J. *British Propaganda at Home and in the United States 1914–1917* (Cambridge, MA: Harvard University Press, 1986)

Stenton, M. *Who's Who of British Members of Parliament* (Hassocks, Sussex: Harvest Press, 1978)

Stewart, D. *The First World War and International Politics* (Oxford: Oxford University Press, 1988)

Swartz, M. *The Union of Democratic Control in British Politics During the First World War* (Oxford: Clarendon, 1971)

Sweetman, J. (ed.). *The Sword and the Mace: Twentieth Century Civil–Military Relations in Britain* (London: Brassey, 1986)

Sylvester, A. *The Real Lloyd George* (London: Cassell, 1947)

Taplin, E. *The Dockers' Union: A Study of the National Union of Dock Labourers 1889–1922* (Leicester: Leicester University Press, 1985)

Taylor, A. J. P. *Beaverbrook* (New York: Simon & Shuster, 1972)

——. *The First World War* (London: Penguin, 1966)

——. *The Troublemakers* (London: Penguin, 1957)

Taylor, H. *The Strange Case of Andrew Bonar Law* (London: Stanley Paul, 1932)

Taylor, R. and N. Young (eds). *Campaigns of Peace: British Peace Movements in the Twentieth Century* (Manchester: Manchester University Press, 1987)

Terrain, J. *Impacts of War 1914–1918* (London: Hutchinson, 1970)

Thompson, M. *David Lloyd George* (London: Hutchinson, 1948)

Thomson, B. *The Scene Changes* (London: Doubleday, 1937)

——. *The Story of Scotland Yard* (London: Grayson & Grayson, 1935)

Thurlow, R. *The Secret State: British Internal Security in the Twentieth Century* (Oxford: Blackwell, 1994)

Tillett, B. 'Who Was Responsible for the War – and Why?', pamphlet (London, 1917)

Tiltman, H. *James Ramsay MacDonald* (London: Jarrolds, 1929)

Trevelyan, C. *From Liberalism to Labour* (London: George Allen & Unwin, 1921)

Turner, J. (ed.). *Britain and the First World War* (London: Unwin Hyman, 1988)

——. *British Politics and the Great War* (New Haven, CT: Yale University Press, 1992)

——. *Lloyd-George's Secretariat* (Cambridge: Cambridge University Press, 1980)

Ullman, R. *Intervention and the War* (Princeton: Princeton University Press, 1961)

Vellacott, J. *Bertrand Russell and the Pacifists in the First World War* (New York: St Martin's Press, 1980)

——. *From Liberal to Labour With Women's Suffrage: The Story of Catherine Marshall* (Montreal: McGill-Queens, 1993)

Wade, R. 'Argonauts of Peace: The Soviet Delegation to Western Europe in the Summer of 1917', *Slavic Review*, 26, 3 (September 1967)

Waites, B. *A Class Society at War: England 1914–1918* (New York: Berg, 1987)

Walker, W. *Juteopolis: Dundee and Its Textile Workers* (Edinburgh: Scottish Academic Press, 1979)

Ward, P. *Red Flag and Union Jack: Englishness, Patriotism and the British Left, 1881–1924* (Rochester: Royal Historical Society, 1998)

Wasserstein, B. *Herbert Samuel, A Political Life* (Oxford: Clarendon, 1992)

Webb, S. and B. *The History of Trade Unionism* (London: Longman Green, 1920 [1894])

——. *Industrial Democracy* (New York: Reprints of Economic Classics, 1965 [1897])

White, S. 'Soviets in Britain: The Leeds Convention of 1917', *International Review of Social History*, 19, 2 (1974)

Whitehead, N. 'The British Population at War', in J. Turner (ed.), *Britain and the First World War* (London: Unwin Hyman, 1988)

Wilkinson, A. *The Church of England and the First World War* (London: SPCK, 1978)

——. *Dissent or Conform? War, Peace and the English Churches 1900–1945* (London: SCM Press, 1986)

Williams, A. *Labour and Russia* (Manchester: Manchester University Press, 1989)

Williams, C. 'The Hope of the British Proletariat: The South Wales Miners, 1910–1947', in A. Campbell, N. Fishman and D. Howell (eds), *Miners, Unions and Politics 1910–1947* (Aldershot: Scolar Press, 1996)

Williams, J. *The Home Fronts: Britain, France and Germany* (London: Constable, 1972)

Wilson, T. 'The Coupon and the British General Election of 1918', *Journal of Modern History*, 36, 1 (March 1964)

Wiltsher, A. *Most Dangerous Women* (London: Pandora, 1985)

Winslow, B. *Sylvia Pankhurst: Sexual Politics and Political Action* (New York: St Martin's Press, 1996)

Winter, J. M. *The Great War and the British People* (Basingstoke: Macmillan, 1986)

———. *Socialism and the Challenge of War: Ideas and Politics in Britain* (London: Routledge & Kegan Paul, 1974)

Winter, J. M. (ed.). *The Working Class in Modern British History* (Cambridge: Cambridge University Press, 1983)

Witherall, L. *Rebel on the Right: Henry Page Croft and the Crisis of British Conservatism, 1903–1914* (Newark, DE: University of Delaware, 1987)

Wood, A. *The Life and Times of Lord Beaverbrook* (London: Heinemann, 1965)

Woodward, D. 'Did Lloyd George Starve the British Army of Manpower Prior to the German Offensive of 21 March 1918?', *Historical Journal*, 27, 1 (1984)

Woodward, L. *Great Britain and the War 1914–1918* (London: Methuen, 1967)

Wrench, J. *Alfred Lord Milner: The Man of No Illusions* (London: Eyre & Spottiswoode, 1958)

Wrigley, C. *Arthur Henderson* (Cardiff: GPC Books, 1990)

———. *David Lloyd George and the British Labour Movement in Peace and War* (New York: Barnes & Noble, 1976)

———. *Lloyd George and the Challenge of Labour* (New York: St Martin's Press, 1990)

———. 'Trade Unions and Politics in the First World War', in B. Pimlott (ed.), *Trade Unions in British Politics* (London: Longman, 1982)

Young, N. 'War Resistance and the British Peace Movement Since 1914', in N. Young and R. Taylor (eds), *Campaigns for Peace: British Peace Movements in the Twentieth Century* (Manchester: Manchester University Press, 1987)

NEWSPAPERS AND PERIODICALS

Aberaman Leader
Britannia
Citizen
Daily Express
Daily Mail
Daily News
Financial Times
Free Man
Herald
John Bull
Labour Leader
Manchester Guardian
Morning Post
New Wales Daily News
Pioneer
South Wales Daily News
Suffragette
The Times
UDC
Western Mail
Yorkshire Evening News
Yorkshire Evening Post

Index